Penguin Cordon Bleu Cookery

Rosemary Hume and Muriel Downes

ILLUSTRATED BY JULIET RENNY

Penguin Books

Penguin Books Ltd, Harmondsworth, Middlesex, England
Penguin Books Inc., 7110 Ambassador Road, Baltimore, Maryland 21207, U.S.A.
Penguin Books Australia Ltd, Ringwood, Victoria, Australia
Penguin Books Canada Ltd, 41 Steelcase Road West, Markham, Ontario, Canada

—

First published 1963
Reprinted 1964, 1965, 1967, 1968, 1969, 1970, 1971, 1972, 1973 (twice)

—

Copyright © Rosemary Hume and Muriel Downes 1963

—

Made and printed in Great Britain
by Cox & Wyman Ltd,
London, Reading and Fakenham
Set in Monotype Plantin

CONTENTS

INTRODUCTION

THIS book is based largely on the teaching of the Cordon Bleu School of Cookery, and we hope it will appeal to all those who study good cooking as well as to the housewife, who has to cope with so many things besides the kitchen.

What tastes good must also look good: one of the most important factors in good cooking is the presentation of the food. Dishes can be made to look irresistible by the right use of form, colour, and garnish, and clever dishing-up. The hostess who combines attractive presentation with delicious food can be proud of her achievement and of the enthusiasm of her guests.

In order to arrive at this enviable state of affairs it is necessary to grasp the essential principles which lie behind all good work in the kitchen. Once they have been understood the technique of cooking is simplified and it is clear why apparently unnecessary processes should be carried out. To memorize a few basic facts is a simple matter, and with the help of this book excellent results will follow in a very short time. These will establish confidence in the cook and arouse her enthusiasm.

A few examples will help to clarify this point. For instance, adding cold milk to a starchy substance like potato makes it tacky; to have a whipped and 'fluffy' mashed potato the milk must be heated. Flour beaten into a creamed cake mixture makes for a tough-textured cake, one that rises in the middle instead of evenly. The flour should be folded in at the last. Again, a batter should be first beaten, *then* allowed to stand before cooking to get rid of the elasticity. Failure to do this results in a tough Yorkshire pudding or pancake.

There are quite a number of points which contribute to good sauce-making: a soft butter and flour roux blends better with the liquid; the liquid should be added at least a third at a time to allow the flour plenty of room to swell, thus ensuring smoothness from the word go; flour thickens but needs cooking too; eggs also thicken, but unless they are mixed with flour they will curdle or separate when boiled; if the sauce is thickened slowly over heat a higher temperature can be reached without the sauce (or soup) 'breaking' as it does if it is boiled quickly.

Finally, the speed of cooking is very important. It is necessary to know when to heat quickly – as in dry frying or grilling steak; or more slowly – for white meat, such as veal or chicken; or to simmer slowly – for stewing cuts.

These are a few of the basic principles. There are people who cannot be bothered with such 'extras' as heating the milk for the mashed potatoes, but there is a technical reason for this, just as there is for heating the dripping to smoking point before putting a joint in the oven to roast, and basting it with hot fat. (In this case the hot fat seals the juices and makes for a more succulent joint.)

These examples may appear to be trivial points, but you will soon find from experience that attention to details such as these makes all the difference. If each part of a process is not right, the dish will not taste as good as it should, or it may have a messy and uninviting appearance.

Modern equipment, electric blenders, deep freezes, and so on, has made the lot of the busy housewife a much easier one. She can now prepare dishes which have in the past been beyond her scope from the technical point of view and because of the time involved. This has been taken into account in the menus suggested for entertaining which are given at the end of this book (page 461). Any prolonged beating, for, say, cakes or soufflés, can be done with advantage in a mixer, and a blender is a help with purée soups – in fact a better result is obtained by using a blender for all creams and purées, and for a prawn butter (page 185), a blender is a must.

By planning your menus to include some dishes that can be made the day before or in the morning, entertaining can be made much easier. This applies to most sweets and all soups; the sweets are then left for turning out or decorating, while the soups need only reheating. On the menus we have starred dishes which can be made in advance; but remember to allow time on the day for finishing. Dishes that are finished too soon look tired, so it is well worth while making time, even at the expense of something not quite so important, to complete a dish or give last-minute touches to a sweet.

As a help to the beginner, the recipes in each chapter of this book are arranged in order of difficulty, from the simple to the more complicated, and we recommend you to try them in this order. Like everything else, cooking has to start from the beginning. You have to learn to walk before you can run; but you may be surprised to find how exciting 'walking' can be – once you begin to see where you are going and to what it is leading.

A NOTE ON QUANTITIES

SOME indication of the quantities to allow when planning a meal and buying food will probably be helpful. The recipes in this book are for four people, unless otherwise mentioned, but it is also useful to know the amount of various foods, both cooked and raw, which should be allowed per person, so that enough and not too much food is cooked for each meal. On the other hand, when ordering foods that are served in individual portions, such as small whole fish, escalopes of veal, and the like, allow one or two over the number of people being catered for. This would apply when cooking a dish of eggs mollet for example – have one more on the dish for appearance. In fact one should never have an 'exact fit' for any dish.

Soups. Three people to a pint of soup is a good average. If plates are used, instead of cups or bowls, less can be allowed – say, four to a pint.

Fish. Fish is less satisfying than butcher's meat. Allow ½ lb. of white fish per head when bought and cooked on the bone. When fillets of fish are served as a first course, one is sufficient if the recipe is elaborate and contains a garnish, but if the dish is simple, such as meunière, allow two; for a main course allow two fillets from a large fish if the meal is a three-course one.

Meat. 4 to 6 oz. per head for stewing or grilling meat without bone. With bone, a middle neck of lamb, for example, not less than ½ lb. a head. Generally speaking the more bone the greater quantity of meat required. For a roast, a minimum of 3½ lb. for four people; this allows for bone weight and should be sufficient for two meals.

Rice. 1 oz. per head for boiled rice for a salad; 1½ oz. for a risotto or pilaff; and 2 oz. per head for rice to serve with curry.

Pastas. 6 to 8 oz. for 4 people is generally sufficient.

THE FIRST COURSE

'FIRST course' perhaps best describes those dishes which may be the prelude to any menu. A wider term than *hors d'œuvre*, which to many conjures up a vision of the *hors d'œuvre variés* of the hotel and restaurant, a first course not only covers foods served *au naturel*, but a variety of simply cooked dishes. Presentation of the first course is of especial importance; owing to its place in the menu it should give a favourable impression both to the eye and palate and pave the way for what is to come.

Preparation of such things as oysters, smoked trout, and so on does not as a rule come within the normal experience of the housewife, and the knowledge of how to present these is sometimes lacking. It is with these two points in mind that directions for presenting the more straightforward type of first course are given here.

Recipes are also included for dishes which require little cooking and for some salads which have their place in this chapter. While it is not usual to serve a large selection of hors d'œuvre at home, a simple and appetizing hors d'œuvre can be prepared with little trouble. This could consist, for example, of a tomato salad, a sardine vinaigrette, and an egg mayonnaise arranged together on one plate for each person. Other salads which may be served as an accompaniment to a main course as well as part of an hors d'œuvre will be found in Chapter 9.

Remember that when toast is served with a first course or savoury it should be made at the last minute, and there should be plenty of it.

MELON

The usual varieties of melon suitable for serving as a first course are:

CHARENTAIS: The normal season is early July to end of August. Charentais are small sweet-scented melons with a particularly delicious flavour, and are usually small enough to serve a half for each person. Cut in half round the melon and scoop out the seeds just before serving. If this is done too early the melon is inclined to dry, and if chilled while cut the flavour will taint other foods in the refrigerator.

The most attractive way to serve them is to embed each half in soup plates on finely chipped or crushed ice.

CANTALOUP: Season late August to end of September. These are large melons, easily recognizable by the natural division into sections on the skin, and with soft orange sweet-flavoured flesh. Like the Charentais they are one of the more expensive varieties. Usually served cut into slices with seeds removed, or whole, filled with different fruits as a dessert.

HONEYDEW: Season mid August until late in the autumn. Honeydews are large green rough-skinned melons with pale yellow honey-flavoured flesh. They are inexpensive and good, but must be perfectly ripe when eaten. Serve cut into thick wedges with the seeds removed, and on individual plates. With the flesh cut into chunks they mix well in a salad of tomato and cucumber.

All melons should be lightly chilled for serving. An ice-cold melon has little flavour. To keep one that has been cut, slip it into a polythene bag and store in the refrigerator. To judge the ripeness of a Charentais or Cantaloup press the top opposite the stalk end and it will give slightly if ripe for eating. A Honeydew is more difficult to judge, as it is a firmer type than the two former. Here it is best to rely on your greengrocer.

When serving melon have a bowl of castor sugar and a small dish of ground ginger to accompany. The pepper mill should also be at hand, as a light dusting of pepper brings out the flavour of melon, especially that of the Cantaloup.

*

Prosciutto Mellone

A popular way of serving melon is with Parma ham, 'Prosciutto Mellone'. The melon may be a Charentais or Cantaloup but the ham should really be Parma. This is a raw smoked delicately flavoured ham, and while the ham fillet, Jambon de Paris, or the Italian Coppa may be used, they do not have the same quality as the Parma. For serving, a section of melon is set on individual plates with wafer-thin slices or rolls of the ham arranged at the side.

Figs with Parma Ham

Ripe figs may take the place of the melon in the preceding recipe.

GRAPEFRUIT

Too well known to need description and now, owing to imports from different parts of the world, in season during most of the year, though like other citrus fruits the winter months are usually the best time to buy them. Choose fruit which is heavy and thin skinned, and chill lightly before preparation and serving. To prepare, cut the grapefruit in half, and cut in between the sections.

Now cut round the outside, slipping the knife under the central core and removing any pips. (A curved, serrated-edged grapefruit knife is the best to use, and means less waste of fruit.) Take the core between the finger and thumb, lift out gently, and the side membranes will then come with it. The grapefruit may be lightly dusted with castor sugar and is ready to serve.

Grapefruit may also be served with various additions such as:

Grapefruit with Ginger

Use stem ginger in syrup. Slice it thinly allowing a small dessert-spoonful for each half of grapefruit. Moisten the ginger with a little of the syrup and sprinkle with brandy just before serving. Put a spoonful of this into the centre of each half of the prepared grapefruit.

Grilled Grapefruit

A simple hot first course, or an accompaniment to a grill or barbecue.

Prepare the grapefruit as usual and add a tablespoon of dry sherry to each half. Dust liberally with castor sugar and set under a pre-heated grill. Leave until the sugar has caramelized slightly, then remove and serve.

Grapefruit with Muscat Grapes

Serve in the autumn when the grapes are at their best and not over-expensive. Besides the English hothouse, other muscat-flavoured grapes can be found in the shops at this time. The sweetness of the grapes combines well with the slight bitterness of the grapefruit.

1 oz. almonds; 3 large thin-skinned grapefruit; 6 oz. Muscat grapes:

DRESSING: 1 tablespoon lemon juice; 1 tablespoon castor sugar; 3 tablespoons olive oil; salt; freshly ground black pepper; 1 dessertspoon chopped mint.

Blanch, split, and shred the almonds. Soak in a small quantity of water for an hour or two, then drain thoroughly. Halve and prepare grapefruit, peel and pip the grapes. Mix the ingredients for the dressing thoroughly, and add the grapes and almonds. If the grapefruit are full of juice, remove a little before putting a spoonful of the grape and almond mixture into the centre of each.

Grapefruit with Lemon Water Ice

Pleasant for a lunch party on a warm day. The ice can be made in the drawer of the refrigerator and half the quantity for the recipe on page 435 (omitting the three oranges and using a whole lemon) is enough for three grapefruit. If wished, the ice may be flavoured with mint; in which case add a handful of mint leaves to the syrup with the lemon rind and leave to infuse. Halve and prepare the grapefruit, dust lightly with castor sugar, and, just before serving, place a dessertspoonful of the ice in the centre of each half. This may be decorated if wished with two or three 'crystallized' mint leaves. For these brush some chosen leaves lightly with egg white, then roll at once in castor sugar and leave on a rack to dry. Mint leaves done this way will keep satisfactorily only for two or three days.

AVOCADO PEAR

Avocados are available throughout the year but the season when they are most plentiful, and inexpensive, is from May to September. The fruit is slightly soft when ripe, and the stone will rattle a little. The flesh should be an even pale green with no dark spots.

The usual, and to many the best, way to serve is to split the fruit in two lengthways, remove the large stone, place one half on individual plates, and fill the centre of each with a sharp vinaigrette dressing. The avocado is eaten with a teaspoon. Other ways of serving are:

Avocados with Green Peppers

Choose ripe avocados. Split in half and remove the stone. For three avocados (which will serve 6 people) take the following:

Combine and shake well together 5 tablespoons of olive oil with 1½ tablespoons wine vinegar, adding salt, pepper, and a pinch of sugar to taste. Sharpen with lemon juice if necessary. Add to this dressing 2 tablespoons each of chopped green pepper (blanched for two minutes in boiling water then drained and refreshed), parsley, and spring onions. Finish with a dash of Tabasco sauce. Place the avocados on individual plates and put a good spoonful of the pepper mixture in the centre of each. Chill slightly before serving.

Avocado Salad (for 6 people)

This may be served individually on lettuce leaves, china soup cups, or in wine goblets.

3 avocados; 3 ripe tomatoes; 1 tablespoon snipped chives; 2 ripe lemons; olive oil; additional lemon juice if necessary; salt and pepper from the mill and sugar to taste.

Peel the avocados. This is easily done by piercing the skin with the point of a stainless-steel knife and running it down from top to bottom of the pear in quarters. Then rip off the skin. Halve the fruit and slice. Scald and peel the tomatoes, quarter, and remove the seeds. Cut each quarter in half lengthways. Cut the rind and pith from one lemon, and cut out the flesh from between the membranes. Grate a little of the lemon rind from the other and squeeze out the juice. Put this with the rind into a bowl and add enough oil to thicken (about 3 to 4 tablespoons). Season to taste and add the chives. Arrange the sliced avocados and tomatoes in layers with the lemon sections cut in pieces, moistening with the dressing between each addition. Chill slightly before serving, with brown bread and butter.

NOTE: Fresh limes can be used in place of lemon but less may be needed as they are more acid in taste.

Avocados with Prawns or Crab (for 6 people)

3 ripe avocados; 3 large tablespoons of shelled prawns, shrimps, or white crab meat; lemon juice; salt and pepper from the mill.

SAUCE: 3 large tablespoons French dressing made with lemon juice in place of vinegar; 3 large tablespoons red tomato chutney, such as Kraft; a small teaspoon of Tabasco sauce.

Halve the avocados, place on individual plates for serving. Sprinkle each with lemon juice, salt, and pepper. Set aside. Combine the ingredients for the sauce, adjust the seasoning, and add the prawns or crab. Spoon this mixture into the centre of each half of avocado. Serve with brown bread and butter.

PINEAPPLE

Pineapple is another fruit which is pleasant for a first course. For this recipe choose a fresh, ripe one, not only for the flavour but for the attractiveness in presentation.

Pineapple Japonais
1 large pineapple; castor sugar; lemon juice.

DRESSING: 1 large egg; 3 tablespoons of tarragon vinegar; 2 tablespoons castor sugar; 3 tablespoons of lightly whipped cream.

Cut the pineapple in two lengthways, remove the core carefully with a grapefruit knife, and cut out the flesh. Slice and replace neatly. Dust with a little sugar and sprinkle with lemon juice. Leave to stand while preparing the dressing.

Beat the egg and add the vinegar and sugar with a pinch of salt. Stand the bowl in a pan of boiling water (or cook in a double saucepan) and stir continually until thick. Turn out to cool. When quite cold, fold in the whipped cream and adjust the seasoning. Coat this over the pineapple just before serving.

Tinned pineapple is better in a mixed salad or in a jelly ring. This American type of salad is very good but depends much on the dressing which accompanies it, and, in fact, a special dressing should be made for each kind of jelly ring.

Pineapple Ring, with cream-cheese dressing
1½ gills pineapple syrup from canned pineapple; juice of two large oranges; ½ gill white wine; 1 tablespoon wine vinegar; 1 dessertspoon sugar; ¾ gill water; ¾ oz. (1 level tablespoon) gelatine; 3–4 tablespoons of sliced or diced pineapple; watercress.

CREAM-CHEESE DRESSING: 4 oz. cream cheese; $\frac{3}{4}$ gill single cream or 'top' milk; salt and pepper.

Rub cheese through a bowl strainer, and beat in the cream by degrees. Season to taste. Set aside.

Prepare the jelly. Mix the syrup, orange juice, wine, and vinegar, together with the sugar. Soak the gelatine for a few minutes in the water then dissolve over gentle heat. Add to the juices and measure for quantity. There should be a pint. Rinse out a pint ring mould with cold water, pour in a small quantity of liquid, and leave until just set. Arrange the pineapple on this and spoon on enough of the cool liquid to cover. Leave this to set then fill to the top with the rest of the liquid. When quite set turn out, fill the centre with a bouquet of watercress and serve the cream-cheese dressing separately.

SMOKED EEL

During the last few years smoked eel has grown in popularity and correctly presented makes an excellent first course. To prepare, the eel is skinned, the flesh cut into long thin strips and arranged on individual plates. Serve with quarters of lemon and brown bread and butter. In some big stores and delicatessens smoked eel fillets may be bought ready sliced; an advantage over buying in the piece. Allow 1 to 2 oz. of the prepared fillet per person, and about half as much again if the skinning and boning is to be done at home.

SMOKED COD'S ROE

This is best bought by the piece and is sold in most delicatessens and some fishmongers. It is at its prime from January to May, and pieces that are soft to the touch should be chosen. Allow $\frac{1}{2}$ to $\frac{3}{4}$ lb. for four. To serve, cut into thick slices without skinning and serve two or three for a portion. Lay them overlapping on individual plates, on a lettuce leaf or with a sprig of watercress and quarters of lemon and brown bread and butter to accompany. Cod's roe may also be bought in jars and is then more suitable for mixing with butter for a pâté, or as a filling for stuffed eggs or tartlets of short-crust pastry.

SMOKED SALMON

This is sold sliced, and should be chosen from a side that is thick and moist-looking when cut. Allow 2 oz. per person for a first course and serve with quarters of lemon and brown bread and butter. If buying a day or two before use, keep in a cool larder and not in a refrigerator. Do not unwrap until ready to arrange the slices on the plates for serving.

SMOKED TROUT

These tend to dry very quickly so buy when they are freshly smoked and soft to the touch. To serve, remove head and skin and take off the flesh from the bone in fillets. Arrange on individual plates, and hand brown bread and butter separately. Horseradish sauce may accompany, though a squeeze of lemon juice goes better with the delicate flavour of the trout.

BUCKLING

A more homely, and less expensive, first course is buckling. This is a smoked herring, so smoked that it is cooked in the process. It is smoked whole, and like trout should be soft; and, as the nature of the herring is oily, moist when bought. Skin and fillet as for smoked trout, but pour over a sharp French dressing and serve garnished with sliced dill cucumber and thinly sliced onion rings. Brown bread and butter should be handed separately.

SARDINES

These may be served as part of a mixed hors d'œuvre; French or Portuguese sardines are considered the best. They are first dressed with a vinaigrette dressing, and should have the skins carefully removed before serving. The bones can also be taken out if wished, though this is not essential as during the canning process they become quite soft.

CAVIAR

Caviar is the roe of the sturgeon, the best thing imported from Russia, and is an expensive luxury. Allow 1 to 2 oz. per person, and serve well chilled, with lemon quarters, racks of hot dry toast, and pats of fresh butter. The traditional accompaniments are 'blinis', yeast pancakes made with buckwheat flour. These are served hot with the caviar and are sometimes layered with sour cream. The most attractive way of presenting caviar is to set the jar or bowl containing it in crushed ice and to hand the accompaniments separately. Black caviar is considered the finest type, the grey coming second. Small tins of Danish 'caviar' are now imported and are excellent for cocktail savouries and sandwiches and very reasonable in price.

Blinis (for serving with caviar)

4 oz. buckwheat flour; ¼ oz. yeast; about ¾–1 gill warm milk and water mixed; 4 oz. plain white flour; 1 egg; 1 egg yolk; 1 tablespoon melted butter; ¼ pint milk and water mixed; 1 egg white.

Place the buckwheat flour in a warm basin, cream the yeast with the warm milk and water, and mix the flour to a thick cream. Cover the basin with a damp cloth and leave to rise in a warm place. Sift the plain flour into another basin with a good pinch of salt and mix to a thick cream with the egg, egg yolk, melted butter, and milk and water. Beat well and then mix into the other batter. Cover again and leave to rise 2 hours. Whisk the egg white and fold into the mixture just before cooking. Blinis should be the size of a small teaplate and are cooked in the same way as drop scones, either in a heavy, lightly greased iron pan, girdle, or straight on a solid topped stove or electric plate. Turn them as the bubbles rise and serve with butter, sour cream, and caviar.

RED CAVIAR

The roe of Canadian red salmon; also reasonable in price, it is
sold in small jars and is good for savouries.

OYSTERS

Perhaps the most famous of first courses, but more often eaten
in a restaurant than at home. It is as well, however, to know how to
prepare oysters in case you should ever want to.

Oysters most easily obtainable here, and perhaps the best
known, are the Whitstable 'natives' – these, though many come
from Whitstable itself, are also cultivated in Cornwall and along
the Essex coast, and are of the same variety. They are sold at a
varying range of prices according to size, and are considered by
many the finest in flavour. English oysters are in season from
September to April, though oysters from other countries are
imported throughout the year. Oysters should be opened just
before eating, and served, half a dozen per portion, on a plate of
crushed ice or special oyster plates, which have an indentation to
hold the shell. Serve with quarters of lemon, tabasco sauce
or cayenne, and brown bread and butter. To open them
easily it is wise to invest in an oyster knife. To open hold the
oyster firmly in one hand and with the other insert the knife at
the side of the shell just by the hinge. With a strong movement
bring it towards the hinge and cut it through, pressing off the top
shell. After opening slide the knife under the oyster (this will
kill it instantly), remove the top shell, and place on the crushed ice
or oyster plate. Serve at once. Oysters preserved in tins or bottles
are suitable for a sauce or soufflé.

Anchovy Rolls
Thin white bread and butter; grated Parmesan cheese; French
mustard; fillets of anchovy.

Soak fillets in milk for 10 to 15 minutes; remove crust from the
bread and butter, spread each slice with the mustard, and sprinkle

this with the cheese. Lay a filleted anchovy on each and roll up.
Bake in a quick oven for approximately 6 to 7 minutes. Serve hot.

Prawn Cocktail

Most kinds of prawns or scampi can be used for a cocktail.
Scampi, however, if bought frozen should, after thawing, be
poached gently in the oven, sprinkled with a little white wine or
lemon juice. The dressing given here may be served as an accompanying sauce to other shellfish.

Allow 1½ oz. of shelled prawns per person. For larger prawns or
scampi 3 to 4 per person. About a good tablespoon of shredded
lettuce for the bottom of each cocktail goblet. Marinade the
prawns in a sprinkling of lemon juice, a good dash of Tabasco
sauce, and freshly ground pepper from the mill.

DRESSING: Sufficient for six. ½ pint mayonnaise or salad cream;
half a red or green pepper chopped and blanched; 2 sticks celery,
chopped; 1 dessertspoon grated horseradish or the same of horseradish cream; 2 tablespoons of sweet tomato pickle (Bicks, Kraft,
or home-made); 2 tablespoons cream.

Combine the ingredients for the dressing in the order given and
adjust the seasoning. Add enough of this to the prawns to moisten
nicely and fill into the goblets on top of the lettuce. Dust with
paprika and, if wished, decorate each with one or two whole
prawns.

Prawn and Orange Cocktail

½ lb. large prawns or scampi; 3 oranges; 1 small onion; 1 lemon;
2 'caps' pimento; ½ gill fresh tomato pulp.

Remove the centre vein from the prawns, place in a shallow dish,
and leave to marinade for 1 to 2 hours in the juice of 2 oranges.
Finely chop the onion, place in a small bowl, and cover with the
lemon juice. Leave ½ to 1 hour. Rub the pimento through a
strainer and prepare the tomato pulp, seasoning it with salt, sugar,
and freshly ground black pepper. Cut the remaining orange into
sections. Mix ¼ gill of the orange juice with the lemon juice

strained from the onion; add the pimento extract and tomato
pulp. Place the prawns and orange in a serving-dish, spoon over
the sauce, and scatter over the chopped onion. Serve with brown
bread and butter. For the pulp more flavour is obtained if tinned
tomatoes are used. Take two or three and rub through the strainer
with the pimento.

Sicilian Prawns

6 oz. boiled, drained, and dried rice; 1½ oz. almonds, blanched
and shredded; French dressing; paprika.

SAUCE: ¼ pint thick mayonnaise; juice of one orange; juice of
½ lemon; 1 to 2 cups pimento sieved; 1 shallot finely chopped;
½ gill strong fresh tomato pulp; 4 oz. shelled prawns.

Mix the rice with the French dressing coloured with the paprika
and add the almonds. Season well. Fill into small dariole moulds
and set aside. Prepare sauce. Combine the ingredients in the order
given, and adjust seasoning. Turn out the moulds and spoon
round the sauce.

NOTE: Make the fresh tomato pulp in the same way as for the
Prawn and Orange Cocktail. If preferred, the rice may be moulded
in a ring mould and the centre filled with the prawns.

German Marinaded Herrings

These should be done with the spiced salted-herring fillets sold
in delicatessen stores, or with salted herrings. The latter should be
soaked for 24 hours in cold water, changing it frequently. After
which dry and fillet.

To marinade in a sweet pickle arrange a layer of thinly sliced
onion rings in the bottom of a deep dish, cover with a layer of
herring fillets cut into pieces, and cover again with onion rings.
Put a thick layer of soft brown sugar until the dish is full. Barely
cover with a good wine vinegar, put on the lid of the dish, and
leave for at least 12 hours. If salted herrings are used add a bayleaf
or two, a few peppercorns, and a dusting of ground mace or allspice
(Jamaican pepper). Serve with a bowl of whipped cream strongly
flavoured with horseradish.

Cod's-roe Pâté

Use freshly smoked cod's roe for preference as it is more delicate in flavour than that from a jar.

12 oz. smoked cod's roe in the piece; 1 shallot finely chopped; 1 cup of fresh white breadcrumbs; a good coffee-cupful of olive oil; lemon juice; tomato juice.

Scrape the roe from the skin, turn it into a mortar or bowl, and pound or beat thoroughly. Soak the crumbs in about half a cupful of cold water, then squeeze dry and add to the roe, pounding well. Work in the oil by degrees. Finish with lemon and tomato juice to taste. Adjust seasoning. The mixture should be light and creamy. A blender is especially useful here to get a good consistency. Serve as for other pâtés with hot dry toast, handing fresh butter, black olives, and quarters of lemon separately.

The following recipe is an anglicized version of the Brandade and is eaten cold.

Brandade

1 lb. white fish, cod, haddock, or turbot; 2 thick slices of white bread; olive oil; lemon juice; 2 cloves garlic, crushed to a cream with salt; ½ pint or more of mayonnaise; capers and sliced gherkins to decorate.

Poach the fish with lemon juice and peppercorns to flavour, leave to cool in its juice, then drain; bone and skin. Cut the crusts from the bread and soak it in a little water and a tablespoon of olive oil; then squeeze as dry as possible. Crush and work the fish well with the bread using either a pestle and mortar or a wooden spoon in a basin. Add gradually 3 to 4 tablespoons of oil, the garlic, a good squeeze of lemon juice, salt and pepper to taste. Stir in 3 to 4 tablespoons of mayonnaise; adjust the seasoning. When you have a creamy but firm consistency pile up in a serving-dish and coat with the rest of the mayonnaise which has been diluted with a little boiling water. Decorate with the capers and gherkins.

Roulades of Smoked Salmon

5 small eggs; 4 oz. smoked salmon; 3 oz. butter; 1 oz. chopped prawns; lemon juice; 1 tablespoon cream; cress to garnish.

Hard-boil the eggs; when cold cut in two and separate the yolks, rubbing them through a bowl strainer. Soften the butter with a wooden spoon, beat in the egg yolks, and when smooth add the prawns, seasoning, and lemon juice to taste. Finish with the cream. Fill mixture into the halves of eggs and reshape. Cut the slices of smoked salmon across and wrap a piece round each half-egg. Fill the remaining mixture into a paper cornet and pipe the top of each roulade to decorate. Set each egg on a round of brown bread and butter or in a boat of short crust pastry. Garnish the dish with cress.

Prawns in Aspic

To keep the delicate flavour of the prawns the jelly should be made with a good fish stock flavoured with white wine rather than vinegar. Aspic made with meat stock or bought aspic is not suitable for this dish.

6 oz. shelled prawns; sprigs of chervil or dill; 1½ pints aspic jelly. Season prawns with a little ground pepper and a sprinkling of lemon juice.

Have ready the jelly and put a good tablespoonful into the bottom of dariole (castle pudding) moulds. When barely set arrange a sprig of chervil or dill on this. Barely cover with cool aspic and leave to set. Fill up each mould with the prawns in layers with the cool jelly. Leave to set. To quicken the process of filling the moulds stand in a roasting-tin with cold water and a little ice round them. To turn out, hold each mould firmly in the hand with the palm across the top and dip into a basin of hand-hot water. Turn at once upside down, tap your hand smartly with the other to loosen the jelly, and slide it out on to a double piece of wet greaseproof paper. Slip a palette knife under each and transfer them to the dish or serving-plates. Serve with a vinaigrette or mayonnaise sauce and brown bread and butter. If chervil or dill

is not available add a tablespoon of chopped parsley to the
prawns when marinading, and place a slice of hard-boiled egg in
the bottom of each dariole before filling up with the prawns and
jelly.

Aspic Jelly
1¼ pints well-seasoned fish stock; ¼ pint white wine; 1½ oz.
gelatine; 2 egg whites; a squeeze of lemon juice.

Put the fish stock and gelatine into a scalded pan and dissolve
over gentle heat; whip the egg whites to a froth and add to the
pan with the wine and lemon juice. Whisk over steady heat until
boiling-point is reached and then allow to boil to the top of the
saucepan undisturbed; draw aside without disturbing the crust
on top and leave to settle. Boil up twice more in the same way.
Stand for 5 minutes and then pour through a scalded cloth.

*

These are two simple first courses which though not often home-
made, it is as well to know how to make.

Potted Shrimps
For ½ lb. peeled fresh or frozen shrimps take 4 oz. butter; 1 teaspoon ground mace; ½ teaspoon mixed spice; ½ teaspoon ground
black pepper; ½ teaspoon paprika pepper.

Put the butter into a saucepan and melt over gentle heat. When
frothing well but before it turns colour, pour off into a basin
and skim well. Put the shrimps into a frying-pan, add enough
of the butter to moisten them well, and add the spices. Toss up
over a brisk heat for two or three minutes until very hot and then
turn into a suitable jar or pot. Press lightly, then spoon over the
rest of the butter, taking care not to add any of the sediment.
  The butter must cover the shrimps and if not sufficient more
must be clarified.

Potted Salmon
Make from cooked salmon that is left over.
To ½ lb. salmon freed from skin and bone take 2–3 oz. butter.

Pound or work the salmon until perfectly smooth. Now work in
the butter, season well and press into small pots so that there is no
gap or crack throughout. Clarify (see above) enough butter to coat
over the top of the pots. Make sure there are no air spaces visible,
then leave to set. Store in a cool place. This will keep for a week
to ten days.

Potted Ham
Made in the same way as the preceding recipe.

Pâté de Foie Gras Truffé
Pâté de foie gras is as much a luxury as caviar. It should not be
confused with the liver pâté in small tins (pâté de foie) or that
which is sold by the pound ready for slicing. The former is suitable for made-up dishes or for cocktail savouries while the latter is
sliced and served with hot dry toast and butter. These pâtés are
imported from France and from other countries and vary in price
according to the quality.

The true pâté de foie gras is made from the liver of a goose
especially fattened for this purpose. A piece or part of the liver
is cooked as a pâté in its own fat with a nugget of truffle. Both
come from Périgord and make a perfect marriage of flavours.
Foie gras may be bought in china pots in varying sizes, in tins or
more expensively *en croûte*. This can be a raised pie of pastry or a
replica of a croûte in china. Both of these are to be seen around
Christmas time in the bigger delicatessen shops or stores. To
serve from the pot or croûte hand it round for the foie gras to be
scooped out with a spoon, or if preserved in a tin, cut into slices
and served on individual plates with hot dry toast and pats of fresh
butter. When toast is called for to accompany any first course or
savoury, it must be made at the last minute and be ample in
quantity. The butter should be unsalted.

For home-made pâtés see Chapter 8, 'The Cold Table'.

Continental Sausages
There are several varieties of these on sale in most delicatessen
shops and stores. Those most easily obtainable are French garlic

sausage, Italian and Danish salami, and both German and Belgian liver sausage. Any of these may be used sliced in a mixed hors d'œuvre or to go with cold meats for an *assiette anglaise*. Liver sausage especially makes a good first course if sliced and served with dill cucumber, hot dry toast, and butter.

Gulls' Eggs

These are a comparatively rare delicacy and therefore expensive, and are only in season for a very short period. It is as well, however, to know how to serve them.

Gulls' eggs are bought ready cooked from a poulterer or fishmonger and arranged in a napkin, unshelled, for people to help themselves. The traditional accompaniment is rock salt from a grinder, and brown bread and butter.

The following two recipes are straightforward and easy to make. They are inexpensive and good.

Eggs Basque

6 hard-boiled eggs; 2–3 caps of pimento, tinned, or 2 fresh peppers shredded and blanched.

DRESSING: 1 finely chopped shallot; 1 teaspoon paprika pepper; 2 tablespoons vinegar; 5–6 tablespoons of oil; salt, pepper, and sugar to taste.

Slice the eggs, arrange in an hors d'œuvre dish. Cut the pimento into strips, and lay over the top lattice-fashion or scatter over the peppers. Combine the ingredients for the dressing thoroughly and adjust the seasoning. Spoon over the dish and serve with brown bread and butter.

Tomato Ring

1 pint of tinned tomatoes; a strip of lemon rind; 4–6 peppercorns; a clove of garlic, well bruised; a bayleaf; salt and sugar to taste; $\frac{3}{4}$ oz. (1 level tablespoon) gelatine; $\frac{1}{2}$ gill water; watercress to garnish; French dressing to accompany.

Put the tomatoes into a pan with the lemon rind, peppercorns, garlic, and bayleaf. Add salt and sugar to taste and bring slowly to the boil. Simmer for a few minutes, then press the pulp through a nylon strainer into a measure. Add the water to the gelatine, allow it to swell, then turn into the tomato liquid. Stir until the gelatine is dissolved, making up if necessary with cold water to just under a pint. Adjust seasoning, adding pepper from the mill to taste. Rinse out a pint ring mould in cold water, pour in the tomato liquid, and leave to set. Turn out and fill the centre of the mould with a bouquet of watercress dipped into the French dressing. Do this immediately before serving. Hand hot anchovy rolls separately, with a sauce-boat of French dressing.

Salad Marguéry
This salad may also be made with flaked tunny fish or sardines in place of the prawns.

4–6 tomatoes, peeled, halved, and seeded; 4 oz. shelled prawns; 1 dill cucumber, thinly sliced; 3 hard-boiled eggs; anchovy fillets.

DRESSING: olive oil; wine vinegar; 1 teaspoon French mustard; 2 tablespoons tomato ketchup or chutney; chopped mixed herbs.

Sauté the tomatoes in oil for 2 minutes, being careful not to over-cook. Season and leave till cold. Split eggs, shred whites, and place them on the bottom of a serving-dish; scatter over the prawns and sieve the yolks on the top. Cover with the sliced cucumber and set the tomatoes on the top, cut side downwards. Split the anchovy fillets into two and arrange on the tomatoes lattice fashion. Combine the ingredients for the dressing and spoon over the salad one hour before serving. Hand brown bread and butter separately.

Herring and Apple Salad
Smoked or salted herring fillets may be used for this or the pickled herring fillets called roll-mops.

8 oz. long-grained rice; 4–6 fillets of herring according to size; ¼ pint milk; 3–4 tart crisp apples.

VINAIGRETTE: 2 tablespoons wine vinegar; 1 tablespoon mixed mustard (German or English); 5 tablespoons oil; salt and pepper from the mill.

Wash the fillets in tepid water, dry, and lay them in a shallow dish. Cover them with the milk and leave for 2 to 3 hours to plump up the fillets. Meanwhile boil the rice in plenty of boiling well-salted water with a slice of lemon and a tablespoon of oil. When just tender, drain, rinse with hot water, and allow to dry in the colander. Mix the ingredients for the vinaigrette well together, adjusting the seasoning. Drain the fillets from the milk and cut them into strips with the scissors. Moisten with half of the vinaigrette, turn rice into a bowl, and fork in the rest of the vinaigrette. Arrange in a serving-dish or salad bowl; peel, quarter, and core the apples, slice them thinly, and arrange them at once on top of the rice. Scatter or arrange the pieces of herring on this, then spoon over the vinaigrette in which the fillets were marinaded.

Salad Niçoise

6 oz. flaked tunny fish, shredded ham, chicken, or prawns; 6–8 oz. of any cooked green vegetables such as broad or French beans, peas, etc.; mixed chopped herbs; ½ a cucumber; 1 lb. tomatoes, peeled and thinly sliced; black olives and anchovy fillets; French dressing.

Put the fish or meat on the bottom of a shallow dish, with the vegetables on top. Scatter over the herbs, cover with the sliced cucumber, and arrange the tomatoes on the top. Make a lattice of anchovy fillets on this and set the black olives between. Spoon over a well-seasoned French dressing. Serve with brown bread and butter.

*

Examples follow of hors d'œuvre made up of different salads. These are arranged in scallop shells, and make an attractive presentation when handed on a big dish for people to help themselves. In default of shells the hors d'œuvre may be arranged on cheese plates.

The recipes which follow are perhaps a little elaborate but are well worth the time and trouble for a fork luncheon.

Egg Mayonnaise and Celery and Anchovy Salad

4 hard-boiled eggs; ¼ pint mayonnaise; 1 small head celery; 8 fillets anchovy, chopped parsley, French dressing.

Cut the celery in fine julienne strips and leave in ice-cold water until wanted. Drain well and mix with a little French dressing. Cut the eggs in halves and place at one side of scallop shells, coat with a spoonful of mayonnaise, and dust with chopped parsley. Fill the other half of each shell with the celery salad and arrange on top two curled anchovy fillets.

Buckling Salad and Potato Mayonnaise

3 buckling; 1 onion; 1 dill cucumber; lemon juice; French dressing; ½ lb. new potatoes; mayonnaise.

Skin the buckling, remove the bone, and divide into neat fillets. Season with black pepper and sprinkle with lemon juice. Slice the onion, blanch and refresh, and mix with the buckling and sliced cucumber. Scrub the potatoes and cook in boiling salted water until just tender, then drain and dry. Peel the potatoes while still hot and dress with a little French dressing; when cold mix with mayonnaise. Place the buckling salad at one side of the scallop shells and the potato mayonnaise at the other side; dust the top with paprika pepper.

Frankfurter Salad and Cabbage Salad

3 frankfurters or 1 small tin; 2 oz. Belgian liver sausage; 2 oz. cooked ham; 4 tomatoes; 1 red or green pepper; French dressing; paprika; tomato purée; French mustard; 6 oz. Dutch white cabbage; 3–4 tablespoons oil; black pepper; salt; 1 tablespoon white wine vinegar.

Poach the frankfurters, allow to cool and cut into slices. Dice the liver sausage and shred the ham. Skin the tomatoes, remove the seeds, and cut into strips. Remove the core and seeds from the pepper, shred, blanch, and refresh. Season the French dressing with paprika, tomato purée, and the mustard. Mix all the ingredients together and moisten with the dressing. Divide the mixture between four shells, putting well to one side, and then fill the other side with cabbage salad. Trim the cabbage, removing outside leaves and core. Shred very finely and then dress with the oil and seasoning. Toss very thoroughly until every shred of cabbage is coated and then add the vinegar.

Danish Tartlets

Shortcrust pastry made with 4 oz. plain flour; 3 oz. mixed lard and butter; 1 egg yolk; 2 tablespoons water.

FILLING: (a) 1 small jar smoked cod's roe; 2 oz. fresh butter; 2 small firm tomatoes; browned almonds.

(b) 1 tin foie gras; 1 oz. butter; 1 tablespoon cream; salt and pepper; hard-boiled egg to garnish.

Make up pastry, line into deep tartlet moulds and bake blind. Prepare filling (a): sieve and work cod's roe with the creamed butter. Season to taste and add a few drops lemon juice. Fill into half the tartlets and arrange a slice or two of tomato on the top. Finish with a browned almond. Prepare filling (b): work foie gras and butter together, add cream, and season to taste. Fill into the tartlets and decorate with the egg white and sieved yolk.

Chapter 2

SOUPS

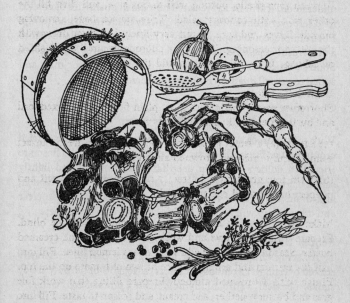

FOR the finer type of soups, such as consommés, veloutés, and fish bisques, it is essential to use a good basic stock, otherwise the result can only be poor. In fact for soups of this kind a special stock should be made and allowed to simmer until strong and well flavoured before straining off.

Vegetable soups, creams, or purées are in a different category, in that milk and water form the basic liquid, though for some recipes a chicken or veal stock may be called for.

Broths, meat or vegetable or a mixture of both, have water as the liquid, making their own stock as the ingredients simmer gently together. These are the soups solid and satisfying enough to be called 'a meal in themselves'.

Recipes and instructions for making the various kinds of stock will be found at the end of this section.

Several recipes representative of each different kind of soup have been given, but there are many more which can be made on the basic recipe. Once the method for each type of soup has been understood, it will be appreciated how small quantities of cooked food left over from a meal can be quickly made into a good soup. For example, cooked spinach or peas can be sieved or blended into a thin freshly made Béchamel or Velouté or left-over Béchamel or Soubise sauce, or mashed potatoes thinned with hot milk and added to a small quantity of freshly sweated vegetables.

GARNISHES

With most purées and cream soups it is usual to serve small fried croûtons, i.e. finely diced stale bread or raw potato. These are fried to a golden brown in deep fat or shallow fat and lightly salted before serving. For potato croûtons dice the potato, blanch, and drain well before frying. Other garnishes both for a clear and cream soup will be indicated in the appropriate recipes.

Scotch Broth

1½ lb. scrag end of mutton or lamb; 1½ oz. barley, previously soaked overnight; 2 onions; 2 carrots; a 'faggot' of herbs (parsley stalks, a bayleaf, a sprig of thyme); about 3 pints of cold water.

Soak the scrag in cold salted water for 12 hours, changing the water once or twice. Then put into a large pan, cover well with the water, and bring slowly to the boil, skimming well. Add barley, salt lightly, cover, and simmer for 40 minutes. Add the onions, chopped, and the carrots, diced, with the herbs. Continue to simmer until the barley and vegetables are well cooked (approximately a further 45 minutes). Remove the herbs, lift out the pieces of scrag, remove the bone, and replace the meat cut into small pieces. Adjust the seasoning and serve very hot.

The consistency of the broth should be thick with the vegetables and meat. If it has to be thinned add more water during the early stages of the cooking so that the flavour is not weakened. A half or whole sheep's head when available may be used in place of the scrag and makes a rich and nourishing broth. Ask the butcher to clean the head, and soak it overnight as for the scrag.

Chicken Broth

Use good chicken stock for this soup made from the liquor from a poached chicken and strengthened with the carcass bones after carving the bird. Strain, cool, and remove all fat.

3 tablespoons finely diced carrot; 2 tablespoons finely chopped onion; 1½ oz. rice; 2 pints strong chicken stock; ½ gill thick cream; 1 dessertspoon chopped parsley.

Put the vegetables, rice, and stock into a pan. Season lightly, cover, and simmer for 35 to 40 minutes. Adjust seasoning and add the cream and parsley. Serve.

Beef Tea

A strengthening broth given in cases of illness or convalescence, where concentrated protein, easily digested, is called for.

2 lb. shin of beef; cold water.

Cut the shin in small squares, pack into a large earthernware jar, casserole, or double saucepan. Salt very lightly (or not at all, if wished). Barely cover with water (about 1 to 1½ pints), set a saucer or lid on top of the jar, stand it in a deep pan of water, and set in a slow oven for 7 to 8 hours, or until the juice is really concentrated. Strain off and serve hot with dry toast.

An Aga slow oven is ideal when making the beef tea in a jar; a double saucepan is more suitable for gas or electric cookers.

Oxtail

This soup may be clear or thick. In either case a strong brown stock well flavoured with vegetables is prepared from the tail and, if to be served clear, clarified as for a consommé. Otherwise the stock is thickened lightly and served with sippets of dried toast or fried bread croûtons.

An oxtail is sometimes rather large for a small household; however, the thickest part of the tail can be used for a stew, and the remainder turned into stock to make a soup for a day or two later.

Thick Oxtail Soup

1 oxtail, jointed and soaked in cold salted water for some hours; beef dripping; 2 onions; 2 carrots, quartered; 2–3 sticks of celery, cut in pieces; a large bunch of herbs (parsley stalks, thyme, and a bayleaf); 6–8 peppercorns; a blade of mace; 1 onion; 1 turnip; 1 carrot, all medium-sized and cut into small dice.

TO FINISH: 1 oz. butter; 1 oz. flour; a wineglassful of port or Madeira; 1 tablespoon mushroom ketchup; sippets of dry toast, i.e. small triangles.

Drain and dry the pieces of oxtail. Heat 2 tablespoons of dripping in a large pan, put in the pieces, and brown well. Draw aside, drain off the fat, and add the vegetables to the pan with the herbs and spices. Well cover with cold water (about $2\frac{1}{2}$ quarts). Salt very lightly, bring to boil, removing any scum that rises, cover pan, then simmer gently for 3 to 4 hours or until the meat is falling from the bones. Half-way through the cooking the lid may be placed half on the pan to allow for a certain amount of evaporation and so help to concentrate the stock. Strain, skim off any fat, and return stock to a pan. Add the diced vegetables and boil gently for 15 to 20 minutes. In the meantime take 2 to 3 tablespoons of meat from the bones and shred. Work butter and flour together to a paste. Draw soup aside, add this kneaded butter in small pieces, and when dissolved reboil. Put in the wine, ketchup, and meat, simmer for 5 to 10 minutes before serving with the toast sippets.

Kidney Soup

6 oz. ox kidney; $1\frac{1}{2}$ pints good brown stock flavoured with chicken giblets; a large faggot or bouquet of herbs (thyme, parsley, and bayleaf); 1 oz. butter; 1 medium-sized onion, finely chopped; $\frac{3}{4}$ oz. flour; 1 teaspoon tomato purée; 1 glass burgundy; 1 dessertspoon redcurrant jelly.

Soak kidney in warm salted water for one hour (to remove the strong taste), then slice and put into a pan with ¾ pint of the stock and the herbs. Simmer for about an hour or until the kidney is tender. Remove herbs, put into a bowl, and set aside. In the same pan melt the butter, add onion, and cook slowly until golden brown, stir in flour, add remaining stock, the kidney and liquor, and the purée. Stir until boiling then add the wine and jelly. Simmer 10 minutes, then pass all through a Mouli sieve. Return to the pan and bind, if necessary, with a little arrowroot. Adjust seasoning and serve with fried croûtons.

Game Soup (1)

1 small raw game-bird (pigeon, grouse, or partridge); 1 tablespoon butter for browning; 2 onions; 2 carrots; 2–3 sticks celery; a large bunch of herbs; 6–8 peppercorns; 1 large glass red wine; 2 pints strong brown stock; 2 flat mushrooms, thinly sliced. For thickening: 1 oz. butter; 1 oz. flour.

TO FINISH: 1 dessertspoon redcurrant jelly; lemon juice.

Brown the bird all over in the butter in a large pan. Remove, add the sliced vegetables, and allow them to take colour also. Replace the bird, add the bouquet, peppercorns, and wine. Cover tightly and simmer on the stove-top or in the oven until the bird is tender (about an hour). Then carve the meat from the breast and set aside. Put the carcass back into the pan with the stock and simmer, uncovered, for another 20 to 30 minutes, then run through a fine strainer. Melt the butter in the pan, add the sliced mushrooms, and after a minute stir in the flour and pour on the stock.

Blend and reboil. Adjust seasoning, add the jelly and a squeeze of lemon juice, and simmer a few minutes. Finish with the meat cut into fine shreds.

A golden sherry may be used in place of the red wine.

Carcasses of cooked game (grouse, pheasant, partridge, etc.) may be used in place of the raw birds. Proceed as above but add the stock with the wine and simmer together for about 1½ hours before straining.

Hare soup is also made in the same way. Usually the back and thighs are served roasted and the trimmings and fore-part turned into soup.

The meat, either from the bird or hare, may be pounded or blended to a purée in place of shredding and worked into the soup with the butter and flour.

Game Soup (2)

Carcasses and pieces of cold cooked game (grouse or pheasant); 1 onion; 1 clove garlic; 1 turnip; 2–3 carrots; a bunch of herbs; a few peppercorns; a blade of mace; 3–4 pints brown stock.
Fresh white breadcrumbs, yolks of 2 eggs; a wineglass of sherry; ½ gill cream (optional).

Break up the carcass and put into a large pan. Add the onion stock with the clove, the turnip, and carrots quartered, the herbs, spices, and stock. Simmer 2 to 3 hours or until the stock is really strong and well flavoured. Strain. Pick off any meat from the bones, pound or blend it with half its weight in breadcrumbs previously soaked in a little of the stock until soft. When smooth, dilute with the stock, season, and bring to the boil. Add the sherry. Beat yolks with the cream (or alternatively with a little of the hot soup) and add to the soup off the heat.

Serve with croûtons of fried bread.

Madrilène

Technically speaking a Madrilène is a clear soup, i.e. a consommé, strongly flavoured with tomato and made with a chicken stock. Minced beef is still used for clarifying.

The following recipe, however, is a simpler version, and while not cleared keeps to the traditional flavour of chicken and tomato.

1 quart strong chicken stock; 1 medium-sized onion; 1 oz. butter; 1 large tin tomatoes; a large bunch herbs; parsley stalks, bayleaf, thyme, and a pared strip of lemon rind tied together; 2 glasses sherry; arrowroot; lemon juice; cream; chives.

Chop onion, soften in the butter, add the stock, tomatoes, and herbs. Season well, using pepper from the mill. Cover and simmer for 40 minutes. Pass through a Mouli sieve. Return to the rinsed-out pan, reduce the sherry to half, and add. Thicken lightly with arrowroot, about a tablespoonful mixed with 2 tablespoons of water. Reboil. Add a few drops of lemon juice, adjust seasoning, and serve. A spoonful of cream may be stirred into each cup just before serving, and the top sprinkled with chives.

The soup should be thin, well-spiced, and piquante in flavour. It can be served iced with a slice of lemon in each cup. In this case omit the cream.

Russian Meat Soup with Cucumber

Made from turkey, goose, or chicken giblets.

2 sets of giblets; 1 lb. gravy beef; 2 onions; a bunch of herbs; kneaded butter (*beurre manié*); 1 dill cucumber; a small cupful of sour cream; cayenne pepper; lemon juice.

Clean and scald the giblets. Cut into pieces with the beef. Brown quickly in a little hot dripping. Then add the onions and herbs with a little salt and peppercorns. Well cover with about $2\frac{1}{2}$ pints of cold water and simmer for about $1\frac{1}{2}$ hours or until the gizzards are tender and the stock strong and well flavoured. Strain through a fine strainer. Return to the pan and thicken with the kneaded butter. Reboil, season highly with the cayenne, and beat in the sour cream. Add lemon juice, to taste, with the cucumber cut into shreds and some of the gizzard cut into thin slices. Serve very hot.

In place of the gravy beef a strong beef stock may be employed.

CONSOMMÉ

A name for clear soup, one that is clarified and strongly flavoured with beef or chicken. A stock should be prepared and allowed to get cold before being clarified so that every particle of grease can be removed. The stock at this stage should be lightly jellied and of a good flavour and colour. Most consommés have a garnish (see page 40), either of vegetable (Julienne or Brunoise) or of herbs (sprigs of chervil or tarragon) or Royal (see page 40), a savoury custard made with either egg white or egg yolk and cream, well seasoned, and left plain or flavoured with tomato purée or anchovy essence.

STOCK FOR CONSOMMÉ: 1 lb. each veal and beef bones; 1 lb. shin or lean beef; onions; carrots; stick of celery; bouquet garni; peppercorns; a little salt; cold water to cover well (3 quarts).

Have the bones broken small; cut the beef into squares. Brown them in a very small quantity of fat, lower the heat, add the vegetables, and let them brown also. Now add the remaining ingredients, and bring slowly to the boil, skimming well. Partially cover the pan and allow to simmer for 2 to 3 hours or until the stock is strong in flavour. Strain and leave till the next day before removing all fat.

For large households, a joint of fresh silverside or aitchbone, of about 3 to 4 lb., may be simmered in water with 2 or 3 veal bones and quartered root vegetables until tender. Meat and vegetables are taken out and eaten as a main course, and the liquid left to simmer uncovered until strong in flavour. The stock is then strained and is available as a base for consommés, aspic jelly, and brown sauces.

For a chicken consommé add a raw chicken carcass or small fowl.

Royal

To one egg white (or yolk) allow 4 tablespoons cream. Break white slightly, but do not make it frothy. Cream yolk. Add cream and seasoning. Flavour if wished. Pour into a small pot or cup. Steam or poach until set. Leave till cold and turn out. Slice and cut into strips or stamp into fancy shapes. Add to the soup before serving.

Consommé Brunoise

1 quart strong stock prepared from bones and gravy beef; ½ lb. raw minced shin of beef; whites and shells of 2 eggs; 1 glass (½ gill) sherry.

BRUNOISE: 1 dessertspoon each finely diced carrot, celery, turnip, and French beans; a nut of butter.

Put the cold stock into a scalded pan (preferably enamel) with the beef, the whites whipped to a froth, and the shells washed and lightly crushed. Whisk over the fire until boiling. Allow the liquid to rise in the pan before drawing it to one side. Leave to settle, then return pan to very gentle heat and simmer for 20 to 30 minutes. Then strain through a scalded cloth. Meanwhile put the vegetables into a small saucepan with the butter, cover, and cook gently until the vegetables are just tender and beginning to colour lightly. Just before serving reheat the consommé, add the garnish and sherry.

Bortsch (clear beetroot)
Prepare as for Consommé Brunoise, adding one raw grated beetroot with the minced beef and a fair quantity of salt before clarifying to counteract the sweetness. Serve a bowl of sour cream and piroshki (see page 48) separately.

VEGETABLE BROTHS

French Onion Soup
1 lb. onions; 2 oz. butter; 1 tablespoon flour; 2½–3 pints well-flavoured stock; 1 small French loaf; grated Parmesan and Gruyère cheese.

Finely chop the onions. Heat a large thick sauce or stewpan, drop in the butter, and whilst foaming add the onions. Cook slowly until a good even brown (about 12 to 15 minutes). Stir in the flour, and after a few minutes, the stock. Simmer for 20 to 30 minutes.

Adjust the seasoning. Slice the bread and lay in a large earthenware casserole; pour on the soup, sprinkle the top with the cheese. Place in a hot oven until brown. Serve very hot.

Tomato Soup
1½ lb. ripe tomatoes or a medium-sized tin of tomatoes; 1 onion; 1 carrot; 1 oz. butter; 1 oz. flour; 1 pint light stock or water; 1 bayleaf; 2 lumps sugar; a pinch of ground mace or nutmeg; salt and freshly ground black pepper.

Wipe tomatoes, cut in four, and squeeze away the seeds (unless you use a tin); strain these and retain the juice. Finely slice onion

PENGUIN CORDON BLEU COOKERY

and carrot. Melt butter in a pan, add the vegetables, cover, and allow to soften for 5 to 6 minutes. Draw aside from the heat, stir in the flour, add the tomatoes, the juice strained from the seeds, stock, bayleaf, sugar, spice, and seasoning. Stir until boiling, simmer for 20 to 30 minutes. Put through a Mouli sieve or strainer, pour back into the rinsed-out pan, and reheat. Adjust seasoning and thicken slightly if necessary with a level teaspoon of arrow-root slaked with a tablespoon of water. Reboil. A little cream may be added to each bowl of soup with a sprinkling of chopped chives on the top. If the tomatoes are lacking in flavour, a teaspoon of the concentrated tomato purée may be added with them. Serve cheese croûtes either separately or in the soup.

Cheese Croûtes

Cut 2 slices of bread, stamp into rounds the size of a penny. Toast these on one side then spread the other with butter into which a little grated cheese has been worked, seasoning it well. Toast until golden brown.

Orange and Tomato Soup

2 lb. tomatoes; 1 onion; 1 carrot; 1 strip of lemon rind; 1 bayleaf; 6 peppercorns; 1 quart light stock; a good pinch of salt; 1½ oz. butter; 1½ oz. flour; ¼ pint single cream; pared rind and juice of half an orange.

Wipe the tomatoes, cut in half, and squeeze to remove the seeds. Slice the onion and carrot and put into a pan with the tomatoes, lemon rind, bayleaf, peppercorns, stock, and salt; cover and simmer until the tomatoes are pulpy (about 30 minutes). Rub through a Mouli sieve or nylon sieve and set aside. Clean out the pan, melt the butter in it, and stir in the flour. Pour on the liquid, blend, and bring to the boil. Meanwhile shred and blanch the orange rind, drain, and set aside. Add the orange juice to the soup, season to taste with salt, pepper, and sugar. Stir in the cream and add the orange rind.

Minestrone

2 oz. small white haricot beans; 2–3 sticks of celery; 1 large

42

onion; 2 tablespoons oil or butter; 2 medium-sized carrots; 2 cloves garlic; 1 oz. raw ham or bacon fat; 1 leek; ¼ of a cabbage or a handful of shelled peas; 3 large tomatoes; ham or meat stock; a large bouquet of herbs.

Soak the beans over night, then drain. Chop onion and slice celery, fry gently for 4 to 5 minutes in the fat, add the beans, the diced carrots, and about 2½ pints of stock. Crush the garlic with the ham fat and add with the herbs. Bring slowly to the boil, season lightly, and simmer for about 1 hour.

Then add the leeks, cut across into ½-inch pieces, the tomatoes, peeled, seeded, and chopped, and the cabbage, shredded, or else peas.

Remove herbs and continue to simmer with the pan covered for a further 30 minutes or until the beans are quite tender, adding more stock if necessary. Adjust seasoning of the soup, then serve with grated Parmesan cheese.

The vegetables for a Minestrone may vary according to the season and a proportion of dried vegetables (peas or beans) or pasta used with the fresh. Raw shredded ham or bacon (2 to 3 oz.) may be added with the garlic if wished. The vegetables should be very well cooked.

Sweet Corn Chowder

4 oz. 'green' streaky bacon; 1 large onion; 1 stick celery; 1 large green pepper, chopped and blanched; 2 medium-sized potatoes, diced; a small bayleaf; ¾ pint water; salt and pepper; 1¼ oz. flour; 1 pint milk; 2 cups sweet corn kernels either fresh, frozen, or from a tin; chopped parsley.

Remove rind from bacon and cut into dice. Frizzle gently until turning colour, then add the onion and celery chopped. When a golden brown, add the pepper, potatoes, bayleaf, and water. Bring to boil, add pepper to taste, and salt lightly. Simmer until potatoes are tender, then draw aside. Blend the flour with ½ cup of the milk and add to the chowder. Stir until boiling. Heat the rest of the milk and add to the chowder with the sweet corn. Simmer a few minutes, dish, and scatter the parsley thickly over the top.

Mushroom and Rice

8 oz. flat mushrooms; 2 medium-sized onions; 1½ oz. butter;
1 oz. flour; 2 pints strong chicken stock; 1 tablespoon rice; 1 bayleaf; 1 tablespoon chopped parsley and mint mixed.

Peel and stalk mushrooms, wash these, and chop finely. Slice
mushrooms thinly. Chop onions, soften them in 1 oz. of the butter
with the chopped peelings and stalks and the sliced mushrooms.
Lay these on the top with a piece of paper pressed down on to
them and a lid on the pan. After 5 minutes, draw aside, add the
rest of the butter, stir in flour, and pour on the stock. Season, stir
until boiling, add the rice and bayleaf. Simmer for 15 to 20
minutes, remove bayleaf, adjust seasoning, and add herbs.

Soupe Normande

1¾ pints water; 2 potatoes; 1 leek; ¼ small cabbage; 1 oz. flageolets;
1 stick celery; sprigged parsley; ½ gill cream.

Bring the water to the boil and add the potatoes, peeled and cut in
quarters, and the leek, split and cut in 2-inch lengths. Season with
salt and pepper, cover, and cook gently for ½ hour. Meanwhile
shred the cabbage (not too finely), blanch, and refresh; wash the
flageolets and leave soaking and cut the celery into 1-inch pieces.
Add all these prepared vegetables to the pan with the washed
parsley and continue cooking for about 1 hour. Just before serving
adjust the seasoning and add the cream.

PURÉES

A purée soup is one made from root vegetables or pulses, i.e.
dried beans, peas, or lentils, previously soaked.

For fresh vegetables, one method is to sweat them, i.e. to soften
in butter without colouring, stir in the flour, the amount depending on the farinaceous quality of the vegetable, and then add the
liquid. Alternatively, the vegetables (fresh or pulse) can be
simmered in the liquid stock or milk before sieving to a purée

and thickened if desired with flour or kneaded butter. Purée soups may be finished with a liaison of egg yolk and cream or milk (see sauces, page 368). This will bind the soup and give it a creamy texture, and for some may take the place of flour altogether, e.g. potato soup.

Care should be taken that a purée is not too thick, but light and flowing though slightly thicker than a cream soup.

*

Potato Soup (Parmentier)
1 lb. peeled potatoes; 1 medium-sized onion; 1½ oz. butter; 1 bayleaf; ½ pint water; 1 pint milk.

LIAISON: 1–2 egg yolks; ½ gill cream.

Slice the onion and potatoes thinly. Melt the butter in a stewpan, add the vegetables, cover tightly, and cook very slowly for about 6 minutes. The potatoes must on no account brown. Draw aside, add the bayleaf, milk, and water. Cover and simmer for 20 minutes. Then pass through a fine Mouli or wire sieve, return to a clean pan, whisk well, and add the liaison. Reheat. Serve with fried bread croûtons. Always add a little of the hot soup to the liaison (for method of preparing it, see page 368) before pouring it into the bulk of the soup.

Artichoke Soup
1½ lb. Jerusalem artichokes; 1 large onion; 2 oz. butter; 1 pint water; 1 pint milk; 1 oz. flour (good weight); 1 egg; ½ gill cream.

Peel artichokes and set aside. Slice onion and soften without colouring in half the butter. Meanwhile slice the artichokes, then add milk, cover the pan, and shake over the heat for 7 to 8 minutes. Pour in the water, season, bring to the boil, and simmer for 15 to 20 minutes, rub through a nylon or fine Mouli sieve, then return to the pan. Blend the flour with ½ gill extra of cold milk, strain into the pan, and stir until boiling. Simmer for a few minutes then beat the egg, add the cream, and add to the soup as for a liaison. Serve with croûtons of bread or potato.

Soup 'Georgette'

½ lb. ripe tomatoes; 1 small head celery; 2 leeks or 1 onion; ½ lb. carrots; 1 oz. each butter and flour; 2 pints water; piece of bay-leaf; pinch of sugar; small pinch ground mace or nutmeg; 1 tea-spoon arrowroot, if necessary; thin cream or 'top' milk (½ gill).

Peel and seed tomatoes, strain these, and reserve the juice. Finely slice onion, celery, and carrots, 'sweat' in the butter, stir in flour. Add tomatoes, juice from the seeds, water, sugar, bayleaf, spice, and seasonings. Stir to boiling-point, simmer for 30 minutes. Sieve and return to pan to reheat. Thicken slightly with arrowroot (which must first be blended with a little water) if required. Correct seasoning, boil 1 minute, stir in cream. Garnish with chopped chives. If necessary thin with a little milk before serving.

White Bean Soup (and Brown or Red Bean Soup)

¼ lb. small white haricot beans; 2 medium-sized potatoes; 1 large onion; 1 oz. butter; a bouquet (parsley stalks and a bayleaf); 1 clove garlic; 2–2½ pints light ham stock or veal stock; 2–3 rashers streaky bacon; 1 dessertspoon chopped parsley, ¼ pint creamy milk or a liaison of 2 yolks and ¾ gill single cream.

Soak beans overnight. Drain and rinse. Slice onion and potato thinly, sweat in the butter without colouring. Add the beans, bouquet, crushed garlic, and stock. Season lightly, but add no salt if ham stock is used. Cover pan and bring very slowly to the boil. This is essential for dried vegetables if they are to be properly cooked.

Simmer until beans are very tender (1½ to 2 hours or longer). Remove herbs and pass through a fine Mouli sieve. Return to the pan, bring the milk to the boil, and whisk it in. Alternatively add the liaison, adjust seasoning. Cut bacon in dice and frizzle until crisp. Dish the soup and scatter the bacon and parsley over the top. Use the same method for brown or red beans, and the same ingredients with the addition of ½ lb. tomatoes and a dessertspoon of tomato purée. The liaison of egg yolks and cream is omitted.

Lentil and Onion Soup

1 pint lentils; 3 oz. onion; 3 pints cold water; a good pinch of salt.

GARNISH: 1 medium onion; chopped fresh or dried mint; croûtons.

Pick over the lentils and wash well. They may be soaked overnight, or, since they are very small, cooked straight away.

Put into a stewpan with the 3 oz. of sliced onion, water, and salt. If the lentils have not been soaked add ½ gill cold water to the pan every half-hour, bringing the pan up to the boil each time. This accelerates the cooking, though it is slightly more extravagant on fuel; but it is a useful method when time is short.

When the lentils are thoroughly soft, pass through a Mouli sieve and if the soup is too thick, thin down with a little 'top' milk. Add the finely chopped onion, which has been cooked in butter till just turning colour. Simmer for 15 to 20 minutes, skimming frequently. Adjust seasoning, and just before serving whisk in a nut of butter. Serve with fried croûtons and a good sprinkling of the chopped mint.

Chestnut Soup

1 onion; 1 carrot; 1 tin whole chestnuts or ¾ lb. fresh chestnuts weighed when peeled (approx 1½ lb. before peeling); 1 oz. butter; 1½–1¾ pints chicken stock; ¾ gill single cream.

GARNISH: 1 apple, quartered, cored, and sliced; butter; chopped parsley.

Slice onion and carrot. Heat butter in a large pan, add the vegetables and nuts, cover, and simmer for 5 to 6 minutes. Add the stock, bouquet, and salt and pepper. Bring to the boil and simmer for 20 to 30 minutes or until nuts are very tender. Pass through a nylon or fine Mouli sieve, return to the pan with the cream. Adjust consistency if necessary, adding a little slaked arrowroot if too thin. Simmer for 2 or 3 minutes. In the meantime fry the apples quickly in the butter until brown, dusting with castor sugar to hasten the process. Turn soup into the tureen, and lay the apples on the top of the soup. Dust well with chopped parsley.

If tinned chestnuts are used, turn the contents of the tin into the pan after the vegetables have been sweated.

Bortsch (for Clear Beetroot Consommé, see page 41)
1 oz. butter; 2 shallots; $\frac{3}{4}$ oz. flour; 1 quart good beef or chicken stock; 1 large cooked beetroot; 1 carton cultured or sour cream.

Melt the butter, add the finely chopped shallot and cook until soft but not coloured; then blend in the flour and stock and stir until boiling. Grate the beetroot, add to the pan with seasoning, and simmer gently until well flavoured with beetroot. Avoid over-cooking or the colour will be spoilt.

Pass the soup through a fine sieve or Mouli, return to the rinsed pan, and reheat carefully. Beat in the cream, adjust the seasoning, and serve with piroshki separately (see below).

Piroshki

DOUGH: $\frac{1}{4}$ lb. flour; 1 egg; 1 oz. butter; $\frac{1}{4}$ oz. yeast; $1\frac{1}{2}$ table-spoons milk; $\frac{1}{2}$ teaspoon salt; $\frac{1}{2}$ teaspoon sugar.

Sift and warm the flour and salt. Cream the yeast with the sugar and dissolve in the warm milk. Beat the eggs and add to the flour with the milk. Beat thoroughly. The dough should be rather soft. Work in the creamed butter and set to rise for 30 to 40 minutes, knock down, then chill until firm. Roll out, stamp into rounds, brush with beaten egg, and put a teaspoon of filling on each. Fold over, shape into a turnover, prove for 10 to 15 minutes, then fry in deep fat.

FILLING: 2–3 tablespoons boiled rice; 1 hard-boiled egg; 2 oz. mushrooms; 6 to 8 spring onions or 1 shallot; $\frac{1}{2}$ oz. butter.

Wash and slice the mushrooms and cook in butter with the chopped or finely sliced onion. Mix all the ingredients in a bowl and season well with salt and freshly ground black pepper.

These piroshki are also served with the clear bortsch and may be baked instead of fried.

CREAMS

A cream soup is one usually made with a green-leaf vegetable first sweated in butter, or one previously cooked to a purée and beaten into a Béchamel sauce. This way will give a smoother texture for certain vegetables, celery for example. The liquid used is light stock or milk and the soups are generally finished with an egg and cream liaison.

It is important not to over-cook a cream soup as it quickly loses its delicate flavour.

*

Cream of Lettuce

2 large heads of lettuce; 1 medium-sized onion, finely chopped; 1 oz. butter; ¾ oz. flour; 1½ pints milk; freshly chopped mint.

LIAISON: 2 yolks of egg mixed with ½ gill cream; or 1 teaspoon arrowroot.

Shred the lettuce finely. Melt the butter, add the lettuce and onion, cover, and stew gently for 5 to 6 minutes. Draw aside, mix in the flour. Bring the milk to the boil, pour on, and add salt and pepper. Simmer for 15 to 20 minutes and pass through a fine sieve. Return to the pan, add the liaison, and bring to the boil. Correct seasoning. Scatter the surface of the soup with freshly chopped mint, and serve with fried croûtons (see page 34).

Cream of Watercress

Make a cream of watercress in the same way, taking 2 bunches of cress and the same amount of other ingredients. Omit the chopped mint.

Cream of Cucumber

1½ pints of white stock (veal or chicken); 2 large cucumbers, peeled and cut into ½-inch slices; a small onion; 1 oz. butter; ¾ oz. flour; salt and pepper; green colouring; chopped mint.

LIAISON: 2 yolks; ½ gill or more of cream or 1 teaspoon arrowroot.

Simmer the cucumber in the stock with the finely chopped onion until soft for 15 to 20 minutes, then rub through a nylon sieve.

Rinse out the saucepan. Make a roux with the butter and flour then add the sieved liquid. Stir until boiling and simmer for 2 to 3 minutes. Cool a little, add the liaison, heat gently until the soup has thickened. Colour delicately, correct the seasoning, and add a little chopped mint. Serve hot or iced with garnish of cucumber 'peas', i.e. scooped out from the cucumber, after peeling, with a pea-sized vegetable scoop. Cook these in boiling water, refresh them, and add to the soup before serving.

Cream of Asparagus

Cream of asparagus is made in the same way using approximately 30 to 40 heads of asparagus or two good-sized bundles 'sprue'. Reserve a few tips for garnish.

Cream of Spinach (1)

1 lb. spinach; 1 oz. butter; 1 shallot or small onion; ¾ oz. flour; 1 pint stock or spinach water; ½ pint milk; ½ gill cream; 1 egg boiled for six minutes; lemon.

Boil the spinach in plenty of salted water, drain, and press. Melt the butter, add the shallot, finely chopped, and soften without colouring. Stir in the flour off the heat, add the stock, blend, and bring to the boil. Season, put in the spinach, and simmer gently for 20 minutes. Put through a Mouli sieve, then return to the pan. Heat the milk and add to the soup. Adjust the seasoning, add a grating of nutmeg and the cream. Chop the egg coarsely and add to the soup just before serving with a squeeze of lemon juice.

Cream of Spinach (2: quick method)

1 small packet frozen spinach purée.

SAUCE: 1½ pints milk; 1 slice of onion; 6 peppercorns; 1½ oz. butter; 1½ oz. flour; salt and pepper.

TO FINISH: 1 oz. butter.

Allow spinach to thaw completely and pour off any liquid. Infuse milk with onions and peppercorns for 10 minutes. Melt butter in pan, stir in flour, strain on flavoured milk, and stir until boiling.

Simmer for 2 to 3 minutes. Draw aside. Beat in the spinach, season, and simmer for 3 to 4 minutes. Finish with the butter.

Cream of Onion

4 oz. onion (approximately 2); 1½ oz. butter; ¾ oz. flour; 1½ pints milk.

LIAISON: 2 tablespoons cream or 'top' milk; 2 egg yolks; 3–4 thin slices of bread.

Boil the milk and slice the onions finely. Melt the butter and, when frothing, add the onions and cook very slowly to soften completely without colouring. When the onions are cooked, add the flour and mix in well over the fire, for 3 to 4 minutes. Draw aside. Add the boiling milk, a little at a time, stirring well to avoid lumps. Bring to the boil, and allow to simmer for 15 to 20 minutes. Remove from the fire, add the liaison of egg yolks and cream, reheat carefully, and adjust the seasoning. Meanwhile cut the bread into rounds the size of half a crown and bake to a pale gold in a cool oven. Place at the bottom of a soup tureen, pour the soup over, and serve.

Crème St Germain

1 small cabbage lettuce; 12 spring onions or 1 small onion; a sprig of mint; 1 quart light veal or chicken stock; 1 pint shelled peas (old peas are best for this); ½ pint shelled young peas; 1 oz. butter; 1 oz. flour; ½ gill cream.

Slice lettuce and onions finely. Put them into a stewpan with the mint, about 1¼ pints of the stock, and the old peas. Simmer until the peas are very tender (about 25 to 30 minutes), take out mint, and pass the soup through a fine Mouli or nylon sieve. Melt the butter, stir in the flour, add the liquid, and bring to the boil, stirring continually; cover and draw aside. Cook the young peas in the rest of the stock until tender and add all to the soup with the cream. Bring again to the boil stirring well. Adjust seasoning and serve.

VELOUTÉS

These soups are made of strong well-flavoured chicken or veal
stock and on the same principle as that of a velouté sauce (see
sauces, page 370). They may take their name from the garnish,
of either shredded chicken, or diced or shaped vegetables, and are
generally finished with a fair proportion of egg yolks and cream.

*

Crème d'Orge (Cream of Barley)
1½ pints well-flavoured jellied veal stock (*fond blanc*); 2 oz. pearl
barley; ½ pint water; 1 oz. butter; ½ oz. flour; ½ pint milk; ½ gill
cream.

GARNISH: 1 carrot; 1 turnip; 2 to 3 tablespoons green peas.

Soak the barley in the water overnight. Next day add both to the
stock, cover, and simmer gently until the barley is tender, about 1
hour. Strain, reserving the liquid and about a tablespoon of the
barley. Prepare garnish by cutting pea shapes from the carrot and
turnip with a vegetable scoop. Cook these with the green peas
until tender, in boiling salted water. Drain and set aside.

Melt butter, stir in the flour, and pour on the barley stock. Stir
until thickening, then add the milk. Bring to boil, season, and add
cream. Simmer for a few minutes before adding the barley and
vegetable garnish.

The root vegetables may be cut into small dice if a pea scoop is
not available.

Lemon Soup
¾ oz. butter; 1 shallot; ¾ oz. flour; 1½ pints strong chicken stock;
1 small lemon; 2 egg yolks; ½ gill cream.

GARNISH: 1 egg white; 1–2 tablespoons cream; salt and pepper.

Melt the butter, add the finely chopped shallot, and cook slowly
until soft but not coloured. Remove from the heat, blend in the
flour, and pour on the stock. Pare the lemon rind, squeeze, and
strain the juice and add to the soup with seasoning and bring to the

boil. Simmer gently for 20 minutes and strain. Meanwhile beat the white lightly, to break it only, and add cream and seasoning. Pour into a cup and poach until firm. Turn out, slice, and cut into decorative shapes. Just before serving add the liaison to the soup, adjust the seasoning, and drop in the garnish.

Iced Mushroom Soup

1¾ pints strong chicken stock, free from grease; 6 oz. mushrooms; 1 level dessertspoon arrowroot; 3 egg yolks; 1 to 1½ gills cream; chives.

Wash mushrooms but do not peel. Push through a sieve or Mouli. Slake the arrowroot with ½ cup of the stock and bring the rest to the boil. Beat in the sieved mushrooms and simmer for 3 minutes. Draw aside and add the arrowroot. Reboil and remove from the heat. Beat cream into yolks, add to the soup as for a liaison, adjust seasoning, and thicken over the heat without boiling. Pour off, when the consistency of thin cream, and chill. Sprinkle the surface of the soup before serving with 'snipped' chives, i.e. cut with scissors.

Walnut Soup

2 oz. fresh walnut kernels; ½ pint milk; 1 oz. butter; 1 medium onion; scant ounce flour; 1 pint chicken stock; bouquet garni; 2 sticks celery.

LIAISON: 2 egg yolks; ½ gill single cream.

Blanch the walnuts, removing as much of the skin as possible, and pass through a nut mill or mincer. Scald the milk, add the walnuts, and leave to infuse. In the meantime melt the butter, add the finely sliced onion, cover, and cook slowly until soft but not coloured. Blend in the flour and stock, season to taste, and stir until boiling. Slice the celery, add to the pan, and simmer gently for 10 to 15 minutes. Strain through a conical strainer and, add to the walnuts and milk. Heat carefully, adjust the seasoning and thicken with the liaison. Serve with fried croûtons (see page 34).

Crème Vichyssoise

3 large well-blanched leeks; 1 oz. butter; 1 stick celery; 3 medium-sized potatoes; 1½ pints jellied chicken stock; ¼ pint thick cream; chives (optional).

Slice the leeks thinly, discarding any green part. Sweat them in the butter, without colouring, until soft. Add the celery and potatoes, also thinly sliced, and the stock. Season lightly and simmer until they are soft. Rub through a fine sieve or Mouli. Adjust seasoning and stir in the cream. Chill. The soup should be very smooth and bland. A few chives or 'snipped' celery tops may be sprinkled on the top before serving.

FISH SOUPS

These may be of the broth type or a rich cream called a bisque. For the latter where a shrimp or lobster butter may have to be made, an electric blender is helpful.

*

Fish Chowder

A thick broth of white fish, potatoes, and bacon. The liquid used is generally milk.

1 lb. fresh haddock, free from skin and bone; ¾ pint water; ½ lb. potatoes, peeled and diced; 2 rashers fat streaky bacon (unsmoked) or a 2-oz. piece salt belly pork; 1 medium-sized onion; ¾ pint creamy milk (or some cream added to it).

Lay the fish in a shallow pan, cover with the water and salt lightly. Poach for 10 to 15 minutes, then lift out carefully and flake. Add the potatoes to the liquid in the pan, cover, and simmer until tender but not mushy. Turn out all into a bowl. Rinse out pan; cut bacon or pork into small lardons, and frizzle gently with the sliced onion (adding a nut of butter if necessary) until golden brown. Add the fish, potatoes, and liquid to the pan and reheat gently. Bring the milk to the boil in another pan and add to the chowder. Adjust seasoning, bring to boiling-point, and serve.

Cream of Fish

¾ lb. whiting or haddock fillet; 1¾ pints good fish stock made from sole bones, well flavoured with vegetables and with the addition of a glass of white wine.

FOR THE VELOUTÉ: 1½ oz. butter; 1½ oz. flour; ¼ pint cream.

TO GARNISH: One or two parsley or chervil sprays.

Skin the fillet, poach gently in a little of the fish stock. Remove and pound it well in a mortar or bowl, or work in a blender.

Melt the butter, stir in the flour, and add the strained stock. Blend and stir until boiling; simmer for a few minutes. Boil the cream and whisk into the soup with the pounded fish. Adjust seasoning. Sprig the parsley or chervil from the stalks and blanch for one minute in boiling water; add to the soup and serve.

Lobster Bisque

1 medium-sized live lobster; 2 tablespoons oil; 1½ oz. butter; 1 glass sherry; 2 shallots, chopped; 2 pints good fish or vegetable stock; a bouquet of herbs.

VELOUTÉ: 1½ oz. butter; 1½ oz. flour; ¼ pint cream.

LOBSTER BUTTER: 1½ oz. fresh butter; coral from the lobster.

Split the lobster, remove the bag from the head and the coral. Reserve this. Heat a large shallow pan, put in the oil and butter, and add the lobster. Cover and cook gently for 4 to 5 minutes, then add the shallot and sherry. Cover again and put into a moderate oven for 15 minutes. Then remove all the meat from the lobster, adding the creamy parts to the coral and reserving the juice from the pan. Put the shells into the stock with the bouquet and simmer for 35 to 40 minutes, then strain. Meanwhile pound, or work in the blender, the lobster meat with the butter and coral until very fine, first reserving some of the tail for garnish. This should be cut into neat slices.

Now make the velouté, using the lobster stock. When boiling simmer a few minutes, draw aside, and whisk in the lobster butter. Adjust seasoning and consistency, if necessary, by the addition

of hot milk, if too thick, or a little slaked arrowroot, if too thin.
Add the cream and pieces of lobster, and reheat carefully without boiling.

STOCKS

A few general rules first:
All stocks should be simmered and not allowed to boil hard. Hard boiling results in a thick and muddy-looking liquid, instead of a semi-clear jelly.
Do not overseason stocks.
To keep any stock satisfactorily, it should be boiled up every day.

*

Bone Stock
For brown sauces, demi-glacé, gravies, etc.

2½ lb. veal and beef bones mixed; 6–8 peppercorns; 6 oz. each onions and carrots; a bouquet of herbs; ½ teaspoon salt; 3 quarts hot water (or enough to cover the bones by two thirds).

Wash or wipe the bones well, keeping them as dry as possible. Break them into small pieces and slice the onions and carrots. Put together into a large stewpan with the vegetables and *rissoler* them well in the oven or on the stove-top. This can be done in a roasting-tin in the oven, if there is no suitable pan, and turned into the soup pot afterwards. Pour on the water, add the bouquet, peppercorns, and salt. Half cover the pan and simmer continuously for 3 to 4 hours or until reduced by about a third.

When a clear *brown stock* is called for (i.e. for a consommé) the liquid, with the bones and meat, should be brought up slowly to the boil and a dash of cold water added once or twice to bring the scum quickly to the surface. Skim well during the process. Add the vegetables when boiling.

A well-reduced brown stock, i.e. jellied when cold, is sometimes called a *fond brun*, and a jellied white stock is called a *fond blanc*.

White stock is made exactly as above but without browning bones or vegetables. Bones used here should be veal and the

vegetables added *after* the liquid has come to the boil and been
well skimmed.

Ordinary Mixed Stock
For small sauces, gravies, broths, etc.

Make with raw or cooked meat bones, chicken carcasses, giblets,
etc., to which may be added bacon rinds and mushrooms, peelings and sliced vegetables (onion, carrot, leek, celery) in proportions of about a third to the total quantity of bone. A bouquet
garni, salt, a few peppercorns and water to cover well, 5 to 6 pints.

Put altogether into a large pan, bring slowly to the boil, skim
and simmer half-covered for 3 to 4 hours. Strain and, when cold,
skim off all fat. This fat can then be clarified and used for dripping, etc., and the stock used within 3 or 4 days. When making
stock of this kind it is best not to mix raw and cooked bones
together; use either all cooked or all raw and break up into as small
pieces as possible, especially in warm weather.

Vegetable Stock
1 lb. carrots; 1 lb. onions; $\frac{1}{2}$ head celery; small piece turnip;
bouquet garni; few peppercorns; $\frac{1}{2}$ oz. butter; 3 quarts hot water;
level dessertspoon salt.

Melt the butter in a large stewpan. Peel and wash the vegetables,
dry and slice them in big pieces. Shake over a slow fire until
brown. Add to the peppercorns salt, herbs, and the hot water.
Bring to the boil, half cover the pan, and simmer for 3 hours or
until the bouillon has a good flavour. It should be reduced by
about a third. Strain off and when cold remove any fat before
using.

Fish Stock
This is used principally for velouté sauces and for fish soups. The
best is made from sole bones; if these are not available plaice bones
can be used but in either case remove the head and trim off the side
fins with the scissors.

Place in a large pan with an onion and carrot to flavour, a few peppercorns, a bayleaf, and a pinch of salt. Pour on enough cold water to cover, bring to the boil, and simmer for 20 to 30 minutes (no longer or the stock will have a bitter flavour). Strain off.

If a strong, well-reduced stock is wanted (sometimes called a 'fumet') boil the liquid down as directed in the recipe.

For a fair quantity of stock, the amount for example that is required for a bisque, use a turbot or halibut head. This gives a good gelatinous consistency.

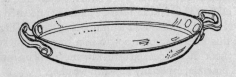

Chapter 3

EGGS AND CHEESE

EGGS

BOILED EGGS (ŒUFS À LA COQUE)

THERE is an art in boiling an egg so that the white is tender and creamy and the yolk soft. The usual way is to plunge the new-laid eggs into fast boiling water, and boil from 3½ to 4 minutes according to taste. Remove at once from the water, set in egg cups, rounded side up, and tap the shell sharply to break the air sac which helps to prevent the egg from hardening.

This method of boiling, however, can toughen the white and in order to get a perfect boiled egg it should be coddled. For this boil the eggs for one minute only, then draw the pan off the heat and leave for 5 minutes. Take out and the white will be a soft creamy texture and the yolk just set. This method is especially suitable for children and invalids as it renders the egg more digestible.

POACHED EGGS (ŒUFS POCHÉS)

Eggs for poaching must be really fresh otherwise the white will detach itself from the yolk when broken into the boiling water. Eggs from battery hens are also liable to behave likewise and should be avoided for cooking in this way. Though egg poachers are available and may save some trouble, they steam the eggs rather than poach them, and in order to get a good-shaped egg, with the white well covering the yolk, the best method is as follows:

Fill a medium-sized saucepan two thirds full with water, and add a tablespoon of white vinegar and half a teaspoon of salt. Bring to the boil. Break an egg into a cup. Stir the water clockwise with a spoon, and when there is a gentle swirl slip the egg into the centre. Follow at once with a second egg, dropping it immediately behind the first. Return pan to the heat and bring up to the boil, the movement of the water will help to throw the white up over the yolk. Draw aside and leave to poach until nicely firm. Remove carefully from the water with a draining spoon and slip into a bowl of hand-hot water. Repeat this process until all the eggs required have been poached. To serve, lift out with the spoon and drain well, holding a piece of muslin or clean cloth underneath. When dry, turn on to a round of hot buttered toast and serve at once.

To keep the eggs for reheating or for use in a cold dish, put them straight into cold water after poaching. To reheat transfer into a bowl of hot water or pour enough boiling water into the cold to bring the temperature up to hand-hot. Be careful that it is not too hot or the yolks will harden. Leave for a few minutes for the eggs to warm through before draining and drying as before. Dishes using poached eggs and suitable for a first course for a luncheon or as a supper dish are listed in the following recipes.

*

Eggs Mornay

5 or 6 eggs; 1 lb. potatoes; ½ oz. butter; about ¼ pint of hot milk; grated cheese.

MORNAY SAUCE: 1 oz. butter; ¾ oz. flour; ½ pint of milk; slice of onion; 6 peppercorns; a bayleaf; a blade of mace; 1 oz. finely grated cheese; ½ teaspoon French mustard.

Poach the eggs and slip them into a bowl of cold water. Boil the potatoes, drain, dry, and crush well with a potato masher. Using a wooden spoon, beat to a light purée with the butter and hot milk. Season to taste and set aside with the lid on the pan. Infuse the onion, bayleaf, and mace in the milk, and pour off. Melt the butter in the pan, stir in the flour off the fire, and strain on the milk. Blend well, return to the pan to heat, and stir continually until boiling. Simmer for 1 to 2 minutes then draw aside, season, and add the cheese by degrees with the mustard. Beat up the potato over the heat and arrange down a fireproof dish for serving. Warm the eggs through, drain and dry, and set on the potato purée. Coat with the sauce, sprinkle with the grated cheese, and brown at once under a pre-heated grill.

Eggs with Nut Butter

4–5 eggs; French bread; 1½ oz. shelled hazel nuts or almonds; 2 oz. butter; lemon juice; 4–5 rashers bacon; 1 bunch watercress.

Poach eggs; slip into warm water. Toast nuts in the oven until brown, then grind or crush. Cut a slice of bread for each egg. Fry in oil or butter until golden brown, drain, and keep warm. Grill bacon until crisp. Drain and dry eggs; set each one on a slice of bread. Put butter into the pan, heat until turning brown, then add nuts and a good squeeze of lemon juice, salt, and pepper. Spoon this at once over the eggs and garnish with the bacon and watercress.

Eggs 'beurre noir'

5 or 6 new-laid eggs; slices of stale bread, or tartlet cases of rich short crust previously baked; 2 or 3 oz. butter; 1 tablespoon

wine vinegar; 1 dessertspoon chopped capers and the same of chopped herbs; salt and pepper from the mill.

Poach the eggs and slip them into hot water. Stamp out a round of bread to fit the eggs, and toast. Alternatively, warm the tartlets in the oven. Lift the eggs from the water, drain, and dry. Set each one on the rounds of toast, or in the tartlet cases, dish, and keep warm. Heat a frying-pan, drop in the butter, and cook over a moderate heat. When turning a nut-brown quickly add the vinegar, capers, herbs, and seasoning. Spoon at once over the eggs and serve.

Eggs Aurore

5 or 6 eggs; rounds of bread (croûtes) for each egg; oil and butter for frying.

SAUCE AURORE: ½ lb. tomatoes; 1 shallot, sliced; ½ oz. butter.

BÉCHAMEL: 1 oz. butter; scant 1 oz. flour; 1½ gills flavoured milk; 2–3 tablespoons cream.

Poach the eggs and slip into cold water. Fry the croûtes until golden brown and set aside. Wipe tomatoes, cut in half, and squeeze to remove seeds. Slice and put into a pan with the shallot and fat. Season and cook to a thick pulp. Rub through a strainer.

Make the Béchamel sauce (see page 369) and beat in the tomato pulp. Boil, adjust seasoning, and add the cream. Warm eggs in hot water, then drain and dry. Heat the croûtes in a hot oven, dish, and set an egg on each. Coat over the sauce and serve at once.

Eggs Bigarade

5 or 6 eggs; ½ pint tomato sauce made with 1 small onion; 1 small carrot; ½ oz. butter; ½ oz. flour; ½ lb. tomatoes; ¼ pint stock; teaspoon tomato purée; a bayleaf; seasoning; 1 large orange; 1 teaspoon orange and lemon juice; 1 tablespoon brown sherry; seasoning.

First prepare the tomato sauce. Slice onion and carrot and cook in the butter for a few minutes without browning; stir in the flour and add the tomatoes cut in half and squeezed to remove the seeds. Add the stock, bayleaf, and seasoning. Bring to the boil, cover, and simmer for 15 to 20 minutes. Meanwhile pare the rind from the orange, using a potato peeler, and cut into thin shreds (Julienne). Blanch in boiling water for 2 or 3 minutes, drain, and refresh. Set aside. Poach the eggs and keep in warm water. Slice the pith from the orange and cut into thin rounds, one for each egg. Arrange in a hot buttered dish and keep warm. Strain the sauce, return to the rinsed pan, reduce a little if necessary, and add the fruit juices, sherry, and seasoning. Finish with a nut of butter. Drain and dry the eggs, set on the rounds of orange, and spoon over the sauce. Scatter over the orange rind and serve at once.

Eggs with Watercress (Cold)
4 to 5 eggs; $\frac{1}{4}$ pint thick mayonnaise; 2 bunches watercress; French dressing; lemon juice; cayenne or tabasco sauce.

Poach the eggs and slip them into cold water. Boil a half-bunch of watercress for 5 minutes, drain well, and sieve. Add this purée to the mayonnaise with a squeeze of lemon and cayenne. Chop the remaining cress coarsely and toss lightly in French dressing. Arrange down the dish; drain and dry the eggs, set on the water-cress salad, and coat with the mayonnaise. Serve with brown bread and butter.

Eggs Mikado (Cold)
5 eggs; 5 oz. Patna rice; 2 to 3 sticks celery; 2 caps pimento; French dressing; $\frac{1}{4}$ pint mayonnaise; sieved hard-boiled egg yolk and finely chopped herbs to finish; watercress.

Poach the eggs and slip into a bowl of cold water. Cook the rice in plenty of boiling salted water until tender, drain, rinse with hot water, and drain well again. Mix, using a fork, with the shredded celery and pimento and add French dressing to taste. Arrange this rice salad in the serving-dish, drain and dry the eggs well, and place on the top. Thin mayonnaise if necessary with a tablespoon of boiling water and coat over the eggs, scatter the sieved egg yolk and chopped herbs over the top. The hard-boiled white may be shredded and added to the rice salad. Put a small bouquet of watercress at each end of the dish.

Eggs Soubise

5 or 6 eggs; 2–3 large Spanish onions; deep fat for frying; 1 egg white; seasoned flour.

SOUBISE SAUCE: 3 large onions; 1 oz. butter.

BÉCHAMEL: 1 oz. butter; scant 1 oz. flour; ½ pint milk flavoured with a bayleaf; a few peppercorns; a blade of mace; 2–3 table-spoons of cream.

Poach the eggs and slip into cold water. Prepare the sauce. Chop the onion, cover with cold water, and bring to the boil. Strain and return to the pan with the butter. Cover and cook slowly until tender. Sieve through a nylon strainer. Prepare the Béchamel and finish with the cream and the onion purée. Adjust the seasoning, cover, and set aside. Slice the Spanish onions into rings about ¼ of an inch thick; put into a bowl with enough of the egg white barely to moisten. Toss about to ensure that the rings are covered with a film of the white. Then scatter in enough of the seasoned flour to coat the onions with a dry 'batter'. Heat the deep fat and when a blue haze rises from it, lower in the basket containing half the onions. Fry until a good golden brown, then turn on to a soft paper to drain.

Reheat the fat and fry the rest of the rings in the same way. Warm the eggs in hot water, drain, and dry well. Lay them on the serving-dish in a half-circle, spoon over the Soubise sauce, and arrange the onion rings at the side. If wished, the eggs may be dished on croûtes of fried bread or on a small quantity of potato purée (see page 357).

Eggs Mariette

6 eggs; 1 lb. tomatoes; 6 oz. shelled prawns; 1 to 2 tablepoons sherry.

CHEESE CREAM: 1 oz. butter; ½ oz. flour; ½ pint milk; 1 oz. grated dry Cheddar cheese and 2 oz. Parmesan cheese (or all Cheddar); chopped parsley.

Poach the eggs and slip them into a bowl of cold water. Set aside. Scald and peel the tomatoes; cut into slices and dust with castor sugar, pepper, and salt. Arrange the tomatoes in a buttered fire-proof dish and put in a moderate oven for 5 minutes. In the meantime prepare the cheese cream. Melt the butter, stir in the flour, and pour on the milk. Stir until boiling, draw aside, and add the cheese by degrees, reserving a tablespoonful. Season with French mustard, salt, and pepper. Warm the eggs, drain, and dry. Re-dish the tomatoes, place the eggs on the top, and scatter over the prawns previously heated in a nut of butter and the sherry. Coat with the cheese cream, scatter over the reserved cheese, and brown quickly under the grill. Dust with the chopped parsley.

Eggs en Croustade Cressonière

RICH SHORT CRUST: 6 oz. plain flour; 3 oz. butter; ¾ oz. shortening (lard or Spry); 1 egg yolk; 1 to 2 tablespoons cold water.

2 to 3 bunches of watercress; ½ oz butter; 1 teaspoon anchovy essence; salt and pepper; 5 new-laid eggs.

SAUCE: ¾ oz. butter; ½ oz. flour; 1½ gills milk; grated cheese.

Make up the pastry, set aside, and chill. Roll out, line into a fluted or plain flan ring and bake blind (see pastry making, page 393).

Poach the eggs, and keep in warm water.

Wash the watercress and chop coarsely. Melt the butter in a shallow pan, add the cress, and cook quickly for 3 to 4 minutes. Add anchovy essence and seasoning. Set aside.

Prepare the sauce, reserving the cheese. Heat the flan case, put in the cress mixture, drain and dry the eggs, and arrange on the top. Coat with the sauce. Sprinkle with the cheese and brown quickly under the grill.

Eggs Duchesse

5–6 eggs; 2 medium-sized onions; 1 oz. butter; 1 teaspoon paprika pepper; 4 oz. mushrooms.

POTATOES DUCHESSE: 1½ lb. potatoes; 1 egg yolk; a nut of butter; salt and pepper; hot milk.

HORSERADISH SAUCE: ¼ pint of velouté sauce made with ½ oz. butter; ½ oz. flour; ¼ pint of strong chicken stock; ¼ pint single cream; 1 tablespoon freshly grated horseradish; lemon juice.

Poach the eggs and slip into cold water. Set aside. Boil the potatoes in salted water until tender, drain, dry, and pass through a 'ricer' or sieve. Return to the pan and beat in the yolk, seasoning, and enough hot milk to make a fairly firm purée. Fill this into a bag fitted with a vegetable rose pipe and pipe on to a buttered baking-sheet, a croustade to hold each egg. Brush them with beaten egg mixed with a large pinch of salt and brown in a moderate oven. Remove and place on the serving dish. In the meantime finely slice the onions and cook in a covered pan with the butter until soft but not coloured. Add the paprika and sliced mushrooms and continue cooking for 3 to 4 minutes. Warm the eggs in hot water, drain, and dry. Place a spoonful of the mushroom mixture at the bottom of each potato croustade, set an egg on the top, coat with a little of the horseradish sauce, and serve the remainder separately.

For the sauce melt the butter, add the flour, cook for a minute, blend in the chicken stock, return to the heat, and stir until boiling. Simmer for a few minutes then add the cream and continue to cook until a syrupy consistency. Add the horseradish and a few drops of lemon juice. Adjust the seasoning.

Eggs en gelée

1½ pints chicken aspic; 5–6 eggs; 3–4 oz. cooked ham; tarragon or chervil leaves to decorate.

ASPIC: To have 1½ pints of aspic it is advisable to clear a two-pint quantity. For this take: 1¾ pints of strong chicken stock free from grease; ½ gill each sherry and white wine; 1 dessertspoon wine vinegar; 2 oz. gelatine; 2 egg whites.

Prepare the aspic first. See that the stock is well seasoned. Put into a large enamel pan, add the wines to the gelatine, and leave for a few minutes, meanwhile whipping the whites to a froth and adding them to the stock with the vinegar. Whisk over moderate heat and when hot add the gelatine. Continue whisking until boiling-point is reached. Let the stock boil undisturbed to the top of the pan, draw aside, and allow to subside. Repeat this process twice more, then stand for 5 minutes before straining through a scalded cloth. Shred the ham, divide it between 5 or 6 small cocottes and add a tablespoonful of aspic to each. When set, drain and dry the eggs and set one in each cocotte. Add enough cool aspic to set each egg in position and leave again to set. Decorate each one with tarragon leaves and carefully fill to the brim with the aspic.

BUTTERED AND SCRAMBLED EGGS

Buttered eggs are those that are cooked to a creamy consistency with plenty of butter. For first-course dishes and savouries various additions can be made either during the cooking (pounded anchovy for example) or when serving with another ingredient, such as devilled shrimps (see page 99) and so on. For the basic recipe allow 2 eggs per person, 1 oz. butter; salt and pepper to taste. Crack eggs into a bowl, beat up with a fork to break them well, season. Melt half the butter in a thick or double saucepan, pour in the eggs, and cook over moderate heat. Stir occasionally at first, using a tablespoon until the eggs begin to set, then more rapidly, using a scraping movement; at this stage draw off the heat and add the rest of the butter in small pieces. Continue to cook for another half minute if necessary, but be careful to keep the eggs soft and creamy. Remove from the heat before they are quite cooked as they will continue to set in the heat of the pan. Turn at once on to hot buttered toast. The following recipes are suitable to serve for a first course for lunch.

*

Buttered Eggs with Tarragon
6 eggs; 3 oz. butter; 1 tablespoon chopped tarragon leaves or other herbs; 1 tablespoon 'snipped' chives; salt and pepper.

Break eggs into a bowl, beat up with a fork, season. Melt two thirds of the butter in a saucepan. Add two thirds of the eggs with the herbs and chives. Cook as described above, and when on the point of setting add the rest of the eggs and butter at once. Serve either on hot buttered toast or with hot dry toast and fresh butter to accompany.

Buttered Eggs with Cheese

Cook as above with chives only. When the remaining egg and butter is added, stir in 4 tablespoons grated Gruyère cheese and 2 to 3 tablespoons cream.

Scrambled Eggs

These are cooked in the same way as buttered eggs, but have less butter and the addition of milk or cream. They may be flavoured or garnished as for buttered eggs.

Take 2 eggs per person; ¾ oz. butter; 1–2 tablespoons milk or cream; salt and pepper. Cook as for buttered eggs, putting the milk into the beaten egg and melting most of the butter at the beginning. A small piece is reserved to be added just before serving. Avoid over-cooking and the addition of too much milk, as this will turn the eggs into watery mixture instead of a light creamy scramble.

Another way of scrambling eggs, especially suitable for children and invalids as being less rich, is to take ½ oz. butter to 2 eggs and 3 tablespoons of milk. Put butter and milk into the saucepan with salt and pepper. Bring to the boil and set aside. Break the eggs directly into the pan and stir continually over gentle heat. After 2 to 3 minutes increase heat and stir more slowly until the desired consistency is reached.

Buttered or scrambled eggs added to chopped hard-boiled eggs for a sandwich filling give a creamy consistency and increase the quantity.

EGGS 'EN COCOTTE' AND 'SUR LE PLAT'

This way of cooking eggs is known in this country as baked eggs. The eggs used should be the freshest possible and are cooked until barely set, either in special oven-ware pots or cocottes, or broken into a shallow buttered dish. Cream, or milk with seasoning, is added and the cocottes put into the oven to cook.

The eggs in the dish (*sur le plat*) may be started on top, and, once the white has begun to set, the dish may be covered and put into the oven for 4 to 5 minutes to complete cooking. Alternatively the dish can be slid under a low grill, uncovered. In this case the eggs are first sprinkled with grated cheese and melted butter, as a protective coating.

Eggs cooked in either of these ways may have any savoury mixture, meat or vegetable, previously cooked, arranged in the bottom of the cocottes, fireproof or copper dish, before the eggs are broken in. In any event the eggs should be lightly cooked as overdone they become unpalatable. Like buttered eggs they will continue cooking after the cocottes or dish has been removed from the oven, and this should be taken into account.

*

Eggs 'en cocotte' with cream
4–5 eggs; 1 oz. butter; ¼ pint thick cream.

Well butter some cocottes, sprinkle them with salt and pepper from the mill. Break an egg into each. Set them in a bain marie and put into a moderate oven (Reg. 4 or 350° F.) for about 6 to 7 minutes or until the whites are barely set and the yolks still soft.

Boil up the cream, well season, and spoon this over the eggs before serving. Serve with hot toast.

As a variation, a spoonful of cooked mushroom, shredded ham, or chicken may be placed at the bottom of the cocotte.

Eggs 'sur le plat' Bonne Femme
2 oz. butter; 1 medium-sized onion, thinly sliced; 2 potatoes peeled and sliced; 4 oz. bacon, cut into strips and blanched to remove salt.

5 eggs; a little cream or 'top' milk; chopped parsley.

If possible, choose a metal dish in which the eggs can be served. The usual type is shallow and round with a curved edge as for an omelet pan. Failing this, first cook the mixture in an ordinary frying-pan, and turn the contents into a fireproof dish before breaking in the eggs.

Melt half the butter in the pan, add the onion and potatoes, season lightly, cover, and cook for 5 to 6 minutes. Take off the lid and add the bacon. Continue to cook, uncovered, for a further 5 minutes. Draw aside, smooth the surface a little, and make 5 depressions with the bowl of a spoon. Break the eggs into these, melt the rest of the butter and sprinkle over with a little cream or milk. Slip the dish into a moderate oven until the eggs are barely set. Dust with chopped parsley and serve at once.

Fillings used for omelets (see page 72) may also form a base for an egg *sur le plat*.

OMELETS

An essential for making a good omelet is a thick pan, preferably of cast iron, as this of all metals is the least inclined to stick. An omelet pan has a curved edge which makes the folding and turning of the omelet an easy operation. Avoid buying too big a pan, a good size is 7 to 8 inches in diameter with a base of 5¾ to 6 inches in diameter. This size is also right for pancakes, and though an omelet pan can be used for all sorts of frying it is better to keep it for omelets and pancakes only and have a larger frying-pan for general use. After making an omelet, it is usually sufficient to wipe the pan round immediately with a damp cloth dipped in salt, but, if used for frying, wash and dry it well, then grease it thoroughly with oil or dripping before putting it away. This treatment will prevent sticking. For a pan that is sticking badly, pour in enough salad oil to cover the bottom and leave for 24 hours. Heat it, pour off the oil, and wipe round with soft paper.

There are two kinds of omelets, the French and the soufflé omelet. The former is nearly always a savoury one, either plain, with herbs or cheese, or alternatively with a variety of fillings. A soufflé omelet, with one or two exceptions, is sweet, flavoured with a liqueur, or filled with fruit of some kind.

When making a French omelet do not have too many eggs in the pan as it is then difficult to get the correct consistency. For a pan the size of that mentioned above three eggs for a plain omelet and two for a stuffed one is the maximum amount. For a larger pan, i.e. 9 to 10 inches in diameter, six eggs is as much as can be managed comfortably.

Ideally when omelets are called for, make them individually for they can then be done to personal taste, well cooked or *baveuse* (soft and runny). For a soufflé omelet a large pan is better, the omelet then being simpler to cook and looking more effective on the dish.

*

French Omelet

3 eggs; $\frac{1}{2}$–$\frac{3}{4}$ oz. butter; 1 tablespoon water.

Break the eggs into a bowl and beat them up with a fork until they will run freely, but are only lightly frothy. Add the water and seasoning. Heat the pan thoroughly, drop in the butter, and while it is still foaming pour in the egg mixture. Leave for 10 seconds to allow the eggs to set on the bottom of the pan, then, with the flat of a table fork, stir round slowly 2 or 3 times to give thick creamy flakes and also to allow the raw egg to drop back on to the hot pan. At this stage, when the omelet is half cooked, grated cheese (about 1 ounce) may be scattered over, or the chosen heated filling spread over the surface. Now start to fold the omelet by tilting the pan away from you and lifting the edge of the omelet nearest to you with the fork. Here any raw egg will run back on to the bottom of the pan. Continue quickly to fold or roll the omelet up (fold if there is a filling or roll if plain). Have ready a hot plate or dish already chosen. Change your grip on the pan so that the handle runs up across the palm between the finger and thumb, and, holding the dish in the other hand, tilt the omelet on to it with a quick movement. Serve at once.

If the omelet is stuffed with, for example, a kidney mixture (see below) it is usual to reserve a good spoonful of this and put it across the top of the omelet when turned out. For a herb omelet, add a good dessertspoonful of chopped mixed herbs, including parsley, to the raw mixture, enough to make it a good green colour.

71

For a plain, cheese, or herb omelet allow two eggs per person; if filled, three eggs is generally sufficient for two people for a first course. When making several omelets, break the total number of eggs required and measure the mixture with a small cup or ladle. This will save time and ensure that each omelet has the correct amount of eggs. Some of the fillings suitable for French omelets are:

a. TOMATO: I shallot; I oz. butter; ½ lb. tomatoes; chopped mint; salt and pepper.

Finely chop the shallot, soften slowly in the butter, then add the tomatoes peeled, quartered, and pipped. Season, add a scattering of the mint, cover the pan, and simmer for about 5 minutes until the tomatoes are just soft.

b. KIDNEYS: I shallot; I oz. butter; 2 lambs' kidneys; I dessert-spoon flour; ½ gill stock; I tablespoon sherry; salt and pepper; ½ teaspoon tomato purée.

Finely chop the shallot, soften in the butter without colouring, then add the kidneys skinned and cut across into slices. Increase heat and sauté briskly until it is turning colour. Draw aside, stir in the flour, add stock, tomato purée, sherry, and seasoning. Bring to the boil and simmer for 5 to 6 minutes. Add a little more stock if the sauce is too thick; the consistency should be that of thick cream.

c. BACON AND POTATOES: 3–4 rashers of streaky bacon; 2 table-spoons of bacon fat or butter; 2–3 cooked or raw potatoes; I tablespoon chopped parsley; salt and pepper.

Remove rind from the bacon and cut the rashers across into strips. Heat the fat in a small frying-pan, add the bacon and the potatoes cut in dice, and fry gently until both are brown. If raw potatoes are used now cover the pan and continue to cook gently until soft. Finish with the parsley and seasoning.

d. WATERCRESS AND GRUYÈRE CHEESE: 2 bunches good watercress; 3 tablespoons thick cream; 1½–2 oz. grated Gruyère cheese; salt and pepper; tabasco sauce.

Chop the watercress rather coarsely, using all the stalks. Boil the cream for a minute then add watercress and toss up over a moderate heat for a few minutes, but do not over-cook. Season well adding a good dash of tabasco. Make the omelet in the usual way, scattering the cheese over the surface when the omelet is half-done; then fill with the watercress, fold over, and turn out.

e. WITH CROÛTONS:

Finely dice some slices of stale bread, enough to make 4 tablespoons. Fry until golden brown in clarified butter (see page 476) or in deep fat. Sprinkle with salt. Make the omelets in the usual way and just before folding scatter a tablespoonful over the surface. When dished, a curl of grilled or fried bacon may decorate the top of each.

For certain fillings, for example spinach *en branche* or purée, the omelet may be coated with a light cheese sauce, a ham omelet with a tomato cream sauce, and so on.

Soufflé Omelet, Sweet

4 large eggs; 2 tablespoons cream or creamy milk; 1 dessertspoon sugar; ½ oz. fresh butter; hot jam or rum; icing sugar; red-hot skewers.

Separate the yolks and whites of egg. Work yolks with the cream and sugar. Whip whites to a firm snow, pour the yolk mixture over them, cutting and folding it in until both are barely incorporated. Heat a large omelet pan (one with a base of 8 inches), drop in the butter, and, while it is still foaming, pour in the mixture. Stir once or twice over a moderate heat, then leave for about a minute to allow the bottom to brown. Slip the pan into the oven (380–400° F. or Reg. 5–6) for 3 to 4 minutes, to set the omelet or put under a moderately heated grill. Quickly spread with hot jam and fold over with a palette knife. Slide on to a hot dish, dust well with icing sugar, have ready the skewers, red hot, and mark across lattice-fashion. If no means of heating the skewers is

available, dust the omelet with castor sugar in place of icing sugar.
Serve at once.

For a rum omelet, heat 2 to 3 tablespoons of rum, light when
the omelet is ready to serve, and pour round.

Other fillings are:

a. Bananas sliced diagonally and fried in butter, dusted with
castor sugar and sprinkled with rum.

b. Strawberries or raspberries mixed with either redcurrant
jelly glaze or Melba sauce (see page 418).

For Omelet Soufflé en Surprise (with ice-cream) see page 435.

Rum Omelet (another method)
4 yolks egg; 3 oz. castor sugar; 6 whites; icing sugar for finishing;
3–4 tablespoons rum.

Add castor sugar to the yolks by degrees and beat well, adding a
little rum to flavour. Whip whites to a firm snow, stir a good tablespoon into the yolk mixture, then cut and fold in the remaining
whites.

Well butter a fireproof dish, sprinkle with icing sugar, and turn
the mixture into the dish. Shape into an oval with a palette knife
and make a depression down the centre and several cuts with the
knife round the sides to facilitate the cooking of the omelet.
Set the dish on the hot-plate for a minute or two then put into a
moderately hot oven (380° F., Reg. 5) for about 7 minutes. Then
remove, dust quickly with icing sugar, and replace in the oven or
brown lightly under the grill. Heat rum, light it, and pour round
the omelet. Serve at once.

Omelet Germiny
5 eggs; salt and pepper; a little clarified butter.

FILLING: 1 bunch small spring onions; ½ oz. butter.

MORNAY SAUCE: 1 oz. butter; ¾ oz. flour; ½ pint milk; 1½ oz.
grated cheese.

Have ready an omelet pan well greased with the clarified butter and keep hot. Cream the egg yolks with the seasoning, fold in the stiffly whisked whites, and pour into the prepared pan. Shake over a moderate heat for about one minute then place in a hot oven (400° F. or Reg. 6) for about 5 to 6 minutes or until barely set. Meanwhile cut the spring onions into one-inch lengths, sauté in butter until soft, and season lightly. Prepare the Mornay sauce in the usual way. Turn the omelet on to a warm serving-dish, place the filling in the centre, and fold in half. Coat at once with the sauce and glaze under the grill.

Omelet Arnold Bennett

5 eggs; 1½ gills cream; 5 oz. cooked, flaked, smoked haddock, i.e. about ½ lb. before cooking and skinning; 2½ oz. butter; seasoning; 2–3 tablespoons grated Parmesan cheese.

Toss the haddock over a quick heat with half the butter and 2 to 3 tablespoons of the cream and allow to cool. Separate the eggs, beat the yolks with a tablespoon of the cream, and season. Whip the whites lightly, fold into the yolks with the haddock, add half the grated cheese. Cook omelet in the usual way in the rest of the butter. Do not fold but slide on to a hot dish, scatter over the rest of the cheese, spoon over remaining cream, and brown at once under a hot grill. Sufficient for 5 to 6 people.

NOTE: The butter may be clarified as for the Germiny. This is a precaution to prevent the omelet over-browning too quickly, or sticking to the pan.

Omelet Soufflé

This recipe is a slightly different type of omelet and one that does not involve last-minute cooking.

5 eggs; 2 tablespoons cream or milk; 2 tablespoons grated Parmesan cheese; ½ oz. butter; salt and pepper.

FILLING: 4–6 oz. flaked cooked smoked haddock; 1 shallot finely chopped; ½ oz. butter; level dessertspoon flour; ¼ pint single cream or creamy milk; chopped parsley (1 teaspoonful).

First prepare the filling. Melt butter, add the shallot, finely sliced, cook slowly until just soft, stir in the flour, pour on the cream or milk, bring to the boil, and add the haddock and parsley. Set aside. Separate the eggs. Beat the yolks with the cream, half the cheese, and seasoning. Whip whites to a firm snow and cut and fold into the yolks. Melt the butter in a fireproof, copper, or enamelled iron dish. Turn the egg mixture into it, shape into an oval, and make a hollow down the middle. Scatter over the rest of the cheese and set the dish in a moderately hot oven (380° F. or Reg. 5 to 6) for 8 to 10 minutes. Reheat the haddock mixture and, when the omelet is ready to serve, spoon it down the centre. Serve at once.

NOTE: Any other filling may be used in place of the fish; shredded ham, prawn or tomato, mushroom, etc.

Spanish Omelets

These are cooked flat in the pan without disturbance and slid out on to a hot dish when set, to be cut like a cake for serving. The eggs are mixed with an assortment of raw or cooked vegetables before cooking.

2 cupfuls of mixed cooked vegetables: green peas, finely diced carrots, green beans, sliced or diced, diced potatoes, etc.; 1 cupful tomatoes, peeled, seeded, and chopped; 3–4 tablespoons olive oil; 1 or more cloves of garlic, chopped; 1 medium-sized onion, sliced; 5 eggs; salt and pepper; level teaspoon paprika; chopped mixed herbs.

Mix the vegetables with the tomatoes and set aside. Heat the oil in a large frying-pan, add the garlic and onion, and fry gently until soft. Turn the vegetables into the pan, season well with the salt, pepper, and paprika, and heat thoroughly. Beat the eggs and pour into the pan. Stir once or twice, then leave until the eggs are barely set. Push the pan under a pre-heated grill to brown, run a palette knife underneath to loosen the omelet, then slide out or turn over on to a flat dish. Sprinkle with the herbs and serve at once.

Potato Omelet

2–3 oz. raw lean ham or gammon rasher; ¾ gill (a wineglass) olive oil; 1 Spanish onion, thinly sliced; 6 oz. (about 2 to 3 potatoes) also sliced or coarsely grated; 4 eggs.

Heat the oil, add the ham chopped, and, after a few minutes, the onion. Continue to fry gently until the onion is half cooked, then add the potato. Season well and cook until soft. Drain off any superfluous oil and add the eggs well beaten. Stir to mix, then leave to allow the underneath to brown. When the mixture is barely set, slide the pan under the grill to brown the surface. When well browned slip or turn out on to a flat dish and serve at once.

The outside should be brown and crisp, the inside soft.

FRIED EGGS

Used mostly as a breakfast or supper dish.

For plain fried eggs and bacon, fry the eggs in plenty of bacon fat or dripping and, if not enough to cover when they are in the pan, baste well with the hot fat while they are cooking. Fry them gently so that the white does not become brown and tough. When the yolk is nicely set, lift out the eggs with a slicer on to a hot dish and surround with rashers of grilled or fried bacon.

*

Deep-fried eggs

These should be round in shape when fried and a light golden brown. The eggs should be as fresh as possible, and the oil used for frying in a small thick saucepan. Heat the oil until a slight blue haze comes from the surface. Break an egg into a cup and slip it carefully into the hot fat. Allow 2 to 3 minutes for frying, then lift out with a perforated spoon to drain thoroughly. This is the easiest method to deep fry eggs, though it is possible to do them in a frying-pan with an inch or so of fat. When fried on one side the egg is turned to allow it to brown on the other. The shape, however, is not so good as when fried in deep fat.

Gascon Eggs

5 eggs; 1 lb. tomatoes; 1 clove garlic; 1 oz. butter; 1 aubergine; oil for frying; 2 slices lean raw ham or gammon rasher, 3–4 oz. in all; chopped parsley.

Peel and slice aubergine, sprinkle lightly with salt, and leave for ½ hour. Meantime scald, peel, and slice the tomatoes. Melt butter in a shallow saucepan, add the garlic, crushed with salt, the tomatoes, salt, and pepper. Cover and cook for 4 to 5 minutes until soft. Draw aside and keep warm. Cut the ham into strips and fry in a spoonful or two of oil for a few minutes, remove and keep warm. Now drain and dry the aubergine and fry the slices in a little extra hot oil until golden brown and tender. Arrange in the bottom of a serving-dish. Keep warm. Deep-fry the eggs, drain, and place on the slices of aubergine. Scatter the strips of ham over the eggs, heat up the tomato, and spoon round the dish. Sprinkle with chopped parsley.

HARD-BOILED EGGS (ŒUFS DURS)

In order to be able to remove the shells easily from hard-boiled eggs lift them carefully into boiling water. Allow 8 to 10 minutes steady boiling from the time they reboil, then plunge them at once into cold water before peeling. Over-boiling will result in a grey lining to the yolk and the white may be tough.

Hard-boiled eggs may be served in many different ways; as a mayonnaise, for stuffing, both hot and cold, and in salads.

*

Egg Mayonnaise

5 hard-boiled eggs; 1 small lettuce; 1½ gills mayonnaise; chopped parsley.

MAYONNAISE: 1–2 egg yolks; ¼–½ pint olive oil; vinegar or lemon juice; salt and pepper, a little dry mustard.

First prepare the mayonnaise. Cream the egg yolks and the seasoning well together. Then add the oil, very slowly for the first two tablespoons until the mixture is thick, and then more rapidly.

Thin with the vinegar when the sauce gets too thick. When all
the oil has been added, finish with the remaining vinegar and
adjust the seasoning. Add a tablespoon of boiling water to bring
the mayonnaise to a coating consistency. Set aside. Cut the eggs
in two, lengthways. Shred the lettuce and arrange in the bottom
of the serving-dish, set the halved eggs on the top and coat with
the mayonnaise. Dust well with the parsley.

Eggs with Anchovies (Cold)
4 eggs; 8–12 fillets of anchovies; 2 oz. butter; fresh herbs.

MAYONNAISE: 1 egg yolk; $\frac{1}{4}$–$\frac{1}{2}$ pint oil; 3–4 teaspoons vinegar
and seasonings; lettuce and watercress for garnish; chopped
herbs.

Hard-boil the eggs, cool quickly, then cut carefully in two lengthways. Soak the anchovies in milk to remove any excess salt and
then pound in a mortar, or work in a basin, until quite smooth.
Add the creamed butter and sieved egg yolks, and season with
freshly ground black pepper.

Prepare the mayonnaise as in the preceding recipe. Fill the egg
whites with the anchovy mixture shaping each half to resemble a
whole egg. Dish the eggs on crisp lettuce leaves and coat with
mayonnaise flavoured with freshly chopped herbs (about a
dessertspoonful). Garnish with watercress.

Egg and Prawn Mayonnaise
5 hard-boiled eggs; 6 oz. rice; 1 cucumber; 6 oz. shelled or
'picked' prawns; half-pint thick mayonnaise; boiling water;
paprika; French dressing.

Peel the eggs and halve them. Boil the rice and drain thoroughly.
Peel the cucumber, cut into four lengthways and across into
small chunks. Thin the mayonnaise with the boiling water to a
cream. Colour the dressing with paprika to a good pink and flavour
it with garlic. Mix enough into the rice to moisten well. Arrange
the rice down the serving-dish, set the eggs on top, and coat
with the mayonnaise. Garnish each side of the dish with the
cucumber and prawns.

Eggs Clamart

5 eggs; I small packet frozen peas; mint; I oz. butter; mayonnaise.

SALAD: 2–3 heads chicory; $\frac{1}{2}$ lb. tomatoes; French dressing.

Hard-boil the eggs and cook the peas in boiling salted water until tender; drain and refresh. Rub the peas through a fine wire sieve and set on one side. Cut the eggs in two lengthways, remove the yolks, and pass also through the strainer. Pound the egg yolk with the softened butter, add the pea purée, and bind with enough mayonnaise to give a soft cream. Season carefully and add finely chopped mint to taste. Fill into egg whites using a bag and plain pipe. Arrange the eggs round a flat serving-dish and fill the centre with the chicory and tomato salad.

Eggs Hongroise

5 or 6 eggs (hard-boiled); 4 onions; butter or oil for frying; thinly sliced tomatoes, 4–6 according to size; paprika pepper; tomato butter.

Slice the eggs and arrange them in the bottom of the serving-dish. Slice the onions thinly and fry until golden brown in the hot butter or oil. Add the peeled and sliced tomatoes, first squeezing them after peeling to remove the seeds. Season and continue to cook for 3 to 4 minutes. Turn this mixture on to the eggs and dust well with paprika pepper. Put the dish into the oven for a few minutes to ensure that it is thoroughly hot. Just before serving, arrange pats of tomato butter on the top.

TOMATO BUTTER: 1–2 oz. butter; I teaspoon tomato purée; a good teaspoonful of Worcester sauce; salt and pepper.

Work the butter together with the purée, Worcester sauce, and seasoning. Spread out about $\frac{1}{4}$ inch thick and leave until quite firm. Then stamp into rounds the size of a two-shilling piece and lift off with a palette knife.

Curried Eggs

1$\frac{1}{2}$ oz. clarified butter or oil; I large onion; I tablespoon curry powder; 1 tablespoon flour; ½–¾ pint of stock (this should be light and can be made from a chicken bouillon cube); 1 tablespoon of redcurrant jelly or apricot jam; a slice or two of lemon; 2–3 tomatoes, peeled, squeezed to remove the seeds, and sliced; 1 tablespoon of mango chutney.

6 eggs; boiled rice (allow 2 oz. per person); fresh chutney to accompany.

First prepare the sauce. Slice or chop the onion, and fry until just coloured in the butter or oil. Add the curry powder and continue to fry for a minute or two. Draw aside and stir in the flour, pour on the stock, bring to the boil, and simmer for 15 to 20 minutes. Now add the jelly and lemon and continue to simmer for another 5 minutes. Adjust the seasoning, add the sliced tomatoes, cover the pan, and set aside. Boil the rice, drain, and dry. Reheat. Prepare the chutney. Halve the eggs and lay in a covered dish. Spoon over the sauce, cover, and gently heat in the oven. Serve with the rice and chutney.

Apple and Mint Chutney (quickly and easily made)
1 large cooking apple; 2 tablespoons good apricot jam; 1 tablespoon vinegar; 1 dessertspoon chopped mint (alternatively a little mint sauce may be used); salt and cayenne.

Peel and grate the flesh coarsely. Mix at once with the jam, vinegar, and mint. Season with salt and pepper. It should be both sharp and sweet.

Stuffed Egg Salad
6 hard-boiled eggs; 3 oz. butter; ¼ pint Béchamel sauce, made with ½ oz. butter; ½ oz. flour; 4 oz. tunny fish; 4 oz. cream cheese or cottage cheese.

RICE SALAD: 6 oz. Patna rice; ½ lb. tomatoes; ¼ pint shelled green peas or a packet frozen peas; 1 small head of celery; 1 red or green pepper; French dressing; cucumber, in season, or diced cooked carrot.

GARNISH: ½ lb. tomatoes; 1 bunch watercress; a few black olives; gherkins.

Cut the eggs in two lengthways; remove the yolks and rub them through a wire strainer. Pound the yolks with the well-creamed butter and divide into two portions. Mix one portion with the flaked tunny fish, pounding well, and the other with the cheese. Season both mixtures and add enough of the cold sauce to bind.

Now prepare the rice salad: Cook the rice in plenty of boiling salted water, drain, and rinse with hot water. Leave to drain. Scald and skin the tomatoes, cut into four, and remove the seeds; cook the peas and refresh until quite cold. Slice the celery and dice the cucumber; cut the pepper in half, remove the core and seeds, and shred, blanch, and refresh. Next prepare the French dressing, using 3 parts of oil to one part of vinegar, seasoning with salt, pepper, mustard, and garlic. Mix the vegetables and rice and moisten with the dressing. Season with extra salt and pepper if necessary.

Arrange the salad in a salad bowl, place the egg whites firmly on the rice, and pipe in the filling. Decorate the eggs with halved olives or sliced gherkins, fill the middle with watercress, and surround the edge of the dish with the quarters of tomatoes.

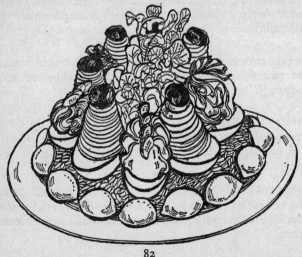

Eggs with Tunny Fish (cold)

3 hard-boiled eggs; 3–4 tablespoons flaked tunny fish; 3 tablespoons Béchamel sauce; 1½ oz. creamed butter or 1 tablespoon mayonnaise.

BÉCHAMEL SAUCE: ¼ pint milk flavoured with bayleaf, peppercorns, and a blade of mace; ½ oz. butter; ½ oz. flour for the roux.

SALAD: ½ lb. cooked French beans; 4 oz. black olives; ½–¾ firm tomatoes, peeled, quartered, and seeded; French dressing lightly flavoured with garlic.

First prepare the Béchamel sauce: Infuse the spices and bayleaf in the milk, strain on to the roux, blend and stir until boiling. Cool. Split the eggs, sieve the yolks, and cream or pound with the tunny fish, sauce, and butter. Season well. Dry the whites, arrange round a serving-dish, securing them in place with a little of the mixture. Put the remaining mixture into a piping bag, fitted with a plain vegetable pipe, and fill into the whites. Mix the salad ingredients together with the dressing and pile up in the centre of the dish. Other fish or meat such as chicken, ham, etc., can be used to replace the tunny fish.

Egg Mousse Niçoise

6 hard-boiled eggs; 1½ gills mayonnaise; ¾ gill light stock or water; 1 level dessertspoon gelatine; pinch cayenne; 1 teaspoon anchovy essence (or to taste); ½ gill partially whipped cream.

Chop the eggs and mix into the mayonnaise. Dissolve gelatine in stock or water and add with the anchovy essence; fold in the cream and turn at once into a plain mould or soufflé dish. Leave to set. Turn out and garnish with strips of anchovy; surround with a salad of tomatoes, black olives, and walnut kernels; garnish with watercress. Other salads may be used in season.

Eggs à la Grecque (cold)

5 hard-boiled eggs; 4–6 oz. smoked cod's roe; 2–3 oz. fresh butter; tomato juice and lemon to taste; a little cream if necessary; ½ pint mayonnaise; 1 level dessertspoonful gelatine; ¾ gill tomato juice.

TOMATO SALAD: 1 lb. firm tomatoes; rind and juice of half a lemon; salt, pepper, sugar; oil.

Cut the eggs lengthways, remove yolks, sieve. Pound or cream
the roe, free from the skin, with the butter, adding tomato and
lemon juice to taste. Add yolks with a little cream if necessary. Fill
back into the whites and reshape. Arrange in a serving-dish.
Dissolve the gelatine in the tomato juice and add to the mayonnaise. When setting, coat over the eggs, slice the tomatoes,
arrange on the dish, and pour over a dressing made with the
lemon juice, oil, and seasonings. Shred rind, blanch, and scatter
over the salad.

Eggs 'Gentilhomme' (cold)

5 to 6 hard-boiled eggs; 2 oz. foie gras or Belgian liver sausage;
1½ oz. fresh butter; 2–3 tablespoons thick Béchamel sauce; salt,
pepper, and mustard.

MAYONNAISE COLLÉE: ½ pint mayonnaise; ¾ gill light stock or
tomato juice; 1 level dessertspoon gelatine.

SALAD: ¾ lb. good tomatoes; 1–2 peppers; 4 oz. button mushrooms; 1 tablespoon oil; 2–3 tablespoons red wine (optional);
French dressing.

Cut the eggs lengthways and scoop out the yolks. Sieve the yolks
and cream with the foie gras, butter, and sauce. Season well.
Wash and dry whites, fill with the mixture, and reshape.
   Prepare sauce by dissolving the gelatine in the tomato juice or
stock, and add whilst still warm to the mayonnaise. Arrange the
eggs round the serving-dish and coat with the mayonnaise when
on the point of setting. Prepare salad by skinning and quartering
the tomatoes and shredding and blanching peppers. Quarter the
mushrooms and sauté quickly in the oil. Add wine and cook
until all the liquid has been absorbed. Mix all the ingredients
together with a well-seasoned French dressing, and pile up in the
centre of the dish just before serving.

Eggs Duxelles

5 hard-boiled eggs; 4 oz. flat mushrooms; 1 oz. butter; 1 shallot;
1 dessertspoon mixed chopped herbs; ½ pint Béchamel sauce;
1½ oz. grated cheese.

Cut the eggs in two lengthways, take out the yolks, and push through a strainer. Slip the whites into cold water. Chop the mushrooms and shallot and cook uncovered in the butter for 5 or 6 minutes. When the mixture is dry, beat in the herbs and 1 to 2 tablespoons of the sauce, together with the sieved yolks. When smooth fill into the whites rinsed and dried and arrange in a fire-proof dish. Beat 1 ounce of the cheese into the sauce and coat over the eggs. Scatter on the rest of the cheese and brown in a hot oven.

Egg Croquettes

4 hard-boiled eggs; 1 dessertspoon chopped parsley; 1 egg yolk; seasoned flour; 1 beaten egg; dried white crumbs; deep fat for frying.

BÉCHAMEL SAUCE: $1\frac{1}{2}$ oz. butter; $1\frac{1}{2}$ oz. flour; $1\frac{1}{2}$ gills milk; slice of onion; $\frac{1}{2}$ a bayleaf, a blade of mace, and a few peppercorns.

First prepare the sauce, and while still warm stir in the parsley, egg yolk, and the chopped hard-boiled eggs. Season well. Turn on to a plate to get quite cold. Divide into equal parts.

Shape on a well-floured board, brush with beaten egg, and roll in the crumbs. Heat the fat until a blue haze rises from the surface, dip in the basket (this is to prevent the croquettes sticking to it), and then carefully put in the croquettes. Lower the basket gently into hot fat and fry until golden brown. Drain well on soft paper and pile up in a hot serving-dish. Garnish with fried parsley and serve at once.

As a croquette should be soft and creamy inside when eaten, it is advisable to make the mixture overnight or at least some hours before shaping. This makes for easier handling. The shape of a croquette is best described as that of a short, fat sausage and, when rolling them on the board, avoid too much flour, as this gets into the mixture and so spoils it. Use two palette knives to shape rather than the fingers and have the beaten egg on a plate mixed with half a teaspoon of salt as this thins the egg and makes a better coating. Have a good quantity of dried white crumbs on a piece of paper and, using the edges of the knives, toss the croquettes in this, one at a time.

Eggs Chimay

3 eggs; 4 oz. mushrooms; 1 oz. butter; 1 small onion; 1 dessert-spoon chopped mixed herbs; 1 raw yolk; seasoned flour; beaten egg; dry white crumbs.

Hard-boil the eggs, wash the mushrooms in salted water, chop finely, and set on one side. Melt the butter in a shallow pan and cook the finely chopped onion slowly until soft but not coloured. Then add the prepared mushrooms and cook briskly until all the moisture has evaporated; season with salt and pepper and add the herbs. Cut the eggs in two lengthways, sieve the yolks, and mix with the raw yolk and mushroom duxelles. Refill on to the egg whites, shaping the mixture well so each half resembles a whole egg. Keep in a cool place until quite firm, then roll lightly in seasoned flour and coat with the egg and crumbs. Fry in deep fat until golden brown, drain, and serve with a piquante tomato sauce.

Eggs à la Reine

3 eggs; 2 oz. white button mushrooms; 1 oz. butter; 3–4 oz. cooked chicken, finely chopped; ¼ pint Béchamel made with ½ oz. butter; ½ oz. flour; ¼ pint milk; 1 raw egg yolk; seasoned flour; beaten eggs; dried white crumbs; deep fat for frying; fried parsley.

VELOUTÉ OR HOLLANDAISE SAUCE (see pages 370 and 376).

Hard-boil the eggs and split in two lengthways. Remove and sieve the yolks, and mix thoroughly with the Béchamel. Chop mushrooms, cook in the butter and add to the mixture with the chicken. Season well and bind with the yolk. Fill into the whites, shape, coat, and deep fry as in the preceding recipe. Garnish with fried parsley and serve with a Velouté or Hollandaise sauce to accompany.

Eggs Phoebe

6 eggs, hard-boiled; 3 oz. streaky bacon; 2 oz. butter; 2 table-spoons chopped mixed herbs (parsley, thyme, chives, etc.); 1 raw yolk; seasoned flour; beaten egg; dried white crumbs.

Dice the bacon and frizzle in a nut of the butter. Turn into a bowl. Split eggs in two, remove yolks, and sieve. Add to the bacon with the remaining butter, herbs, and yolk. Cream well and season. Fill into the whites, but sandwich them together to form a whole egg, allowing plenty of filling so that the two halves are slightly apart. Roll in seasoned flour, beaten egg, and crumbs. Fry in deep fat and serve with a pepper and tomato sauce.

SOFT-BOILED EGGS (ŒUFS MOLLETS)

Like poached eggs these can be cooked some hours before, and kept ready for serving cold or to be reheated.

Eggs Mollet are served principally as a first course dish for a lunch or as a main dish. They should be served on a purée of some kind, or in a pastry case before coating with the appropriate sauce. Eggs cooked in this way will retain their soft yolk if immediately plunged into cold water after boiling, and this is the reason why they are boiled for a longer time than the breakfast egg. To cook, lift the eggs into fast-boiling water, take the time from when the water reboils, and allow 5 minutes boiling time, 6 minutes if the eggs are very fresh. Then put them into cold water and leave for 8 minutes. Now peel carefully, first cracking the shell gently all over with the back of a spoon. When the shell is a mosaic, peel off a band round the centre with the side of the thumb. The end pieces will then slip off easily. Put the eggs into cold water until wanted. For reheating, see poached eggs, page 60.

Eggs Mornay, Aurore, Mikado, Soubise, en Croustade Cressonière, and Duchesse can be used for eggs mollet or poached.

*

Eggs 'Mollet à l'Indienne'
5 eggs; 4 oz. Patna rice (boiled as for rice salad on page 82); shredded pimento to garnish.

CURRY CREAM SAUCE: 2 tablespoons oil; 1 tablespoon chopped onion; 1 clove garlic; 1 level dessertspoon curry powder; 1 good teaspoon tomato purée and $\frac{1}{4}$ pint water, or $\frac{1}{4}$ pint strong fresh tomato juice; 1–2 slices lemon; 1 tablespoon apricot jam; $\frac{1}{2}$ pint mayonnaise.

Soft-boil the eggs as on page 87. Peel and keep in cold water while preparing the sauce. Soften the onion in the oil with the chopped garlic. Add the curry powder and cook for a few minutes, then stir in the tomato purée and the water. Add the lemon slices and seasoning. Cook gently for 7 to 10 minutes, then stir in the jam and boil up well. Strain. When cold add enough to the mayonnaise to flavour nicely. Drain and dry the eggs. 'Tease' the rice with a fork to make sure the grains are quite separate, then arrange down the centre of the serving-dish. Place the eggs on the rice, and coat with the sauce. Garnish with the pimento and dust with paprika pepper.

NOTE: Any curry mixture left over should be kept for future use. If wished, a larger quantity can be made and stored in a screw-top jar. Use a hot curry powder for preference.

Eggs Crécy

5 eggs; 1 lb. new baby carrots; $\frac{1}{2}$ oz. butter; salt; pepper; lemon juice; 1 dessertspoon chopped parsley.

SAUCE: $\frac{1}{2}$ oz. butter; $\frac{1}{2}$ oz. flour; $1\frac{1}{2}$ gills milk; $1\frac{1}{2}$ oz. grated Gruyère cheese.

Scrape or peel the carrots, leave whole or quarter according to size, and put into a pan with half the butter, salt, pepper, and water barely to cover. Cook until tender and the liquid is reduced to a glaze. Draw aside and finish with the remaining butter, a squeeze of lemon juice, and the parsley. Meanwhile soft-boil the eggs according to directions on page 87, and slip into warm water to reheat. Prepare the sauce as for a Mornay (page 369). Drain and dry the eggs. Arrange the carrots round a serving-dish. Put 2 or 3 tablespoons of the sauce on the centre of the serving-dish and set the eggs on this. Coat them with the rest of the sauce and serve at once.

Eggs Mollet Florentine

5–6 eggs; 2 lb. spinach; 1 oz. butter; grated cheese to finish.

MORNAY SAUCE: 1 oz. butter; 1 oz. flour; $\frac{1}{2}$ pint milk; 1 oz.

grated Cheddar cheese; 1 oz. grated Parmesan cheese; salt; pepper; French mustard.

Soft-boil the eggs, according to directions on page 87. Cook the spinach in boiling, salted water; drain, press dry, and toss up over the fire until hot with the butter. Keep warm. Prepare the Mornay sauce. Warm the eggs in hot water. Arrange the spinach on the serving-dish and drain and dry the eggs. Place on top. Spoon over the sauce; dust with a little extra grated cheese and brown under the grill.

Eggs Mollet with Ham
5 new-laid eggs; 5 thin slices of ham; 3 oz. macaroni; grated cheese to finish.

BÉCHAMEL SAUCE: ¾ pint milk; slice of onion; bouquet garni; 6 peppercorns; 1¼ oz. butter; 1 oz. flour; a spoonful of grated cheese to finish.

Soft-boil the eggs according to directions on page 87. Meanwhile cook the macaroni in plenty of boiling, salted water until tender, drain and refresh, and put at the bottom of a well-buttered gratin dish. Keep warm. Prepare the Béchamel sauce. Warm the eggs, drain, and dry. Wrap each in a slice of ham and arrange on the macaroni. Spoon over the sauce, dust with grated cheese, and brown under the grill.

Eggs Mollet Benedictine
5 new-laid eggs; 5 slices of thinly cut ham; 2–3 tablespoons white wine.

HOLLANDAISE SAUCE: 2 tablespoons tarragon vinegar; 1 egg yolk; 2 oz. butter; slice of onion; 6 peppercorns; a blade of mace.

VELOUTÉ SAUCE: 1¼ oz. butter; 1 oz. flour; ½ pint strong chicken stock.

Soft-boil the eggs according to directions on page 87. Prepare the sauces (see pages 370 and 376), first the Hollandaise then the

Velouté, and keep warm. Place the slices of ham in a buttered fire-proof dish, moisten with the wine, and slip into a moderate oven to heat through. Warm the eggs, drain, and dry. Roll each in a slice of hot ham and arrange in the serving-dish. Beat the Hollandaise sauce into the Velouté and spoon over the eggs and ham. Glaze quickly under the grill before serving.

Eggs 'Mollet en Croustade' (cold)
4–5 eggs; 1 cucumber; ½ lb. puff pastry; ¼ pint thick mayonnaise; freshly grated horseradish.

Soft-boil the eggs according to directions on page 87. Prepare a pastry case for each egg and in this place a spoonful of blanched, diced cucumber with a little chopped mint. Place the egg on top and coat with mayonnaise to which has been added the horse-radish to taste and a dessertspoon of boiling water. The pastry case may be a bouchée or a tartlet case, the latter baked blind (see page 393).

Eggs 'Mollet en Surprise'
4–5 eggs.

SOUFFLÉ MIXTURE: 1 oz. butter; scant ½ oz. flour; 1 gill milk; 1½ oz. Parmesan cheese; 3 eggs.

Soft-boil the eggs according to directions on page 87. Prepare the soufflé mixture (see page 92). Have ready prepared and well buttered a soufflé dish size 1 (see page 91), put a layer of the soufflé mixture in the bottom, drain and dry the eggs, and arrange them in the dish. Cover with the rest of the mixture. Dust the top with grated cheese and browned crumbs and bake in a moderately hot oven (Reg. 6 or 400° F.) for 12 to 15 minutes. Serve at once.

Flemish Eggs
8 eggs; 1 oz. butter; 1 tablespoon French mustard; 1 large table-spoonful chopped parsley; 4–6 oz. shelled prawns or shrimps; 1½ gills cream; 2 oz. grated Gruyère cheese.

Soft-boil the eggs, peel, and, while still warm, chop them coarsely on a hot plate. Have ready the butter, melted in a shallow pan, and add the eggs with the mustard, parsley, and prawns. Season with salt and pepper, and add the cream. Shake the pan up over a moderate heat for a few minutes and turn into a buttered fireproof dish. Scatter the cheese over and brown lightly under a preheated grill. Serve at once.

HOT SOUFFLÉS

These are comparatively simple to make, the only difficult point to judge being the right moment to take the soufflé from the oven. However, provided this is correctly set and preheated, the shelves adjusted so that the soufflé cooks in the centre of the oven, and the time given in the recipe adhered to, there should be little margin for error.

When ready to take from the oven, the soufflé should be well risen, firm to the touch, and of a good colour. The correct consistency of a soufflé when served is fluffy and lightly set, with the exception of the centre which is creamy. Care should be taken to choose the right-sized dish for the amount of mixture being made, so that the soufflé appears at the correct height above the dish when baked, approximately 2 to 3 inches. Soufflé dishes, or cases as they are called, are numbered in sizes underneath the dish, and indication will be given in the following recipes of the size to use.

Hot savoury soufflés are a useful vehicle for any leftovers, and the basic mixture may be either of cheese or tomato, or kept plain. Soufflés should be served straight from the oven to the table and not kept waiting. If you want to make a soufflé for more or fewer than four people, alter the ingredients proportionally, but remember to use one more egg white than yolk.

*

TO PREPARE A SOUFFLÉ CASE: Cut a band of greaseproof paper about 7 inches wide, and sufficiently long to go round the outside of the dish with an overlap of 3 to 4 inches. Fold over one of the edges of the paper to the depth of about 1 to 2 inches. Butter the top half of the paper and wrap it round the dish, the fold should be on the bottom half. Tie the paper round with fine string and set the dish on a baking-sheet or tin. As a rule the dish is not buttered, this makes it easier for the soufflé to rise.

Cheese Soufflé

1½ oz. butter; 1 oz. flour; 1½ gills milk; 4 egg yolks; 5 egg whites; 1½ oz. each of grated Parmesan and Gruyère cheese, mixed; salt; cayenne and paprika pepper; a little extra grated Parmesan cheese; browned crumbs.

Prepare the soufflé case (size 2), set on a baking-tray.

Melt the butter in a fair-sized saucepan, stir in the flour, add the milk, and stir until boiling. Cool slightly, beat in the yolks, one at a time, adding salt and cayenne pepper to taste; then work in the cheese. Whip whites to a firm snow and stir in one large tablespoon to soften the mixture a little, then quickly fold in the remainder. Turn the mixture into the prepared case, sprinkle the top with cheese and browned crumbs, and bake in a moderately hot oven for about 20 to 25 minutes. Remove paper, dust with paprika, and serve at once.

Soufflé Napolitana

CHEESE SOUFFLÉ MIXTURE: 1 oz. butter; ½ oz. flour; 1 gill milk; 3 egg yolks; 4 whites; 1½ oz. each grated cheese, Parmesan and Gruyère mixed; salt; cayenne and paprika pepper.

FILLING: 1 oz. spaghetti, boiled until tender; 3–4 tablespoons rich tomato sauce (al sugo, see page 104); a nut of butter.

Prepare a soufflé case No. 2 about 6 inches diameter. Heat spaghetti with the tomato sauce and butter, set aside.

Make the soufflé mixture, and turn one-third into the bottom of the dish. Layer with half of the spaghetti, then with a third of the soufflé, and complete in this way. Finish with cheese and brown crumbs. Bake as for cheese soufflé.

Other soufflés can be made in this way using a cheese soufflé as a base, for example with (a) shredded ham mixed with tomato sauce, (b) sautéd mushrooms, or (c) cooked fish of any kind.

Vegetable soufflés, spinach, artichoke, carrot, and so on, are made with a basic Béchamel sauce of 1 oz. butter, 1 oz. flour, and $\frac{1}{2}$ pint flavoured milk, to which is added 4 heaped tablespoonfuls of the vegetable purée. The mixture should be well seasoned and 4 egg yolks and 5 whipped whites incorporated.

For a tomato soufflé, the same amount of butter and flour is called for, but tomato juice or fresh tomato pulp is used in place of milk for the basic sauce.

Haddock Roulade
A soufflé in a slightly different form.

$\frac{1}{2}$ lb. smoked haddock weighed when cooked and flaked; 4 eggs; $\frac{1}{2}$ gill thick cream; 1–2 tablespoons grated cheese, preferably Parmesan.

FILLING: 3–4 hard-boiled eggs; $\frac{1}{2}$ pint Béchamel sauce made with $1\frac{1}{2}$ oz. butter; a good 1 oz. of flour; $\frac{1}{2}$ pint flavoured milk; chopped parsley.

First prepare the filling. Make the sauce, chop the eggs coarsely, and add with a good spoonful of chopped parsley. Keep warm.

Crush and pound the haddock to a purée. Separate the eggs and work the yolks and cream into the purée, season lightly, and finish with two-thirds of the cheese. Whip whites to a firm snow, and fold into the mixture as for a soufflé. Have ready a thick baking-sheet with a raised edge, lined with a buttered paper, or make a paper case size 12 by 9 inches. Turn the mixture on to this, smooth over, and dust with the rest of the cheese. Bake in a hot oven (400° F. or Reg. 6) for 10 to 15 minutes. Turn out on to a sheet of greaseproof paper dusted with Parmesan, peel off the paper, and spread thickly with the sauce. Roll up as for a Swiss roll and tilt on to the serving-dish. Serve at once.

Instead of the haddock other ingredients may be used: salmon, vegetable purées, and so on.

CHEESE

Cheese in the kitchen is generally an adjunct rather than a complete dish, though there are certain exceptions such as a fondue or toasted cheese.

Certain types of cheese are better for cooking than others, especially Parmesan and Gruyère. The latter, rich in fat and delicate in taste, is the classic cheese for a fondue, while the hard, dry Parmesan has a sharp, distinctive flavour and is the proper accompaniment for all pasta dishes. It is also the best cheese for a gratin as it browns well. In a sauce or soufflé the ideal mixture is Parmesan and Gruyère in equal proportions. Mozzarella, another Italian cheese, is a good cheese for cooking, as, unlike other cheeses, it does not become stringy when heated. It is principally used sliced on the top of certain dishes for grilling or baking.

For everyday use, any good, well-flavoured cheese such as Cheddar or Cheshire is perfectly satisfactory, provided it is reasonably dry and can be finely grated. Moist cheese is difficult to handle and inclined to lump when grated, and is best grated directly over a dish rather than sprinkled on with the fingers.

For toasted cheese or Welsh Rarebit, Leigh – a Lancashire cheese – is considered the best; this is not always possible to get, and a well-matured, dry Cheddar is a good alternative.

The right place on the menu for cheese is at the end rather than at the beginning; for example, a plain cheese soufflé is more appreciated as a savoury than as a first course. Cocktail savouries may also contain cheese, and here curd cheese, well seasoned and flavoured, is popular.

The following cheese dishes may be served as a main course for a luncheon or as a substantial savoury.

*

Crêpes Gruyère

BATTER: 3½ oz. plain flour; 2 whole eggs; 1 dessertspoon each oil and melted butter; 1¾ oz. grated Gruyère cheese; salt; pepper; 1½ gills–½ pint milk and water mixed.

FILLING: ¾ pint thick Béchamel sauce made with 2 oz. butter; 2 oz. flour; ¾ pint flavoured milk.

FINISHING: 1 oz. grated cheese; ½ oz. butter; 1 tablespoon chopped parsley.

Sift flour into a bowl, break in the eggs, add oil and butter, and pour in 1½ gills of the liquid by degrees, stirring well. When well beaten, add the cheese, salt, pepper, and cayenne and leave for ½ hour. Meantime prepare the Béchamel sauce, season well, and set aside. Heat a pancake pan, add a few drops of oil, and when hot pour in a good tablespoon of the batter – enough to make a fairly thin pancake. When brown on one side, turn and cook on the other for ½ to 1 minute. Turn on to a rack. If the batter is too thick, add the rest of the liquid. Continue cooking the pancakes, stacking them one on top of the other until the batter is finished. Fill the pancakes with a good tablespoonful of the sauce, roll up like a cigar, and arrange them in a buttered fireproof dish. Scatter over the cheese and dot with the butter. Brown well in a quick oven (400° F. or Reg. 6) for 7 to 10 minutes. Sprinkle with the parsley and serve very hot. See page 401 for a more detailed description of cooking pancakes.

Gougère

For a main course this is generally cooked in one dish, the cheese mixture being arranged round the sides and the centre filled with a salpicon of fish, vegetables, or game before baking. For a savoury, individual ramequins or ovenware cocottes are two-thirds filled with the mixture and if wished a spoonful of chutney or devilled ham, tomato relish, and so on, first put into the bottom of each.

CHEESE CHOUX PASTRY: $\frac{1}{4}$ pint water; 2 oz. butter; $2\frac{1}{2}$ oz. sifted plain flour; 2 eggs; 2 oz. finely diced Gruyère or Cheddar cheese.

PRAWN AND TOMATO SALPICON: 1 medium-sized onion; $\frac{3}{4}$ oz. butter; $\frac{1}{2}$ oz. flour; $\frac{1}{4}$ pint light stock; 2 tablespoons tomato chutney or relish; 2 large tomatoes, peeled, quartered, and pipped; 4 oz. frozen prawns; salt; pepper; grated cheese; chopped parsley.

First prepare the pastry. Boil the water and butter together; when bubbling draw aside and shoot in the flour all at once. Beat until smooth for about $\frac{1}{2}$ minute; cool. Beat in the eggs, one at a time, and continue to beat until the mixture is glossy looking. Then stir in the cheese and season well with salt, pepper, and mustard. Set aside. Slice the onion and soften in the butter without colouring; stir in the flour, add the stock, and bring to the boil. Draw aside, add the chutney, tomatoes and prawns, and seasoning.

Butter an oval fireproof dish, about 10 inches in length, and arrange the cheese mixture round the edge in a thick border. Turn the salpicon into the centre and dust the whole with grated cheese. Bake in a hot oven (400° F. or Reg. 6) for about 35 to 40 minutes. Serve very hot, dusted with chopped parsley. For individual ramequins allow 15 to 20 minutes baking time.

Quiche Lorraine

This well-known cheese-and-bacon flan is equally suitable for a main course or a savoury, and with less cheese is good as a first course. As a savoury, make up as small tartlets using a fluted cutter to stamp out the pastry to line the moulds. For a perfect quiche, cream instead of milk should be used.

PASTRY: 6 oz. plain flour; pinch of salt; 3 oz. butter; 1 oz. Spry; a little cold water to mix.

FILLING: 1 egg and 1 yolk; 1 oz. grated cheese; seasoning; 1 gill milk; 2 oz. bacon; 1 small onion or 12 spring onions; ½ oz. butter.

Make the pastry and line into a 7-inch flan ring. Then prepare the filling by beating the eggs in a basin, adding the cheese and seasoning and milk. Melt the butter in a small pan, add the bacon, diced, and the onions, finely sliced; if using spring onions leave them whole. Cook slowly until just golden in colour, then turn the contents of the pan into the egg mixture. Mix and pour into the pastry case. Bake at Reg. 5–6 until firm and golden brown (about 30 minutes). Serve hot or cold.

*

The recipes which follow should take their place as a savoury rather than a main course.

Welsh Rarebit

6 oz. dry, well-matured Cheddar or Leigh cheese; 1½ oz. butter; good ½ gill brown ale; salt; pepper; cayenne; squares of fresh dry or hot buttered toast.

Grate the cheese. Melt the butter in a shallow saucepan or small sauté pan, add the ale with the cheese and plenty of seasoning. Set the pan on a gentle heat and stir continuously until smooth and creamy, but do not get more than just hot, otherwise the mixture will be stringy. Turn at once on to the toast arranged in a hot dish and serve.

Toasted Cheese

1 oz. butter; ¾ oz. flour; 1½ gills creamy milk; 2 oz. grated cheese (Cheddar or Cheshire); salt; pepper; French mustard; squares or small rounds of hot buttered toast.

Melt the butter, stir in the flour, pour on the milk, and stir until boiling. Draw aside. Beat in the cheese by degrees and season well. Have ready the toast arranged in the serving-dish and spoon over the sauce to cover well. Brown under a hot grill.

Cheese Aigrettes (or Beignets)
Cheese choux pastry; deep fat bath; grated Parmesan cheese.

Prepare the same quantity of cheese choux pastry as for Gougère (see page 96).

Heat the fat until a very faint blue haze rises from the surface. Drop in the mixture carefully a teaspoonful at a time, allowing plenty of room for the mixture to rise. Increase the heat slightly and continue to fry the aigrettes for about 7 minutes or until well puffed up and golden brown. Lift out with a draining spoon, drain on soft paper, and dust with Parmesan. Serve very hot. Care must be taken to have the fat at the correct temperature. If it is too hot the aigrettes will brown before they have time to swell, and if not hot enough they will not set and will disintegrate before rising. The temperature of the fat, if a thermometer is used, should be 380° F.

Cheese Sablés
3 oz. plain flour; salt; cayenne pepper; 3 oz. butter; 3 oz. grated cheese; beaten egg.

Sift the flour with salt and a small pinch of cayenne into a mixing-bowl; add the butter and cut into small pieces with a round-bladed knife. Rub the butter into the flour, add the cheese, and press together into a paste. Roll out fairly thinly and cut into two-inch strips. Brush with beaten egg and cut each strip into triangles. Bake in a moderate oven (375° F. or Reg. 5) to a good golden brown (about 10 minutes).

SAVOURIES

These nowadays are more frequently served in place of a sweet than as an additional course, and so can be reasonably substantial. If, however, one is to follow a sweet, it should be small (not much more than a mouthful), piquante, and above all hot. In either event savouries should be simple, for the menu may have contained at least one rich course, and to fulfil its traditional function the savoury should clean the palate.

The classic savouries are 'Angels on Horseback' – oysters wrapped in bacon, cooked quickly under the grill or in a hot oven, and served on hot buttered toast; 'Devils on Horseback' – prunes cooked in red wine and stuffed with an almond and anchovy fillet, then wrapped in bacon and cooked and served in the same way; and the cheese savouries mentioned above. Marrow bones are also classic, and, though a little out of fashion, certainly deserve a mention. Properly served and presented they make the best of savouries.

HOT SAVOURIES

Marrow Bones

Ask your butcher for marrow bones suitable for a savoury, and he will then cut them into even-sized lengths.

Allow one per person with one or two over. In order to keep the marrow in the bone it is advisable to cover the top of each with a flour and water paste. Place the bones upright in a steamer or in the saucepan with boiling water to come two-thirds of the way up the bones. Cover the pan, and, if steaming, allow 50 minutes to 1 hour. If boiling, less time can be given.

To serve, remove the flour and water paste and wrap each bone in a strip of clean linen cloth, such as a napkin. Stand upright on a dish and serve with hot dry toast. To eat, a piece of the toast is laid on a plate and the marrow is scooped out with a marrow spoon (a thin elongated spoon) or the blade of a small knife on to the toast, and is then well dusted with pepper before eating.

Devilled Shrimps with Cheese Cream

Croûtes of bread the size of a 5s. piece (1–1½ inches in diameter) fried golden brown in hot oil or butter.

4 oz. picked shrimps, fresh or frozen; salt; pepper, cayenne or tabasco; 1 large tablespoon tomato chutney; ½ oz. butter.

CHEESE CREAM: ½ oz. butter; ½ oz. flour; ¼ pint creamy milk; 1½ oz. grated cheese; salt; pepper; mustard.

First prepare the croûtes, drain, and keep warm. Toss the shrimps up over the heat with the other ingredients when thoroughly hot, dish the croûtes, and pile the mixture up well on to each. Keep warm, prepare the cream as for the sauce, finishing with the cheese added by degrees, and season lightly. Spoon over the croûtes and brown well under the grill. Serve very hot.

This savoury may be varied by using cooked mushrooms.

Kebabs St Jacques

4 scallops; water; lemon juice; 4–5 peppercorns; a small bayleaf; 4 thin rashers streaky bacon; 1½ oz. butter; stale white bread; 1 bunch watercress; French dressing.

Poach the scallops for 3 to 4 minutes in water, barely to cover, lightly acidulated with the lemon juice, and the peppercorns and bayleaf to flavour. Draw aside and cool in the liquid. Remove the crusts from the bread and shred the crumb with a fork to give 4 to 6 large tablespoons of coarse breadcrumbs. Fry these gently in the butter until golden brown, stirring from time to time. Turn into the serving-dish and keep hot. Remove the rind and *rust* from the rashers and spread them out with the blade of a knife so that they are very thin. Divide in two. Drain and cut the scallops in half. Wrap each piece in a half rasher, and skewer on to a cocktail stick. Grill on both sides until nicely crisp or put into a hot oven for 5 to 6 minutes. Arrange the kebabs on the crumbs and surround with the cress dipped into the dressing. Serve at once.

*

Chicken livers skewered with tiny rolls of bacon and a scrap of bayleaf also make a good savoury served on fingers of toast spread with anchovy butter. Among the simpler savouries are mushrooms on toast; these can be varied by using the peelings and stalks, with one or two extra mushrooms finely chopped and cooked with a nut of butter to a paste, then spread on to the whole mushrooms. Dust with Parmesan cheese and cook these on a buttered baking sheet for 6 to 7 minutes in a hot oven before serving on croûtes of hot buttered toast.

Herring roes are also a classic savoury. Soft roes are used, lightly rolled in well-seasoned flour before frying in hot oil or clarified butter.

COLD SAVOURIES

These have their place in the menu but are more suitable for a lunch or a fork supper than for a dinner.

*

Camembert Frappé

1 Camembert; 1 Demi-sel cheese; a little hot milk; 2–3 table-spoons whipped cream.

Cut away the rind from the Camembert and pound or work until smooth. Cream the Demi-sel with the hot milk to make it the same consistency as the Camembert. Blend the two cheeses together and add the cream. Fill into small dariole moulds, cover the top with waxed or greaseproof paper, and place in the ice-making compartment of the refrigerator for at least 12 hours. The mixture should be light and creamy before putting into the moulds. Sieve the Camembert before working if a mortar is not used. Serve with hot water-biscuits.

Chapter 4

PASTAS AND RICE

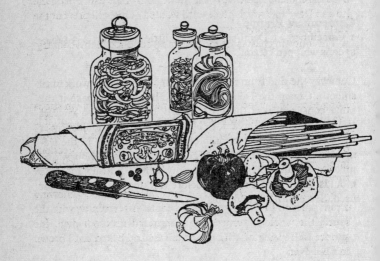

PASTAS

UNDER this heading come such farinaceous dishes as macaroni, spaghetti, noodles, and many others too numerous to be listed here.

Italian in origin, *pasta* is literally a paste made of flour and water (sometimes with the addition of egg) then rolled out thinly and formed into various shapes before being dried ready for cooking. In some shops, principally in big towns, pasta such as noodles or ravioli may be bought freshly made, though these can be made at home. Each kind of pasta is cooked in the same way, that is, first simmered (hard-boiling will toughen them) in stock or water until barely tender, then strained and finished with butter, cream, or the appropriate sauce. Care must be taken that it is not over-cooked but remains nicely firm. A good test is to be able to cut it through with the thumb-nail. Once this stage is reached, strain at once and rinse with a jug of hot water. Return to the pan and finish according to the recipe. If the pasta is not to be used immediately add enough hot water, or stock, if that has been the cooking liquid, to cover the bottom of the pan. Put on the lid and leave in a warm place until wanted. This will prevent the pasta from becoming sticky.

The following pastas are the ones most common in this country.

MACARONI

Long tubes about the thickness of a pencil and in Italian shops can be bought in varying sizes. Though macaroni is sold cut, it is best to buy it in lengths, which can be broken if wished. It should be cooked in lengths of about 3 inches according to the directions given above, putting it into plenty of boiling salted water. Cooking time is approximately 15 to 20 minutes.

Macaroni is best served in a cream or Mornay sauce, allowing 1 pint sauce to ½ lb. macaroni for 4 people. After mixing with the sauce, the whole is turned into a buttered fireproof dish, the surface well sprinkled with grated cheese and baked until brown in a hot oven.

SPAGHETTI

Like macaroni, spaghetti can be bought in fine or medium thicknesses and is a thin rod of pasta. Buy in lengths and avoid breaking it before cooking. If the ends are lowered gently into the boiling salted water, they will soften immediately so that the whole can be easily curled round into the pan. Cooking time, 12 to 15 minutes; finish as for the general directions for pasta (above). Though good in a cream sauce, spaghetti is even better with a strong-flavoured tomato sauce, or *à la Bolognese*, that is with a rich, brown sauce of meat and/or chicken livers.

*

Spaghetti with Tomato (Napolitana)
½ lb. spaghetti; grated Parmesan cheese.

TOMATO SAUCE: 1 lb. ripe tomatoes; 1 medium-sized onion; 1 oz. butter; 1 level dessertspoon flour; 2 cloves garlic; a bayleaf; several parsley stalks and a spray of thyme; scant ¼ pint stock or water; ½ oz. butter to finish.

First prepare the sauce. Wipe and halve the tomatoes; squeeze over a strainer to remove the seeds, then reserve the juice with the tomatoes. Slice the onion thinly and soften in the butter without colouring, i.e. with the lid on the pan. Stir in the flour, add the garlic, crushed, the herbs, and stock. Bring to the boil, season well with salt, pepper from the mill, and a pinch of sugar. Add the tomatoes and juice, cover and simmer for 20 minutes or until pulpy. Meanwhile cook the spaghetti, drain, rinse, and keep warm. Rub the sauce through a strainer, first removing the herbs, and return to the rinsed-out pan. Boil until really thick (about 10 minutes) with the lid off the pan, stir occasionally and more frequently towards the end. Finish with the butter. Mix enough of the sauce into the spaghetti to coat it thoroughly. Shake up over the heat, adjust the seasoning, then turn into a hot dish, scatter over some Parmesan cheese, and serve hot with a bowl of more cheese separately.

It is important that the sauce should be a rich, red colour, and coat the spaghetti without too much falling on to the dish. In fact, it is more of a pulp than a sauce, and when tomatoes are plentiful in summer a further ½ lb. may be added and the flour and stock omitted. At other times in the year a better result is obtained by using the canned tomatoes, 2 cupfuls for the above quantity. A teaspoonful of tomato purée may also be added to help concentrate the flavour.

Spaghetti Bolognese
½ lb. spaghetti; butter; grated Parmesan cheese; chopped parsley.

SAUCE BOLOGNESE: ¼ lb. chicken's or calves' liver or raw minced steak; 1 large onion; 1 oz. dripping or oil; 1 level dessertspoon flour; ½ pint good stock; a bouquet garni; 1 teaspoon tomato purée, or a tablespoon of well-reduced tomato pulp; 1 clove garlic; a dash of Marsala or sherry.

Chop the onion finely and dice the liver. Melt the dripping in a
sauté pan or shallow saucepan, add the onion, cook for several
minutes, then add the liver and sauté briskly until brown. Draw
aside, stir in the flour, pour on the stock, season, and bring to the
boil. Add the herbs, tomato purée, and the garlic, crushed with a
large pinch of salt, and finish the seasoning with some freshly
ground pepper. Simmer, stirring occasionally until thick and
rich, 40 minutes to 1 hour. Add the sherry and remove the herbs.
Meanwhile cook the spaghetti, drain well, and return to the pan.
Add a good knob of butter, cover with a cloth, and leave in a
warm place until the sauce is ready. Pile the spaghetti up in a hot
dish and spoon over the sauce. Serve at once, well dusted with
chopped parsley and with a dish of grated Parmesan handed
separately.

VERMICELLI

Resembles very fine spaghetti and is used mostly as a garnish in
clear soup, or crushed dry as a coating for a rissole. It may also
be cooked and finished as for any spaghetti dish.

LASAGNE

These are squares of pasta, either green (*lasagne verde*, flavoured
with spinach) or plain. It can be made at home with a pasta as for
ravioli (page 107) and dried lightly before boiling, or may be
bought from most Italian or delicatessen stores in packets. After
boiling, the lasagne is layered alternately with a meat sauce and a
cream sauce.

*

Lasagne
¾ lb. green lasagne pasta (ravioli paste flavoured and coloured with
cooked sieved spinach cut into thin sheets about 4 by 3 inches
wide).

MEAT SAUCE: 1 oz. butter; 1 oz. flour; 1 onion; 1 small carrot;
1 small stalk celery; ¾ lb. finely minced beef; ¼ lb. finely minced
lean pork; seasoning; 1 heaped teaspoon tomato purée; 1 glass
white wine; about ½ pint stock.

CREAM SAUCE: 1½ oz. butter; 1¼ oz. flour; ¾ pint milk or about ½ pint milk and ¼ pint single cream; grated Parmesan cheese; grated nutmeg.

First prepare the sauces. For meat sauce, melt the butter, add the finely diced vegetables, and cook slowly until soft, add the meats, and continue cooking for 10 to 15 minutes. Season with salt and freshly ground pepper, add the tomato purée, the wine, and about ⅓ of the stock. Simmer very slowly for 1 hour adding the remaining stock a little at a time. The sauce should be thick. Prepare the cream sauce in the usual way, finishing with the cream and seasoning with a little grated nutmeg. Simmer the lasagne a few at a time in a large pan of boiling water, remove with a strainer, drop into cold water. Drain and spread on a clean damp towel. Butter a fireproof dish and cover the bottom with a thin layer of the meat sauce, then cover that with a layer of the cream sauce and a dusting of grated cheese. Arrange a layer of the prepared pasta over the sauces with ends turning up the side of the dish. Repeat this layering until the dish is full (at least 6 layers) finishing with the sauces and cheese. Bake in a moderately hot oven (380° F. or Reg. 5) for about 20 to 25 minutes.

NOODLES OR TAGLIATELLE

Ribbons of pasta of varying widths. The narrow ones may be flavoured with spinach or tomato, or left plain. Cook as for other pasta.

CANNELONI

Large fat tubes of pasta, partly cooked by boiling, then usually filled with a minced-meat mixture or spinach and cream cheese as for ravioli. Cooking completed in a tomato sauce or gravy. Alternatively, cannelonis may be small pancakes filled with a savoury mixture and coated with a light cheese sauce.

*

Canneloni

BATTER: 4 oz. flour; 1 egg; 1 yolk; 1 tablespoon oiled butter; salt; pepper.

FILLING: 1 lb. spinach; 2 oz. milk or cream cheese; salt; pepper.

MORNAY SAUCE: ½ pint milk; ¾ oz. butter; scant ¼ oz. flour; 2 oz. finely grated cheese; a slice of onion and carrot; bouquet garni.

Prepare batter as for pancakes. Allow to stand ½ hour. Fry small pancakes, stack them, and set aside.

Blanch the spinach in boiling water for 5 minutes, drain, and press. Chop and mix the cheese and seasoning. Fill this mixture into the pancakes, roll up, and arrange in a buttered fireproof dish. Prepare Mornay sauce, coat over the cannelonis, and brown in a quick oven for 7 to 10 minutes.

RAVIOLI

Small squares or rounds of pasta filled with the mixture as for cannelonis. They are first simmered gently in stock or water and then finished in a well-flavoured tomato sauce.

*

Ravioli

DOUGH: ½ lb. plain flour; a large pinch salt; 2 beaten eggs; 1 tablespoon olive oil; 2–3 tablespoons water or milk.

FILLING: 4 oz. cooked ham or chicken or a mixture of both; 1 teaspoon chopped herbs or parsley; 2 tablespoons thick Béchamel sauce; tomato sauce (see page 104); Parmesan cheese.

First prepare the paste. Sieve the flour with the salt on to a slab or board. Make a well in the centre and pour in the eggs and oil using the fingers of one hand. Begin to work up to a firm dough, gradually drawing in the flour and adding the water as required. Now knead well as for bread until the dough is perfectly smooth. This will take 5 to 6 minutes. Cover with a cloth and leave for 15 minutes.

Prepare the filling. Chop the meat finely or mince. Mix with the herbs and Béchamel. Season well. Roll out the paste as thinly as possible. It is advisable to take half at a time, and if at all elastic leave for 10 or 15 minutes after rolling out.

Brush over half the paste with water and arrange at regular intervals (between 2 and 3 inches apart) small heaps of the filling. Fold over the other half of the paste and press firmly round each mound with a small ball of the dough. Cut out with a small fluted round cutter, or with a pastry wheel into squares. Leave for half an hour or longer before cooking. Any dough left over may be rolled out very thinly and then left until all elasticity has disappeared before cutting into strips for nouilles and so on. If to be dried, cover with a piece of paper and leave for a day or so until quite crisp.

Cook the ravioli gently in boiling stock or salted water for 20 to 30 minutes. Lift out carefully with a draining spoon and lay on a buttered fireproof dish. Have ready about ½ pint tomato sauce (see page 104), or the sauce may be made with the stock in which the raviolis were cooked. Spoon the sauce over the raviolis and set the dish in a moderate oven (350° F. or Reg. 4) for 10 minutes. Dust with grated Parmesan cheese before serving and also hand a bowl of cheese separately.

GNOCCHI

These may be classed under this main heading, though they are not strictly speaking a pasta. There are three different kinds: Romana, made of polenta (maize meal) or coarse semolina; Parisienne or French gnocchi, made in a similar way to choux pastry; and potato gnocchi. The two former may be served as a first or main course, while the last is usually an accompaniment to a meat dish.

*

Gnocchi Romana
1 pint milk and water mixed; 1 onion; a bayleaf; 5 tablespoons of polenta (maize meal) or coarse semolina; ½ oz. butter; 1½ oz. grated cheese (Parmesan for preference); salt; pepper; French mustard.

Add the onion and bayleaf to the milk and water and bring
slowly to boiling-point. Take out the onion and bayleaf, stir
in the polenta or semolina, add salt and pepper, and cook slowly
for 10 to 12 minutes, stirring frequently. Add a little more
liquid if the mixture is too solid. Remove from the heat, beat
in the butter and cheese, and adjust the seasoning, adding ½
teaspoon of the mustard. Spread out on to a tray or large dish.
The consistency should be that of very thick cream and the
thickness of the mixture ½ to ¾ inch. Leave until quite cold, then
cut into squares and arrange round a well-buttered dish with the
pieces overlapping. Sprinkle well with grated cheese and melted
butter and brown in a quick oven for 12 to 15 minutes. Fill the
centre of the dish with the chosen sauce – tomato, cheese, mushroom, etc. – before serving.

Gnocchi Parisienne

1½ gills milk; 4 oz. butter; 6 oz. flour; 4 eggs; 3 oz. grated cheese.

Boil the milk and butter together, draw aside, and at once add all
the flour. Beat until smooth. Cool, then add the eggs one at a time
and the cheese. Season well with salt and pepper and French
mustard. Poach in dessertspoonfuls in boiling salted water for
10 to 12 minutes. Drain, dry on a napkin, and arrange in one
layer in a buttered, fireproof dish. Coat with a Mornay sauce,
sprinkle with grated cheese, and bake for 12 to 15 minutes in a
moderately hot oven.

Potato Gnocchi

1 lb. potatoes; ¼ lb. plain flour; 1 small beaten egg; 1 dessertspoon
butter; salt, pepper, and nutmeg.

Boil, drain, and dry the potatoes. Push through a ricer or wire
sieve, add the butter, flour, seasoning, and enough egg to
bind the mixture together. Shape into a sausage on a floured
board. Cut into small pieces and roll each with a fork. Throw
them into boiling salted water and poach gently for 10 to 15
minutes. Drain and return to the pan with a little melted butter.

RICE

A cereal that repays care and attention, for boiled rice is something so easy to do and yet often difficult to accomplish to perfection. Much depends on the type of grain, and how it has been treated. Unpolished and brown rice will give the best results in this case, as they are unlikely to become sticky after boiling.

There are several methods of boiling rice. In China and the Middle East they prefer to cook their rice covered by two or three 'fingers' of cold water on the top and continue until all the water has been absorbed and the rice is dry. This is an excellent method but needs judgement of heat and the right tempo of cooking to get perfection. For the less experienced, the following method is simpler and gets rid of the excess starch if the rice is not of the first quality.

Choose a large saucepan, enamel or aluminium, to hold 2 to 3 quarts of water. Fill it and add a dessertspoon of salt and a slice of lemon. Heat, and when the water is bubbling throw in the rice ($\frac{1}{2}$ lb. to 3 quarts of water). Stir with a fork and boil hard for about 12 minutes, when the rice should be tender but firm. The grains should not look blown. Check the boiling at once, either by throwing in a cup of cold water or by draining immediately into a colander. Pour over a large jug of hot water (even if the rice is to be served cold) and with the handle of a wooden spoon make drainage holes. Leave for at least $\frac{1}{2}$ hour before using. The rice may then be 'forked' into a buttered dish for reheating or into a bowl for mixing with a French dressing for a salad. When fairly large amounts are boiled, spread the rice out on to a tray or large dish, teasing it with a fork, after draining it well in the colander. Allow 2 oz. per person for curry, $1\frac{1}{2}$ oz. for a risotto or pilaff, and 1 oz. for a salad.

The main varieties of rice are:

PATNA or PATNA TYPE: now grown in Siam, a long grain, suitable for boiling and some pilaffs.

SPANISH JAP or JAVA rice: a thick, short, stubby grain, right for milk puddings when the maximum amount of liquid can be absorbed. May be used for risottos, though for perfection an Italian rice is essential.

CAROLINA: a cross between the long and short grain and one most used for puddings.

ITALIAN RICE: large, thick, white, or reddish grains, principally for risottos.

WILD RICE: imported from America and, as its name implies, really wild. The grain is immensely long and thin and the rice is something of a delicacy. Usually eaten plainly boiled and finished with butter. It is expensive.

*

Risotto Milanese

1 medium-sized onion; 2 oz. mushrooms; 1 clove garlic; 1½ oz. butter; scant pint of good meat or vegetable broth; pinch of saffron soaked in an eggcupful of hot water for ½ hour before using*; 6 oz. Italian rice; 1 oz. Parmesan cheese.

Slice the onion, slice or quarter the mushrooms, chop and crush the garlic with ½ teaspoon salt. Melt 1 oz. of the butter in a thick saucepan, add the onion, and soften slowly, only allowing it to colour a delicate brown. Add the rice (do not wash it). Cook for a few minutes, then add the mushrooms and cook quickly for a minute or two, stirring constantly. Add a good pint of the broth, the garlic, saffron, seasonings, and bayleaf. Simmer till the rice is soft but not mushy and the consistency is that of thick cream, adding more broth from time to time as the rice absorbs it, the whole occasionally stirred and kept gently simmering. When the rice is just cooked, draw off the fire, remove the bayleaf, adjust the seasoning, powder the top with the grated cheese, dot over the remaining butter, cover, and leave for 4 to 5 minutes. Stir round lightly with a fork and turn at once into a hot dish.

Cooked beef marrow is sometimes used to finish the risotto in place of the last half an ounce of butter (i.e. scooped from a freshly boiled marrow bone).

Pilaff

1 large onion; ½ lb. long-grained rice; a good pinch of saffron; 2 oz. butter; 1¼–1½ pints stock; 1½ oz. cheese.

* This soaking brings out the colour and flavour of the saffron. The water in which it has been soaked should be used in the recipe too.

Melt two-thirds of the butter, add the finely sliced onion, cover, and cook slowly until soft but not coloured. Add the rice, fry for a few minutes until the rice looks clear then add salt and pepper, the saffron soaked as for the risotto, and 1¼ pint of stock. Bring to the boil, cover tightly, and put into a moderate oven for 20 to 30 minutes, or until the grains are tender and the stock absorbed. Add the extra stock if necessary, and with a fork stir in the rest of the butter and the cheese. To this basic recipe may be added shredded 'leftovers' of chicken, ham, and so on with the rice or stirred in during the cooking.

As the above two recipes show, the difference between a risotto and a pilaff is that one is cooked on top heat resulting in a soft cream and using a thick-grained rice; the pilaff made with a long-grained rice, cooked in the oven with all the liquid added at once and so giving a dry and flaky consistency.

Another useful dish though strictly speaking not a pilaff is one made with boiled rice. This takes little time to make and prepare and the ingredients may vary according to taste, and to where the dish appears in the menu.

Shrimp Pilaff

½ lb. Patna or long-grained rice, previously boiled and dried; 1 onion, sliced; 1 lb. tomatoes; 1 large green pepper; 2 oz. butter; 4 oz. 'picked' or fresh shrimps or prawns.

Cook the onion in half the butter, add the shrimps and one third of the tomatoes, peeled and cut into thick slices, and the pepper shredded and blanched. Cover and cook gently for 4 to 5 minutes. Put remaining butter into a large pan, add rice, and toss over hot fire. Season well. Fork in the mixture lightly. Pile up on a hot dish and surround with remaining tomatoes, cut in halves, dotted over with butter and set in the oven for 4 to 5 minutes.

Paëlla

Paëlla is a classic Spanish dish where the main ingredient is rice with an assortment of fish and meat. It is a good effective dish for a party. Abroad special pans for cooking paëlla are sold, though a large deep frying or sauté pan answers quite well.

3 tablespoons olive oil; 6 oz. long-grained rice; 1 medium-sized onion, sliced; 3 oz. ham or bacon cut in wide strips; 1–2 pinches saffron (previously soaked); 2–3 joints chicken or rabbit; ½ pint prawns, mussels, or other shellfish; 4 oz. rock salmon or firm white fish (cut into nuggets); 2 cups of tinned or fresh pimento; 2 tablespoons of cooked peas; 1–1½ pints light stock or water; seasoning; chopped parsley.

Choose a deep large frying-pan. Heat oil in it till smoking, add rice, onions, and bacon. Stir over moderate heat till rice turns white; add saffron. Draw aside and arrange the meat, fish, prawns, sliced pimento, and peas on the top.

Season well. Pour over the stock, cover with a piece of greased paper and a lid, and cook in a moderate oven for 30 to 40 minutes till the rice is tender and the stock absorbed. *Do not stir* and serve at once well sprinkled with chopped parsley.

NOTE: If a young roasting chicken is used joint and brown the pieces in oil before adding to the rice.

Cooked chicken, rabbit, etc., can also be used in this way. For a simple Paëlla use bacon and fish and pimento and peas to decorate.

Chapter 5

FISH

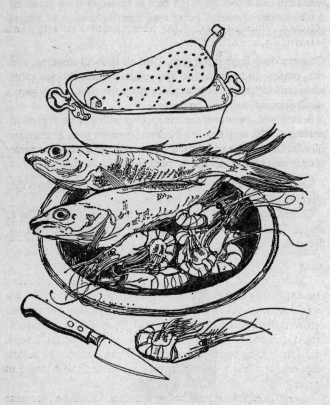

FOR the purpose of cooking, fish falls into four natural categories: sea-water; fresh-water; shellfish; and smoked fish.

Sea-water fish are divided or classified as round or flat fish and white or oily fish. In a white fish any oil is confined entirely to the liver, for example cod, halibut, etc. Consequently the flesh is delicate and very easy to digest. In an oily fish the natural oils are distributed throughout the flesh, giving it a very high nutritative value, for example herring, mackerel, etc.

All fish, unless dried, salted, or smoked, should be eaten very fresh, and it is fair to say that when it smells 'fishy' it is stale and not at its best.

CHOICE: When buying from the fishmonger the following points are an indication of freshness:

1. The flesh should feel firm and the tail be quite stiff.
2. The eyes should be bright and not sunken in the head.
3. The gills should be red and the body be covered with a natural slime or plenty of scales.

PREPARATION:

Cleaning: Wash the fish under the running cold tap and remove any scales by scraping with the back of a knife from the tail to the head; avoid over-handling and so damaging the flesh. The fish will most likely have been gutted by the fishmonger but the cook must check this and remove any black skin left inside the cavity; rub this gently with the corner of a damp cloth dipped in salt and it will come away quite easily. If however this has not been done or the fish has been bought direct from the quay-side it is quite simple.

For *large round fish* such as cod or haddock, slit them just below the head along the belly to the vent. Remove the intestines, wash well, and reserve the liver if liked (the liver of red mullet and cod are considered a delicacy, also the roe). Wash the roe carefully as the membrane is easily broken. It may be cooked inside small fish like herring but in the case of large fish it should be cooked separately; it has a quite different texture and takes longer to cook.

Small round fish such as herring and mackerel can be cut across the shoulders, so removing the head and intestines in one operation. Some fish (this is done either for appearance or because the flesh is delicate), generally salmon, sea or river trout, and red mullet are cleaned through the gills; the gills are cut away before cooking and the fish most carefully washed along the backbone to remove any congealed blood. It is then dried thoroughly to avoid diluting the cooking liquor or the flavour of the accompanying sauce.

Flat fish (for example sole, plaice, or halibut) that swim with the dark skin uppermost are cut in an arc or half-circle immediately below the head on the dark side. After removing the scales and cleaning fish, remove the fins, cutting from the tail towards the head, trim the tail, and the fish is ready for skinning and filleting.

SKINNING: The fine skin of small haddock and whiting can be removed while the fish is whole if the dorsal and central fins are removed first. To do this cut the fins, with a thin strip of skin, from the tail towards the head. Then, holding the head firmly in one hand, grip in turn the bony pieces just under the gills and rip the skin on each side down towards the tail. Do not attempt to skin these small fish after filleting as the flesh is delicate and breaks easily. Fillets of larger round fish such as cod, and fillets of plaice and lemon sole, are skinned in the following manner. Place the fish skin-side down on a wooden board. Lift the skin carefully from the tail and grasp a small piece between the fingers and thumb, using a little salt to prevent slipping. Now hold a knife at an angle to the skin and, using a sawing motion, push the flesh away from the skin.

Dover or Black Sole is skinned whole. After trimming the fins, lift the skin on the black side at the cut where the fish was cleaned and slip the thumb under about one inch of skin right around the fish. Then using salt to prevent slipping pull the skin firmly from the tail to the head. Repeat this process for the white skin on the underside.

Round fish such as cod, haddock, and mackerel are, after trimming, cut down the back, with the knife kept on top of the backbone; cut along the fish lifting the top fillet right off. Now insert the knife under the bone and, keeping it as close as possible and working from the head to the tail, cut the bone from the fish.

FILLETING (removing the bones): This is best learnt by watching an expert rather than by trying to follow instructions, but with care and a thin filleting knife the art can soon be mastered.

Herring and small river trout which are not divided when filleted, are cut down to the vent with scissors or knife and then if the thumbnail is inserted and the fish opened down to the tail the bone may be pulled easily from the tail to the head.

Flat fish: cut the fish down the centre back bone from the head to the tail; now working from the head and keeping the knife close to the bone cut in sweeping strokes from the right to the left until a fillet is lifted. Turn the fish round and lift the second fillet in the same way but this time work from the tail. Repeat this on the other side of the fish to obtain four fillets in all.

METHODS OF COOKING

1. BOILING: really a misnomer as fish cooked in liquid should have only gentle heat applied and the temperature must not exceed 190° F. It should in fact poach for best results and this may be done in a pan on top of the stove or a fire-proof dish in the oven. The cooking liquid is known as a court bouillon (see page 123), and this can vary from the simplicity of salted water using $\frac{1}{2}$ oz. salt to 1 quart water, and milk flavoured with lemon, to a vegetable broth acidulated with white or red wine or vinegar. The choice of court bouillon is dictated by the type of fish and the way in which it is to be served which can be quite plain with a sauce handed separately, coated with a sauce made from the cooking liquor, or finished with butter.

This method of cooking is suitable for whole fish such as codling, haddock, salmon, etc., or steaks and cutlets from very large fish.

2. BAKING is a method suitable for whole stuffed fish or cutlets which are basted frequently during their cooking with hot fat or oil; sometimes an aromatic marinade is used but whatever is chosen should only be sufficient to moisten the fish during the cooking period, not to cover. Small whole fish such as red mullet and mackerel are frequently baked *en papillote*; in this case each fish is enclosed in buttered greaseproof paper, parchment, or foil, and the necessity for basting is eliminated.

3. FRYING: *Shallow fat frying* is used for small whole fish fillets and cutlets. The only preparation necessary after cleaning is a quick roll in seasoned flour, but other coatings may be used such as

medium oatmeal on herrings or even egg and crumb on fillets of fish. The fat used should be oil, good dripping, a mixture of oil and butter, lard, or commercially prepared fat. Any fat left in the pan after this method of cooking must be strained into a clean dry bowl, covered when quite cold, and kept exclusively for fish.

Deep fat frying: a method excellent for fillets of fish and small whole fish such as whiting, smelts, and sole. The fish must be protected from the great heat of the fat by a coating such as egg and crumb or batter. By reason of this the fat can be used for a variety of ingredients as the coating is sealed immediately it touches the hot fat and so there is no danger of it being tainted with a fishy flavour. The exception to this rule of coating is whitebait, which because of its size is simply rolled in seasoned flour. In this case the fat must be kept as after shallow-fat frying. Suitable fats are vegetable oils, block suet, clarified lard or dripping, or commercially prepared fat.

4. AU GRATIN: Fillets, cutlets, and small whole fish are covered with a prepared sauce, finished with crumbs and butter, possibly but not necessarily cheese and then cooked and served in the same dish. The success of this simple method of cooking depends on the size of the dish and the thickness of the sauce. The fish should be flat and cover the base of the dish; in this way the juices that exude from the cooking fish will blend evenly with the sauce if this consistency is correct at the beginning.

5. GRILLING: Good for small oily fish, viz. herring and mackerel, as the heat is so intense it crisps the skin, making it particularly appetizing. Also suitable for whole sole, mullet, and steaks of turbot and halibut, but in this case the fish needs basting continually with clarified butter and to improve the finished appearance it should be dipped first in milk and then in seasoned flour before cooking.

6. À LA MEUNIÈRE: A method for small whole fish such as trout, herring, whiting, etc., and fillets of sole. It is frying, but in clarified butter only. The fish is placed undrained in the serving-dish and finished with lemon, finely chopped parsley, seasoning, and butter cooked to a golden brown. When cooking *à la meunière* the choice

of frying-pan is important and it must be large enough to allow the butter to flow freely and for steam to escape between the fillets or small fish as they cook. There should be room to turn the fish with ease but if the pan is too large and a large area is uncovered by fish the clarified butter will scorch and the flavour of the dish will be ruined.

7. AU BLEU: Small whole fish such as trout can be cooked in this way, but it is a method only possible when live fish are available. They must be stunned and rapidly cleaned through the gills to avoid handling as it is the natural slime of the fish that turns blue when the fish is immersed in the court bouillon (see page 123). The court bouillon must be prepared with vinegar not lemon, as it is the vinegar that produces the blue tinge on the skin, but a red-wine court bouillon is especially good for fresh-water fish, particularly if it is used to prepare an accompanying sauce, but whichever is chosen, there must be sufficient liquid to cover the fish.

8. STEAMING: Fillets of fish or cutlets can be placed on a buttered plate, seasoned lightly, covered with milk and a pat of butter with greaseproof paper and a second plate on the top, and cooked over a pan of gently simmering water. This method of cooking is most suitable for invalids or people with delicate digestions.

BASS (BAR)

A round, silvery fish found in both fresh and sea water in season from May to July. Small fish can be cooked as trout, *à la meunière*, fried, or grilled, and large fish poached, as salmon, with an accompanying sauce.

BLOATER – *see Herring* (page 134)

BREAM (BRÈME)

A round fresh-water fish of poor flavour as it lives mainly in ponds and slow-running rivers. It can be grilled and served with a good sauce (say Tartare or Bercy) or marinaded and then baked.

SEA BREAM (BRÈME DE MER)

A round fish in season all the year round, but at its best from
July to October. It has a pink tinge to the skin which is covered
with large, tough scales. The flesh is coarse in texture and the
flavour dull. It can be poached whole or stuffed with bread and
herb or mushroom stuffing and baked; or any recipe for fillets
of sole or plaice may be used.

BRILL (BARBUE)

A flat sea-water fish in season from September to May,
best in the winter months. It is similar in shape to turbot but the
skin is a pale sandy brown. It has good, firm flesh with a yellowish
tinge and can be cooked as turbot or sole.

*

Brill Juliette

1½–2 lb. brill, filleted; 6 oz. button mushrooms; ¼ pint white
wine; lemon; 2 aubergines; 4 tomatoes; butter; chopped parsley.

SAUCE: ½ pint Béchamel sauce made with 1½ oz. butter; 1¼ oz.
flour; ½ pint milk infused with peppercorns, mace and bayleaf;
1 shallot; 2–3 tablespoons cream.

Skin the fillets cut in half, wash and dry, and lay in a buttered
fire-proof dish. Slice the mushrooms finely, scatter them over the
fish, season with salt and a squeeze of lemon, and pour over the
wine; cover with a thickly buttered paper. Set aside.

Peel and slice the aubergines, sprinkle with salt, and leave ½
hour. Peel the tomatoes and cut in halves. Dry the aubergines,
fry in butter until brown and tender, and keep warm. Fry the
tomatoes in the same pan. Cook the fish in a moderate oven for
15 to 20 minutes.

Drain the liquid from the fish into a small pan, add the finely
chopped shallot, and reduce to about ½ gill. Have ready the
Béchamel, add the reduced wine, stir until boiling, and add the
cream. Simmer a few minutes.

Arrange the aubergine down the centre of the serving-dish,

set the fillets on top, and spoon over the sauce. Garnish with the tomatoes and dust with chopped parsley.

Brill Durand

1½–2 lb. brill, filleted; 1 glass white wine; a squeeze of lemon.

VEGETABLE GARNISH: 3 medium carrots; 1 turnip; 2 medium onions; ½ oz. butter; 1 glass white wine; bouquet garni; 4 tomatoes.

TO FINISH: ¾ pint cream; chopped parsley.

Skin the fish, trim, fold, and place in a buttered dish, with seasoning, the wine, and lemon; cover with a buttered paper and leave ready for poaching in a moderate oven for 10 to 15 minutes.

Slice the root vegetables into rounds and place in a shallow saucepan with the butter, wine, herbs, and seasoning. Cover with a paper and lid and cook until the liquid is absorbed and the vegetables tender (about 15 minutes). Do not allow to colour. Remove the herbs and add the tomatoes, skinned, pipped, and shredded, and heat carefully.

When the fish is cooked, strain the liquor from the fish into a small pan and reduce by half. Add the cream slowly, season well, and bring to the boil. When thick add the parsley.

Place the vegetables on a hot serving-dish, arrange the fish on the top, and spoon over the sauce.

Brill à la Bretonne

2–2½ lb. brill; 2–3 potatoes; bouquet garni.

DUXELLES: ½ lb. mushrooms; 2–3 shallots; 2 oz. butter; seasoning; chopped parsley and rosemary; 1 glass white wine; 4 heaped tablespoons fresh breadcrumbs; 1 egg.

Wash and dry the fish, trim, and cut from head to tail on each side. Lift each fillet in turn and cut away the backbone, keeping the fish in shape. Season inside with salt and pepper.

Wash the mushrooms in salted water, squeeze dry, and chop finely. Chop the shallots, place in a saucepan with the butter, cover, and cook slowly until soft but not coloured. Stir in the mushrooms, seasoning, and herbs and continue cooking for a further 2 to 3 minutes. Pour on the wine and let it reduce, then add the breadcrumbs and bind with the beaten egg. Allow to cool. Stuff the fish with the mushrooms duxelles and put in a well-buttered dish. Surround with a fine julienne of (raw) potatoes (see page 478), season lightly, moisten with a glass of water, and bake in a moderate oven for 35 to 40 minutes.

CARP (CARPE)

A fresh-water fish, round and red in colour. It can grow to a large size and attain great age. Like many of the fresh-water fish it has a closed season, from 16 March until 15 June. It is eaten more on the Continent than here. It needs careful preparation as it is inclined to be muddy in flavour, and is best served with a well-flavoured red wine (see Eels en Matelote, page 127) or Bercy sauce.

COD (CABILLAUD)

A deep-sea fish in season all the year round, but at its best from May to October. It has fine, creamy flakes and lends itself to many ways of cooking. Fresh, it can be bought whole, in fillets, or in steaks as the fish can weigh from 1¼ to 20 lb. The best selected fish weigh 9 to 10 lb. The roe is sold separately, either fresh or smoked. The liver is used in the manufacture of cod-liver oil and the tongues are considered a great delicacy. Fillets of cod are also sold smoked. These are good, although not to be compared with smoked haddock, and can be cooked in exactly the same way. Cod is also salted. The fish are split, salted, and dried and exported in large quantities to France, Spain, and Italy where it has a more ready sale than in this country. It is known as 'Morue' and must be thoroughly washed and soaked before cooking. The true 'Brandade' (see page 173) is prepared with this fish. Some people think the flesh of cod dull and watery but this is invariably due to lack of skill in cooking, and if the following treatment is given before attempting even the most simple recipe, it is fit to grace any table. Wash and dry the fish, rub the skin with cut fresh lemon, and sprinkle lightly with salt. Leave in a cool place for ½ to 1 hour, then tip away any liquid, wipe the fish, and follow the chosen recipe.

*

Boiled Cod with Egg Sauce

1½–2 lb. steak of cod.

COURT BOUILLON: 1½–2 pints water; 1 sliced carrot; 1 onion stuck with a clove; bouquet garni; 6 peppercorns; 2 tablespoons vinegar.

EGG SAUCE: ¾ pint milk; slice of onion; blade of mace; 4 peppercorns; ½ bayleaf; 1 oz. butter; ¾ oz. flour; 2–3 hard-boiled eggs.

First prepare the court bouillon by putting all the ingredients together into a pan. Salt lightly, bring to the boil, and simmer with the lid on the pan for 15 to 20 minutes. Cool a little before putting in the fish tied in a piece of muslin. Bring slowly to the boil, then reduce the heat and poach or simmer very gently for 20 to 25 minutes.

Meanwhile prepare the sauce. Infuse the herbs and spice in the milk until well flavoured, then strain. Melt the butter, add the flour off the fire, and blend in the liquid. Replace on the heat and stir continually until the sauce boils; allow to boil for several minutes to cook the flour thoroughly and to bring the sauce to a creamy consistency. Season and add the hard-boiled eggs rather coarsely chopped.

Lift out the fish carefully, drain, remove the skin, and dish on a folded napkin. Garnish with parsley and serve the sauce separately.

Cod au Gratin Mornay

1½ lb. cod fillet; 1 tablespoon brown crumbs; 1 tablespoon grated cheese; 1 tablespoon melted butter.

MORNAY SAUCE: 1 oz. butter; scant 1 oz. flour; ½ pint milk; seasoning; a pinch of grated nutmeg; 2 oz. grated cheese, half Parmesan and half Gruyère is best.

First prepare the fish. Cut into even-sized pieces and place in a buttered fireproof dish (see note on page 118). Melt the butter, remove from the heat, and blend in the flour and the milk. Season with salt and pepper and stir continuously over a gentle heat until boiling. Cook for a few minutes, then draw aside and beat in the cheese a little at a time. Add the nutmeg and reheat carefully to make sure all the cheese is melted, but do not allow to boil. Spoon the sauce over the fish and dust with the mixed crumbs and cheese. Sprinkle with the melted butter and bake in a moderate oven for 20 to 25 minutes.

Spiced Cod

1½–2 lb. steak of cod; salt and pepper; 1 level teaspoon each paprika and ground ginger; 2 large onions; 2 lemons; 2 sprays parsley; white wine or dry cider.

Skin and bone the fish and cut into neat steaks. Mix the spices with a little salt and freshly ground black pepper; rub into the fish.

Slice the onions, cover with cold water, bring to the boil, drain, place at the bottom of a fireproof dish, and set the fish on top.

Pare the rind from one lemon cut into fine shreds. Cook until tender and keep on one side. With a serrated-edged knife cut the pith away from both lemons, slice the flesh into thin rounds, and lay on the fish. Chop the parsley coarsely and scatter over. Pour enough wine or cider into the dish barely to cover the fish, cover, and cook in a very moderate oven for about 1 hour. Allow to get quite cold, then dust with extra chopped parsley and the prepared lemon rind before serving.

Cod à l'Indienne

1½–2 lb. cod; a little oil for frying – about 5 tablespoons; 6 oz. boiled rice to accompany.

SAUCE: 2 medium onions; 2 tablespoons oil; 1 level tablespoon curry powder; 1 level tablespoon flour; ½ pint light stock or water; ½ oz. almonds, blanched, shredded, and soaked in a coffeecupful of boiling water; 1 large tablespoon mango chutney; lemon juice; salt, pepper, and sugar to taste; 1 teacupful fresh skinned and quartered tomatoes.

First prepare the fish (see note page 123) then prepare the sauce. Chop the onions, fry till barely coloured in the oil, add the curry, and after a few minutes the flour. Continue to fry and after 2 or 3 minutes moisten with the stock. Simmer uncovered for 15 to 20 minutes. Add the almonds and the liquid and continue simmering a further 15 minutes. Add the chutney and seasonings. Finally, add the tomatoes and set aside.

Skin and bone the fish, cut into thick fillets, roll in seasoned flour, and fry quickly in hot oil. When a good brown, drain and pile in the centre of a serving-dish. Boil up the sauce and spoon enough over the cod to moisten well. Send the rest of the sauce to table in a sauce-boat and hand the rice separately.

Cod Portugaise
1½–2 lb. steak of cod; ½ pint salad oil; ½ lb. onions; 6 cloves of garlic; ¾ lb. tomatoes; salt; cayenne pepper; 3 sweet red peppers – fresh or canned; chopped parsley.

First prepare the fish, then cut into 'nuggets', about 1½-inch cubes, dredge with flour, and fry quickly in hot oil. Drain and place in a casserole. In the meantime take 2 good tablespoons of the frying oil and in this fry the finely sliced onion and the chopped garlic. When just turning colour, add the skinned and seeded tomatoes, season with salt and cayenne pepper, and simmer gently for 10 minutes. Spoon this mixture over the fish, cover with the blanched sliced peppers, and cook in a moderate oven for about 10 minutes. Sprinkle with chopped parsley and serve.

Fillets of Cod Cubat
1½–2 lb. steak of cod; 8 oz. mushrooms; ½ oz. butter; 1 dessert-spoon chopped mixed herbs; ¼ pint thick Béchamel sauce, made with 1 oz. butter; 1 oz. flour and ¼ pint flavoured milk; pinch of ground mace.

MORNAY SAUCE: ¾ oz. butter; ¾ oz. flour; ½ pint milk; 1½–2 oz. grated cheese (Parmesan and Gruyère mixed); French roll.

Skin and bone the fish, divide into cutlets, place in a well-buttered dish, season, and sprinkle well with lemon juice. Cover with a thickly buttered paper, and cook in a slow to moderate oven for 15 minutes.

Make a Béchamel sauce. Wash and finely chop the mushrooms without peeling them. Sauté in the butter until the purée will come from round the sides of the pan; add seasoning and herbs, mix with the Béchamel, and set aside.

Now make the Mornay sauce. Melt the butter, add the flour, pour on the milk, and stir continually until boiling. Draw aside, beat in the cheese, and add mustard, salt, and pepper to taste.

Reheat the mushroom purée, and spread down the centre of a serving-dish. Arrange the cod fillets on the top and coat with the Mornay sauce. Sprinkle with Parmesan cheese and glaze under the grill. Garnish with croûtes of the French roll fried in butter.

COLEY OR SAITHE

A round fish similar in size and shape to fresh haddock, and in season throughout the year. The skin is dark and the flesh rather grey, but full of flavour, and it whitens during cooking. It is sold in fillets, and sometimes in steaks in the north of England, and is good fried, but any recipe for fresh haddock or cod can be used.

DAB (CARRELET) – see Flounder (page 128)

EEL (ANGUILLE)

Found in fresh and sea water, the flesh is rich but the bones are small and troublesome. They must be skinned before cooking. To do this, cut off the head, lift the skin, and peel back, pulling down and inside out, towards the tail.

*

Jellied Eels
2 lb. eels; 1 pint good fish stock, made from sole bones or a turbot

head; 1 onion stuck with a clove; 1 carrot; bouquet garni; salt; pepper; lemon juice; parsley.

Prepare the eels and after washing thoroughly cut in 3-inch lengths and put them in a stewpan with the stock and flavourings. Simmer gently for about ½ hour and leave to cool a little in the liquid. Lift the pieces of eel carefully and arrange in small soufflé dishes or a deep baking-dish. Strain the liquor, add the parsley, and pour over the eels. Leave to set.

To serve, turn from the small dishes or cut in squares from the baking-dish as individual portions. Hand brown bread and butter.

Fried Eels
2 lb. eels; seasoned flour; 2 tablespoons oil; 2 oz. butter; 1 clove garlic; juice of ½ lemon; seasoning; 1 teaspoon chopped parsley.

Prepare the eels, cut into pieces 2 to 3 inches long, and roll in the seasoned flour. Heat the oil until smoking, drop in the butter, and add the eels at once. There must be enough room for the steam to escape between the pieces of fish or they will stick, so do not overfill the pan; rather fry in two batches if the pan is small.

Lift the eels carefully and place in a hot serving-dish. Add the chopped garlic to the pan and cook until golden, then add the lemon juice, seasoning, and parsley and pour over the fish. Serve very hot.

Eels 'en matelote'
2 lb. eels; 1 oz. butter; 1 onion; 2 glasses red wine; ½ pint fish stock; bouquet garni; 1 doz. pickling onions; 1 oz. butter; 1 doz. button mushrooms; kneaded butter (see page 368); chopped parsley; croûtons of fried bread.

Prepare the eels, wash thoroughly, dry well, and cut in 3-inch lengths. Melt the butter in a shallow stewpan, add the finely chopped onion and prepared eel, and cook gently until golden brown. Flame with the red wine, allow to reduce by half, and then add the stock. Season with salt and pepper, add the herbs, and simmer very gently for about 20 minutes. Blanch the onions, drain, and return to their pan with the butter and cook until golden; then add the mushrooms and continue cooking for 2 to 3 minutes.

Remove the bouquet garni from the eels, add the onions and mushrooms, and thicken the sauce with kneaded butter; continue cooking for 10 minutes.

Pile the fish in the centre of a hot serving-dish, pour over the sauce, dust with chopped parsley, and surround with the croûtons.

For *Smoked Eel* – see page 18.

FLOUNDER (CARRELET)

A flat fish, similar to plaice but the dark skin is a lighter brown, mottled with dark brown. It is inferior to plaice, but any recipe given for plaice or sole can be used.

GRILSE

A young salmon weighing around 3 to 8 lb., returning from the sea to the river to spawn for the first time.

HADDOCK (EGLEFIN OR AIGLEFIN)

A large round fish in season all the year round, it has firm white flakes with a delicate flavour and is easily recognized by the dark line running down each side and the black finger mark just behind the head. Legend calls this St Peter's mark. The fish is sold whole, or in cutlets, steaks, and fillets. Small fish filleted are packed and sold as block fillets. Haddock is also sold smoked, the larger fish are filleted and smoked, but those which are most highly esteemed weigh from ¾ to 3 lb. and are split and then smoked. They are known as *Finnan Haddocks* and the best come from Aberdeen. The very small fish filleted and smoked are known as golden cutlets. Aberdeen smokies are small haddock gutted and smoked whole. They are stronger in flavour than Finnan but can be cooked in the same way.

It is important when cooking smoked haddock to cover it with liquid as it becomes dry and hard. Various methods can be used: boiling water, or a mixture of water and milk, can be poured over, the dish covered and left for 10 minutes; it can be simmered gently in reduced milk on top of the stove, or even poached in milk or water.

*

Haddock Maître d'Hôtel
1½ lb. fresh haddock fillets; 1 oz. butter; seasoning; ½ lemon; 4 tablespoons cream; tablespoon chopped parsley.

Wash and dry the fish and cut into portions. Butter a fireproof dish, lay in the fish, and season with salt and freshly ground pepper. Moisten with the lemon juice and spoon over the cream. Cover with a thickly buttered paper and bake in a moderate oven for 10 to 15 minutes. Serve dusted with the chopped parsley.

Haddock Bonne Femme
1½ lb. fresh haddock fillets; 1 tablespoon brown crumbs; 1 tablespoon melted butter.

SAUCE: 1 shallot; 3 oz. mushrooms; 1½ oz. butter; ¾ oz. flour; ½ pint light stock or potato water; salt; pepper; nutmeg; squeeze of lemon.

Skin the fish and set in a buttered fireproof dish.

Now prepare the sauce. Wash the mushrooms in salted water (do not remove the stalks or peel) and chop finely. Melt half the butter in a saucepan, add the finely chopped shallot, and cook gently until just beginning to colour; then add the mushrooms and cook briskly for about 3 to 5 minutes to evaporate any moisture. Draw away from the heat, drop in the remaining butter, and blend in the flour and the stock. Season with salt, pepper, and a grate of nutmeg, add the lemon juice, and stir over a gentle heat until boiling. Simmer for a minute or two, cool slightly, and then spoon over the fish. Dust with the brown crumbs and pour over the melted butter. Bake in a moderate oven for 20 to 25 minutes.

Haddock Hongroise
5 small fresh haddock fillets (1½ lb. weight); a squeeze of lemon juice; ½ gill water.

SAUCE: 2 oz. mushrooms; 1½ oz. butter; scant 1 oz. flour; 1 heaped teaspoonful paprika; ½ pint milk; 1 cap canned pimento.

Wash and dry the fillets, remove the skin, and place in a buttered fireproof dish. Season with salt and a few peppercorns. Add the lemon juice and water, cover with a buttered paper, and poach in a very moderate oven for about 15 minutes.

Wash the mushrooms, slice finely, and place in a saucepan with half the butter; cover and simmer for 2 minutes. Remove the pan from the fire, drop in the remaining butter, and when melted stir in the flour, paprika, and milk. Blend until smooth, return to the fire, and stir until boiling. Strain on the liquid from the fish, reduce for a minute or two, then add the pimento finely sliced.

Arrange the fish on a serving-dish and spoon over the sauce.

Kedgeree

2 oz. butter; 8 oz. cooked, flaked smoked haddock; 6 oz. boiled rice, well dried; 2 hard-boiled eggs; 1 raw egg; 2–3 tablespoons cream or creamy milk.

Melt two-thirds of the butter in a pan, put in the fish, and shake over the fire until thoroughly hot. Add the rice and hard-boiled eggs, coarsely chopped, and seasoning. Shake and stir over the heat with a fork for a few minutes. Add the raw beaten egg and enough cream or milk to moisten nicely. Reheat, stirring occasionally, and turn out.

Smoked Haddock Flan

RICH SHORTCRUST PASTRY: 6 oz. plain flour; 3 oz. butter; 1 oz. shortening; egg yolk and water to mix.

1 lb. smoked haddock; 1 small bunch spring onions or the shredded green part of a leek; 2 hard-boiled eggs; Béchamel sauce made with 1 oz. butter; ¾ oz. flour and ½ pint flavoured milk; 1 lb. potato purée bound with 1 egg yolk; grated cheese to finish.

Line a 7- to 8-inch flan ring with the pastry and bake blind.

Cook and flake the fish and blanch the spring onions or leek. Place the fish at the bottom of the flan case, put the onions over and the quartered eggs round. Spoon over the sauce and pipe the potato purée across the top, lattice fashion. Sprinkle with grated cheese and brown in a quick oven.

Smoked Haddock Mousse

1 lb. smoked haddock on the bone or ¾ lb. smoked fillet; 2 eggs, hard-boiled; cold Béchamel sauce made with ¾ oz. butter and ¾oz. flour and ½ pint milk; ¼ pint mayonnaise; scant ½ oz. gelatine; ½ gill light stock or water; ½ gill cream.

TO FINISH: 2 hard-boiled eggs; 1 pint aspic jelly.

Have ready the fish, cooked, skinned, and flaked, and the eggs chopped. Mix the sauce and mayonnaise together. Dissolve the gelatine in the stock over a gentle heat and add the sauce with the fish and eggs. Lightly whip the cream and fold into the mixture. Turn into a soufflé case to three-parts full and leave to set. Decorate the top with sliced hard-boiled egg and spoon over enough cold aspic to hold them in position. Leave to set and then fill the dish with more aspic.

HAKE (COLIN)

A large, round fish caught off the west coast and in the Irish Channel. Similar in appearance to cod but with a sharp, pointed face like pike. The flesh is friable and the bones are easy to remove, and because of this it is a fish very suitable for creams and mousses. It can also be cooked as cod or turbot.

*

Mousseline de Poisson

1¼ lb. hake (or 1 lb. fresh haddock fillet); 3 egg whites; 1½ gills cream; ½ gill milk.

VELOUTÉ SAUCE: 1 oz. butter; ¾ oz. flour; 1½ gills fish stock made from the bones and skin; ½ gill top milk.

Remove all skin and bone from the fish and pass through the

mincer. Check the weight; there should be ¾ lb. Put the minced fish in a bowl over ice and beat well with a wooden spoon. Break the egg whites slightly with a fork and beat them into the fish very slowly. Rub through a fine wire sieve or use an electric blender. Beat in the cream a little at a time and when it is all absorbed add seasoning. Use plenty of salt; this will thicken the mixture, then stir in the milk very slowly. Turn into a buttered oval dish or ring mould, cover with buttered paper, and poach in the oven in a bain-marie until firm (about 15 to 20 minutes). Leave for a minute or two before turning out. Serve coated with the velouté sauce and garnished, if liked, with shrimps or mushrooms.

Petits Pains de Poisson Margot

¾ lb. cutlet of hake; Béchamel sauce made with 1 oz. butter; 1 oz. flour; 1½ gills flavoured milk; 1 egg; 1 egg yolk; 12 button mushrooms.

SAUCE: 1 oz. butter; 1 oz. flour; ½ pint fish stock; ½ gill milk; 2 tablespoons cream; 1 oz. picked shrimps.

First prepare the Béchamel sauce and leave to cool. Remove the skin and bone from the fish, mince, and then pound thoroughly with the cold sauce. Add the eggs and season to taste.

Trim the mushrooms and cook quickly with a nut of butter, seasoning, and a squeeze of lemon.

Butter 8 to 12 small dariole moulds. Place a cooked mushroom at the bottom of each and fill to within ¼ inch of the top with the fish cream. Cover each mould with a 'twist' of buttered paper and cook *au bain-marie* for 15 to 20 minutes in a moderate oven.

Meanwhile, prepare a good stock with the skin and bones of the fish flavouring it with white wine or lemon, vegetables, and herbs. Melt the butter, add the flour, and cook lightly. Blend in the stock, stir until thickening over gentle heat, then add the milk and bring to the boil. Simmer for 5 minutes, then add the cream and shrimps. Unmould the fish creams and spoon over the sauce.

HALIBUT (FLÉTAN)

A flat-fish similar in appearance to turbot, in season throughout
the year. It grows to a great size and is generally sold in steaks and
cutlets. The flesh being firm and rather dry it needs careful cooking and a good sauce to be palatable. Any recipe for cod or turbot
is suitable.

*

Halibut Dimitri

1½ lb. steak of halibut; ½ oz. butter; ½ gill water; seasoning.

SAUCE: 1 oz. butter; 1 oz. flour; ½ pint milk infused with half a
bayleaf, a slice of onion and 6 peppercorns; 2 tablespoons cream.

TO FINISH: 8–10 anchovy fillets.

Wash and dry the fish and place in a buttered fireproof dish.
Pour over the water, season, and cover with a buttered paper and
cook gently in the oven for about 20 minutes. Meanwhile prepare
the sauce, cover, and set aside.

Take up the fish, remove the centre bone and skin and divide
into four neat pieces. Strain the liquor from the fish into the sauce
and simmer together; adjust the seasoning and add the cream.
Place the fish on a hot serving-dish, spoon over the sauce, and
garnish each portion with a lattice of anchovy fillets. Serve with
small steamed potatoes tossed in parsley.

Halibut Dugléré

1½ lb. steak of halibut; ½ oz. butter; ¼ pint water; ½ gill white wine;
a squeeze of lemon; seasoning.

SAUCE: 1 oz. butter; 1 oz. flour; liquor from the fish; ½ gill top
milk or single cream; 2 tomatoes, concasséd; 1 teaspoon chopped
chives and parsley.

Prepare the fish, place in a buttered fireproof dish, pour over the
water, wine, and seasonings, and cover with a buttered paper.
Cook gently for about 20 minutes in a very moderate oven.

Melt the butter, remove from the heat, and blend in the flour
and then the liquor strained from the fish. Season with salt

and pepper and stir until boiling, then add the cream and simmer together for 2 to 3 minutes.

Remove the centre bone from the fish and divide into portions. Add the prepared tomatoes and herbs to the sauce; adjust the seasoning and make sure the tomatoes are really hot; spoon the sauce over the fish and serve at once.

HERRING

A small, round fish with oily flesh found in abundance round the shores of Great Britain; when fresh are covered with silvery scales and they are at their best from May to October. Fresh, they lend themselves to many ways of cooking, but it is often the simpler methods that find the most favour, such as grilling whole, split, rolled in oatmeal and fried, or soused. They are cured and preserved in numerous ways and many are packed in barrels in salt; the majority of these are exported, often returning to this country after further processing. At home the most popular forms of preserved herring are kippers and bloaters. Kippers are herrings split and smoked over oak chips, whilst bloaters are herrings gutted and cured whole.

*

Grilled Herrings
4 herrings; seasoning; a little oil; sprays of fresh parsley.

MUSTARD SAUCE: see page 375.

Clean and prepare the fish and then make 3 or 4 cuts at an oblique angle to the backbone on each side of the herring. Season with salt and pepper and brush lightly with oil. Preheat the grill and brush the rack with oil. Grill the herrings gently for about 4 to 5 minutes on each side until the skin is crisp and golden brown. Serve garnished with sprigs of fresh parsley and mustard sauce handed separately.

Fried Herrings in Oatmeal
4 herrings; seasoning; about 4 tablespoons medium oatmeal; oil or good dripping for frying.

Clean and prepare the fish. Split open and remove the backbone. Score the skin in 2 or 3 places and season the fish with salt, pepper, and a squeeze of lemon. Roll them in the oatmeal, pressing it in well with a palette knife. Heat the dripping and when it is smoking put in the herrings, cut side down, and fry golden brown on each side, allowing 7 to 10 minutes in all. Drain on kitchen paper and serve on a hot dish garnished with sprigs of fresh parsley. If the herrings contain roes, roll these in a little seasoned flour, fry separately, and use as garnish.

Soused Herrings
4 herrings; ¼ teaspoon ground mace; 1 bayleaf; 2 cloves; 6 peppercorns; 2 allspice; salt; brown malt vinegar and water in equal quantities, about ¾ pint; 1 medium onion, sliced.

Split and fillet the herrings, roll up from head to tail, and place in a fireproof dish. Heat the vinegar with all the spices and seasonings to boiling-point and allow to cool. Pour the cold vinegar and spices over the fish and bake in a very low oven (325° F., Reg. 3) for about 1 hour.

KIPPERS: When plump and freshly cured they are best dotted with butter and grilled, but to give a very succulent result place in a shallow dish, pour over boiling water, cover, and stand 5 minutes, then drain well, dot with butter, and grill until crisp.

BLOATERS: These can be grilled or split, rolled in seasoned flour, and fried in the same way as herring. Preparation and time of cooking is the same.

LING

A white fish with firm flesh, similar to cod but rather lacking flavour. It is frequently salted, and should be cooked as cod.

MACKEREL (MAQUEREAU)

A round oily fish, a little larger than a herring, found in great numbers during the summer months swimming in shoals round the coast. They have distinct markings and no scales, but a pearly sheen which disappears when the fish is stale. It must be eaten very fresh as the flesh decomposes quickly, but when fresh the flesh is firm and delicious. Mackerel can be cooked in exactly the same way as herring but the following recipes are particularly good.

*

Grilled Mackerel with Green Gooseberry Sauce

4 mackerel; seasoning; a squeeze of lemon; a little oil.

GREEN GOOSEBERRY SAUCE: ½ lb. green gooseberries; 1 table-spoon castor sugar; 2 oz. butter; scant ½ oz. flour; ½ pint hot water; good pinch of chopped fennel; salt; pepper; nutmeg.

Top and tail the gooseberries, put them into a pan of boiling water and simmer gently until turning yellow. Strain and pass through a nylon sieve or strainer and sweeten with the sugar. The purée should make about ¾ gill or a small cupful. Prepare the sauce by melting ½ oz. of the butter and adding the flour off the fire. When well mixed, pour on the hot water, bring to the boil, draw aside, and add the rest of the butter, piece by piece, and then the gooseberry purée. Finish with the fennel and seasoning to taste, adding a little grated nutmeg.

Trim the mackerel and make about four diagonal cuts across the flesh on either side of the fish. Season with salt and freshly ground black pepper and sprinkle well with lemon juice. Brush with oil and grill for 10 to 15 minutes, depending on the size, until brown and crisp. They can also be split and boned and grilled, and in this case grill the cut side first for about 8 to 10 minutes and the skin side for only 3 minutes.

Serve on a hot dish, garnished with lemon, and hand the goose-berry sauce separately.

Baked Mackerel with Watercress and Anchovy Butter

4 mackerel; seasoning; ½ lemon.

WATERCRESS AND ANCHOVY BUTTER: ½ bunch watercress; 1½ oz. unsalted butter; 4 fillets anchovy or anchovy essence to taste.

Trim and fillet the fish and place the fillets skin side down in a
lightly buttered fireproof dish; season with salt and plenty of
freshly ground black pepper and moisten with the lemon juice.
Bake in a moderate oven for 10 to 15 minutes.

Meanwhile blanch the watercress, refresh, and drain. Chop
finely with the anchovies or work both in a blender. Soften the
butter with a wooden spoon and add the watercress purée by
degrees. Season with a squeeze of lemon and extra anchovy
essence to taste. Shape into 8 neat 'pats' and chill.

Place the fish in a clean, hot dish and place a pat of savoury
butter on each fillet before serving.

Mackerel Algérienne
3–4 mackerel, according to size; ½ lemon; chopped parsley.

SALPICON: 2 green or red peppers; ¾ lb. ripe tomatoes; ½ oz.
butter; 1 shallot; 1 clove garlic; 1 teaspoon paprika pepper.

Split and bone the mackerel, wash, and dry well. Place the
fish in a fireproof dish, season with salt and freshly ground black
pepper, and squeeze over a little lemon juice. Bake in a moderate
oven for about 20 minutes. Meanwhile prepare the salpicon.

Shred the peppers, blanch, and refresh; skin the tomatoes,
remove the seeds, and slice. Melt the butter, add the finely
chopped shallot, and cook until soft; then add the tomatoes, the
garlic crushed with salt, and the paprika. Stew slowly to a rich
pulp, then add the peppers and continue cooking for 2 to 3
minutes; spoon this mixture over the fish and serve garnished
with thin slices of lemon and chopped parsley.

MULLET – RED (ROUGET)

A small, round fish with a rosy pink skin and delicate friable white
flesh. It is known as the woodcock of the sea as after cleaning
quickly through the gills it is cooked with the liver in the fish.
This is considered to be a great delicacy but if preferred it can be
cleaned in the usual way. In season from May to September.

Red Mullet 'en papillote'

4 red mullet; 4 tablespoons oil, or melted butter; seasoning; lemon juice.

Cut four large ovals of greaseproof paper of a size to enclose each fish. Brush the papers with oil or melted butter, place a prepared fish on each and season with salt and pepper and a squeeze of lemon. Wrap up each fish, place in a fireproof dish, and bake in a moderate oven for 12 to 15 minutes.

Have ready a very hot dish, break away the paper, and lift the fish very carefully as the skin and flesh of the mullet is easily damaged. Serve quite plain or with a little extra melted butter.

Red Mullet with Fennel and Lemon

4 mullet; 4 tablespoons oil or melted butter; seasoning; 1 shallot; 2 roots Florentine fennel; 1 lemon; 1 oz. butter; chopped parsley.

Trim and prepare the mullet and make three or four diagonal cuts across the flesh on each side of the fish. Season with salt and freshly ground pepper and leave to marinade in the oil or butter and finely chopped shallot while preparing the fennel.

Cut the fennel into thick slices and blanch in boiling, salted water for 2 to 3 minutes, then drain well. Remove the peel and pith from the lemon with a serrated-edged knife and cut into segments. Melt the butter and add the fennel and sauté until just tender. Season with salt and pepper and add the lemon and chopped parsley.

Brush the grill rack with oil and preheat the grill. Lift the mullet from their marinade and grill for 8 to 10 minutes, moistening them with oil as necessary during cooking. Arrange the fish on a hot serving-dish and pile the fennel and lemon at each end.

Red Mullet Angers

4 red mullet; 2 glasses white wine and 1 glass water to make ½ pint liquid; a squeeze of lemon; seasoning; bouquet garni; 1 shallot; ½ oz. butter; 3 egg yolks; 3 tablespoons thick cream; 1½ oz. unsalted butter.

Trim and prepare the mullet and place in a sauté pan (or frying-pan) with the wine, water, and seasonings. Bring very gently to simmering-point, draw the pan to the side of the stove, cover, and leave to poach for 10 minutes.

Chop the shallot, place in a saucepan with $\frac{1}{2}$ oz. butter, and allow to cook slowly until golden; then tip on the liquor from the fish and allow to reduce by half. Thicken with the liaison of egg yolk and cream (see page 368), remove from the heat, beat in the unsalted butter a little at a time, and pass the sauce through a conical strainer.

Lift the fish carefully on to a cold serving-dish and add any extra liquid left in the pan to the sauce. Spoon the sauce over the fish and allow to get quite cold before serving.

MULLET – GREY

A round fish, larger than red mullet, with beautiful firm white flesh. They are caught off the coast of Cornwall during the summer and autumn months and can be cooked in the same way as cod.

PILCHARD

A small, round oily fish, similar to a herring but with a tough skin. It is caught off the Cornish coast and may be found in local fish shops, but in the main pilchards are canned. Like herring they are very nutritious. If you buy fresh ones, fry them like sprats.

PLAICE (PLIE)

A flat fish with a greyish-brown skin with bright orange spots. It is one of the most commonly used fish in this country. The flesh is rather tasteless and so it is generally served fried either whole or in fillets with a savoury butter or well-flavoured sauce as an accompaniment, but any recipe for sole can be used.

*

Fried Fillets of Plaice

Fillets of plaice; 2 tablespoons flour; salt and pepper; beaten egg; dried white crumbs.

Skin the fillets, wash, and dry well. Roll the fillets in the flour sifted with the seasoning, then brush with beaten egg and coat with the crumbs. Press the crumbs on well using a palette knife and place in a wire basket, ready for frying.

Heat the fat until a faint blue smoke rises from the surface and make sure there is sufficient to cover the food. Lower the frying-basket gently into the fat and cook until golden brown. Lift the basket and drain, first over the pan and then turning the fish on to a wire rack or crumpled kitchen paper. Serve piping hot, and if it has to be kept warm never cover or the crispness will be spoilt. For the same reason sauce should be served separately. Garnish the dish with sprays of fried parsley. To fry parsley, have ready good sprays of parsley, washed and thoroughly dried, with the main stalk removed. Turn out the heat from under the fat-bath, wait for a minute (there must be no blue haze), and then lower the parsley very gently into the fat. When the bubbling subsides the parsley will be quite crisp and should be bright green.

Plaice 'en goujons'
Fillets of plaice; 2 tablespoons flour; salt and pepper; beaten egg; dried white crumbs.

Skin the fillets, wash, and dry well. Cut them diagonally into finger-like strips and prepare and fry in the same way as the fried fillets. Serve piping hot piled in an entrée dish with a piquante tomato sauce handed separately.

PIKE

A round fresh-water fish easily recognized by its long, sharp head. It has a cruel-looking face and is indeed a great fighter. The flesh is white and friable, which makes it very suitable for creams, stuffings, and quenelles. If plainly cooked in a court bouillon it needs a well-flavoured accompanying sauce.

*

Quenelles de Brochet
6 oz. pike, free from skin and bone (whiting, hake, or codling

can be used); salt; pepper; grated nutmeg; 1 oz. butter; ½ oz. flour; ½ gill milk; 2½ oz. butter; 1 egg white; 2 egg yolks; 2–3 tablespoons thick cream.

Cut the fish into cubes and pound with the seasonings in the pestle and mortar until smooth. Prepare a panada with the 1 oz. butter, flour, and milk, and allow to get quite cold. Work the cold panada into the fish, then add the creamed butter, the unbroken egg white, and the egg yolks. Pass through a fine sieve or work in the blender, then add the cream very slowly, beating well between each addition. Keep the mixture in a cool place for 1 hour then shape and poach for 10 minutes (see below). Serve in a cream or velouté sauce.

SHAPING:

1. The mixture can be placed in small quenelle moulds, which may be bought.

2. Shape with two dessertspoons in the same way as meringues, cleaning the spoons in a small bowl of hot water after making each quenelle.

3. Use a piping-bag fitted with an éclair pipe and cut away the mixture cleanly with a knife when the desired size and length is obtained.

4. Most simply of all the mixture can be rolled and shaped by hand on a lightly floured board.

POACHING: Have ready a sauté pan or frying-pan full of boiling, salted water. Slide in only just enough quenelles to cover the bottom of the pan as they rise during cooking. Draw the pan to the side of the stove, cover, and allow barely to simmer for 10 minutes. Lift carefully and drain on a cloth before serving in a sauce.

ROCK SALMON

The fishmonger's name for the common cat fish, rock eel, or nurse. It is sold skinned and the flesh is firm with a pinky tinge. It is used in great quantities by the fried-fish trade but is good for fish stews or a matelote.

SALMON

A pink-fleshed, oily fish with superb firm flesh, caught in rivers of the northern hemisphere that flow to the sea. The season varies around the coast of the British Isles from early February to September, some rivers being earlier than others. A salmon is $3\frac{1}{2}$ years old or over (younger, it is called grilse) and reaches a great size. It is covered with bright silvery scales and when very fresh there is a thick buttery curd between the flakes, which disappears within hours of being caught. The flesh is rich and very satisfying and it is sufficient to allow 4 oz. per head when catering, although when ordering whole fish it must be remembered that the head is about one fifth of its length and weight, so choose, where possible, fish with small head and tail and broad shoulders. Chilled or frozen Canadian and Pacific salmon can be bought outside the season of the home-caught fish.

Salmon can be cooked in various ways. For a very large function or for the cold table in hotels and restaurants the fish is cooked whole; for smaller parties in a private house it is more usual to choose a thick piece cut from the middle of the fish, weighing anything from $1\frac{1}{2}$ to 3 lb. Cutlets or steaks of salmon $\frac{3}{4}$ to $1\frac{1}{2}$ inches thick are suitable for individual portions and grilling. When the fish is cooked whole it is not necessary to remove the scales, indeed it is better to leave them on as they give protection to the delicate skin, making it easier to remove before serving. To poach salmon it must be covered in liquid and so for a whole fish a fish kettle with a drainer is essential. However, it is possible to cook a thick steak in the oven, but it must be basted frequently with the cooking liquid.

Times for Cooking

Whole fish over 5 lb.	8 mins. per lb.
Whole fish under 5 lb. and large steaks	10 mins. per lb.
Whole fish under 2 lb.	15–20 mins. per lb.
Steaks and cutlets, depending on thickness	12–15 mins.

Thick steaks or large pieces of salmon can also be steamed. They should be prepared, seasoned lightly, and wrapped in buttered foil or parchment paper; allow 20 minutes to the pound and leave to cool without unwrapping. This is an excellent method of preparing salmon for the deep freeze.

*

Boiled Salmon

$2\frac{1}{2}$ lb. steak of salmon; court bouillon made with $1\frac{1}{2}$ pints water; juice of $\frac{1}{4}$ lemon; 2 glasses white wine; 1 level teaspoon salt; 6 peppercorns; bouquet garni.

Clean the fish, making sure that all the blood near the backbone is scraped away, and dry well. Tie the fish carefully round with tape, but not too tightly as the salmon will swell during cooking, or wrap in muslin. Place underside down in a fish kettle or shallow stewpan, pour over the court bouillon, which should be still warm, and bring to the boil. Reduce the heat, cover the pan, and calculate the cooking time (see previous notes) from now. The liquid must just tremble throughout the cooking; on no account must it boil or the delicate skin will break and the flesh be damaged. Drain the fish quickly, remove the skin, and serve on a napkin. Garnish with a spray of parsley and hand 'fish' potatoes and Hollandaise sauce separately.

For the fish potatoes, cut some medium-sized potatoes in quarters lengthways, and pare the sharp edges to shape them into

ovals. Boil until three parts cooked, drain, and return to the pan.
Cover with a piece of muslin, then the lid. Set on a gentle heat to
complete the cooking.

Grilled Salmon Cutlets

4 steaks of salmon, cut ¾-inch thick; 2 tablespoons oil; 1 small
onion, sliced; salt; freshly ground black pepper; a squeeze of
lemon.

FOR SERVING: 2 oz. maître d'hôtel butter.

Prepare the fish and leave to soak in the oil and seasonings for up
to 1 hour. If there is no time for marinading, just brush well on
both sides with oil. Heat the grill and scrape any of the marinade
adhering to the fish. Grill for 5 minutes on each side and then a
further 2 minutes on each side, making 14 minutes in all.

Have ready the maître d'hôtel butter and spread about ⅓ of
this on a warm dish. The dish must only be warm as the butter
should soften, not oil. Remove the skin and centre bone from the
salmon, arrange on the prepared dish, and place the remaining
butter on the top of each cutlet.

Salmon Gourmets

4 steaks of salmon; ¾ gill white wine; lemon juice; 1 slice onion;
6 peppercorns; sprig of parsley.

SAUCE: 4 tablespoons Tarragon vinegar; blade of mace; 6 peppercorns; 3 yolks of egg; 4–6 oz. butter; ¼ teaspoon tomato purée;
grated rind of ½ orange.

GARNISH: 3 tomatoes; 2 oz. button mushrooms.

Poach the fish in the white wine, lemon juice, and seasonings in
a moderate oven for about 15 minutes.

Meanwhile prepare the sauce. Reduce the vinegar with the
peppercorns and flavourings to 1½ tablespoons. Strain on to the
creamed egg yolks, add a small nut of the butter, and whisk until
thick over gentle heat; then add the remaining butter by degrees.
Set aside.

Prepare the garnish. Skin the tomatoes, cut in four, squeeze away the seeds, and cut into neat shreds. Slice the mushrooms and cook quickly in a nut of butter, a squeeze of lemon juice, and seasoning.

Strain the liquor from the fish, reduce to 1 tablespoon, and add to the sauce with the tomato purée and the orange rind. Remove the skin and bone from the salmon and arrange in a warm serving-dish. Add the garnish to the sauce and spoon over the fish. This may be glazed quickly under the grill if liked.

Cold Salmon Mousse

¾ lb. steak of salmon; Béchamel sauce made with 1 oz. butter, 1 oz. flour, 1½ gills flavoured milk, and seasoning; 2 oz. butter; 1–2 tablespoons cream; 1–2 tablespoons sherry; 1–2 drops carmine.

TO FINISH: ½ pint aspic jelly; sliced cucumber, or a few sprays of dill or chervil.

Poach the salmon in the oven, covering it with a hot court bouillon prepared without vinegar, which helps to keep the colour of the fish; allow to cool in the liquid, then remove the skin and bone. Prepare the Béchamel sauce and turn on to a plate to cool quickly. Cream the butter until quite soft and half-whip the cream.

Pound the salmon in a pestle and mortar or work well in a bowl with a large wooden spoon or the end of a rolling-pin. Add the sauce by degrees with plenty of seasoning. Fold in the butter, cream, and sherry; do not over-work at this stage or the mixture will curdle. Add the carmine with discretion and only if the fish is not a good pink. Turn into a size-2 soufflé case, smooth over the top, and set in a cool place for about 10 minutes to firm.

Run over a thin layer of aspic and, when set, arrange the garnish on the top, dipping it first in a little liquid aspic. Set the garnish in another layer of aspic and then fill to the top of the dish with the rest.

Salmon Mousse Nantua

¾ lb. steak salmon; Béchamel sauce made with ¾ oz. butter; ¼ oz. flour; ½ pint flavoured milk and seasoning; ½ pint mayonnaise;

1 level dessertspoon powdered gelatine dissolved in 3 tablespoons light stock or water; 2 tablespoons cream; 1 egg white; 2 oz. picked prawns or shrimps.

GARNISH: watercress; hard-boiled egg, and extra prawns if wished.

Prepare the salmon and sauce as in the preceding recipe and, when both are ready, pound well together and work in *half* the mayonnaise. Season well and add the warm gelatine, the half-whipped cream, and chopped prawns. Whisk the egg white until stiff, fold into the salmon mixture, and turn at once into a lightly oiled mould and leave to set.

Thin the remaining mayonnaise with boiling water or a little tomato juice and season carefully with Tabasco or a 'point' of cayenne.

Turn out the mousse, coat with the mayonnaise, and garnish suitably.

Salmon Cutlets en Chaudfroid

4 steaks of salmon; ½ pint mayonnaise; 1 dessertspoon oil; 1 shallot, finely chopped; 1 level teaspoon paprika; 1 level teaspoon tomato purée; juice from the seeds of the tomatoes; ¼ pint aspic jelly; 1 teaspoon gelatine.

TO FINISH: ½ pint aspic jelly; a few sprigs of chervil or 3 thin slices of cucumber for each steak; 4 tomatoes; 2 oz. picked prawns or shrimps.

Poach the fish in the oven, well covered with hot court bouillon (see page 123). Allow to cool a little in the liquid, then remove the skin and bone and bind each cutlet in muslin; press between two plates until cold.

In the meantime, soften the shallot in the oil, add the paprika, tomato purée, and strained juice from the tomato seeds, and cook for 2 to 3 minutes; strain and cool.

Place the fish steaks on a cake rack with a plate underneath.

Flavour the mayonnaise with tomato and paprika mixture; dissolve the gelatine in the aspic over gentle heat and add to the mayonnaise. When on the point of setting baste over the salmon steaks. Decorate each steak with the chervil or cucumber slices each dipped in aspic and then baste again with cold liquid aspic.

Arrange on a serving-platter and garnish with a salpicon of the tomatoes and prawns and chopped aspic jelly.

SARDINE

The young or 'fry' of pilchard, they are caught off the coast of Brittany, south of Spain and Portugal, and in the Mediterranean where they are landed in great numbers. The majority are canned in olive oil and used for hors d'œuvres (see page 19) but a few are sold fresh and are delicious fried until crisp and golden and served with lemon, or baked *au gratin*.

SEA TROUT OR SALMON TROUT

A fish similar in shape and habitat to the salmon, but it is rather longer and narrower and never attains quite the size or weight of salmon. The flesh is not so firm and the flavour more delicate, and for this reason it is generally cooked whole. Salmon trout can be cooked and served in the same way as salmon. In season May to July.

*

Salmon Trout 'en gelée'
2½–3 lb. sea trout; 1½ pints court bouillon flavoured with white wine, vegetables, and herbs; 2 oz. gelatine; 1 tablespoon wine vinegar; ½ gill sherry; 2 egg whites.

GARNISH: ½ pint prawns; ½ cucumber; 1 bunch watercress.

Trim the trout, vandyke the tail, and wash well, taking care to scrape away the blood that lies against the backbone and to remove the gills if this has not been done by the fishmonger. Curl the fish slightly and place, underside down, in a fish kettle or fireproof dish and pour over the well-seasoned court bouillon while still warm. Poach for 25 to 30 minutes in the fish kettle but for 35 to 45 minutes if baking in the oven. On no account must the liquid around the fish boil, and when baking in the oven baste frequently. Allow the fish to cool in the court bouillon and then lift carefully on to a board or large dish. Remove any specks of fat floating on the surface of the liquid with kitchen paper, strain into a clean saucepan, add the gelatine, etc., and prepare an aspic jelly (as directed on page 26).

Snip the skin along the top of the trout and remove carefully, leaving the head and tail intact. Cut through the backbone just below the head, ease a knife along the bone, and then gently lift it up and out towards the tail; cut the bone just short of the tail.

Run a little aspic over the serving-dish and leave to set. Lift the trout, using a fish slice and palette knife for support, and place on the prepared dish.

Slice the cucumber finely; peel the shell from the tails of the prawns but do not remove the heads. Arrange the prawns along the top of the fish and then baste with cold liquid aspic. Decorate the dish with the cucumber and watercress and hand a mayonnaise or sauce verte separately.

SKATE (RAIE)

A curiously shaped fish, rarely seen whole in the fishmongers but sold cut in pieces or 'wings'. In season August to April. It needs more careful preparation than most fish as the black skin is covered with a rather heavy slime with a number of small barbs or nodules and should be washed well and scrubbed lightly. The black skin is always removed before serving. The extra trouble is worth while as the flesh is thick and creamy and most digestible. Skate can be dipped in batter and deep-fat fried or cooked in a court bouillon.

*

Skate 'au beurre noir'
1 wing of skate weighing about 1½–2 lb.

COURT BOUILLON: 1 quart water; 1 level dessertspoon salt; 1 wineglass vinegar; 1 medium onion, sliced; bouquet garni; 6 peppercorns.

BEURRE NOIR: 2 oz. butter; 2 tablespoons wine vinegar; salt and pepper; 1 dessertspoon capers; 1 teaspoon chopped parsley.

First prepare the court bouillon. Put all the ingredients in a pan, bring to the boil, and simmer for 5 minutes and allow to cool.

In the meantime prepare the skate. Cut into portions and place in a shallow stewpan. Strain over the court bouillon, bring slowly to the boil, then draw aside and allow barely to simmer for 25 to 30 minutes. Lift out the pieces with a fish slice, drain thoroughly, gently scrape away the skin from both sides, and arrange in a serving-dish. Keep hot.

Heat a frying-pan, drop in the butter, and cook gently to a deep nut brown. Pour over the fish. Add the vinegar to the pan and the seasoning, and reduce to half; sprinkle capers and parsley over the fish and pour over the reduced vinegar. Serve at once.

Skate 'au fromage'

1½–2 lb. wing of skate; 1 tablespoon wine vinegar.

SAUCE: ¾ pint milk infused with 1 onion stuck with a clove and a bouquet garni; 1½ oz. butter; 1¼ oz. flour; 2 oz. grated cheese.

GARNISH: small croûtes of fried bread.

Prepare the fish, cut into portions, and place in a shallow pan with water to cover, the vinegar, and a level dessertspoon of salt. Bring to the boil, draw the pan to the side of the stove, cover, and allow to simmer very gently for 25 minutes.

Make the sauce, using the method described for Béchamel on page 369, and when cooked beat in half the cheese. Sprinkle half the remaining cheese on the bottom of a buttered gratin dish.

Drain the fish thoroughly and gently scrape away the skin from both sides. Arrange the pieces of skate in the prepared dish, spoon over the sauce, and scatter over the rest of the cheese. Bake in a hot oven until brown and garnish with the croûtes of fried bread.

Skate with Orange

1½–2 lb. wing of skate; 1 small onion; 1 oz. butter; 2 oranges; 1 teaspoonful chopped parsley and thyme; 1 small teaspoon wine vinegar.

Prepare the fish cut into portions and cook in acidulated water (that is, water with lemon juice or vinegar added) in the same way as in the previous recipe. Drain thoroughly, remove the skin, arrange in a serving-dish, and keep hot.

Chop the onion very finely, put into a small frying-pan with half the butter, and cook slowly until soft but not brown. Peel one orange and slice into rounds; add the rest of the butter to the pan, put in the orange slices, dust with sugar, and fry quickly, until turning colour, and arrange on the fish. Add the juice of the other orange to the pan with the herbs, seasoning, and vinegar. Boil up and pour over the fish.

SMELTS (ÉPERLAN)

A small round fish with a silvery almost transparent look and a faint smell of cucumber, it is found in salt and fresh water, being of the salmon species, and is in season from June to September. The flesh is very delicate in flavour and the fish is always cleaned through the gills and then the gills removed. They are generally seen prepared in this way, packed in small boxes. The most popular and usual way of preparing smelts is to coat with egg and crumb or to dip in batter and deep-fat fry, but they can be cooked *au gratin* or poached and served with a thin tomato sauce.

SOLE – DOVER

A flat, white fish, long and oval in shape, with fine, firm flesh. It is distinguished by its dark, almost purple, brown rough skin and is caught off the shores of this country in the North Sea from Yorkshire to Kent, in the Channel off the south coast of Ireland, and in the Mediterranean. Sole is held in high esteem by all cooks and can be prepared in many ways. It is available through-out the year but is at its best from April to January. Slip soles are small fish weighing no more than 12 oz.

*

Sole Maintenon

1½–2 lb. sole, filleted.

COURT BOUILLON : 2 glasses white wine; ¼ pint water; blade of mace; 2 allspice; bouquet garni; salt; pepper.

VELOUTÉ SAUCE : 1¼ oz. butter; 1 oz. flour; ½ pint court bouillon; 2 egg yolks; 2 good tablespoons thick cream; ½ gill fresh tomato sauce or small teaspoon tomato purée and court bouillon to make ½ gill; ¼ lb. button mushrooms.

Place the bones and the fish trimmings in a pan with all the ingredients for the court bouillon and simmer gently for 20 to 30 minutes, then strain. Poach the fillets in a buttered dish covered with a little of the fish fumet in a moderate oven for about 8 to 10 minutes.

Meanwhile prepare the velouté sauce. Melt the butter, add the flour, and cook gently to a straw colour; blend in the fish fumet and stir until boiling. Work the egg yolks and cream together and add the sauce away from the fire. Add the tomato sauce or purée and the sliced mushrooms previously cooked in a little butter. Spoon the sauce over the fish and serve.

Sole Normande

1½–2 lb. Dover sole; ½ glass dry white wine or cider; a squeeze of lemon; 1¼ oz. butter; 1 oz. flour; ¼ pint vegetable stock; ¼ pint double cream.

Trim and skin the fish, cut off the head, wash and dry well, and place in a buttered gratin dish. Moisten the fish with the wine and lemon; season with salt and a few peppercorns, cover with a well-buttered paper, and poach in a moderate oven for about 15 to 20 minutes. Meanwhile prepare the vegetable stock, allowing it to reduce well to strengthen the flavour.

Melt the butter, blend in the flour, and cook gently to a straw colour. Tip on the stock, stir until smooth, and then bring to the boil; strain in the liquid from the fish and simmer together for 2 to 3 minutes.

Place the sole in a fresh, warm dish, add the cream to the sauce, heat carefully, and pour over the fish.

Sole Walewska

1½–2 lb. Dover sole, filleted; 4 crayfish tails or slices of lobster meat; 4 slices truffle; ½ pint fish fumet made from the bone with seasoning and vegetables to flavour; 1 oz. butter; ¾ oz. flour; ½ gill single cream; 1 oz. grated Parmesan cheese.

Prepare the fillets, fold neatly, and place a slice each of lobster and truffle on each fillet. Lift carefully into a buttered gratin dish and pour over ½ gill of the fish fumet, and cover with a buttered paper. Poach in a moderate oven for 8 to 10 minutes.

In the meantime prepare the sauce with the remaining fish fumet, butter and flour in the usual way, then add the cream and cheese. Reheat without boiling and adjust the seasoning.

Place the fish on a hot serving-dish, spoon over the sauce, and glaze under the grill or in a quick oven.

Sole Meunière aux Raisins

2 1¼-lb. soles, filleted; 2–3 oz. butter; juice of ½ lemon; 1 dessert-spoon chopped mixed herbs and parsley.

GARNISH: ½ lb. muscat or green grapes; lemon juice; chopped parsley.

Wash and dry the sole. Keep wrapped in a cloth in the refrigerator until just before cooking. Peel and pip grapes, sprinkle with lemon juice, and put in a warm place to heat gently. Roll the fillets in seasoned flour. Heat the pan and drop in a third of the butter; when foaming lay in the fillets and fry until nicely coloured on both sides. Arrange in the serving-dish. Wipe out the pan, reheat, and drop in the rest of the butter. When a light brown, quickly add the lemon and herbs with salt and pepper. Pour over the fish whilst foaming and scatter over the grapes. Dust with chopped parsley.

Soles Fourrées

4 small slip soles; 2 oz. butter; 6 tablespoons fresh white crumbs.

FILLING: ½ oz. butter; scant ½ oz. flour; 1 gill milk; 2 oz. picked prawns; 2 oz. mushrooms; 1 tablespoon cream.

GARNISH: 1 bunch watercress.

Skin and lift the fillets on both sides and remove the backbone. Then prepare the filling. Melt the ½ oz. butter, add the flour away from the fire, and blend in the milk and seasoning. Stir until boiling and reduce for 2 minutes. Wash and quarter the mushrooms, toss quickly in butter over the fire, and add to the sauce with the prawns and cream.

Reshape the soles, lay on a buttered baking-sheet, fill with prawn mixture, brush over with melted butter, and scatter over the white crumbs. Sprinkle again with melted butter, then bake in a moderate oven, basting occasionally, for 20 to 30 minutes. Serve with 'bouquets' of crisp watercress.

Sole Colbert

4 slip soles weighing 12 oz. each; seasoned flour; beaten egg; dry white crumbs; deep fat for frying; 2 oz. maître d'hôtel butter.

Skin and trim the soles, leaving on the heads, and wash and dry well. Cut down the centre of the backbone on the white underside of the fish and lift the fillets to the fin bones on this side only. Dust the fish and the underside of the raised fillets with a little seasoned flour, then coat with the egg and crumbs, pressing the crumbs on well. Fry the fish in smoking hot fat to a deep golden brown. Drain well on kitchen paper, then carefully lift away the backbone. Fill the centre of each fish with the maître d'hôtel butter and serve immediately.

Sole Andalouse

2 1¼-lb. soles filleted; 4–6 peppercorns; a slice of onion; lemon.

RICE SALAD: 4 oz. long-grained rice; 1 teacupful cooked peas; 2 caps canned pimento; French dressing.

SAUCE: ½ pint mayonnaise; 1 clove garlic; 1 level teaspoon tomato purée; 1 level teaspoon paprika.

GARNISH: 1 cap pimento; 1 bunch watercress; 2 large tomatoes.

Skin the fillets of fish, fold, and lay in a buttered dish. Season with salt, add the peppercorns, onion, and a squeeze of lemon and a little water, and poach in a moderate oven for 8 to 10 minutes. Allow to cool in the liquid. Meanwhile prepare the rice salad (see page 82) and place in a serving-dish.

Crush the clove of garlic with a little salt and work into the mayonnaise with the tomato purée and paprika; thin with a little juice from the canned pimento and adjust the seasoning.

Arrange the sole on the rice, spoon over enough sauce to coat each fillet, and decorate with strips of pimento. Garnish the dish with bouquets of watercress and sliced tomatoes. Hand any extra separately.

Sole Niçoise

2 1¼-lb. soles; 4–6 peppercorns; slice of onion; lemon; 6 oz. long-grained rice cooked and well drained; French dressing; ½ pint mayonnaise; anchovy essence; anchovy fillets; ½ lb. tomatoes; 8–12 black olives.

Prepare and cook the fish as in the preceding recipe. Moisten the rice with a very little French dressing and then add enough mayonnaise to bind; place this on the serving-dish and arrange the fish on top. Add anchovy essence to taste to the mayonnaise, spoon over the fillets of sole, and decorate with a lattice of anchovy fillets. Garnish the dish with sliced tomatoes and stoned black olives mixed with French dressing.

Sole 'en éventail'

A dish suitable for a cold buffet. The recipe will serve eight and as the name implies should resemble a fan.

2 1¼-lb. soles, filleted; ½ lemon.

FISH MOUSSELINE: 1 lb. whiting; 2 egg whites; ¼ pint cream.

MAYONNAISE COLLÉE: ½ pint mayonnaise; ½ gill aspic jelly; 1 teaspoon gelatine.

GARNISH: sliced truffle or sliced cooked button mushrooms; 1½ pints aspic jelly.

Trim the fillets and wash and dry and flatten carefully with the blade of a heavy knife or cutlet bat. Prepare the fish mousseline following the instructions on page 131. Spread the top half of each fillet on the skin side with the mousseline or farce, draw the tail section over, and smooth the sides. Each fillet should look

like the section of a fan, broad at the top and quite pointed at the end. Place in a buttered dish and squeeze over a little lemon; cover with buttered paper and poach in a very moderate oven for 10 to 15 minutes.

Dissolve the gelatine in the liquid aspic over a gentle heat and add the mayonnaise. Place the fillets of fish on a cake rack and, when quite cold, coat with mayonnaise collée which should be thick and on the point of setting. Decorate each fillet with a motif cut from a slice of truffle or use 3 or 4 slices of mushroom, dipping each piece of decoration in aspic before placing in position. Baste with cool aspic and leave to set.

Dish on a bed of chopped aspic and finish with aspic croûtons.

Sole au Vin Blanc

2 1¼-lb. soles, filleted; 1 onion; 1 carrot; 1 stick celery; bouquet garni; lemon; ½ pint water; ¼ lb. mushrooms.

SAUCE VIN BLANC: 1 glass white wine; 1 finely chopped shallot;

6 peppercorns; blade of mace; 1 egg yolk; 2 oz. butter; 1¼ oz. butter; 1 oz. flour; ½ pint fish stock.

Fillet and skin the sole, wash and dry them, fold and place in a buttered fireproof dish with a squeeze of lemon juice; season with salt and peppercorns and cover with a buttered paper. Set on one side. Place the fish bone and skin in a saucepan with the vegetables to flavour, cover with the water and seasoning, herbs and lemon juice, and simmer gently for 20 to 30 minutes. Strain and measure – there should be ½ pint.

Meanwhile prepare the first part of the white-wine sauce. Reduce the wine on the shallot and seasonings to a teaspoonful. Strain on to the beaten egg yolk, stand the bowl in a bain-marie, add a nut from the 2 oz. quantity of butter, and beat until thick. Then add the remaining butter, a small piece at a time, beating well. When it is the consistency of whipped cream, cover and set aside. Place the prepared sole in a very moderate oven to poach for about 10 minutes. Wash and trim the mushrooms, slice or quarter, depending on their size, and cook quickly with a nut of butter, seasoning, and a squeeze of lemon.

Now continue with the sauce. Melt the 1¼ oz. butter, add the flour, and cook slowly until a pale straw colour. Remove from the heat, add the measured fish stock, and blend until smooth. Season, return to the heat, stir until boiling, and then leave to simmer for 5 minutes. Arrange the fillets of sole in a warm serving-dish and scatter over the mushrooms. Beat the butter sauce into the velouté and spoon over the fish. Glaze under the grill before serving.

Filets de Sole Suchet

1½ lb. sole, filleted; 1 wineglass white wine; a squeeze of lemon; 2 medium-sized carrots; a sherry glassful of Madeira or sherry; 2 medium-sized ripe tomatoes.

SAUCE: 1½ gills Béchamel made with 1 oz. butter, ¾ oz. flour, 1½ gills flavoured milk and seasoning, the fumet from the fish, 2 tablespoons cream.

FARCE: ½ lb. whiting; white of 1 egg; ¾ gill cream.

Fillet and skin the sole. Make the farce by working the fish with the egg white added by degrees, then beat in the cream and season finally with salt and pepper. Spread the soles thickly with the farce, fold over, and lay in a lightly buttered fireproof dish. Pour over the white wine and lemon and cover with a buttered paper.

Cut the red part of the carrots into fine strips and put into a small pan with a nut of butter and the sherry. Cover and simmer till tender.

Poach the fish for 10 to 15 minutes, strain liquor into the Béchamel sauce, simmer to a creamy consistency, and add the cream and lastly the carrots. Cut the tomatoes in half after skinning and grill lightly. Arrange the sole in a serving-dish, coat with the sauce, and garnish each fillet with the half tomato.

Sole Joinville

PANADE: 1½ gills milk; 2 oz. butter; 2½ oz. flour; 2 eggs; ½ gill cream.

¾ lb. fresh haddock or cod weighed when skinned, boned, and minced; 4 slip soles, filleted with the bones.

VELOUTÉ SAUCE: 1 oz. butter; ¾ oz. flour; 1½ gills fumet made from the sole bones; ½ gill single cream or creamy milk.

PRAWN BUTTER: shell from the prawns; 1 oz. fresh butter.

GARNISH: 12 large prawns; ½ lb. button mushrooms.

First prepare the panade. Bring the milk and butter to the boil. When boiling, draw off the heat and at once add the flour. Beat until smooth, then leave till cold. Put the minced fish into a bowl, work in the panade with the eggs, and when thoroughly mixed add the cream and season well. Well butter a ring mould, line the fillets of sole, skinned side uppermost, into the mould, making sure that they overlap slightly so that there is no gap between them. Fill the fish farce into the mould and fold the ends of the fillets over the top. Cover with a piece of thickly buttered paper and cook in a bain-marie in a very moderate oven for 40 to 45 minutes or until firm to the touch.

Meanwhile prepare the garnish. Take off the body shells

only of the prawns and set them aside for the sauce. Put the prawns between two plates with a little melted butter and set them in the oven for 5 minutes to warm through.

Wash the mushrooms and cook them with a nut of butter and a squeeze of lemon juice for 4 to 5 minutes; season and set aside.

Prepare the sauce. Pound the prawn shells in a mortar with the butter until smooth, then rub through a fine sieve or strainer. Set aside. Make the velouté sauce as usual and beat in the prawn butter off the heat. Adjust the seasoning.

Turn out the mould on to a hot serving-dish and with a clean cloth wipe up any juice that may come away from the fish. Coat with the sauce, fill the centre with some of the mushrooms, and garnish with the prawns.

SOLE – LEMON

A flat white fish easily distinguished from the black sole as it is more oval, the fins wider, and the skin smooth and of a sandy brown colour. While it can be cooked in the same way as Dover sole, it is best to choose the simpler and less costly recipes as although good the flesh is inferior to that of Dover sole.

SPRATS

Small round fish with oily flesh similar to a herring but when fully grown no more than five inches long. They can be distinguished from herring by their serrated bellies. The fry are caught in large numbers in estuaries of rivers around the coast and are sold as Whitebait. Sprats are sometimes smoked and they are found hanging in the fishmongers tied in small bundles; they are also salted in barrels and called Norwegian anchovies.

*

Fried Sprats

Wipe the sprats, roll in seasoned flour and shallow fat. Fry or dip in fritter batter (see page 401) and deep-fat fry. Serve very hot with fried parsley and fingers of lemon.

STURGEON

A large fish with a long head and snout, caught in the cold

rivers of Russia and Scandinavia but found occasionally in the north of England and Scotland. Known as a royal fish when caught here, it must be presented or offered to the Crown. It is most famous for its roe, known as caviar, but it also gives us isinglass, the purest form of gelatine. The flesh of the sturgeon is meaty and is in fact said to resemble veal. It is good stuffed and baked whole or, if cut in steaks, crumbed and fried. It is also smoked like salmon and is imported into this country. It is sold cut in thin, wafer-like slices and served with lemon.

TROUT

A small, round fresh-water fish found in rivers and lakes, the colour of its flesh depending on its habitat and feeding. The type most commonly found at a fishmonger's is the rainbow trout bred in specially conditioned tanks: it has white, delicate flesh, weighs from 6 to 10 oz., and can be poached, grilled, or fried *à la meunière*.

When cleaning it, it is important to remove any blood against the backbone and to check that the gills have been removed. Do not remove the head before cooking as when the eyes turn white it is a good indication that the fish is cooked.

*

Truite au Four
5 even-sized trout; seasoned flour; melted butter; 1½ gills cream; chives.

Trim, wash, and dry the trout and dust with seasoned flour. Lay on a baking-sheet brushed with melted butter and spoon over more butter to coat the fish. Bake in a hot oven to crisp the skin for about 7 to 10 minutes, basting occasionally. Meanwhile season the cream and boil for several minutes to thicken slightly. Add a tablespoon of 'snipped' chives and set aside. When the trout are nice and brown, dish them and pour over the boiled cream immediately before serving.

Trout Genève

4–6 trout; 2 glasses white wine; ¼ pint water; a squeeze of lemon;
1 onion; 1 carrot; bouquet garni; seasoning; 1 oz. butter; 4 oz.
button mushrooms; 2 shallots; 3 oz. breadcrumbs; 2 oz. butter;
1 lemon.

Clean the trout, prepare a court bouillon with the wine, water,
and flavourings, and when tepid poach the trout in this. Drain
the fish, remove the skin, place in a serving-dish, and keep warm.
Melt the 1 oz. butter and sauté the quartered mushrooms and
finely chopped shallots: set aside. Strain the court bouillon, add
the crumbs, and simmer for 5 minutes. Remove from the heat,
beat in the remaining butter, a small piece at a time, and add the
mushrooms and a good squeeze of lemon. Spoon this sauce over
the trout and surround with thin slices of lemon.

Truite aux Amandes

4–6 trout.

COURT BOUILLON: 1 pint water; 1 onion; 1 carrot; 1 stick
celery; bouquet garni; 1 slice lemon; 1 glass white wine.

2 oz. almonds; 2 oz. fresh butter; seasoning; lemon juice.

First prepare the court bouillon. Place the water, vegetables,
herbs, and seasoning in a pan and simmer gently for 30 minutes.
Strain and allow to cool. Wash, dry, and trim the trout and place
in a fireproof dish, cover with court bouillon, and poach in the
oven for 15 to 20 minutes. Meanwhile blanch and shred the
almonds. Drain the fish when cooked, carefully remove the skin,
and arrange in the serving-dish.

Heat the butter in a small pan, add the almonds, and cook
slowly, until toasted to a pale golden brown. Add the lemon juice,
salt, and freshly ground black pepper to taste and pour over the
fish. Garnish with bouquets of watercress and serve at once.

Trout Vénitienne

4–6 trout; ½ glass white wine; ½ gill water; a squeeze of lemon;
1 small cucumber; a handful of spinach; 2 sprigs of tarragon and

chervil; ½ oz. butter; ½ oz. flour; ½ pint hot water; 2 egg yolks; 2 oz. butter; 2 shallots.

Fillet the trout. Poach the fillets in a little white wine and water, a squeeze of lemon juice, and a few sprigs of tarragon and chervil. In the meantime dice and blanch the cucumber and prepare the sauce.

Boil a handful of spinach with sprigs of tarragon and chervil. Drain. Press and pass it through a sieve or blender. Put on one side. Melt the butter in a saucepan, add the flour off the fire, and pour on ½ pint hot water; add salt, pepper, and the egg yolks. Stir briskly with a whisk until coming up to the boil, then draw aside and stir in by degrees 2 oz. of butter. Mix in enough of the green purée to make good colour and flavour.

Pour off the liquor from the fish into a saucepan, add two finely chopped shallots, and reduce to a syrupy consistency – strain into the sauce, adding a squeeze of lemon and seasoning if necessary. Arrange the fish in a hot serving-dish, add the cucumber to the sauce, and spoon over.

Trout Vinaigrette
5 river trout; court bouillon.

VINAIGRETTE DRESSING No. 2: see page 381.
1 cucumber; 1 bunch good watercress.

Trim the trout and lay in a fireproof dish. Pour over enough court bouillon to cover, and poach for 15 to 18 minutes in a moderate oven. Cool, then drain, and leave a short while before skinning. Now prepare the vinaigrette dressing. Peel the cucumber, shred, and moisten it with a little French dressing. Mix with the cress broken into small sprigs. Dish the trout, spoon over the vinaigrette, and garnish with the salad.

Trout 'en gelée'
4–6 even-sized trout; 1½ pints court bouillon; 2 pints aspic jelly made with sole bone stock; sprays of fennel or dill or sliced cucumber to garnish.

First prepare the court bouillon (see page 123), simmer gently for 30 minutes, strain, and allow to cool. Clean the trout, trim their fins and tails, and poach in the court bouillon for about 15 to 20 minutes. Allow to cool in the liquid and then drain, remove the skin, and carefully remove the backbone.

Have ready the aspic and when cold pour a little on the serving-dish and leave to set. Brush the trout with aspic and then arrange on the serving-dish. Garnish with the dill or cucumber and baste with extra cold aspic. Hand plain or green mayonnaise separately.

Trout Nantua

5 river trout; a little water; lemon juice and seasonings for poaching.

SAUCE: ½ pint mayonnaise; a good ½ gill fresh tomato juice; a dash of tabasco; salt; pepper; 2 oz. prawns.

GARNISH: ½ cucumber; a few watercress stalks; French dressing.

Trim trout and poach 15 to 20 minutes. Cool in the liquid then lift out carefully and remove the skin and bone. Dish and set aside. Mix the tomato juice with the mayonnaise and seasonings. Mix in the prawns and spoon over the fish. Have ready the cucumber, thinly sliced, and the watercress stalks, chopped. Mix together with a little French dressing. Arrange the salad at the side of the dish or serve separately.

Smoked Trout – see page 19.

TUNNY (THON)

An enormous shark-like fish caught off the coasts of France, Spain, Portugal, and Italy. It has very firm flesh which is good cold with a garlic mayonnaise, but, like the sardine, it is better known in this country canned. The 'meat' is not at all fishy in flavour and indeed it combines well with veal, chicken, and eggs.

TURBOT

One of the best of the white fish – in fact a few years ago was considered the finest fish, but, like clothes, the fashion in food changes, and today sole has taken pride of place. Turbot grows to an enormous size, the flesh being firm, rich, and creamy white, and the skin, which is considered a delicacy, very gelatinous. Small fish weighing about 6 lb., known as chicken turbot, can be bought whole or filleted, but the larger fish are generally cut into large pieces suitable for cooking whole or in slices.

Turbot should be soaked in cold water with a little salt and lemon juice to whiten the flesh prior to cooking. If a whole fish is being cooked, make an incision down the length of the backbone on the dark-skin side and calculate the cooking time by allowing 10 minutes to the pound. Turbot steaks ½ inch thick or fillets will only need 8 to 10 minutes if poached on top of the stove. A little extra time must be given if the oven poaching method is used.

*

Turbot Aurore
2-lb. piece of turbot.

COURT BOUILLON: 1 pint water; 1 glass white wine or a dash of wine vinegar; 1 onion; 1 carrot; bouquet garni; salt; 4 peppercorns; a slice of lemon.

'Fish' potatoes cut from 3 large potatoes; ½ pint prawns; parsley.

AURORE SAUCE: 1½ lb. ripe tomatoes; 1 shallot; ½ oz. butter; 1 level teaspoon tomato purée; ½ pint Béchamel sauce made with 1½ oz. butter; 1¼ oz. flour; ½ pint flavoured milk, and 2–3 tablespoons cream.

Prepare the fish and the court bouillon (see page 123). Place the turbot on the drainer in a fish kettle with the white skin uppermost and pour over the court bouillon. Bring slowly to simmering-point, draw to the side of the stove, and allow to cook well below boiling-point. If cooking in the oven in a fireproof dish baste frequently.

Meanwhile prepare the sauce. Wipe the tomatoes, cut in half and squeeze to remove the seeds. Slice and put into a pan with the sliced shallot, butter, and purée. Season well and cook to a pulp. Rub through a strainer. Make up the Béchamel sauce and add the tomato pulp. Bring to the boil, adjust the seasoning, and finish with the cream.

Cut the potatoes in quarter lengthways and trim the sharp edges to make them oval in shape. Boil until three-quarters cooked, drain. Return to the pan, cover with muslin, then the lid, and set on a gentle heat to complete the cooking.

Drain the fish well, dish on a folded napkin and garnish with the potatoes, prawns, and parsley. Hand the Aurore sauce separately.

Turbot 'en soufflé'

4 steaks turbot; 1 glass white wine; ½ glass water; slice of onion; 6 peppercorns; 1 bayleaf; 6 oz. mushrooms; ½ oz. butter.

SOUFFLÉ MIXTURE: 2 oz. butter; 1¾ oz. flour; liquor from the fish, reduced to ½ gill; ¾ pint milk; ½ gill cream; 2 eggs; 2 tablespoons grated cheese; 1 tablespoon brown crumbs.

Prepare the fish, set in a buttered fireproof dish, and pour over the wine and water. Season, add the onion and bayleaf, and cover with a buttered paper. Poach in a moderate oven for about 10–15 minutes, then remove the black skin and bone. In the meantime prepare the sauce.

With the butter, flour, and milk mixed in the usual way, when boiling add the reduced fish stock and cream, season well, and beat in the two egg yolks. Slice the mushrooms and cook quickly in the butter. Whisk the egg whites until stiff, but not dry, and fold into the sauce. Put a small quantity of this on the bottom of a fireproof dish and arrange the fish on the top with a spoonful of mushroom on each piece. Spoon over the rest of the sauce, sprinkle with the cheese and crumbs, and bake in a moderate oven for 15 minutes.

WHITEBAIT

The fry of herring, sprat, or pilchard caught in the estuaries of rivers around the coasts of Britain. It is served as a first-course dish, fried until crisp and golden brown, and served with fingers of lemon and brown bread and butter.

*

Whitebait

Allow 4 oz. per head; 2–3 tablespoons flour; seasoning; deep fat for frying; 1 lemon; brown bread and butter.

Pick over, discarding weed and any damaged fish, but do not wash. Sift the flour with the seasoning and roll the fish in it until evenly coated. Shake gently to remove the surplus.

Heat the deep fat until just below haze point and place only enough whitebait in the frying-basket to cover the bottom. Plunge the basket into the fat and cook until the bubbling subsides – after 2 to 3 minutes, no more. Drain the basket first over the fat bath and then on a plate, and tip the whitebait on to a rack or crumpled kitchen paper. Continue cooking the entire quantity of whitebait in the same way, reheating the fat between each batch. When complete, reheat the fat bath until the fat is smoking freely, turn all the fish into the basket, and fry a second time until crisp and golden. Drain and serve piled in an entrée dish with fingers of lemon and brown bread and butter handed separately.

WHITING

A round, white fish, light and silvery in colour, with delicate flesh which is friable and very easy to digest. It is the best fish to use for soufflés but it lends itself to various other methods of cooking. Because of its friable nature it is difficult to transport and so is dismissed by many people 'as food for the cat' but near the sea and prepared by expert fishmongers it comes into its own. Skinned and filleted, each fish weighing between $\frac{1}{2}$ to 1 lb., it is good cooked very simply.

*

Whiting au Gratin

4 whiting, filleted (about $1\frac{1}{2}$ lb.); $\frac{1}{4}$ lemon; $\frac{1}{2}$ oz. butter; 1 level tablespoon brown crumbs; 1 tablespoon grated cheese.

SAUCE: $\frac{1}{2}$ pint milk infused with 1 slice of onion; bouquet garni and 6 peppercorns; 1 oz. butter; $\frac{3}{4}$ oz. flour.

Wash and dry the fillets of fish and place in a lightly buttered fireproof dish. The fillets may be folded if liked but the bottom of the dish must be covered. Season the fish lightly and moisten with the lemon juice. Prepare the sauce and spoon it over the fish. Mix the crumbs and cheese together, scatter over the dish, and dot with any remaining butter. Bake in a moderate oven (350° F., Reg. 4) for about 20 to 25 minutes.

Whiting Alsacienne

4 whiting filleted ($1\frac{1}{2}$–2 lb.); a squeeze of lemon; seasoning; $\frac{1}{2}$ gill water.

CABBAGE: $\frac{1}{2}$ Dutch white cabbage; 1 medium onion; 1 oz. butter.

SAUCE: $1\frac{1}{4}$ oz. butter; 1 oz. flour; $\frac{1}{2}$ pint milk; 2 oz. grated cheese; a little French mustard.

Prepare the fish, and fold the fillets evenly and place in a buttered fireproof dish with the lemon, seasoning, and water; cover with a buttered paper and keep ready for cooking.

Shred the cabbage finely, cutting away any hard centre core. Slice the onion, put in a stewpan with the butter, cover with a paper and lid, and cook slowly until soft but not coloured (2 to 3 minutes). Add the cabbage, stir well, and season with salt and freshly ground black pepper; cover with a buttered paper and lid and cook slowly until tender (about 30 minutes) on top of the stove (or for 45 to 50 minutes in the oven).

Cook the fish for 15 to 20 minutes in a moderate oven (350° F., Reg. 4) and prepare the sauce. Add the liquor from the fish to the sauce, and beat in two-thirds of the cheese, a little at a time; reheat carefully without boiling and adjust the seasoning. Spoon the cabbage down the centre of a hot serving-dish; arrange the fish on the top and coat with the sauce. Dust the top with the reserved cheese and brown in the oven or under the grill.

Whiting Orly

3 whiting filleted (1–1½ lb.); fritter batter, No. 1 or 2 (see page 401); deep fat for frying; sprays of parsley; tomato or tartare sauce.

Wash and dry the fish very well and cut each fillet in 3 or 4 long strips. Prepare the fritter batter and heat the deep fat until a faint blue haze appears. Dip each piece of fish into the batter and twist two or three times before lowering into the hot fat. Fry until crisp and golden and drain well. Serve piled on a hot entrée dish garnished with fried parsley. Hand a piquante, tomato, or tartare sauce separately.

Whiting 'en Dauphin'

4 small whiting (8 oz. each); 4 mushrooms for garnish; 2 egg whites; ¼ pint cream; 2–3 tablespoons milk.

DUXELLES SAUCE: 1½ oz. butter; 2 tablespoons mushroom stalks and peelings; 1 shallot; 1 oz. flour; 1½ gills fish stock; 1 gill top milk.

Skin and fillet the whiting, mince half the fish, and prepare a good stock from the bones. Make a fish mousseline with the minced fish, egg whites, and cream as directed on page 132, and work in the milk. Spread the farce on each fillet and roll up. Set upright in a buttered gratin dish, sprinkle with lemon juice and a little water, cover with a buttered paper, and poach in the oven for 25 to 30 minutes.

In the meantime prepare the sauce. Melt half the butter in a saucepan, add the finely chopped shallot and mushroom peelings, cover, and cook slowly until quite soft. Remove from the fire, add the remaining butter, blend in the flour, and tip on the fish stock. Stir over gentle heat until the sauce begins to thicken, add the milk, and continue stirring until the sauce boils; adjust the seasoning. Cook the mushrooms for garnish in a little butter with seasoning and a squeeze of lemon juice.

Dish the stuffed fillets in a hot serving dish. Spoon over the sauce and garnish each fillet with a mushroom cap.

NOTE: The fish farce can also be flavoured with a little duxelles if liked.

Steamed Whiting Soufflé

4 oz. filleted whiting.

PANADA: ½ oz. butter; ½ oz. flour; ½ gill fish stock or milk; 2 small eggs; cayenne; salt and lemon juice; ½ gill cream.

Shred the fish finely, make the panada (avoid over-cooking – it should be *just* brought to the boil, no more) and allow to cool. Place the fish and panada in a mortar and pound well; add the beaten eggs by degrees and continue pounding. Rub through a fine wire sieve or use a blender. Add seasonings and lightly fold in the cream. Place in a prepared tin, cover with a twist of greased paper, and steam gently for 45 minutes until firm. Turn on to a hot dish and coat with an anchovy or velouté sauce.

MISCELLANEOUS FISH DISHES

Fish cakes

1 lb. fresh cod fillet; ½ lb. potatoes; ½ oz. butter; ½–1 gill hot milk; beaten egg and dried white crumbs for coating.

Wash the fish, dry well, sprinkle lightly with salt, and allow to stand for 15 to 20 minutes.

Tip away any liquid that has accumulated and place the fish in a buttered dish; add a squeeze of lemon and cover with a paper. Cook in a moderate oven for about 15 to 20 minutes. Meanwhile cook the potatoes in boiling salted water and, when tender, drain and shake over heat until dry. Push them through a sieve or potato ricer. Flake the fish, remove skin or bones, and add to the potato with the butter, seasoning, and enough hot milk to bind the mixture together. Divide into equal portions, shape neatly, and then roll in seasoned flour. Brush with beaten egg and cover with the prepared crumbs. Fry in smoking hot fat until golden brown on both sides. Drain well and serve garnished with sprigs of fried parsley, and hand a tomato sauce separately.

Fish Pie

1 lb. fresh cod or haddock fillet; ½ oz. butter; 2 hard-boiled eggs or 1 small tin champignons de Paris; 1 egg; 1 teaspoon chopped parsley; 1 lb. potatoes; ½ oz. butter; ½–1 gill hot milk; 1 oz. grated cheese.

SAUCE: ½ pint milk infused with 1 slice of onion, bouquet garni and 6 peppercorns; 1 oz. butter; ¾ oz. flour.

Skin the fish and place in a fireproof dish with seasoning and a squeeze of lemon. Cover with a buttered paper and cook in a moderate oven for 15 to 20 minutes. In the meantime cook the potatoes and beat to a purée with the butter and hot milk. Prepare the sauce and add the flaked fish and sliced, hard-boiled eggs or mushrooms; season well, add the beaten egg and parsley, and pour in a buttered pie dish. Cover with the creamed potatoes; sprinkle over the grated cheese and brown in a quick oven.

Fish Croquettes

½ lb. flaked cooked fish (¾ lb. fresh haddock or cod fillet); 1½ gills milk; 1 slice onion; ½ bayleaf; blade of mace; 1½ oz. butter; 1½ oz. flour; 1 egg; dried white crumbs and beaten egg for coating; deep fat for frying.

Infuse the milk with all the flavourings and strain. Melt the butter and draw away from the heat. Blend in the flour and milk. Stir over the fire until boiling and allow to simmer a minute or two. Beat the fish into the sauce a little at a time, adjust the seasoning and add the beaten egg. Turn on to a plate or dish and allow to get quite cold. Divide in eight equal portions, roll and shape on a floured board, then coat with the beaten egg and crumbs. Heat the deep fat until smoking and make sure there is enough to cover the croquettes completely or they will split. Fry until golden brown, then drain well and serve garnished with fried parsley. Serve with a tomato sauce or a Tartare or Hollandaise sauce.

Matelote Normande

A good mixture of fish, such as 1 lb. rock salmon; 2 6-oz. steaks of

turbot; 4 scallops; 20 pickling onions; 3 oz. butter; ½ pint white
wine or dry cider; 1 tablespoon flour; 5–6 spoons cream.

Heart-shaped croûtons of fried bread; chopped parsley.

Clean and prepare the fish, cutting it into neat pieces. Melt the
butter in a sauté pan and when very hot but not coloured add the
fish and cook a few minutes on each side, but do not allow to
colour. Moisten with the cider, season with salt, pepper, and
bouquet garni, and add the onions that have been partly cooked
in a little butter. Cover and allow to cook over a very gentle heat
for 20 minutes, then remove the fish and onions and reduce the
liquid in the pan by half. Knead the butter and flour and add to
the pan. When the sauce is thick and creamy, add the fresh cream
and season well. Replace the fish and onions and simmer together
for 2 to 3 minutes.

Dish the Matelote, surround with the croûtons fried in butter,
and dust with the parsley. This can also be served in a vol-au-vent
case.

Matelote Bonne Femme
1½ lb. steak of cod; 6 scallops; 1 onion; 1 carrot; 1 stick celery;
bouquet garni; lemon; ½ pint water; 1 glass white wine; kneaded
butter; 6 long slices of bread and butter for frying; garlic.

GARNISH: 2-oz. rasher green streaky bacon; 12 button onions;
¼ lb. button mushrooms.

Cut the fish into six even-sized steaks, wash, and set on one side.
Place the fish bone and skin in a pan with the vegetables, water,
squeeze of lemon, herbs, and seasoning and simmer very gently
for 20 to 30 minutes. Strain and allow to cool.

Put the fish steaks and scallops in a sauté pan, cover with the
fish fumet and wine, and cook very gently for about 15 minutes.

Meanwhile prepare the garnish. Cut the bacon into small
strips and blanch. Cover the onions with cold water, bring to the
boil and strain. Add a good nut of butter to the pan, a teaspoonful
of castor sugar, cover, and cook slowly until brown and tender.

Remove the lid from the pan, add the bacon, and allow to brown.
Cook the mushrooms in a little butter with a squeeze of lemon and
seasoning. Trim the slices of bread, rub each side with a little
crushed garlic, and fry golden brown in butter. Arrange these
croûtes in a serving-dish.

Carefully remove the cod steaks from the sauté pan and place
on the croûtons. Cut each scallop in two and arrange on top of
the cod. Keep warm. Thicken the liquid in the pan with the
kneaded butter, baste over the fish, and finish with the garnish.

Brandade Parisienne

1½ lb. salt or fresh cod; 4 oz. potatoes; ¼–½ pint olive oil; 1 clove
garlic; 1½ gills Béchamel sauce; hot milk; slices from a thin
French loaf.

For *salt cod*, soak overnight and then poach in water for about
30 minutes – do not overcook. If using *fresh cod*, wash and dry and
sprinkle with salt. Leave for 30 minutes, drain away any liquid
and wipe well with a cloth. Squeeze over a few drops of lemon
juice, cover with buttered paper, and poach in a moderate oven.
Then flake and chop the salt or fresh fish. Have the potatoes
freshly boiled and push through a wire sieve or ricer. Add to the
fish and turn both into a double saucepan. Heat the oil in a small
pan, crush the garlic lightly, and fry in the oil until turning yellow.
Beat the oil into the fish and potato with the Béchamel sauce,
adding seasoning and hot milk until the mixture is light and
creamy. The sauce, oil, and milk must be added slowly.

Pile in a hot dish and surround with croûtes of bread rubbed
with garlic and fried until golden brown in hot oil.

Vinaigrette de Poisson

1 lb. steak of turbot; 2–3 large cooked beetroot; 4 small cooked
potatoes; 1 dessert apple; 1 pickled cucumber; 1 teacupful
cooked peas; about 5 tablespoons salad oil; 2 tablespoons wine
vinegar; garlic crushed with salt; sugar to taste; ½ pint mayonnaise.

GARNISH: ½ pint prawns; lettuce hearts and watercress.

Cook the turbot in salted water, allow to cool, remove the skin and bone, and flake into a bowl. Dice the beetroot, potato, and apple and add to the fish with the sliced cucumber and peas. Work in the oil and vinegar with two forks and season well with salt and sugar. Add a little freshly ground black pepper and leave to mellow for 20 minutes, then mix in enough mayonnaise to bind the fish and vegetables together. Pile the vinaigrette in the serving-dish, coat with the remaining mayonnaise, and arrange the garnish round.

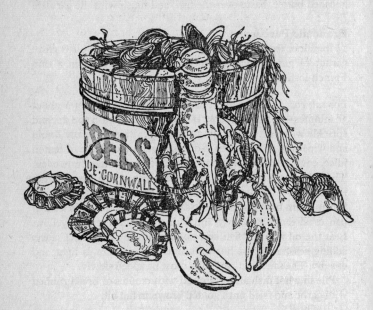

SHELLFISH

Shellfish should be eaten very fresh as because of their general habitat and method of feeding the flesh decomposes quickly. It is best to buy the shellfish alive, but failing this purchase only from a shop having a quick sale and where you are confident that lobsters and crabs are boiled daily.

Shellfish can be cooked in the plainest of court bouillons, namely salted water, and indeed it is not uncommon for them to be boiled in sea water, but, if they are to be eaten cold, the following liquid is recommended:

Court Bouillon for Shellfish

2 onions; 1 carrot; 1 oz. butter; $\frac{1}{4}$ pint white wine; juice of $\frac{1}{2}$ lemon; $1\frac{1}{2}$ pints water; bouquet garni; 6 peppercorns; 1 teaspoon salt.

Slice the onion and carrot, put into a pan with the butter and cook very slowly until soft and golden; moisten with the wine and water and add all the other ingredients. Bring to the boil and simmer gently for 20 minutes. Plunge in the shellfish, cook for the required time, and leave to cool in the liquid.

CRAB

In season May to September. Choose crabs with a rough shell and large claws. They should be heavy for their size and always freshly boiled. The male or cock crab is considered the finer and can be distinguished by its claws, these being larger than the female's. To boil, allow 15 minutes per pound and cool in the court bouillon. To dress, first remove the big claws and set aside. Twist off the small claws, removing at the same time the under-shell or body of the crab. Set aside.

Take out and throw away the small sac that lies in the top of the big shell; any green matter in the big shell; and the gills or spongy fingers that lie round the big shell.

With a teaspoon, scrape out into a small bowl all the brown creamy part which lies round the sides of the big shell. Take a cloth and, holding the big shell firmly, break down the sides which are marked naturally. Wash and dry the shell thoroughly. Remove the small claws and set aside. Cut the body of the crab in two and with a skewer pick out all the white meat into a bowl, taking care not to break off fine pieces of shell. Crack the big claws and shred all the meat, breaking it well. Put all the white meat together. Cream the brown part thoroughly. Season it well with pepper, salt, and mustard. Add dry breadcrumbs (about 2 tablespoons) and, if the mixture is stiff, add a spoonful of cream.

Arrange this mixture across the middle of the shell and pile white meat up at each side. The crab may be decorated with sieved, hard-boiled yolk of egg and chopped parsley. The shell is laid in the middle of the ring of claws made by sticking the small claws one into another. Surround with crisp lettuce leaves. Serve with mayonnaise, tartare sauce or sharp French dressing, and brown bread and butter.

*

Devilled Crab

1 dressed crab or $\frac{1}{2}$ lb. frozen crab meat; 2 oz. butter; 1 shallot; 1 tablespoon brandy; 2 tablespoons cream or Béchamel sauce; 2 tablespoons white breadcrumbs; 1 tablespoon dry grated cheese; 1 teaspoon French mustard; salt; pepper; a dash of anchovy essence and Worcester sauce; cayenne; 2 small bananas.

Put the crab meat in a bowl. Melt 1 oz. butter, add the very finely chopped shallot, and cook until soft. Add the brandy and work into the crab meat with the cream or sauce, breadcrumbs, and cheese. Season well with all the condiments, and replace the mixture in the shell or in a gratin dish. Dust with crumbs or a little extra cheese and bake for 5 to 10 minutes in a hot oven. Place sliced bananas fried in the remaining butter on top and serve with thin, hot biscuits (water biscuits, for example).

Crab Soufflé

$\frac{3}{4}$ oz. butter; 1 teaspoon paprika pepper; 1 teaspoon curry powder; 12 oz. crab meat (preferably white); a few drops of Tabasco sauce; salt; freshly ground black pepper; $\frac{1}{4}$ pint Béchamel sauce made with $\frac{1}{2}$ oz. butter and $\frac{1}{2}$ oz. flour; 1–2 tablespoons cream; 3 egg yolks; 4 egg whites; grated cheese; a few browned crumbs.

Melt the butter in a stewpan, add paprika and curry powder, and cook for 1 minute. Draw aside, add crab meat and tabasco, and season well. Warm over the fire, adding the Béchamel and cream. Draw aside and mix in the yolks. Whip the whites to a firm snow, cut and fold into the mixture, and turn into a prepared soufflé case. Scatter the top well with the cheese and a few crumbs. Bake in a moderate oven until well risen and firm to the touch –

20 to 25 minutes. A prawn or shrimp soufflé may be made in the same way, using a pint of shelled prawns and ¼ pint Béchamel.

CRAYFISH (ÉCREVISSE)

A fresh-water shellfish like the lobster in appearance only very much smaller. After cooking it is bright pink in colour and has a most delicate flesh. It is used mostly as garnish.

CRAWFISH (LANGOUSTE)

A rock lobster, is similar to a lobster but it has no large claws and the head is broad and ugly. The shell is darker in colour, rather rough and very hard. The flesh, although sweet, is coarse in texture. It can be cooked in the same way as lobster.

LOBSTER (HOMARD)

At their best from March to October but in season throughout the year. The shells range from brilliant prussian blue to a greeny-black which changes to the familiar cardinal red in cooking. The hen lobster is esteemed for the spawn which can be used for lobster butter to colour and flavour sauces, but the flesh of the cock lobster is finer and firmer in texture. The head and body of the cock is narrower and longer than the hen's. Lobsters should always be bought alive, particularly if a hot dish is being prepared. It is only in this way that twice cooking can be avoided and perfection attained. Like crab, a lobster should be heavy for its size. Avoid those covered with barnacles as these can be an indication of age.

How to kill a live lobster: Cover the lobster tail with a cloth, hold firmly with the left hand, and, using a sharp knife, pierce through the head at the small cross mark or indentation that lies about half-way along the head. The lobster is killed immediately.

*

Boiled Lobster
Choose medium-sized lobsters and allow ½ per person; court bouillon (see page 173) to cover.

Plunge the lobster into the boiling court bouillon and then boil gently for 20 minutes for lobsters up to 1 lb., for 30 minutes for 1 to 1½ lb., and for ¾ hour for over 2lb.

When cold, drain well, wipe and rub the shell with a little salad oil, and split the lobster in half; remove the small bag or stomach in the head and the dark line running down the tail but leave the soft creamy mixture in place. Crack the large claws and carefully ease out the meat. Twist off the smaller claws which can be kept for garnish, or, if there is time to spare, the sweet flesh can be removed by rolling the handle of a wooden spoon along the claw. Lift out the tail meat from each half, cut in thick scallops and replace it the red side up in the opposite half shell. Place the claw meat in the head. Serve garnished with crisp lettuce hearts or watercress. Hand mayonnaise separately.

Lobster 'Cordon Bleu'

2 cooked lobsters weighing about 1 lb.; ½ pint mayonnaise; 1 clove garlic; 1 teaspoon tomato purée; juice from canned pimentoes; 6 oz. boiled rice; French dressing (see page 381); 1 teaspoon paprika; 1 bunch watercress.

Cook and dress the lobster as directed in the preceding recipe. Prepare the mayonnaise; crush the garlic with a little salt to a smooth cream, and add to the mayonnaise with the tomato purée and pimento juice. Spoon this sauce over the lobster meat. Set the lobsters on a serving-dish and garnish with watercress. Whisk the paprika into the dressing, pour over the rice, and mix well with a fork; add extra seasoning if necessary and serve in a separate dish.

Lobster Mousse (to serve 6–8 people)

2 medium-sized live lobsters (1½ lb. each); court bouillon; ½ pint velouté sauce made with 1 oz. butter, 1 oz. flour, and ½ pint court bouillon in which the lobster was cooked; 1½ gills mayonnaise; 1 dessertspoon gelatine dissolved in ½ gill court bouillon; ½ gill cream; salt; pepper; paprika.

FINISH: ½ gill thick mayonnaise; tomato juice.

Prepare the court bouillon, boil the lobsters for ½ hour, and leave to cool in the liquid. Make the velouté sauce (see page 370) and turn on to a plate to cool. Remove the meat from the shells of the lobsters, put the tail of one aside for garnish, and chop all the remaining meat. Combine the cold sauce and mayonnaise, dissolve the gelatine over a gentle heat, and add to the mixture with the lobster and seasoning. Half-whip the cream, fold into the mousse, and fill into a lightly oiled tin or soufflé case. Leave to set. Turn out, coat with the mayonnaise thinned with a little tomato juice, and arrange the sliced tail meat on the top.

Lobster Thermidor

2 live lobsters weighing ¾ lb. each, or 1 lobster weighing 1½ lb.; 1 tablespoon oil; 1½ oz. butter; 1 good tablespoon chopped shallot; 1 teaspoon chopped tarragon; 1 teaspoon chopped chervil; 1 teaspoon chopped parsley; 1 wineglass (¾ gill) white wine; 1½ gills thick Béchamel sauce made with 1 oz. butter, ¾ oz. flour, and 1½ gills milk; 1 gill single cream; a little French mustard; paprika; salt; 3 tablespoons grated Parmesan cheese; browned crumbs.

Kill and split the lobsters; remove the stomach and intestine. Warm the pan, add the oil and butter, and put in the lobsters cut side down. Sauté gently for 5 minutes, then cover and put in a moderate oven for 15 minutes.

Meanwhile make the Béchamel sauce. Put a nut of butter into a shallow pan, add the chopped shallot and herbs, cook for one minute, add the white wine, simmer for 5 minutes, then stir in the sauce and cream. Simmer until thick, then add the cuisson from the cooked lobster.

Remove the meat from the shell and claws of the lobster; cut the tail meat into thick scallops. Chop the head and claw meat. Add the chopped meat to the sauce with mustard, paprika, and salt to taste with 2 tablespoons of the Parmesan cheese. Put this mixture into the cleaned and trimmed shells, lay the tail scallops rounded side up on top, spoon on any remaining sauce, and sprinkle with the remaining cheese mixed with the crumbs. Lay on a baking-sheet, bake for 5 minutes at Reg. 5, then glaze under the grill. Dish on to a folded napkin and serve hot.

Lobster Newberg

1 live lobster weighing 1½ lb.; 1 oz. butter; 2 tablespoons brandy; 1 glass sherry; ¼ pint cream; 3 egg yolks.

Kill the lobster, cut the head in two lengthways, discard the stomach, and divide the tail across in 3 or 4 scallops. Crack the claws carefully, but do not attempt to remove the flesh. Lift away any coral, mix with an extra ounce of butter, and set on one side.

Heat the ounce of butter in a sauté pan, put in the lobster, and cook gently until the shell changes colour (about 5 minutes), then flame with the brandy. Tip on the sherry, simmer for 1 minute, and pour over the cream. Season with salt and pepper, cover, and cook for 20 minutes. Remove the pieces of lobster, take it out of the shell, and keep it warm. Thicken the juices in the pan with the egg yolks; adjust the seasoning and spoon over the lobster. If the coral was available add it to the sauce after thickening with the egg yolks.

Lobster Américaine

1 large lobster weighing about 2 lb.; 1½ tablespoons oil; 2 tablespoons brandy; 2 oz. butter; 1 small onion; ¾ lb. concasséd tomatoes; ½ clove garlic; 1 glass white wine; bouquet garni; 1 level teaspoon tomato purée; ¾ oz. flour; 1 breakfast-cup cooked vegetable mirepoix (carrots, turnips, and French beans); 1 wineglass stock; 6 oz. boiled rice.

Kill the lobster and cut as for Lobster Newberg. Crack the shell of the claws. Remove the coral. Scoop out the soft, creamy meat from the head and set on one side. Heat the oil in a sauté pan, put in the pieces of lobster, and cook until the shell turns red and the flesh is firm (about 5 minutes). Flame with the brandy. Add half the butter to the pan, put in the finely chopped onion, and cook slowly for 5 minutes; then add the tomatoes, garlic crushed with salt, and herbs, and moisten with the white wine. Simmer for

10 minutes. Remove the lobster from the pan and add the mire-poix and the stock if necessary. Cream the remaining butter with the coral, the creamy substance, and the tomato purée and flour, and work into the pan off the fire. Reboil and adjust the seasoning. Return the lobster to the pan, reheat gently, and then dish. Serve the plainly boiled rice separately.

Lobster with Mushrooms

2 small lobsters weighing ¾ lb. each; 1 oz. butter; 1 glass sherry.

SAUCE: 2 shallots finely chopped; ½ oz. butter; 1 heaped tea-spoon paprika; 1 glass white wine; 1½ gills thick Béchamel made with 1 oz. each butter and flour; ½ gill cream.

MUSHROOM SALPICON: 8 oz. mushrooms; 1 oz. butter; salt and pepper; 2 tablespoons thick cream; 1 dessertspoon chopped parsley.

Split the lobsters and remove the stomach and the dark line run-ning down the tail. Heat the butter in a large sauté pan, put in the lobsters cut side downwards, and sauté for 4 to 5 minutes to firm the flesh; then flame with the sherry, cover, and cook in the oven for 10 to 15 minutes.

Prepare the salpicon. Slice or quarter the mushrooms, cook for 3 or 4 minutes in the butter, add seasoning, cream, and parsley. Set aside.

Prepare the sauce. Soften the shallots in the butter without colouring, add the paprika and, after a minute or two, the wine. Reduce to a half then beat in the Béchamel. Reboil, adjust the seasoning, add the cream and the strained cuisson from the lobsters, and reduce until thick. Take up the lobsters, remove the flesh carefully, and cut into slices. Pour a spoonful of the sauce into each tail shell, arrange the slices on top, and coat with the rest of the sauce. Fill the salpicon into the head shells and serve at once.

Lobster Pancakes

PANCAKE BATTER: 4 oz. plain flour; 1 egg; 1 egg yolk; 1 table-spoon melted butter or salad oil; ½ pint milk; salt and pepper.

FILLING: 1 cooked lobster weighing about 1 lb.; 1 oz. butter; 1 level teaspoon paprika; Béchamel sauce made with 1 oz. butter; 1 oz. flour and ½ pint milk flavoured with onion, peppercorns, and mace; 1 level teaspoon tomato purée; 2 tablespoons cream.

SAUCE: ¼ lb. button mushrooms; ½ oz. butter; ¼ lb. tomatoes; 2 tablespoons brandy or dry sherry; ¼ pint cream; seasoning.

FINISH: 2 tablespoons grated Parmesan cheese.

Prepare the batter, leave to stand at least 1 hour, then fry very thin pancakes (see page 401).

Slice the lobster meat and toss in the butter with paprika to colour and flavour. Add the tomato purée and Béchamel sauce. Season well and add the cream. Put a good spoonful of the lobster mixture on each pancake, fold over, and put in a well-buttered dish to keep hot. Slice the mushrooms and put into a pan with the butter over moderate heat for 2 to 3 minutes. Skin the tomatoes, cut in quarters, scoop away the seeds, and cut in thin strips. Add to the mushrooms with the brandy, cream, and seasonings. Increase the heat, boil rapidly for one minute, and spoon over the pancakes. Dust with the Parmesan cheese and glaze quickly under the grill.

MUSSELS (MOULES)

These are at their best from October to March and the medium-sized ones have the finest flavour. They are found in sand-banks around the coasts of this country and many are imported from France and Holland. It is essential that mussels are alive just prior to cooking as they decompose very quickly and one dead mussel can be a potential cause of food poisoning. Discard any that remain open after being tapped sharply with a wooden spoon or the back of a knife.

The preparation and washing of mussels is most important. First they must be washed and scrubbed one by one under a running tap, or in a bowl, and put into a fresh bowl of clean water. Trim away any weed that should be hanging from the shell and, if any mussel seems unusually heavy for its size, prise it open with a small sharp knife. It may be full of mud or sand and this would ruin the whole dish. After the first scrubbing, thoroughly shake the mussels in the fresh bowl of water and then lift them with the hands into a colander – do not tip them as any sand would just be poured on the top. Repeat this washing and lifting twice and the mussels will be ready for cooking and free from sand. If cooking has to be delayed by force of circumstances, cover the mussels with fresh water and add a tablespoon of fine oatmeal. This will feed and plump the mussels and help to keep them alive.

*

Moules Marinière

2 quarts mussels; 1–2 shallots, finely chopped; freshly ground pepper; 1 glass white wine; 1 wineglass water; a large bouquet garni with an added stick of celery; kneaded butter to thicken lightly; 1 dessertspoon chopped parsley.

Well wash and scrub the mussels. Put into a large pan with the shallot, pepper, and liquid and bouquet. Cover and bring up to the boil, shaking the pan occasionally. Simmer for a minute or two, then draw aside and pour off the liquid into a saucepan. Thicken with the kneaded butter, reboil, and add the parsley. Turn the mussels into a deep dish or soup tureen, remove the top shell, and pour over the sauce.

NOTE: If a richer sauce is preferred, the strained liquor from the mussels can be thickened with a liaison of 2 egg yolks and $\frac{1}{2}$ gill cream in place of the kneaded butter.

OYSTERS

In season from September to April and are at their very best served *au naturel* (see page 21); but they make an excellent savoury (for Angels on Horseback, see page 99). They can also be served hot if liked.

PRAWNS (CREVETTES)

There are many varieties of prawns with a wide difference in

size. Before cooking they are almost transparent and those found
in rocky pools around the shores of this country are sold by the
pound ready boiled by the fishmonger. The smaller ones,
having a softish shell, are good for prawn butter and sauces (see
below), and the larger ones with hard shells are particularly
suitable for hors d'œuvres and garnishes. There are now, however, many prawns imported from overseas which are sold
frozen, invariably cooked and shelled before freezing. The giant,
Mediterranean prawns are sold by the dozen and are served with
brown bread and butter and a sauce or mayonnaise seasoned with
extra mustard.

*

Brioches aux Crevettes
Freshly baked brioche – allow one per head.

FILLING: large prawns; allow 3–4 for each brioche.

PRAWN SAUCE: 1 oz. butter; ¾ oz. flour; 1½ gills fish stock; ½ gill
cream; prawn butter made with 1 oz. butter, shells from the
prawns and a little carmine.

Cut the top from the brioche, scoop out some of the soft crumb,
brush the outside with a little melted butter, and set in the oven to
heat through.

Shell the prawns leaving the head on one for each brioche for
garnish and set the required number to warm between two
buttered plates. Remove the eyes from the shells and pound the
shells and any prawns over with the butter and a drop of carmine
for colour. Rub through a sieve and set on one side. Melt the
butter, add the flour, and cook gently to a straw colour; blend in
the fish stock and season and stir until thickening. Add the cream
and bring to the boil. Cover the pan and keep warm.

Fill the brioche with the prawns moistened with a little of
the sauce, replace the cap, and set in a serving-dish. Remove
the sauce from the heat, beat in the prepared prawn butter, and
adjust the seasoning and serve separately.

Prawns Maison
4–6 courgettes; 2 oz. butter; 2 shallots; 1 level teaspoon tomato

purée; 6 oz. prawns; ½ oz. butter; 2 tablespoons sherry; ½ pint Mornay sauce; grated cheese.

Wipe the courgettes and wrap in well-buttered greaseproof paper, allowing 1½ oz. butter for this. Bake in a moderate oven until tender (380° F., Reg. 5) about 45 minutes. Cut off the top of each courgette and using a teaspoon carefully remove the centre. Melt ½ oz. butter, add the finely chopped shallot and cook until soft. Work in the tomato purée, add the courgette pulp, season well and fill into the skins.

Toss the prawns in the remaining butter, flame with the sherry and divide between the courgettes. Spoon over the Mornay sauce, sprinkle with a little grated cheese and brown under the grill or in a hot oven.

Timbale à l'Indienne
6 oz. rich shortcrust pastry (see page 384); 6 oz. prawns; 3 hard-boiled eggs; 3 oz. cooked rice.

CURRY SAUCE: 2 small onions; 1 oz. butter; 1 dessertspoon curry powder; Béchamel sauce made with 1 oz. butter, 1 oz. flour, and ¾ pint flavoured milk; 1–2 tablespoons cream.

Line the outside of a charlotte mould or a deep sandwich tin and bake blind. Chop the onions very finely, cook until soft but not coloured in the butter, then add the curry powder and cook for 3 to 4 minutes. Add the Béchamel sauce. Simmer together a few minutes then add the cream and seasoning if necessary.

Fill the pastry case with the prawns, quartered eggs, and rice, layering them with the sauce. Dust the top with paprika pepper and hand any remaining sauce separately.

Prawn and Egg Galette
PUFF PASTRY: 6 oz. plain flour; 6 oz. butter (see page 388).

½ pint milk; slice of onion; blade of mace; salt; pepper; bouquet garni; 1½ oz. butter; 1¼ oz. flour; 6 oz. prawns; 3 hard-boiled eggs.

Set the puff pastry and then prepare the filling. Scald the milk with the onion, spices, and seasonings and leave to infuse for a few minutes. Melt the butter over gentle heat, blend in the flour, strain on the milk, and bring slowly to the boil, stirring continually. Add the prawns and quartered eggs, adjust the seasoning, cover with a buttered paper, and leave to get quite cold. Roll out the pastry and cut into two rounds the size of a dessert plate, one $\frac{1}{8}$ inch thick and the other about half as thick. Place the thin round on a damp baking-sheet, spread the prawn and egg filling over the centre, damp the edges, and cover with the second round of pastry. Press down round the edge and brush over with an egg glaze. Decorate the top and then bake in a hot oven (Reg. 7 or 425° F.) for about 20 to 25 minutes.

Prawn Soufflé
See Crab Soufflé page 174.

SCALLOPS (COQUILLES ST JACQUES)

In season from October to March and, like all shellfish, should be bought alive. When alive, the shell is tightly closed and unless the correct knife is available they are quite difficult to open as the scallop is attached to the shell by a very strong muscle. They are generally opened and cleaned by the fishmonger but, should this have to be done in the kitchen, put the scallops in a quick oven for a few minutes. They will soon open. Clean away the beard, which is the dark frill around the scallop, wash them and dry well. Handle with care as the bright orange section, the roe, is particularly delicate.

Scallops can be fried or poached in liquid and served in a sauce, but, whichever method of cooking is used, only a gentle heat must be applied or they will be tough. Because of this use butter for frying, not oil, and take care when poaching that the cooking liquid does not boil.

*

Scallops Nature
6 scallops; ½ oz. butter; seasoning; ½ gill cream; 2 tablespoons fresh breadcrumbs.

Wash the scallops and dry well. Melt the butter and brush a little over the bottom of 4 deep shells. Halve or quarter the scallops, depending on their size, and place in the shells. Season with salt and pepper and a squeeze of lemon. Spoon over the cream, sprinkle with the crumbs, and moisten with the remaining melted butter. Bake in a moderate oven for 8 to 10 minutes.

Fried Scallops
6–8 scallops; 1 tablespoon seasoned flour; 1 oz. butter; Hollandaise Sauce.

Wash and dry the scallops very well and roll in seasoned flour. Melt the butter in a small sauté pan, put in the scallops, and fry gently until golden brown on both sides – about 8 minutes in all. Serve on a hot dish with the Hollandaise Sauce handed separately.

Scallops Mornay
6 scallops; white wine and water for poaching; lemon; a slice of onion; a few peppercorns; 1 bayleaf.

MORNAY SAUCE: 1 oz. butter; 1 oz. flour; ½ pint milk; 1 oz. each Parmesan and Gruyère cheese; 1–2 tablespoons cream; a little extra grated cheese for finishing.

Wash and dry the scallops, put into a shallow pan, pour over a wineglass of water, half a glass of white wine and a good squeeze of lemon. Add the onion, peppercorns, and bayleaf, cover, and poach *gently* for 5 to 7 minutes.

Melt the butter, add the flour, mix, and pour on the milk. Blend and thicken over the fire. Add a wineglass of the liquor from the scallops and allow to boil for 3 or 4 minutes, then draw aside and beat in the cheese by degrees. Adjust the seasoning and finish with the cream. Cut the scallops into 3 or 4 pieces and place in a gratin dish or arrange in the deep shells. Mask well with the sauce and dust a little extra cheese over each. Brown under a hot grill or in a quick oven.

Scallops Parisienne

6 scallops; ½ gill white wine; ¼ pint water; 1 sprig parsley; ½ bayleaf; 6 peppercorns; 1 oz. butter; 1 shallot; ¼ lb. button mushrooms; ¾ oz. flour; ½ gill milk; a little melted butter; 1 tablespoon brown crumbs.

Prepare the scallops and put into a pan. Cover with wine and water, add the salt and parsley, bayleaf, and peppercorns. Poach for 5 minutes. Take out and cut each scallop into 4 or 5 pieces. Melt the butter in a saucepan, add the shallot finely sliced, the mushrooms cut in quarters, cover, and cook for about 5 minutes. Draw aside and add the flour and the strained liquor from the scallops. Stir until boiling, simmer a few minutes, add the milk by degrees, then reduce rapidly to a creamy consistency. Add the scallops and fill into the deep shells. Scatter over browned crumbs and a little melted butter and brown under the grill.

Scallops Chapon Fin

6 scallops; water and lemon juice for poaching; 6 peppercorns; ½ bayleaf; slice of onion; 1 shallot; 1 oz. butter; 2 oz. button mushrooms; ½ oz. flour; 1 glass red wine; 1 glass light stock; 1 clove garlic; 1 level teaspoon tomato purée; 2 concasséd tomatoes; potato purée; a little melted butter; browned crumbs.

Poach the scallops for 5 to 6 minutes in water, barely to cover, a few drops of lemon juice, and the flavourings. Turn out into a bowl. Chop the shallot very finely and put into a pan with half the butter, cook for 1 minute, then add the mushrooms washed and quartered. Sauté for 2 or 3 minutes, take out the mushrooms, and add the rest of the butter and the flour. Allow the flour to colour slightly, then add the flamed wine and stock. Crush the garlic with a little salt and add to the pan with the tomato purée and mushrooms and stir until boiling. Simmer 10 to 15 minutes, then add the scallops cut in quarters and the tomatoes. Fill back into the shells, pipe round the potato purée, and sprinkle with the

crumbs and melted butter. Brown in a quick oven for 7 to 10
minutes.

Scallops Maison
6 scallops; 1 glass white wine; ½ glass water; peppercorns; 1 bayleaf.

FOR THE SAUCE: ¾ oz. butter; a good ½ oz. flour; 1 medium onion;
1 level teaspoon curry powder; 1 level teaspoon tomato purée;
¼ pint milk; 1 tablespoon ground almonds or walnuts; 1 coffee-
cupful boiling water; juice of ½ lemon; 2 tablespoons cream.

Put the scallops into a pan, add the wine, peppercorns, and bayleaf. Poach for 6 to 7 minutes and cool in the liquor. Melt the
butter in a pan, add the finely sliced onion, and after a few minutes
the curry powder and flour. Fry gently for a minute or two, then
add the tomato purée and milk. Bring to the boil and simmer for 5
minutes. Meanwhile pour the boiling water on to the almonds,
leave for 10 to 15 minutes, then strain through a muslin. Add this
'milk' to the sauce, sharpen with lemon, then add the cream.
Simmer to a creamy consistency, drain the scallops, cut in four,
and add to the sauce. Serve in the deep shells with boiled rice
coloured with paprika.

SCAMPI

The name given to a very large prawn caught in the Bay of Naples
but now accepted as the name for Dublin Bay prawns, which are
in fact langoustines or baby crawfish. They can be bought fresh
or boiled in the shells but to satisfy the great demand for scampi
by the restaurants they are imported in vast quantities, deep
frozen and packed raw but ready shelled.

*

Fried Scampi
1 lb. Dublin Bay prawns.

FRITTER BATTER: 4 oz. flour, a 'nut' of yeast, a teacup of warm
water, 1 tablespoon of oil; large sprays of parsley for garnish.

ALABAMA SAUCE: $\frac{1}{2}$ chopped green or red pepper; 4 sticks chopped celery; 1 clove crushed garlic; $\frac{1}{4}$ pint cream dressing; $\frac{1}{2}$ gill tomato chilli sauce, or tomato chutney; 1 tablespoon grated horseradish.

Prepare the fritter batter. Sieve the flour into a warm basin, cream the yeast with a teaspoon of sugar, add the water and add to the flour. Beat until smooth, stir in the oil, and leave in a warm place for about 30 to 40 minutes or until the mixture is well risen. Season with salt and pepper before using.

Shell the prawns or allow to thaw if frozen ones are being used, dip in the batter, and fry in smoking-hot fat until golden brown. Drain well and, when the fat has cooled a little, fry the well-dried parsley until crisp. Meanwhile prepare the cream dressing and then mix all the ingredients together for the Alabama sauce. Dish the prawns, garnish with the parsley, and hand the sauce separately.

Scampi Provençale

1 lb. scampi; white wine and water for poaching or butter for frying; peppercorns; 'bouquet', and a slice of onion for flavouring; the wine and water or butter; 2 tomatoes concassés; 2 oz. button mushrooms, quartered and sautéd.

SAUCE: 2 shallots finely chopped; $1\frac{1}{2}$ glasses white wine; a bouquet garni; $\frac{1}{2}$ oz. butter; $\frac{1}{2}$ oz. flour; a few mushroom peelings chopped; 1 clove garlic crushed; 1 teaspoon tomato purée; $\frac{1}{2}$–$\frac{3}{4}$ pint good stock.

First prepare the sauce. Simmer the shallots with the bouquet and the wine until it is reduced by half; set aside. Melt the butter, add the flour, and, when brown, add the rest of the ingredients. Simmer for 15 to 20 minutes, then add the reduced wine and continue to cook until syrupy.

Poach the scampi in the wine and water, or roll in seasoned flour and sauté lightly in a little butter. Add mushrooms and tomatoes to the sauce; simmer a minute or two, spoon over the scampi, and serve.

Scampi Hongroise

1 lb. scampi; seasoned flour; butter for frying; saffron rice or plainly boiled rice.

SAUCE HOLLANDAISE: 2 tablespoons wine vinegar; a slice of onion; 2–3 peppercorns; $\frac{1}{2}$ bayleaf; 1 egg yolk; 2 oz. butter.

HONGROISE SAUCE: $1\frac{1}{4}$ oz. butter; 1 dessertspoon chopped shallot; 1 heaped teaspoon paprika; scant ounce flour; $\frac{1}{2}$ pint light veal stock; $\frac{1}{4}$ pint strong fresh tomato pulp; 2–3 tablespoons cream.

First make the Hollandaise sauce, cover, and set aside. Then prepare the Hongroise sauce. Soften the shallot in the butter without colouring, add paprika and flour, and cook for a few minutes. Pour on the stock and tomato pulp, stir until boiling, add the cream, season, and simmer for a few minutes. Draw aside and beat in the Hollandaise sauce by degrees. Keep warm.

Roll the scampi in the seasoned flour, fry quickly in the butter, and dish at once in a hot dish. Just before serving, pour over the sauce and serve with the rice. For saffron rice, fork a pinch of saffron, previously soaked in boiling water, into boiled rice with a little melted butter. Warm as for Simla rice.

Scampi Gustave

1 lb. scampi; 1 oz. melted butter; salt; pepper; a dash of tabasco.

VIN BLANC SAUCE: 1 shallot, finely chopped; 1 glass white wine; 2 egg yolks; $1\frac{1}{2}$ oz. butter; $\frac{1}{2}$ gill cream; lemon juice; $1\frac{1}{2}$ gills velouté sauce made with $\frac{3}{4}$ oz. butter, $\frac{1}{2}$ oz. (good weight) flour, and $1\frac{1}{2}$ gills fish stock.

GARNISH: 1 doz. cooked asparagus tips; 2–3 ripe tomatoes; 2 oz. mushrooms, quartered; butter.

First prepare the sauce. Simmer the shallot in the wine until reduced to half. Pour on to the yolks, well worked together with a nut of the butter. Thicken over gentle heat, adding the rest of the butter by degrees. Finish with the cream and lemon. Now add the velouté sauce and heat gently without boiling. Set aside in a bain-marie.

Prepare the garnish. Peel, quarter, and pip the tomatoes; pass through the butter. Do the same with the mushrooms, sliced, and the asparagus tips.

Poach the scampi in the butter with the seasoning for about 6 to 7 minutes. Arrange in a serving-dish, put the garnish on the top, and coat over the sauce. Glaze lightly under the grill before serving.

SHRIMPS

All the recipes given for prawns can use shrimps instead.

Chapter 6

MEAT

It is important to know how to choose good meat for, though the butcher will guide you to a certain extent, all the responsibility should not be left with him. Meat, to be tender, must be properly hung. Most good butchers do not sell it before it is ready, but sometimes circumstances – market conditions and so on – force them to do so. If bought then the meat should, before cooking, be kept for several days in a cool larder or refrigerator (depending on the weather).

Well-hung beef is dark red in colour and the fat is the colour of Jersey cream. The prime cuts, sirloin for example, have a slight marbling of fat through the meat; other medium cuts such as top-side lack this and so need more careful cooking to make them tender. Fat is so necessary to keep meat moist and juicy and to give flavour that a certain proportion must be left on a cut whether roasting, stewing, or braising. For this reason veal, being an immature meat and having little or no fat, is frequently larded or barded before cooking. In a ragout or stew a fair amount of fat gives the gravy a rich and gelatinous quality and helps to thicken it.

Lamb and veal as young and tender meat are not hung as long as beef, while offal should be eaten as fresh as possible.

ROASTING

True roasting is done on a spit over an open fire and though this has always been acknowledged as the best method it is only during the past few years that it has been made possible in the modern kitchen. Manufacturers have evolved both gas and electric spits usually combined with a grill, which give excellent results.

In default of a spit the joint may be set on a rack or grid in the roasting-tin. If the grid is not used, place the joint – particularly a round or sirloin of beef – on its edge rather than laid flat on the cut side, as the part which comes in contact with the tin may get hard and over-brown.

For oven roasting (virtually baking), pre-heat the oven to the correct temperature, first setting the shelf at the right height to take the joint comfortably. Put the roasting-tin in the oven with 3 to 4 tablespoons of dripping, depending on the size of the joint. When it is smoking, take it out, set the meat either on the grid or straight on to the tin, baste well, and put back in the oven. Cook according to the weight of the meat, basting every 10 to 15 minutes until done.

Average Roasting Times and Temperatures*

BEEF: 15 to 20 minutes to the pound and 15 to 20 minutes over. Oven temperature: 425° F., Reg. 7, decreasing to 400° F., Reg. 6.

* Roasting times for spit roasting are roughly the same as those given here; but a schedule comes with each spit-roaster.

LAMB OR MUTTON: 20 minutes to the pound and 20 minutes over. Oven temperature: 400° F., Reg. 6, decreasing to 380° F., Reg. 5.

PORK: 25 minutes to the pound and 25 minutes over. Oven temperature: 400° F., Reg. 6.

VEAL: 20 minutes to the pound and 20 minutes over. Oven temperature: 400° F., Reg. 6.

The time of cooking will vary depending on the thickness of the joint and this must be taken into consideration. Any small joint should be roasted not less than 45 minutes in all, irrespective of weight.

Dish the joint on a hot dish, keep warm, and strain off the fat carefully, leaving about a tablespoon in the tin with the sediment to make the gravy. If lamb or mutton is being roasted, fry a slice or two of onion in the fat to give colour and flavour as these meats do not yield as much gravy as beef. Add about a level dessertspoon of flour, scrape and stir this well over gentle heat to collect all the sediment, and pour on about ¼ pint of stock, or more, depending on the thickness of the gravy required. Make the stock from the bone, or if not available vegetable stock, or water in which potatoes have been boiled. Bring to the boil, stirring well, season, and skim if necessary. Strain into the gravy boat. The thickness of the gravy should vary a little with each meat: for sirloin of beef, lamb, or veal it should be only lightly thickened; for pork it should be slightly thicker.

POT ROASTING

This method calls for little attention and is particularly suitable for meat and poultry which need long, slow cooking or are inclined to be dry and lacking in flavour. The process is simple. The joint is well browned in dripping, or in oil and butter mixed, in a thick deep pan or casserole with a tight-fitting lid. The heat is then lowered and root vegetables – onion, carrots, and celery – added, either whole or quartered, with a bouquet garni, a few peppercorns, and very little salt. No liquid, or at most $\frac{1}{2}$ gill of stock or a glass of wine (depending on the recipe being followed) is poured in and the lid tightly closed. The pan is set on slow enough heat to ensure gentle cooking either on the stove top or in the oven. A medium-sized joint – one of $2\frac{1}{2}$ to 3 lb. – will take 2 to 3 hours to be really tender.

The joint is served whole with the gravy well skimmed, and thickened if wished with arrowroot or kneaded butter. The vegetables can also be served with the meat, but as these will have imparted their flavour to the gravy and would moreover be overcooked, it is better to serve a freshly cooked vegetable separately.

BOILING

A method of simmering in water with root vegetables to flavour. The classic joints cooked in this way are:

SILVERSIDE OR TOPSIDE OF BEEF: Serve with small carrots, onions, and dumplings. The meat may be salted or fresh; if salted, put the joint into cold water and bring slowly to the boil, skimming well before adding the vegetables. If the joint is a large one, add the vegetables about $1\frac{1}{2}$ hours before the end of the cooking time. Dumplings, pieces of suet pastry the size of golf balls (see page 385), are best cooked separately in some of the liquor taken from the pan. To be really light they should be boiled rather than simmered, with the lid on the pan and plenty of room allowed for them to swell. Cooking time is 30 minutes.

SALT PORK: A piece from the leg, hand, or belly of pork. Serve with pease pudding; this goes well with the rich meat and is especially good with belly pork.

BOILED MUTTON: A leg or half leg. Simmer in water with vegetables to flavour. Serve with a caper sauce (see page 375).

For all the above joints allow 25 minutes to the pound simmering time and 25 minutes over.

GRILLING

A method allied to spit roasting in that the food is cooked by radiant heat. Grilling in the domestic kitchen is done either by electricity or gas; charcoal grills are also on the market but these are used for out-of-door barbecues. Infra-red grills are also available and instructions for grilling times are given with the grill.

Heat the usual type of gas or electric grill for at least 5 to 7 minutes before starting to grill. Wait until the grill is red hot and keep the griller pan underneath during this time. As a general rule the food should be not more than 3 inches away from the grill at the start of cooking. Once the food (a thick steak, for example) is well browned on both sides and needs more cooking, lower the griller rather than the heat.

If the grill is not very satisfactory, a good result can be got from using a thick frying-pan, particularly for steaks. Set the pan on full heat for several minutes, pour in about a dessertspoon of oil or dripping, just enough to make a film over the bottom of the pan, and lay in the meat.

Cook on full heat for the given time, turning once only. It may be necessary to lower the heat before the correct stage is reached, but this must not be done until both sides are well browned. This process is known as 'dry frying' and only the minimum of fat should be used to prevent sticking. For dry frying allow 2 to 3 minutes less time than for grilling as the heat is more intense.

Meat may be brushed with oil before grilling. This applies especially to rump steak and will prevent any possible scorching or hardening of the meat. Do not salt the meat before grilling as this will draw out the natural juices and so prevent browning. Turn the meat once only when well browned.

The following table gives a guide to the time allowed for grilling steaks, chops, cutlets, etc. For a mixed grill the ingredients are added to the griller at different times as these vary depending on what is being cooked. (See the recipe for a mixed grill on page 223.)

GRILLING TIMES

STEAKS: Rump ¾–1 inch thick; fillet, 1–1½ inch thick. Allow 6 to 7 minutes for rare; 10 to 12 minutes for medium rare. Sirloin or

Porterhouse steaks, i.e. cut from the wing rib, usually about $\frac{3}{4}$ inch thick, are best dry or pan fried. Allow 6 to 7 minutes for medium rare.

CUTLETS: $\frac{3}{4}$–1 inch thick, allow 6 to 7 minutes.

PORK CHOPS: $\frac{3}{4}$–1 inch thick, allow 10 to 15 minutes.

KIDNEYS (lamb's): allow 6 to 7 minutes.

SAUSAGES: 6 to 7 minutes for chipolatas or small sausages; 8 to 10 minutes for large sausages.

In addition to timing, a test for judging when meat is sufficiently grilled is to press it with the finger. If it is soft and gives under pressure it is rare, while if it is firm yet resilient it is medium, and, if really firm, well done. The surface must in every case be very well browned and can, especially for chops and cutlets, be almost charred.

Chops and cutlets are not served underdone but should be a delicate pink when cut; the same applies to kidneys, although these may be more underdone to taste. Sausages must be thoroughly cooked.

Most grills should be accompanied by a savoury butter. This may be served separately, or a pat put on the steak or cutlet just before serving. The most usual savoury butters are:

MAÎTRE D'HÔTEL: for steak, mixed grills, and fish.
2 oz. fresh butter; 1 dessertspoon chopped parsley; lemon juice; salt and pepper to taste.

Work the butter on a plate with a palette knife and when soft add the other ingredients. Shape into pats and chill before using.

ANCHOVY: for mutton chops or cutlets and for fish.
2 oz. fresh butter; anchovy essence; freshly ground black pepper; 4 fillets anchovy.

Work the butter on a plate with a palette knife; pound or crush the anchovies, add to the butter with pepper and enough essence to colour a delicate pink and strengthen the flavour.

ORANGE: for lamb cutlets, steak, and fish.

2 oz. fresh butter; grated rind of $\frac{1}{2}$ an orange; 1 teaspoon of the juice; 1 teaspoon tomato purée; salt and pepper.

Work together as above.

Other butters, such as garlic and mint, are made in the same way.

SHALLOW FRYING

This is a method used for the smaller cuts of meat and for poultry.

The depth of fat varies according to the cut and kind of meat and may be good dripping, salad oil, or clarified butter. Some-times a mixture of oil and butter is used; oil to give colour and crispness and butter for flavour. Frying is done on a moderately brisk heat, especially when dripping or oil is the chosen fat, but less hot if butter or clarified butter is used. The food should be turned only once when nicely browned on one side, and may be drained on paper. Generally speaking, food fried without a coat-ing is not drained but dished at once; this, however, is indicated in the recipe as is the time of cooking.

STEWING

Stews or ragouts are of two kinds, white and brown. A white stew is considered to be a little less complicated to make than a brown one, but both share a common rule in that the stewing must be slow and gentle. Boiling will toughen the meat and makes for too much reduction in the gravy.

White stews are made with 'white' meat, i.e. lamb or veal, and can, with advantage, when not a prime cut, be previously soaked in salted water before cooking to whiten and to remove any strong flavour. These stews are sometimes known as fricassées or blanquettes.

For a brown stew, made from beef or mutton, care must be taken to brown the pieces of meat quickly on all sides, but not over-much, as this renders it dry and tasteless. A 'gulyas' is a Hungarian stew of beef, mutton, or pork with a large proportion of onion and well flavoured with paprika.

BRAISING

A method of cooking by moist heat which is ideal for those cuts of meat which call for long, slow cooking to make them tender. Braising can also be applied to game and poultry.

For a braise, choice of the right pan or casserole is essential as the joint must fit snugly into the pan. It should be thick and solid and of iron, enamelled iron, or cast aluminium, with a close-fitting lid, oval or round in shape. The joint is first browned in this, taken out, and replaced by a bed of diced vegetables (a mirepoix), then the pan is covered and the vegetables allowed to 'sweat' for 7 minutes or so. The meat is replaced and enough jellied stock added barely to cover the 'mirepoix'. The pan is again covered and set in a slow oven for the necessary time.

The amount of liquid is important; only a small quantity is required so that the bulk of the meat will cook gently in the steam rising from the bottom of the pan. When the meat is very tender it is served according to the recipe. The liquid or gravy in the pan should be strong, clear, and well reduced, and may, if it is wished, be lightly thickened, though this is not usual. Joints for braising may be marinaded, a process designed to make the meat more tender and give flavour. Marinades consist of wine, usually red, with oil, root vegetables, and herbs, and the time for soaking, or marinading, may vary from 12 hours to 3 days or longer depending on the recipe being followed.

SAUTÉING

A quick method of cooking for the best cuts of meat and poultry, and, like braising, choice of the correct pan is an essential part of the process.

Sauter means to fry the chosen meat briskly in butter, clarified butter, or olive oil, until well browned, then liquid – wine and/or stock – is added barely to cover the meat and the cooking completed in this concentrated sauce. The dish takes its name from the additional ingredients added during the cooking.

A sautoir or sauté pan is in fact a deep frying-pan with straight sides and a lid which allows ample space for browning and for the maximum reduction of the sauce. For this reason do not attempt to sauté in a saucepan but rather improvise with a frying-pan and the odd lid.

BEEF

FILLET

This cut is best known for steaks and tournedos but also makes an excellent roasting joint for a dinner party or for the cold table. For roasting the fillet may be larded (see page 480) to give additional fat and to add to the appearance. For steaks, cut the fillet before trimming into slices 1 to $1\frac{1}{2}$ inches thick and grill or dry fry. Tournedos are cut from the 'eye' or centre of the fillet after this has been trimmed and so are smaller in size. They vary from $\frac{3}{4}$ to 1 inch in thickness and are cooked as for fillet steak. The fat which lies on the fillet is considered a delicacy and small nuggets of this may be cooked with the tournedos and a piece set on the top of each before serving. Tournedos are usually accompanied by various garnishes and sauces and it is from these that the dish may take its name.

SIRLOIN

A cut used principally for roasting and for steaks but is also good for a sauté. To roast, a piece of sirloin should weigh not less than $3\frac{1}{2}$ to 4 lb., especially if from a large animal, and should contain the undercut or fillet. This joint may be boned and rolled, though it will be more juicy if roasted on the bone. As this, however, is a large joint for a small household, it can be boned and the top half of the sirloin rolled and tied for roasting. The fillet is taken out and kept for steaks and the bone is used for stock. (For times of roasting and oven temperatures see page 192.) Classic accompaniments to roast beef are Yorkshire Pudding and Horseradish Sauce (see pages 200 and 379). The gravy is lightly thickened. In addition to roast potatoes, creamed swedes, marrow, or courgettes and creamed cabbage go particularly well with beef.

Yorkshire Pudding

4 oz. plain flour; 1 egg; ½ pint milk and water mixed.

Sift the flour with a good pinch of salt into a mixing-bowl, make a well in the centre, and drop in the egg. Start adding the milk and water to the egg, gradually drawing in the flour. When about half the liquid has been added, beat thoroughly until air bubbles break on the surface, then whisk in the remaining milk. Cover and stand in a cool place for at least ½ hour.

Heat 1 tablespoon of dripping in a Yorkshire pudding-tin and when it is smoking tilt and rotate the tin to cover the surface with the hot dripping. Pour in the batter and bake in a hot oven (425° F. or Reg. 7) for 20 to 30 minutes until well risen and crisp. Cut into squares for serving.

RUMP STEAK

This cut is best as steaks for grilling or dry frying. It is excellent in flavour but to be really tender it must be well hung. Have it sliced not less than ¾ to 1 inch thick.

WING RIB

This is primarily a roasting joint and like sirloin is best in a large piece. It may also be boned and rolled.

AITCHBONE

A fair-sized cut of 3 lb. and upwards with no bone. Excellent for roasting, pot roasting, or braising.

TOP RUMP AND TOPSIDE

These cuts are largely sold for roasting as the meat can be divided into small easily carved joints. Being exceptionally lean the meat is inclined to be a little hard when roasted and so these cuts are better pot-roasted or braised. If roasted, however, the meat will be more tender if left underdone. Topside is also sold salted for boiling.

CHUCK OR BLADE BONE STEAK

A cut from the shoulder. Used for steak pies and puddings and all ragouts or stews.

TOP RIB

An inexpensive roasting joint with a fair proportion of fat; it is especially good when served cold. Top rib is known as 'Jacob's Ladder' as it rises considerably in the oven when roasting. Plenty of room, therefore, should be allowed between the shelves.

BUTTOCK STEAK OR SECOND STEAK

Mostly for braising as a piece of stuffed steak and for beef olives. Can also be used for stews.

BRISKET AND FLANK

Cuts well streaked with fat and especially suitable for salting or spicing for eating cold.

SHIN

A lean cut, rich in albumen and used primarily for beef tea, strong stocks and consommés. Like chuck steak, it is gelatinous and so is good for stews, but needs long, slow cooking.

SKIRT

A cut that lies below the fillet and is ideal for steak and kidney pies or puddings and as a tender cut for sautés.

CLOD OR STICKING

Very good for beefsteak pudding and pies, especially when skirt is not obtainable.

Beef Ragoût

1½ lb. chuck steak; 4 medium onions; 4 medium carrots; 1 tablespoon dripping; 1 tablespoon flour; 1 pint stock; a bouquet garni;
1 clove garlic; 1 teaspoon tomato purée; salt; pepper.

Cut the beef into large squares and the onions and carrots in
quarters. Chop the garlic, add a good pinch of salt, and crush
with the point of the knife to a cream. Heat a thick enamelled
iron or aluminium casserole, put in the dripping, and when it is
smoking lay in the pieces of meat to cover the bottom of the
casserole closely. Fry briskly until brown on one side then turn
and brown on the other. Take out the meat, add the vegetables,
and fry rather more slowly until beginning to colour. Draw off the
heat and pour off the surplus fat, leaving 1 tablespoonful. Stir in
the flour, cook slowly for a minute or two, then add the stock,
crushed garlic, and tomato purée. Bring to the boil, season
lightly, replace the meat, and add the bouquet garni. Cover and
simmer gently on the stove-top or in the oven (340° F. or Reg. 3)
for about 1½ to 2 hours or until the meat is really tender. Remove
the bouquet, adjust the seasoning, and spoon into a hot casserole
for serving. Serve with a mousseline of potatoes.

Carbonnade of Beef

1½ lb. chuck steak or sticking; 2 tablespoons dripping; 2 onions;
1 level tablespoon flour; 1 clove garlic; ½ pint brown ale; 1 pint
hot water; bouquet garni; salt; pepper; a pinch of grated nutmeg and sugar; 1 teaspoon vinegar; 2 slices of bread about ¼ inch
thick or a French roll; French mustard.

Cut the meat into large squares. Slice the onions. Chop and crush
the garlic with a little salt. Heat the dripping in a stewpan,
and when it is smoking put in the meat to cover the bottom
of the pan and brown quickly on both sides. Lower the heat
slightly, add the onions and brown also. Dust with the flour,
pour on the ale and water, add the garlic, bouquet and season with
the salt, pepper, and vinegar and stir until boiling. Turn into
a fireproof casserole, cover closely, and cook gently in the oven
(340° F. or Reg. 3) for 2½ to 3 hours. Remove the crust from

the bread and cut each slice into four, or slice the French roll. Forty minutes before serving, take out the bouquet, skim off any fat from the casserole, and spoon on to the bread. Spread thickly with the mustard and arrange on top of the casserole, pushing the bread down below the surface to make sure it is well soaked with the gravy. It will float again to the top. Put the casserole back into the oven uncovered for the rest of the time or until the bread forms a good brown crust.

Beef Goulasch

1½ lb. chuck steak; 2 large onions; 2 tablespoons dripping; 1 level tablespoon paprika pepper; 1 tablespoon flour; 1 dessertspoon tomato purée; ¾–1 pint stock; a bouquet garni; a clove of garlic; salt; pepper; 1 red pepper; 2 large tomatoes; 2–3 tablespoons sour cream or yoghourt.

Cut the meat into large cubes. Slice the onions, chop and crush the garlic to a cream with a good pinch of salt. Heat the dripping in a stewpan, brown the meat in this, and then take out the pieces; lower the heat and put in the onions. Fry for a few minutes then add the paprika and, after 1 minute, the flour, tomato purée, garlic, and stock. Stir until boiling, replace the meat, and add the bouquet and a little salt and pepper. Cover and simmer gently on the stove-top or in a moderately slow oven for about 2 hours. In the meantime, shred and blanch the pepper, peel the tomatoes, removing the hard core and seeds, and then slice them. When the meat is tender add the pepper and tomatoes, simmer 2 or 3 minutes, and then turn into a casserole for serving. Spoon the cream over the top and serve with nouilles or plainly boiled potatoes.

Steak and Kidney Pudding

1½ lb. beefsteak; ½ lb. ox kidney; 1 small onion; 1 dessertspoon finely chopped mixed herbs; salt; pepper; seasoned flour; ¾ lb. suet crust (see page 385).

Cut the steak and kidney into ½-inch cubes. Chop the onion finely. Prepare the suet crust. Grease a 7-inch pudding basin well.

Take two-thirds of the pastry, roll out to about 1 inch thick, flour the surface well, and fold over. With the hands, work up the ends of the folded edge so that it takes the rough shape of the basin. Now roll the pastry lightly to make each layer ¼ to ½ an inch thick. Lift up the pastry and insert into the basin. Roll the pieces of steak and kidney in the seasoned flour and fill the basin with the meat, seasoning with salt, pepper, and the herbs. Pour in enough cold water to fill the basin to two-thirds. Roll out the rest of the pastry, cover the top of the basin, and pinch well round the edge. Trim it off neatly. Have ready a piece of clean linen cloth, dip in boiling water, and wring out. Flour the surface, make an inch pleat in the centre to allow for rising, and lay over the pudding. Tie round and knot the four corners of the cloth over the top. Submerge the basin in a large pan of fast boiling water and boil steadily for 3 to 4 hours. Replenish with boiling water from time to time when necessary. To serve, take off the cloth and pin a folded napkin round the basin. Send to the table with a jug of of boiling water. When the pudding is cut some water is poured in to augment the gravy.

Steak and Kidney Pie

1½ lb. buttock steak, clod, or skirt; ½ lb. ox kidney; seasoned flour; 1 small onion; 1 dessertspoon chopped parsley; stock or water; ½ lb. flaky pastry made with ½ lb. flour and 3 oz. each butter and lard (see page 386).

Make the pastry and set aside.

Chop the onion finely; cut the steak and kidney in ½-inch cubes and roll in the flour. Fill into a 7-inch pie dish, scattering the onion and parsley between the layers. Fill the dish two-thirds full with the stock. Roll out the pastry, cut a strip to cover the edge of the pie dish, pressing it down well, and lay the rest of the pastry over the dish. Trim round the edge and 'knock up' with the back of a knife. Pinch lightly on the edge to decorate and finish with 'leaves', etc. Make a hole in the centre with the point of a knife and brush with beaten egg mixed with a large pinch of salt. Bake in a hot oven (425° F. or Reg. 7), for 35 to 40 minutes, then wrap a

doubled sheet of wet greaseproof paper over and round the pie
and continue cooking at 350° F. or Reg. 4 for 1½ hours or until the
steak is tender.

Bitkis

4–6 oz. stale crumb of bread (about 2 thick slices); 1 small onion;
1 lb. good minced steak; 1 oz. minced fat if the steak is very lean;
1 tablespoon chopped parsley; about ¼ pint cold water; seasoned
flour; dripping; ½–¾ pint tomato sauce (see page 378); 2–3 tablespoons sour cream.

Cut the crusts off the bread and just cover the slices with cold
water. Chop the onion finely, add to the steak, fat, and parsley.
Squeeze the soaked bread dry in a piece of muslin, crumble and
mix with the steak. Work together well, kneading it like bread, or
work in the mixer adding the ¼-pint of water by degrees. The
mixture should be perfectly smooth, light, and short in texture.
Season well. Shape into small cakes, about 2½ inches in diameter
and ¾-inch deep, on a wet board. Roll lightly in the flour and fry
quickly until brown on both sides in hot dripping. Lift straight
into a fireproof dish. Have the tomato sauce ready and pour over
the bitkis. Cook in a moderate oven (360° F., Reg. 4) for 25 to 30
minutes. Ten minutes before serving, spoon the cream over the
dish.

Braised Beef

MIREPOIX: 2 large carrots; 2 large onions; 2 sticks celery; 1
small or 1 half turnip.

2–2½ lb. topside of beef; 2 tablespoons dripping.

A large bouquet garni; 1½ gills to ½ pint good bone stock; fresh or
tinned vegetables to garnish.

Dice the vegetables for the mirepoix.

Brown the meat all over in the hot dripping in the braising
pan. Take it out, lower the heat, and add the mirepoix. Cover
and cook gently 6 to 7 minutes. Set the meat on the vegetables,
add the bouquet, and pour round the stock. Season lightly, cover

the pan, and put into the oven (325° F., Reg. 3) for about 2 hours or until very tender.

In the meantime, prepare the garnish. This may be simple and time-saving. For example, a tin of small carrots, drained and tossed up over the heat with butter and chopped parsley, or braised celery or leeks. More elaborately, a selection of vegetables in season, such as French beans, carrots, and young turnips, cooked separately, may surround the dish. To serve, take up the beef and slice if wished. Strain the gravy and reduce until syrupy. Dish the beef with the garnish and spoon the gravy over the meat.

Braised Beef Mâconnaise (for 6)

MARINADE: 1 onion; 1 carrot; 1 clove garlic; 2 tablespoons olive oil; 6 peppercorns; a pinch of salt; 2 glasses Mâcon.

3 lb. aitchbone or topside of beef; 2 tablespoons oil; 1 large onion; 1 large carrot; 1 clove garlic; bouquet garni; ¼ pint bone stock; 1 glass Mâcon; 4–6 oz. button mushrooms, or 1 small tin 'champignons de Paris'; ½–¾ lb. button onions for glazing (see page 353).

SAUCE: 1 shallot; 1 tablespoon oil; 1 tablespoon flour; ½ pint jellied stock.

Prepare the marinade. Thinly slice the onion and carrot, chop the garlic. Combine with the other ingredients. Bring to the boil, simmer for 1 minute, and leave till cold. Lay the meat in a deep dish and pour over the marinade. Leave 12 hours or longer, turning the meat over from time to time.

When ready to cook, slice the onion and carrot, chop and crush the garlic with salt, wipe the meat, and reserve the marinade. Heat the oil in the braising-pan, brown the meat on all sides, take out, lower heat, and put in the vegetables. Fry until turning colour, replace the beef, and add the garlic, bouquet, stock, and wine. Season, cover, and braise slowly in the oven about 2½ to 3 hours, basting and turning the meat occasionally. Skim any oil from the surface of the marinade and strain.

Prepare the sauce. Soften the shallot in the oil, add the flour, and cook to a russet brown; draw aside, stir in the stock and

marinade, bring to the boil, and cook uncovered for 15 minutes.
Prepare the glazed onions. Wash, trim, and quarter the mushrooms or drain the liquor from the tin. Add to the sauce and continue to simmer 5 minutes. Take up the meat when tender; reduce
the liquor in the pan by half and strain it into the sauce. Boil up
well and skim. Slice as much beef as is needed, arrange in a
serving dish, spoon over some of the sauce, and garnish with the
onions. Serve the rest of the sauce separately.

Beef Olives Provençale

4–5 thin slices of buttock steak, each weighing 4–5 oz. and
approximately 5 inches in size.

FARCE: 6 oz. minced pork, veal or sausage meat; 1 small onion;
1 oz. butter; 2 large tablespoons fresh white crumbs; 1 dessertspoon mixed chopped herbs and parsley; 1 small egg, beaten;
salt; pepper; 5–6 green olives.

FOR BRAISING: 1–2 tablespoons beef dripping or oil; 2 onions;
2 carrots; a stick of celery; about ½ pint good bone stock; bouquet
garni.

TO FINISH: ½ lb. tomatoes; chopped parsley.

Bat out the slices of steak if necessary, though the butcher will
do this if asked. They should be as thin as a veal escalope. Cut in
half.

Prepare the farce. Chop the onion finely, soften in the butter,
and when cool mix with the pork, crumbs, and herbs. Add enough
of the egg to moisten nicely. Shred the olives and add to the
farce, season and spread on to the slices of meat. Roll up and tie
securely with thread. Dice the vegetables.

Heat the fat in a stewpan, brown the 'olives' all over, take out
and set aside. Put in the vegetables, allow them to colour, then
place the 'olives' on top. Pour in the stock, add the bouquet and
bring to the boil. Cover tightly and cook in a slow to moderate
oven (350° F., Reg. 3) for about 1½ hours or until very tender.
Meantime peel, seed, and slice the tomatoes. Take up the 'olives',
remove the threads carefully, and keep warm. Strain the gravy,

return to the pan, thicken slightly with kneaded butter or arrow-root, and add the tomatoes. Simmer 1 to 2 minutes. Dish the olives in a casserole or on a potato purée and spoon over the gravy. Dust with chopped parsley.

Sauté of Beef Chasseur

2–2½ lb. sirloin or 1½ lb. skirt; 2 tablespoons oil; 1 dessertspoon butter; 3 shallots or 1 small onion; 1 tablespoon flour; 1 glass white wine; 1 dessertspoon tomato purée; 1 clove garlic; bouquet garni; ½ pint good jellied stock; ½ lb. button mushrooms; stale bread for croûtes; oil for frying; chopped parsley.

Bone the meat if using sirloin and cut into 2-inch squares. Chop the shallots finely; chop and crush the garlic with salt. Trim, wipe, and quarter the mushrooms. Cut 6 or 7 triangular or heart-shaped croûtes from the bread. Heat a sauté pan, add in the oil and when hot drop in the butter. While foaming put in the meat quickly and sauté briskly until nicely coloured on both sides. Take out, reduce heat, and add the shallots. After a few minutes stir in the flour and continue cooking until a good russet brown. Draw aside, blend in the wine, tomato purée, garlic, and stock. Stir until boiling, put in the bouquet and meat. Cover and simmer gently 35 to 40 minutes. Fry the croûtes in very hot oil until golden brown; drain and set aside. Ten minutes before the sauté is done add the mushrooms. When the meat is tender adjust the seasoning, dish the meat, and reduce the sauce rapidly if necessary. Spoon over the dish and surround with the croûtes. Dust with the parsley. Serve with a purée of celeriac mixed with potato.

Roast Fillet of Beef with Mushrooms

2½–3 lb. fillet; larding bacon; beef dripping.

GARNISH: 12 large even-sized mushrooms; 1 shallot; 2 oz. butter; 3 large tablespoons fresh breadcrumbs; 1 dessertspoon chopped fresh thyme and parsley; 1 tablespoon grated Parmesan cheese.

TO ACCOMPANY: clear thin gravy or a Madeira sauce (see page 374); potatoes Anna or Château (see pages 360 and 359).

Weigh and tie up the fillet if necessary. Lard it if wished and set on a grid. Pre-heat the oven to 450° F., Reg. 8. Put 3 large table-spoons of dripping into a roasting-tin large enough to take the grid, heat in the oven until the fat is smoking, then set the grid and fillet in the tin. Baste and roast for approximately 45 to 50 minutes for medium rare. Baste frequently and lower the heat after half an hour if the meat is getting too brown.

In the meantime prepare the garnish. Peel and stalk eight of the mushrooms. Wash the remaining four with the stalks and peel-ings. Chop them and the shallot finely. Cook in half the butter for 5 to 6 minutes, increasing the heat gradually to drive off surplus moisture. Draw aside, season well, and stir in the crumbs and herbs. Fill this mixture on to the mushrooms and scatter over the cheese. Melt the rest of the butter, well brush a baking sheet with it, and set the mushrooms on this. Sprinkle them with the remaining butter and slip into the oven 10 to 15 minutes before the beef is ready. To dish, take up the beef, set on a hot dish, and surround with the mushrooms. To make the gravy, pour off all the fat leaving only the sediment in the tin. Add about ¼ pint good strong stock and mix well over a moderate heat. Season and strain. Spoon a little of this round the fillet and serve the rest in a gravy boat. Use the Madeira sauce in the same way. If wished, the fillet may be carved, i.e. cut in slices about ¼ inch thick, before dishing.

Entrecôte of Beef Bordelaise
3 lb. top part of sirloin, boned and tied securely; 2–3 tablespoons oil or good dripping; 6–8 oz. mushrooms.

SAUCE BORDELAISE: ½ pint demi-glace sauce (see page 373); 1 large teaspoon tomato purée; 1 shallot; 1 level teaspoon paprika; 1 large glass red wine; 1 large marrow bone.

Roast the meat in a hot oven, basting frequently with the oil or dripping; allow 50 minutes to 1 hour. In the meantime prepare the sauce. Chop the shallot finely, put it into a pan with the pap-rika and wine, and simmer until reduced by half. Add to the demi-glace with the tomato purée and continue to simmer for 5 or 6 minutes. Scoop the marrow out of the bone, cut into dice, and poach for 2 or 3 minutes in salted water; drain. Strain the sauce, return to the pan, and add the marrow; set aside. Sauté the mushrooms, whole or quartered, in a good nut of butter. Dish the meat, surround with the mushrooms, and serve the Sauce Bordelaise separately.

Tournedos Béarnaise
4–6 tournedos; Béarnaise sauce (see page 377).

First prepare the Béarnaise sauce and set aside.

Trim the tournedos. Pre-heat the grill and griller; set the tournedos on the grid and grill 4 to 5 minutes on each side for medium rare. Dish on a hot dish and put a teaspoonful of the Béarnaise on the top of each tournedos immediately before serving, or if preferred the sauce can be served separately and a nugget of grilled fat placed on top instead. Two or three spoonfuls of gravy made from the juices in the griller pan may be poured round the dish and the tournedos set on a croûte of fried bread if wished.

Steak 'au Poivre'
4 fillet steaks cut 1–1½ inches thick; 1–2 tablespoons black peppercorns; oil; butter; watercress to garnish.

Prepare the steaks at least two hours before wanted. Crush the peppercorns with a rolling-pin; beat the steaks lightly, roll in the peppercorns, and press in well. Brush with oil and leave to marinade.

Grill or pan-fry in a little butter for 7 to 8 minutes, depending on thickness. Dish the steaks. Add an extra ounce of butter to the pan, cook to a good 'noisette'. Season with salt and a squeeze of lemon and pour over the steaks. Serve garnished with 'bouquets' of watercress. Potatoes Lyonnaise may accompany (page 358).

Steak 'farci foie gras'
1½–2 lb. rump steak cut about 1½ inches thick; salad oil.

FARCE: ½ oz. butter; 1 shallot; 2 oz. mushrooms; 1 oz. ham; 2–3 tablespoons fresh breadcrumbs; 1 small tin foie gras; salt; pepper.

TO FINISH: ¾ oz. butter; a good squeeze of lemon juice; 1 dessert-spoon chopped parsley; watercress.

First prepare the farce. Finely chop the shallot and soften in the butter. Wash the mushrooms, chop finely, and add to the pan; cover and cook 4 to 5 minutes. Chop the ham and add to the mixture with the crumbs, off the heat. Season, turn out, and cook. Cut the steak at one side to form a pocket, add the foie gras to the farce, mix well, and fill into the steak. Sew up with thread or fasten with poultry pins; brush with oil and grill 4 to 5 minutes on each side. Remove the thread or pins, dish, and keep warm. Heat a small pan, drop in the butter, and when a light brown add season-ing, the lemon juice, and parsley. Spoon over the steak and serve at once. Garnish with a little watercress.

Médaillons de Bœuf à la Russe

6 tournedos cut from the small end of the fillet; 1–2 tablespoons brandy; clarified butter for frying.

SALPICON: 10 oz. even-sized 'open' mushrooms; 1 oz. butter; 12 green olives, turned; ½ wineglass stock; juice of ½ lemon; 1 car-ton (3–4 tablespoons) sour cream.

POTATOES ANNA: 1½–2 lb. even-sized potatoes; 2–3 oz. butter.

First prepare the potatoes. Well butter a thick frying-pan 8 or 9 inches in diameter. Slice the potatoes thinly, arrange neatly in the pan to fill completely, adding small pieces of butter and salt and pepper between the layers. Cover tightly, cook on a moderate heat 20 to 25 minutes, then slip the pan into a slow to moderate oven to complete cooking.

In the meantime, marinade the tournedos in the brandy with a sprinkling of ground black pepper. Sauté the mushrooms in the butter, season, add wine or stock, and reduce slightly. Add cream and olives and set on low heat while cooking the tournedos.

Season highly and fry in the clarified butter rapidly for approximately 3 minutes on each side. Add the marinade and any cooking juices to the salpicon. Turn out the potatoes on to a large dish, arrange the tournedos on the top, and pour round the salpicon. Serve very hot.

Tournedos Périgord (for 6)

6 croûtes of bread cut to fit the tournedos; 10 oz. white button mushrooms; fresh or clarified butter; 6 tournedos; 3 tablespoons brandy; ¼ pint thick cream; ¾ pint demi-glace sauce (see page 373); 1 tin pâté de foie, or 2 oz. liver pâté.

Fry the croûtes in butter until golden brown. Set aside. Reserve 6 button mushrooms for garnishing and brown them in a little butter. Keep warm.

Sauté the tournedos in butter allowing 3½ to 4 minutes on each side; take out and keep warm. Add the mushrooms to the pan and continue to sauté for 1 minute. Add 2 tablespoons of brandy, the demi-glace, and cream. Boil up quickly to reduce a little and season. In the meantime work the rest of the brandy with the foie gras; spread on to the croûtes, set a tournedos on each, and arrange in a hot dish. Spoon over a little of the sauce and arrange the mushrooms from the sauce at each end of the dish. Serve the rest separately. Garnish the top of the tournedos with a browned mushroom. Serve very hot.

Fillet of Beef Chancelière (for 6)

2 lb. fillet of beef; fat bacon for larding (optional); 1 onion; 1 carrot; good dripping; ¾ pint demi-glace sauce; 1 small glass Madeira.

GARNISH: *Croquettes of celeriac:* 1 root celeriac; seasoned flour; beaten egg; white crumbs and grated Parmesan cheese in equal portions.

Lard the beef if wished, tie up neatly, and brown all over in a little hot dripping. Draw aside and take out the beef. Slice the onion and carrot, add to the pan, fry for a few minutes then stir in the demi-glace and Madeira. Bring to the boil, replace the beef, season, cover, and cook gently for 25 minutes, turning the beef occasionally.

In the meantime prepare the garnish. Cut the celeriac into thick fingers, boil until just tender, drain and dry. Roll the pieces in seasoned flour, brush with beaten egg, and roll again in the crumbs and cheese. Make sure they are well coated. Fry in shallow fat, oil, or butter until golden brown. Set aside. Take up the beef, slice if wished, and arrange on a serving-dish. Reduce the sauce rapidly for a minute or two, strain, spoon a little over the meat, and serve the rest separately. Pile the garnish at each end of the dish.

Beef 'en croûte'

2 lb. fillet of beef; 4 oz. button mushrooms; 1 dessertspoon chopped mixed herbs and parsley; butter; ½ lb. quantity puff pastry; egg for glazing; watercress to garnish.

Trim and tie up the fillet. Pepper it and brown it quickly all over in hot butter, then roast in a quick oven for 10 minutes. Take out and allow to get cold. In the meantime slice the mushrooms, sauté in butter for a few minutes, draw aside, add the herbs, and cool.

Roll out the puff pastry to a rectangle. Divide it in two, one piece two-thirds larger than the other. Put the mushroom mixture on the larger piece, lay the beef on top, and press up the pastry round it. Lay the other piece of pastry over the top, brush with egg glaze, and decorate with 'fleurons'; bake in a hot oven for 35 to 40 minutes, or until well browned. Serve hot or cold, garnished with watercress.

Beef Niçoise with Anchovy Loaf (for 6)

1½ lb. fillet of beef; 2–3 tablespoons olive oil for roasting; 1 pint aspic jelly (this can be made from the powdered, bought aspic, and a glass of sherry added in place of the same amount of water).

SALAD: 1 large aubergine; 1 lb. tomatoes; 1 onion; 2 green peppers.

DRESSING: 1 teaspoon paprika; 1 clove garlic; 1 carton sour or 'cultured' cream; lemon juice or wine vinegar to taste.

GARNISH: 3 hard-boiled eggs; ¼ lb. black olives.

Roast the fillet in a quick oven for about 35 minutes and allow to cool.

In the meantime prepare the salad. Slice the aubergine, score the surface with a knife, sprinkle with salt, and leave 20 to 30 minutes; then drain away the liquid and dry in a cloth. Skin and quarter the tomatoes and flick away the seeds; slice the onion; halve the peppers, remove the core and seeds, and shred finely.

Heat 2 tablespoons of olive oil in a frying-pan and colour the aubergine on either side. Reduce the heat, add the sliced onion to the pan, and continue cooking until soft but not coloured, adding extra oil if necessary; then add the peppers and seasoning and cook 2 to 3 minutes. The aubergine should now be tender. Increase the heat under the pan, add the tomatoes, and cook briskly for 1 minute. Turn into a dish to cool. Crush the garlic with a little salt to a cream and work into the sour or cultured cream with the paprika. Season with freshly ground pepper and add the vinegar or lemon to taste.

Carve the beef, arrange in overlapping slices round a flat serving-dish. Brush well with cool aspic giving two or three coats. Spoon the salad into the centre of the dish, quarter or slice the eggs, and stone the olives. Garnish the dish with these and serve the dressing separately. Serve with a hot anchovy loaf.

Anchovy Loaf

1 loaf light or French bread; 3–4 oz. fresh butter; anchovy essence; 6 anchovy fillets; pepper.

First prepare the anchovy butter. Soak the fillets in a little milk for half an hour to soften them. Drain and chop. Cream the butter, add the chopped fillets and enough essence to flavour well, and colour the butter a delicate pink.

Cut the bread in even slices down to the crust but not right through. Spread the butter between each slice, tie the loaf securely with string or tape, and set on a baking-tin. Spread any remaining butter on the top and sides. Bake in a moderate oven until crisp and golden brown, about 10 to 15 minutes (400° F. or Reg. 6). Serve hot with the string removed. Hand the loaf for people to break off or cut a slice as wanted.

LAMB AND MUTTON

Lambs may vary a little in size but the best are small, with moderate covering of firm white fat. The meat is a soft to dark red in colour. Lamb also calls for hanging but for less time than beef. For roast lamb the classic accompaniments are mint sauce, or mint jelly, green peas, and new potatoes.

LEG

This is the leanest cut and so must be well basted while roasting. Though primarily a roasting joint it is excellent braised. The weight varies from 3 to 5 lb.

LOIN

Rather a fat cut and so inclined to be wasteful. Used for chops but good boned and stuffed and either roasted or braised.

SADDLE

A choice and expensive joint suitable for a large party. A saddle is a double loin taken from the top end down to the tail. The weight averages 8 to 10 lb. and is generally sufficient for that number of people. A saddle may be served plainly roast with clear gravy, mint sauce, or redcurrant jelly and with young vegetables to accompany or to garnish the dish. For a more elaborate presentation, the saddle is carved and a farce or stuffing of some kind, such as a soubise or duxelles, put between the slices. The whole is then reshaped and brushed with a meat glaze (i.e. strong clear bone stock reduced to a syrup, or melted butter) and a scattering of Parmesan cheese. The saddle is returned to the oven for a further 5 to 10 minutes to brown. To roast, use a good dripping or wine and butter, basting frequently. Allow approximately 2 hours for a saddle of 8 lb. with the oven temperature at 380° F. or Reg. 5–6. Be careful not to over-cook; the meat should be delicately pink. To carve – and this for a plain roast may be done in the dining-room – slice down the length of the fillet on each side of the backbone. If carved in the kitchen, replace the slices on the bone and brush over with meat glaze before serving.

BEST END OF NECK

For cutlets and noisettes and for a small joint. The whole best end consists of 6 to 7 cutlet bones and averages $1\frac{1}{2}$–2 lb. in weight. For cutlets and a plain roast the neck should be chined only and the bones sawn through 2–3 inches from the top.

TO PREPARE NECK FOR ROASTING

Cut away chine bone and use for the gravy. Cut off the 'flap', the piece containing the tops of the cutlet bones, and set aside. Slice the fat away from the top of the bones to a depth of about 2 inches. With a small knife cut away the gristle from between the cleared bones and scrape them clean. Make sure that the fat side of the neck has been skinned and then score it lattice fashion with the point of the knife. Roast the neck and the 'flap' according to the recipe being followed. When done the meat may be carved before serving and the 'flap' cut into pieces.

TO PREPARE CUTLETS

Cutlets can be bought ready cut and trimmed, but it is more economical to prepare them at home. When buying a piece of best end of neck, take note of the size. If the neck is small two bones must be allowed for each cutlet, though a medium-sized whole best end will yield five cutlets of about $\frac{3}{4}$ to 1 inch thick. Cutlets should not be thinner than this as the 'nut' of meat will tend to curl in cooking and become dry.

TO CUT AND TRIM

Remove chine bone from the neck. If this has not already been done by the butcher the bone must be sawn through from the underside, taking care not to damage the meat, and the top bones also sawn through. Both these pieces are cut off and the top or flap can be divided and cooked and served with the cutlets if wished. With a sharp knife cut down between the bones and slightly nearer to one bone than the other. Take two bones if necessary to make a plump cutlet. Now cut out any second bone and trim off surplus fat but leave a good rim round the nut of meat and the small piece which lies just under it. Scrape the top of the bone clean.

TO PREPARE NOISETTES

Noisettes are boned cutlets and to prepare them the best end is not chined but left plain. To bone, start at the chine bone and, with a sharp knife, cut down to and then along the cutlet bones keeping the knife well on the bone and working with short, even strokes. Season the surface of the meat and roll up tightly starting at the chined end. Cut off some of the end-fat piece if necessary; there should be enough to wrap once round the nut of meat. Tie at 1 to 1¼-inch intervals with fine string, then cut between to form a noisette.

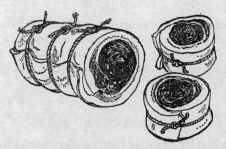

Cutlets and noisettes are frequently served fried, either plain or with a coating of egg and crumbs. In this case they call for a greater depth of fat than ordinary shallow frying. Clear dripping, oil, or oil and butter mixed may be used and should come half-way up the sides of the cutlet or noisette. If the fat is too shallow the meat will not be completely cooked and there may be an ugly white line where the fat has not reached. Care must be taken when frying in dripping or oil. These fats reach a high temperature and if, for example, noisettes that have been egged and crumbed are put into a fat which is too hot they will brown before having had their correct time for frying. If this should happen, take them out while still golden brown and set on a grid. Put this into a moderately hot oven for 5 minutes or so to complete cooking. Fried in butter the temperature is much lower so that the meat should be cooked when the outside is nicely browned.

CROWN ROAST

This joint, generally served at a dinner party, is prepared by the butcher. It consists of two best-end necks turned outwards before being skewered together to form a circle. The crown is roasted with butter and wine or dripping at the temperature for lamb and allowing $1\frac{1}{4}$ to $1\frac{1}{2}$ hours. Served with a strong gravy, the centre of the crown may be filled with spring vegetables and the top bones finished with a cutlet frill. A crown roast will serve 6 to 8 people.

SHOULDER

A good cut for roasting either plain or boned and stuffed. The meat is particularly sweet and well flavoured and has a moderate amount of fat which keeps it moist and juicy. One of the best joints for eating cold, especially if kept after cooking for that purpose. Weights range from $2\frac{1}{2}$ to $3\frac{1}{2}$ lb.

MIDDLE NECK AND SCRAG

Both these cuts are inexpensive and good for stews both white and brown. Middle neck has more meat than scrag, the latter being particularly suitable for broths. Double scrag – rounds cut right across the neck – may be pot-roasted or braised, and though these pieces have a fair amount of bone (a fact which must be taken into account when ordering) the meat is sweet and lean.

BREAST

When lean this cut is good boned and stuffed and either pot-roasted or braised. The butcher will bone and roll it for you.

CHUMP ENDS

These small pieces are from the end of the loin. Like scrag they have their full share of bone, but cooked with plenty of vegetables they make a good and very inexpensive dish.

MUTTON

Good mutton is full of flavour and is good for roasting, boiling, and braising. The joints are the same as, but naturally heavier than, lamb and so may be a little large for the average household. Mutton should be well cooked and served when roasted with a soubise (onion) sauce or redcurrant jelly and lightly thickened gravy. Haricot or butter beans are frequently served in place of roast potatoes. Leg or shoulder of mutton may also be boiled or pot-roasted.

*

Roast Lamb with Casserole of Mushrooms

Choose a best-end of neck, a shoulder or leg. Prepare the neck as in the directions on page 216. The other joints are left plain or may, especially the leg, be stuck at intervals with slivers of garlic or sprigs of parsley. To do this, make incisions with the point of a small knife and press into them 1 or 2 cloves of garlic cut into strips, or the parsley. The amount of garlic depends on personal taste but brings out the flavour of the lamb, as does the parsley. Use this in the same way but insert the sprigs at more frequent intervals. Rub the joint well with butter, 1½ to 3 oz. according to size, grind over some pepper from the mill, cover with paper, and put in a preheated oven. For time and temperature see page 192.

In the meantime prepare the casserole of mushrooms. When

the lamb is cooked, dish and make the gravy. If serving with a vegetable in a sauce do not thicken it but have it strong and clear. Serve small roast potatoes with the lamb.

Casserole of Mushrooms

1 lb. artichokes cut in pieces the size of a walnut; ½ lb. button mushrooms; 1 oz. butter; 1 oz. flour; 1 pint milk (or ½ stock and ½ milk); salt; pepper; 1–2 tablespoons thick cream; nutmeg or mace.

Boil the artichokes in milk and water until barely tender. Drain, add a nut of butter, and set aside. Trim the mushrooms. Melt the butter and toss the mushrooms in this over a quick fire. Mix in the flour, milk, and seasoning, stir until boiling, add the artichokes, cover the pan, and simmer 10 minutes. Finish with the cream. In summer, replace the artichokes with baby new potatoes and in this case do not serve potatoes with the meat.

Haricot of Lamb

3 oz. haricot beans.

2½ lb. double scrag or 2 lb. middle neck of lamb; 2 tablespoons dripping; 3 medium-sized onions; a large bouquet garni; 1 tin tomatoes (about ½ pint); chopped parsley.

Soak the beans for 12 hours, then simmer gently in salted water for a good hour.

Trim the pieces of lamb if necessary; it will have been already cut by the butcher. Quarter the onions and heat the dripping in a shallow stewpan. Brown the meat in this, take out, and put in the onions. Cook slowly until brown, replace the meat, season, and add the bouquet, tomatoes, and beans drained from the liquor. Cover tightly and cook slowly for a good hour or until the meat and beans are tender. Adjust the seasoning, remove the herbs, turn carefully into a casserole, and dust thickly with the chopped parsley.

Stuffed Breast of Lamb

1 good breast of lamb, boned; 1 large onion; ½ lb. sausage meat;

1 dessertspoon chopped mixed herbs; a little dripping; 2–3 carrots; 2 large onions; clove of garlic; ½ pint stock or water; level dessertspoon flour; 1 dessertspoon chopped parsley to finish.

Chop the onion, cook in a spoonful of the dripping to soften, and add to the sausage meat with the herbs, parsley, and plenty of salt and pepper. Spread this mixture on the inside of the breast roll and tie up or sew with fine string.

Heat 2 spoonfuls of dripping in a thick pan, brown the meat in this, then add the carrots and onions cut in quarters. Shake over the fire for a few minutes to allow the vegetables to colour slightly, drain off as much fat as possible, and pour in the stock. Add the clove of garlic, season, cover, and cook slowly 1½ to 2 hours.

When the meat is tender, lift out carefully and remove the string. Slice and lift on to a hot serving-dish, surround with the vegetables, and strain the gravy into a small pan. Skim off the fat, add a dessertspoon to the flour, mix and stir this into the gravy, reboil, and season. If too thick add a little extra stock or water to thin. Finish with the parsley and spoon over the meat.

Navarin of Lamb

1½–2 lb. middle neck of lamb; 2 medium-sized onions; 2 medium-sized carrots; 1 small turnip; 1–2 tablespoons dripping; 1 teaspoon sugar; 1 tablespoon flour; about 1 pint water; bouquet garni; chopped parsley.

Trim the pieces of neck, quarter the onions, and cut the carrots and turnip into very thick match-shaped pieces. Heat the dripping in a shallow stewpan, brown the meat on all sides, take out, and put in the vegetables. Dust with the sugar and fry until well coloured, shaking the pan frequently. Be careful that they do not get over-brown and so give a bitter flavour to the navarin. Stir in the flour carefully and continue to fry for a few minutes. Add three-quarters of the stock, bring to the boil, and replace the meat. Top up with the remaining stock so that the meat is barely covered, add the bouquet, seasoning, and cover the pan. Simmer half an hour, then remove the lid, turn the pieces over, and continue to simmer for a further half-hour uncovered. When the meat is tender and the gravy nicely reduced, dish and sprinkle well with the parsley.

Braised Leg of Lamb

1 small leg of lamb, about 3 lb.; 2 oz. butter; vegetables for braising (2 large carrots, 2 large onions, 2 sticks celery, 1 small turnip); 1 glass white wine; ¼ pint jellied veal or chicken stock; bouquet garni.

Brown the leg carefully all over in the butter, then take out and put in a plateful of the braising vegetables cut into dice. Cover the pan and allow to sweat 6 or 7 minutes, then replace the leg, pour in the wine and stock, add the bouquet, cover, and braise gently about 1½ to 2 hours. Take up and dish, strain the gravy, thicken lightly if wished, and adjust the seasoning. Serve with potatoes Savoyade and braised celery.

Shashlik (Kebabs of Lamb)

6–8 long metal skewers; special kebab skewers can be bought for this.

1½ lb. boned lamb (a small half shoulder is a good cut); 2 onions; fresh bay leaves; pepper from the mill; a little oil; boiled rice for dishing.

Cut the lamb into 1-inch cubes and the onions into quarters. Pull these apart into pieces and put on a dish with the lamb; season well with pepper and sprinkle with oil. Leave an hour or two or longer. Thread the pieces on to the skewers alternately with a piece of onion and bayleaf. Brush with oil. Cook under a hot grill, turning once only, allowing about 4 or 5 minutes on each side. Dish on a bed of hot boiled rice. If wished a devilled sauce can accompany. When serving, it is usual to push the meat gently off the skewer on to the rice; this can be done at table or in the kitchen.

Mixed Grill

4 lamb cutlets; 4 kidneys; ½ lb. chipolata sausages; 2–3 good
tomatoes; ½ bunch watercress; Maître d'Hôtel butter (see page
196).

While the grill is heating prepare the ingredients. Trim the cutlets; skin and split and skewer open the kidneys; halve the
tomatoes and season; pick over the watercress. If the griller pan
will not hold all the ingredients grill the sausages and tomatoes
first. Place the tomatoes cut side downwards on the grid with the
sausages, slide the pan under the grill, and after 3 or 4 minutes
turn the tomatoes over. Dot the tops with a few pieces of butter
and dust with castor sugar. Turn the sausages also and return to
the grill for a further 3 or 4 minutes, then arrange in a hot dish.
Place the cutlets and kidneys rounded side uppermost on the
grid and slide the pan in close under the grill. Allow about 3½ to 4
minutes on each side, then dish and garnish with a little watercress
before serving at once. A little gravy may be made by adding a
dash of hot stock or water with salt and pepper to the pan.
Serve with Maître d'Hôtel butter. Bacon or liver may also be
included in a Mixed Grill.

Loin of Lamb Lyonnaise

2–2½ lb. loin of lamb; 2–3 tablespoons dripping.

STUFFING: 1 small onion; 1 oz. butter; 4 oz. minced raw pork;
2 tablespoons fresh white crumbs; 1 tablespoon chopped
parsley; 1 teaspoon chopped lemon thyme or mixed dried herbs;
grated rind ½ lemon; a little beaten egg.

ONION FONDU: 2 large Spanish onions; 1 oz. butter.

GRAVY: 1 level dessertspoon flour; ¼–½ pint strong stock made
from the bones.

Remove bones from the meat, brown them lightly in a pan with
an onion and carrot. Add herbs and seasoning, cover with water,
and leave to simmer gently. Prepare the stuffing. Chop the onion

finely, soften in the butter in a small covered pan without colouring, turn into a bowl, and mix with the pork, crumbs, herbs, and seasoning. Bind with the egg. Spread the stuffing over the meat, roll up and secure with poultry pins and fine string. Heat the dripping and when it is smoking put in the meat and baste well. Cook about 1 hour in a hot oven (400° F. or Reg. 6) basting well.

In the meantime prepare the onion fondu. Slice the onions finely, blanch in salted water, and drain. Melt the butter in a small sauté pan, add the onions, season with freshly ground black pepper, cover, and cook very slowly to a rich golden brown.

Take up the meat and keep warm while making the gravy. Turn the onion fondu on to a serving-dish, remove the poultry pins and string from the meat, carve it, and arrange on the top. Baste with a little of the gravy and serve the rest separately.

Neck of Lamb Portugaise

2 lb. best end neck of lamb; 3 oz. walnut kernels; 1 tablespoon butter; 1 medium-sized onion; 3 tablespoons white crumbs (1½ oz.); 1 tablespoon chopped parsley; grated rind of ½ lemon; beaten egg; salt; pepper.

FOR ROASTING: wine and butter.

Bone the lamb, score the fat and season the surface of the meat. Grind the nuts through a Mouli grater. Chop and soften the onion in the butter and add with the dry ingredients to the nuts. Moisten with the lemon and egg, but do not get it too wet. Roll up and fasten with poultry pins or sew with fine string and a trussing needle. Spread with the butter and pour over a glass of white wine. Roast in a moderate oven for about 45 to 50 minutes, basting well.

In the meantime prepare the GARNISH:

3 large tomatoes; chopped basil or lemon thyme; green olives; 2–3 rashers unsmoked bacon; olive oil.

Skin the tomatoes, cut them in half, and set them on a fireproof plate. Salt on the cut side and turn over to drain a little. Shred the

olives and bacon and mix together. Sprinkle the surface of the
tomatoes with the herbs, pile a spoonful of the olive mixture on
each, and sprinkle well with oil. Just before serving put into the
oven for about 5 or 6 minutes or pass under the grill until nicely
brown and crisp. Dish the lamb and surround with the tomatoes.
Serve a plain gravy separately.

Shoulder of Lamb Chasseur (for 6)

1 small shoulder of lamb; wine and butter for roasting.

STUFFING: 1 oz. butter; 1 small onion; ½ lb. sausage meat; 1 small
tin chestnut purée; 1 dessertspoon mixed chopped herbs; salt
and pepper; 1 small beaten egg; ½ pint demi-glace sauce; 2
tomatoes; a little stock.

Bone out the shoulder. Prepare the stuffing. Chop the onion
finely, soften in the butter, and add to the rest of the ingredients
for the stuffing. Fill into the shoulder, sew up with fine string or
fasten with poultry pins. Spread a doubled sheet of greaseproof
paper with 1 to 2 oz. butter, grind some black pepper over it, and
wrap over and round the lamb. Set in a roasting-tin, pour round a
glass of white wine, and roast in a moderately hot oven (400° F.
or Reg. 6) for about 1¼ hours. At the end of half an hour remove
the paper, baste well, and continue to roast, turning the joint
over from time to time. Scald and peel the tomatoes. Cut out the
stalks, squeeze to remove the seeds, and cut each into 4 or 5
pieces. Have ready the demi-glace sauce. Take up the lamb,
take out the string or pins, set on a hot dish, carve a few slices,
and keep warm. Pour off the fat and rinse out the tin with a little
stock. Strain into the demi-glace, add the tomatoes, and boil up
well. Spoon a little over the meat and serve the rest separately.

Leg of Lamb Duxelles

1 small leg of lamb, about 3 lb.; garlic, butter, and white wine
for roasting; grated Parmesan cheese; watercress to garnish.

DUXELLES FILLING: ½–¾ lb. mushrooms; 1 oz. butter; thyme
and parsley; 2 shallots, finely chopped; 3 tablespoons white
breadcrumbs.

Rub the leg well with butter, stick it with slivers of garlic, wrap in paper, set in a roasting-tin, and pour round a glass of the wine. Roast in a moderately hot oven allowing 15 to 20 minutes to the pound. When half cooked, remove the paper and baste frequently until done. Remove, cool slightly, then take up and strain the juice from the pan, removing any excess fat. De-glaze the pan with a little extra wine and good stock, season, strain, and add to the juice. Thicken with a little kneaded butter or slaked arrow-root. Set aside.

While the lamb is roasting prepare the filling. Wash and chop the mushrooms finely. Melt the butter, add the shallots, and after a minute the mushrooms with a tablespoon each of chopped thyme and parsley. Cook briskly 5 to 6 minutes, draw aside, and add the crumbs and seasoning. Slice the lamb carefully and insert the filling between each slice. Reshape. Replace the leg in the roasting-tin, work 1 to 2 oz. of cheese with the same amount of butter, and spread over the surface of the meat. Ten minutes before serving put into a very hot oven to brown and to heat well through. Dish on a hot dish with a little of the gravy round and the rest served separately. Garnish with watercress. Small roast potatoes or boulangère potatoes may accompany, as may a green salad.

Lamb Cutlets Doria

1½–2 lb. best end neck of lamb chined; seasoned flour; beaten egg; dry white crumbs; approximately 1 gill oil and 1 oz. butter for frying; 1 large cucumber; 12–18 spring onions according to size; ¾ oz. butter; a little chopped mint.

TO ACCOMPANY: a brown or mousseline sauce (see pages 373 and 377.)

Divide the neck into cutlets and trim. Flour, egg, and crumb them and set aside.

Peel the cucumber, split into four lengthways, then cut across in 2-inch lengths. Trim the onions, leaving on about 2 inches of the green top. Blanch these with the cucumber in boiling water and drain well. Melt the butter in a shallow pan, add the onions and cucumber, season and cover. Simmer 5 to 7 minutes, shaking the pan occasionally. Directly the cucumber is cooked draw aside and add a little freshly chopped mint.

Fry the cutlets in the hot oil and butter, turning once only. Dish them *en couronne* and pile the cucumber in the centre. Hand the sauce separately.

Lamb Cutlets Périnette

2 lb. best end neck of lamb, chined; 4 tablespoons fresh white crumbs; 2 oz. ham; clarified or fresh butter for frying; beaten egg.

SALPICON: 1 lb. tomatoes; 2–3 caps tinned pimento or 1–2 fresh red peppers; 1 leek; 1 oz. butter; 1 teaspoon tomato purée; 1 teaspoon paprika.

Divide the meat into cutlets, trim and roll in seasoned flour. Chop the ham with the crumbs. Brush the cutlets with the egg and roll in the crumb mixture, pressing it well on.

Prepare the garnish. Peel and slice the tomatoes, shred the pimentos, or blanch if fresh peppers and set aside. Cut the white part of the leek into thin rounds and the green into shreds. Blanch the latter and set aside. Soften the white part of the leek in the butter, add the purée, paprika, tomatoes, and pimentos. Season well, cover the pan, and simmer 3 to 4 minutes.

Fry the cutlets until golden brown on both sides, or 6 to 7 minutes. To serve, arrange *en couronne* with the tomato salpicon in the centre. Scatter over the shredded leek before serving.

Cutlets Soubise

1½–2 lb. small best end of neck, chined only; 1 onion; 1 carrot; bouquet garni; 1 glass white wine; ½ glass stock.

SOUBISE: 3 large onions; 1 oz. butter; salt; pepper.

BÉCHAMEL: 1½ oz. butter; 1½ oz. flour; ½ pint flavoured milk; ½ gill cream.

TO FINISH: Fried onion rings (see vegetable chapter); potato purée.

Remove the chine bone and flap. Lay the neck in a shallow stew-pan, fat side downwards. Slice the onion and carrot and put round with the bouquet garni, wine, and stock. Cover tightly and simmer gently 40 to 50 minutes. Draw aside and keep hot.

In the meantime prepare the potato purée and slice the onions for the soubise. Blanch and drain very well. Return to the pan with the butter, press a piece of greaseproof paper right down on top of the onions, and cook slowly until tender but not brown. Sieve or put into a blender. Strain the juice from the lamb, keeping the meat in the pan. Measure ¼ pint and take off any fat. Make the Béchamel, add to it the lamb stock and onion purée, and boil up together. Adjust the seasoning and finish with the cream. Keep warm. Fry the onion rings and heat the potato purée. Take up the meat and slice into cutlets. Arrange a small quantity of the potato purée down the centre of the serving dish and set the cutlets on this; coat with the sauce and garnish with the onion rings.

Lamb Cutlets 'en cuirasse'

1½–2 lb. best end neck of lamb, chined only; ½ lb. puff pastry; 1 oz. butter; 1 shallot; 6 oz. mushrooms; 2 oz. cooked ham; 2 teaspoons tomato purée; chopped parsley.

Remove the chine bone from the meat, divide into cutlets and trim well. Pan-fry or grill the cutlets and allow to cool. Make the puff pastry. Next prepare the HACHIS:

Melt the butter, add the finely chopped shallot and cook slowly 2 to 3 minutes until soft but not coloured. Stir in the mushrooms, finely chopped, and continue cooking a further 3 minutes. Add the tomato purée, shredded ham, and parsley and turn on to a plate to cool.

Roll out the pastry and cut into pieces about the size of your hand, spread a spoonful of the *hachis* on each, put on a cutlet, and cover with another spoonful of the mushroom mixture. Fold over the pastry leaving a piece of bone showing; brush with beaten egg and cook in a hot oven 15 to 18 minutes (425° F. or Reg. 7). Serve with new potatoes and a sauce chasseur. The bones may be topped with a cutlet frill (which may be bought at a stationer's).

Noisettes Papillon

6 noisettes cut from a 2-lb. piece of best end; 1 glass sherry; fresh or clarified butter for sautéing; 6 large mushrooms; ¾ gill stock; 1 teaspoon tomato purée.

Marinade the noisettes in the sherry for 1 hour. In the meantime prepare and cook the potatoes and peel the mushrooms. Sauté the noisettes in the butter, take out and keep warm. Sauté the mushrooms 4 to 5 minutes, then arrange in the serving-dish and set a noisette on each. Add the stock and purée with any marinade that is left to the pan, season, and boil up well. Pour round the dish and garnish with potatoes or serve them separately.

Noisettes Milanese

2 lb. best end neck of lamb; chopped herbs; clarified butter for frying.

SPAGHETTI MILANESE: 5 oz. spaghetti; 2 oz. lean ham; 2 oz. mushrooms; 1½ gills strong tomato sauce (see page 378).

Prepare the noisettes from the neck, scattering the surface of the meat with the chopped herbs before rolling up. Set aside.

Poach the spaghetti in boiling, salted water. Slice the mushrooms and cook in a little butter. Shred the ham. Strain off the spaghetti, rinse with a little hot water, and drain well. Add the mushrooms and ham to the tomato sauce and bring to the boil. Reheat the spaghetti in ½ oz. butter and pour on the sauce. Cover and keep warm. Pan-fry the noisettes in the clarified butter for 7 to 8 minutes; arrange round a serving-dish and pile the spaghetti in the centre. A little gravy may be made from the juices in the pan to accompany the noisettes.

Noisettes Louisette

2 lb. best end neck of lamb; a little oil; 1 glass sherry and the same of stock.

SALPICON: 4 oz. lean ham; 1 cucumber; 1 oz. butter; 1 small onion; 1 dessertspoon chopped mint; 2 tablespoons thick cream.

Prepare the noisettes from the neck. Pan-fry them in the oil, drain off, and de-glaze the pan with the sherry and stock. Set aside.

Chop the onion finely and shred the ham. Peel the cucumber, cut into coarse julienne shreds, blanch, and drain thoroughly. Heat a sauté pan, put in the butter and onion. Cook gently 2 to 3 minutes, then add the cucumber, the shredded ham, mint, salt, and pepper. Shake up over the heat, then finish with the cream. Arrange the noisettes *en couronne* in a serving-dish and turn the salpicon into the centre. Reheat the gravy and spoon over the noisettes.

VEAL

Good veal should be a pale rosy pink in colour and needs little or no hanging to make it tender and palatable. An immature meat, it has little or no fat and so this is frequently introduced by barding, i.e. a piece of pork or bacon fat laid over the surface of the meat, or larding – 'sewing' – the meat with strips of the same fat. Joints or cuts of veal lend themselves best to a roast, pot-roast, or to a sauté. The meat is inclined to be dry, so must be kept well basted and have some rich and well-flavoured sauce or garnish as an accompaniment. Roast stuffed veal is a traditional English dish with its savoury stuffing and garnish of bacon. Cuts of veal are:

BREAST

Used for blanquettes or boned and stuffed as a galantine.

SHOULDER

The best cut is the oyster from the blade bone. For blanquettes, ragouts, and stuffed for a pot-roast or braise. Trimmings, as well as those from the leg, for 'pie' veal.

LOIN

As chops or, if not too big, boned, stuffed, and roasted.

LEG

The prime cut and contains the fillet, a small round and particularly tender piece which runs down the leg and which is used for 'grenadins', the equivalent of a tournedos in beef. It may also be roasted. Escalopes, ½-inch slices of meat about 3 to 4 inches by 2 to 3 inches are also taken from the leg. These are batted or flattened out by the butcher to as much as half again in size. If for any reason they have to be done at home, lay each one between two pieces of waxed or oiled greaseproof paper and beat well with a cutlet bat or the base of a heavy frying-pan. Escalopes can be cooked in a variety of ways.

KNUCKLE

Also from the leg (shin), this is valuable for blanquettes, ragouts, and stocks, being particularly gelatinous.

HEAD

See offal (page 250).

Roast Stuffed Veal

3 lb. oyster of veal; 3–4 tablespoons good dripping; 8 thin rashers of streaky bacon; stock for the gravy made from the bone.

FORCEMEAT: 1 small onion; 2 oz. butter; 4 oz. fresh breadcrumbs; grated rind of ½ a lemon; 1 tablespoon chopped parsley; 1 dessertspoon chopped thyme or marjoram; a little beaten egg to bind; salt and pepper.

Bone out the meat; season the cut surface. Chop the onion finely and soften in the butter without browning. Mix with the crumbs, lemon rind, and herbs. Moisten with beaten egg and season well. Spread over the meat, roll up, tie securely, or fasten with poultry pins. Heat the dripping in the tin in the oven, preheated and set at 400° F. or Reg. 6. Put in the meat, baste, return the tin to the oven, and roast for about 1½ hours, basting frequently. Remove the rind and rust from the rashers, spread each one out under the blade of a knife, then roll up and thread on to a skewer, or if preferred cut each rasher in half and leave unrolled. The rolls should be baked 10 minutes before the meat is ready until brown and crisp, or the bacon may be grilled if left as rashers.

Dish the meat, removing the string, surround with the bacon, and keep warm. Strain off the dripping leaving 1 to 2 tablespoons with the sediment in the tin. Dust with the flour, cook for a minute, then pour in a cup of stock. Boil well, season, strain into the sauce boat.

Blanquette of Veal

2 lb. breast of veal; 2 onions; 2 carrots; a large bouquet garni.

FOR THE SAUCE: $1\frac{1}{2}$ oz. butter; $1\frac{1}{2}$ oz. flour; $\frac{1}{4}$ pint single cream or creamy milk; 1–2 egg yolks; a squeeze of lemon juice.

Cut up the veal into nice-sized pieces. Soak in plenty of cold salted water overnight to whiten the meat. Drain and put into a large pan with cold water to cover, add a slice of lemon and salt. Bring to the boil, drain, and refresh. Return to the pan, barely cover with cold water, bring slowly to the boil, skim well, add a little salt and the bouquet. Simmer for about 45 minutes. Quarter the vegetables and add, first removing the slice of lemon. Continue to simmer until the meat is very tender. Strain off the liquor but keep the meat and vegetables covered in the pan.

Prepare the sauce; melt the butter, stir in the flour, and cook for a minute or two until a pale straw colour. Draw aside. Measure 1 pint of the veal stock, pour this into the roux, blend and return to the heat. Stir until boiling and cook rapidly for 3 to 4 minutes. Add half the milk and adjust the seasoning. Cream the yolks with the remainder and add as for a liaison. Finish with a squeeze of lemon. Take out the bouquet and pour the sauce over the meat and vegetables. Gently shake the pan to mix them together, leave for 5 minutes on the side of the stove, reheat if necessary, and turn into the serving-dish. Serve accompanied by boiled rice or a purée of potatoes.

Ragoût of Veal Créole

$1\frac{1}{2}$–2 lb. tender veal from shoulder or leg; 2 tablespoons oil;

1 tablespoon butter; 2 small onions; 1 clove garlic; 3 rashers bacon or a 3–4 oz. piece; 1 dessertspoon flour; 1 teaspoon tomato purée; ½ pint good stock; 1 glass white wine; a bouquet garni.

PILAFF: 4 oz. long-grained rice; 4 oz. mushrooms; 4 tomatoes; 1 large green pepper; 1 oz. butter.

Cut the veal into 1½-inch cubes. Slice the onions, chop the garlic, cut the bacon into lardons, and blanch. Brown the veal in the hot oil and butter, lower the heat, and add the onions, garlic, and bacon. Continue to cook until all are nicely coloured, shaking and stirring occasionally. Dust in the flour, mix and add the purée, stock, wine, and bouquet. Bring slowly to the boil, cover, and cook gently on the stove-top or in the oven (340°F. or Reg. 3 to 4) for 50 minutes to 1 hour or until tender.

In the meantime, prepare the pilaff. Boil, refresh, and dry the rice. Slice the mushrooms; peel, seed, and shred the tomatoes; seed and shred the pepper. Melt the butter in a sauté pan, add the mushrooms, and cook 3 to 4 minutes; then add the tomatoes and pepper and continue to cook for a further 4 minutes. Season well and add the rice. Fork up well together until thoroughly hot. Draw aside.

Dish the veal at one end of the serving-dish, reduce the gravy if necessary, and spoon over the veal. Pile the rice at the other end of the dish. When peppers are not available take 2 to 3 tablespoons cooked green peas.

Veal Forestière

2–2½ lb. veal cut from the leg or shoulder; 1 oz. butter, preferably clarified; 1 small onion; 4–6 oz. small chipolata or cocktail sausages; 4–6 oz. slice of unsmoked bacon; 1 glass white wine; 1 large bouquet of herbs; 4–6 oz. button mushrooms; 1 wineglass good stock; kneaded butter made with 1 dessertspoon each butter and flour.

Tie up the veal to make a neat joint (or the butcher may do this for you) and brown all over in the butter. Take out. Chop the onion finely, remove the rind from the bacon, cut into lardons, and blanch. Add the onion, bacon, and sausages to the pan and allow

to brown. Take out the sausages and replace the veal together with
the wine and herbs. Cover the pan tightly and simmer about 1
hour. Add the mushrooms and sausages and continue to cook for
a further 7 minutes. Take up the veal, slice and arrange it in the
serving-dish. Keep warm, add the stock to the pan (first removing
the herbs), and thicken with the kneaded butter. Boil up well and
spoon over the dish. Garnish the dish with glazed onions (see
page 353) if wished.

Fricandeau of Veal à l'Oseille

2½–3 lb. veal cut in a long tapering piece from the shoulder or leg;
larding bacon; 2–3 rashers streaky fat bacon; 2 large carrots
and 2 large onions; 1 wineglass white wine; ¾ pint stock; a bouquet
garni.

Trim and tie the meat to make a neat joint, and lard it. Spread the
rashers on the bottom of a large stewpan. Cut the vegetables in
rounds and place on the bacon. Cover and sweat 6 to 7 minutes.
Set the veal on top and add the wine, stock, and bouquet. Bring to
the boil and braise in the oven at 330° F. or Reg. 3 for about 2
hours, basting from time to time. Take up the veal, strain the
gravy, skim if necessary, and return to the pan with the veal. Put
back uncovered into the oven, raise the heat to 360° F. or Reg. 4,
and continue to cook, basting frequently, until brown and well
glazed.

In the meantime prepare the purée of sorrel.

PURÉE OF SORREL: 2 lb. sorrel; ½ oz. butter; scant ½ oz. flour;
1 teacup thick Béchamel; ½ cup cream; 1 small egg; salt and
pepper.

Wash and blanch the sorrel for 10 minutes. Drain, press, and rub
through a sieve. Make a brown roux with the butter and flour.
Lay the sorrel on this (do *not* mix) and leave for 20 minutes, then
mix well and beat in the Béchamel and egg. Stir over moderate
fire and use when a thick cream. If sorrel is unobtainable, spinach
may be substituted.

Take up the veal and slice. Spoon the sorrel down the serving-

234

dish and arrange the veal on top. Reduce the gravy if necessary and spoon a little over the dish. Serve the rest separately.

Veal Orloff

2½–3 lb. fillet or leg of veal; 1–2 oz. butter; 1 glass white wine; ¼ pint stock; root vegetables for braising; ¼ lb. button mushrooms, sliced and cooked; 1½ gills Mornay sauce (see page 369); 2 large onions, chopped, softened in butter, and sieved.

SOUBISE: 2 large onions; 3 oz. thick-grained rice; ¾ oz. butter; a good ¼ pint stock; 1 egg yolk; 1 tablespoon cream.

Tie up the veal neatly. Brown all over in butter, then braise with the wine, stock, and vegetables to flavour. Allow about 1 to 1½ hours to cook.

In the meantime prepare the Soubise. Chop the onions, soften them in the butter, add the rice, flavouring, and stock. Bring to the boil, cover, and cook in the oven until very soft. Sieve or beat thoroughly to form a purée. Add the yolk and cream.

Take up the veal, make the gravy, and set aside. Slice the meat, spread each slice with the purée and the cooked mushrooms. Reshape on the serving-dish.

Prepare the Mornay sauce and add the puréed onions to it. Coat this over the veal and brown in a quick oven 12 to 15 minutes. Serve the gravy separately with new potatoes and sautéed cucumber.

Sauté of Veal Martini

1½–2 lb. shoulder of veal; 2 oz. butter; 4 onions; 1 oz. flour; 1 glass white wine; ½ gill dry vermouth; 1 pint veal stock; seasoning; bouquet garni; ½ lb. mushrooms; 1 egg yolk; 1 teaspoon lemon juice; ¼ pint cream; 6 oz. boiled rice; 1½ oz. butter; 1½ oz. grated Parmesan cheese.

Slice the onions thinly. Cut the meat into 1½-inch cubes, brown in the butter, then add the onions and allow them to take colour. Stir in the flour and after a minute or two the white wine and vermouth. Pour on enough of the stock barely to cover, season, and add the bouquet. Cover and simmer 40 minutes. Slice the mushrooms, add to the sauté, and cook for a further 10 minutes or until the veal is tender. Work the yolk and cream together and add to the sauté off the fire as for a liaison. Draw aside. Melt the butter in a sauté pan, put in the rice, and toss up on brisk heat. When thoroughly hot stir in the cheese with a fork. Dish the sauté and rice together or separately.

Sauté of Veal Marengo

2 lb. oyster or fillet of veal; 4–5 tablespoons oil; 1 large onion; 1 tablespoon flour; 1½ glasses white wine; scant pint good stock; 1 lb. tomatoes or ½ pint fresh tomato purée; 1 clove garlic; 6 oz. mushrooms; bouquet garni; 6 croûtes of bread; chopped parsley.

Cut the meat into large cubes, heat the oil in a sauté pan, and colour the meat on all sides. Drain off all but 1 tablespoon of the oil, add the onion, dust with the flour, and cook slowly 5 to 6 minutes until golden. Add the wine and stock and stir until boiling. Reduce the heat and add the garlic, crushed with salt, the herbs, and tomatoes. If using fresh tomatoes, wipe, cut in half, and squeeze away the seeds. Cover the pan and cook gently on top of the stove or in the oven for about 45 minutes. In the meantime, prepare the mushrooms and croûtes. Wash the mushrooms in salted water and dry well. Do not peel. Cut in halves or quarters depending on size. Cut triangular croûtes and fry golden brown in hot oil. Remove the meat from the pan with a draining-spoon and reduce the liquid to about ¾ pint, then strain. Replace the meat and add the mushrooms and sauce. Cover and simmer very gently for 15 minutes. Serve surrounded with the croûtes and dust with chopped parsley.

Veal Chops Singalese

5 veal chops; 2 oz. butter, fresh or clarified; 1 shallot; 1 level teaspoon curry powder and the same of paprika; 1 level dessert-spoon flour; 1½ gills jellied stock, veal or chicken; ½ gill thick cream; salt and pepper.

GARNISH: ½ lb. spring onions, well trimmed but leaving 1–2 inches of the green stalk on the bulb; 1 oz. butter.

Sauté the chops in the butter until golden brown, take out, and keep warm. Lower the heat, add the chopped shallot and spices to the pan, and after 1 minute stir in the flour. Draw aside, add the stock, stir until boiling, season, and replace the chops. Cover, simmer on top of the stove, or place the pan in a moderate oven for 15 to 20 minutes.

In the meantime, prepare the garnish. Blanch the onions in boiling water for 3 minutes. Drain and sauté gently in a covered pan in the butter for 6 to 7 minutes. Dish the chops and keep warm. Reduce the sauce a little and add the cream. Boil up well and strain over the dish. Either scatter the onions over the chops or put a small bunch on each.

Veal Chops Bonne Femme

4–5 veal chops; 1½ oz. butter; 4 oz. gammon rasher; 12–18 button or pickling onions; 4 oz. button mushrooms; 1 tablespoon flour; 1 glass white wine (optional); ¾ pint stock; a bouquet garni; 3 small potatoes or 6–8 baby new potatoes; chopped parsley.

Trim the chops, brown in the butter in a shallow stewpan, draw aside, and take out. Cut the gammon into lardons, blanch with the onions, and drain. Quarter the mushrooms and add to the pan with the bacon and onions. Sauté until turning colour, stir in the flour, add the wine and stock, and bring to the boil. Season, replace the chops with the bouquet. Cover and simmer on the stove-top or in the oven (350° F. or Reg. 4) for 20 minutes.

In the meantime, quarter the potatoes lengthways or, if new, leave whole. Trim away the sharp edges of the quarters, blanch, and add to the pan. Continue to cook for a further 20 minutes or until both meat and potatoes are tender. Dish and sprinkle with chopped parsley.

Ossi Buchi

If possible go to a Continental butcher to get the 'ossi buchi' properly cut. They are round slices of veal, about 1 inch thick, taken from the knuckle, and have the bone in the centre.

5 ossi buchi (about 2–2½ lb.); 2–3 tablespoons olive oil; 1 large onion; 1 carrot; 2 cloves garlic; 1 level tablespoon flour; ¾ lb. ripe tomatoes, concasséd, or 1 small tin tomatoes; 1 heaped teaspoon tomato purée; 1 glass white wine; 1½ gills good stock; a bouquet garni.

Brown the ossi buchi in hot oil in a large stewpan or iron casserole. Draw aside and take them out. Slice the onion and carrot and chop the garlic; add to the pan, cover and sweat 4 to 5 minutes, then stir in the flour, add the tomatoes, purée, wine, and stock. Season and bring to the boil. Replace the veal, add the bouquet, cover and cook slowly for about 1½ hours on the stovetop or in the oven. Take up carefully, dish the ossi buchi, strain the sauce, and reduce if necessary. The sauce should be rich, red, and full of flavour and just enough to coat the ossi buchi. Serve with rice or pasta. If wished all stock may be used in place of the wine.

Escalopes à l'Orange

5 escalopes; 2 oz. fresh butter; 1 dessertspoon flour; 2 good oranges; 1 tablespoon brandy or a small glass of sherry; 1 gill good stock; salt; pepper; chopped parsley or snipped chives in season.

Sauté the escalopes in the butter until nicely brown. Take them out and draw the pan aside. Stir in the flour. Grate the rind of 1 orange into the pan, add the strained juice, the brandy, and stock. Bring to the boil, season well, replace the escalopes, cover, and simmer for 10 minutes.

In the meantime, slice the peel and pith from the second orange and cut the flesh into rounds, one for each escalope. Warm between two plates. Dish the escalopes, set an orange-round on each, and spoon over the sauce. Sprinkle with parsley.

Escalopes à la Crème

5 escalopes; 1 shallot or a small onion; 4 oz. white button mushrooms; 1 oz. fresh butter; 1½ wineglasses white wine; 1 glass stock; kneaded butter; ½ gill thick cream; tarragon leaves or chopped tarragon.

Chop the shallot finely and slice the mushrooms. Heat the sauté pan, drop in the butter, and, when it is foaming, put in the escalopes. Sauté briskly 3 to 4 minutes on each side, take out, add the shallot and mushrooms, sauté a few minutes then add the wine. Reduce a little, replace the escalopes, pour on the stock, and add salt and pepper. Bring to the boil and cover the pan. Simmer 6 to 7 minutes. Draw aside, add about a tablespoon of the kneaded butter in small pieces, shaking the pan to introduce it easily into the sauce. Reboil and add the cream. Adjust the seasoning and cook for a minute or two. Dish the escalopes, boil up the sauce well, and spoon over the dish.

Wiener Schnitzel

5 thin escalopes measuring about 5 inches by 3; seasoned flour; 1 beaten egg, seasoned and with a few drops of oil added; dry white crumbs; clarified butter for frying or a mixture of oil and butter.

For each escalope a thin slice of lemon and ½ teaspoon capers; a slice of gherkin cut lengthwise; a squeeze of lemon juice; chopped parsley.

Roll the escalopes in flour, shake, brush with egg, and roll and press in the crumbs. Heat the butter in a large frying-pan, lay in the escalopes, and fry over a moderate to slow fire for about 7 to 10 minutes, turning once only. At the end of this time they should be a deep golden brown. Serve at once on a hot, flat dish and garnish the middle of each 'schnitzel' with a slice of lemon and the capers and gherkin on top of the lemon. Add a squeeze of lemon to the butter remaining in the pan and strain over the dish. Dust with chopped parsley and serve immediately.

Escalopes Italienne

5 thin escalopes; 1½ oz. butter; 1 small onion; 1 glass Marsala or sherry; 1 dessertspoon flour; 1½ gills veal stock; ½ teaspoon tomato purée; a bayleaf; salt and pepper.

GARNISH: 2 lb. spinach; butter; 1–2 tablespoons thick cream;

½ lb. ripe tomatoes; 1 clove garlic; 5 slices Mozarella or Gruyère cheese.

Chop the onion finely. Brown the escalopes in the butter, adding the onion just before they are ready. Flame with the Marsala. Take out the escalopes, stir in the flour, stock, and purée, bring to the boil, add the bayleaf, and season. Replace the veal, cover and simmer 10 to 12 minutes. In the meantime cook and purée the spinach, put an ounce of butter in the pan, and when a noisette add the spinach and dry off thoroughly. Finish with the cream. Season. Scald the tomatoes and slice them. Crush the garlic with salt. Sauté for a minute only in a dessertspoon of butter (i.e., 'pass' through the butter). Set the spinach down the centre of the serving dish, arrange the escalopes free from sauce on the spinach, and cover with the tomatoes. Lay the cheese on top and brown under the grill. Boil up the sauce, strain, pour a little round the dish, and serve the rest separately.

MISCELLANEOUS VEAL DISHES

Veal and Ham Pie

8 oz. flaky pastry.
1½ lb. shoulder of veal or pie veal; 4 oz. lean ham or gammon rasher; 3 hard-boiled eggs; 1 dessertspoon each finely chopped onion and parsley; a little grated lemon rind; salt and pepper; good jellied stock.

Cut the veal in pieces 1 to 1½ inches square and the ham into strips. (If gammon is used remove the rind and rust, cut into strips, and blanch.) Arrange the meat, ham, quartered eggs, onion, and parsley, etc., in layers till the pie dish is filled, doming the top slightly. Pour in enough stock to fill the dish three-parts full. Roll out the pastry, cover the dish, decorate, and cook as for Beefsteak Pie (see page 204).

Veal Cream with Tomatoes

¾ lb. finely minced raw veal.

PANADE: 1½ oz. each butter and flour; 1½ gills water; 2 eggs; ½ gill cream.

FILLING: 1 oz. butter; 1 shallot; 2 oz. mushrooms; 1 level dessert-spoon flour; ½–¾ gill stock; 2 oz. ham.

VELOUTÉ SAUCE: 1¼ oz. butter; 1 oz. flour; good pint veal stock; ½ gill cream; 4 tomatoes, concasséd; 1 teaspoon chopped parsley.

First prepare the panade. Melt the butter, blend in the flour and the water, and bring to the boil. Turn on to a plate to cool.

Prepare the filling. Chop the shallot and slice the mushrooms. Melt the butter, add the shallot and mushrooms, cook gently 5 to 6 minutes, stir in the flour and stock, and bring to the boil. Draw aside, add the shredded ham, and allow to cool. Beat the panade into the veal, season well, adding a pinch of ground mace. Work in the eggs and finish with the cream. Turn into a well-buttered plain mould, make a hollow in the centre with a wet spoon, and put in the filling. Cover with buttered paper and poach or steam the cream for about 45 minutes.

In the meantime, prepare the velouté sauce, finishing with the cream, concasséd tomatoes, and parsley. To dish, turn out the cream and coat with the sauce. If preferred, the cream may be left unfilled and a mushroom sauce made in place of the velouté and tomato.

Fricadelles

1 lb. finely minced veal; 2 oz. minced pork fat; 1 small onion; 1 teaspoon chopped thyme; 5 oz. stale white bread with the crust removed; milk; about ¼ pint cold water.

TOMATO SAUCE (see page 378): 2–3 tablespoons sour cream or yoghourt; 8–10 black olives; 1 lemon.

Soak the bread in enough milk to cover well for half an hour. Squeeze dry in a piece of muslin, crumble into a bowl. Chop the onion very finely and add with the veal, fat, and thyme. Season and work thoroughly together (kneading as for bread), adding the water by degrees. Season very well with salt, pepper, and paprika.

Shape into small balls about the size of a marble, roll lightly in flour, and fry quickly in the oil or butter until brown. Lay in a deep fireproof dish and spoon over the tomato sauce, which should just cover. Cook gently in the oven for 15 to 20 minutes. Stone the olives and cut the lemon into eight pieces. Add the sour cream to the sauce, shaking the dish gently to mix it in without breaking the fricadelles. Serve in the dish and garnish with the olives and lemon quarters.

PORK

Good pork has pale pink flesh with a fair proportion of very white fat and no smell.

All pork must be thoroughly cooked and, as it is not the most digestible of meats, it should not be given to children or invalids.

The traditional accompaniments to roast pork are herb force-meat balls, or stuffing, and apple sauce with roast potatoes and creamed cabbage. The cuts of pork are:

LOIN

For roasting or pot-roasting and for chops. Loin should have the skin or 'crackling' which is, however, frequently removed before selling in order to cut away some of the fat. For roasting the crackling should be scored, i.e. marked in strips with a sharp knife (this is done by the butcher). When roasted this becomes golden brown and crisp and so makes a good contrast to the rich meat. To crispen the crackling, spoon over 1 to 2 tablespoons of boiling water 5 minutes before dishing. Loin should also be chined to make carving easier and can be stuffed by slitting the meat at 1½-inch intervals and pressing forcemeat down each cut. If the joint is not stuffed, the forcemeat may be formed into small balls, egged, crumbed, and fried.

FILLET

This is the leanest cut of pork, having no fat whatsoever, and is the strip of meat that lies under the loin. Each fillet weighs 8 to 12 oz. and may be cooked in several ways. Roasted, they are first slit, stuffed, wrapped in bacon, and well basted with a little good dripping. The oven should be hot (400° F. or Reg. 6) and the roasting time 45 minutes. Slice the fillets diagonally before serving with a lightly thickened gravy.

LEG OR HALF LEG OR JOINTS CUT FROM THE LEG

For roasting, see the notes about crackling under Loin. Ample time should be allowed for cooking (see the temperature and time chart for roasting, page 193).

SPARE-RIB AND CUTS FROM THE SHOULDER

These make good small roasting joints, and may also be pot-roasted. Serve as for roast pork.

*

Roast Spare Rib of Pork

2–2½ lb. spare rib of pork; good dripping; stock for gravy.

ACCOMPANIMENTS: apple sauce (see page 379); roast potatoes (see page 357).

FORCEMEAT BALLS: 1 oz. butter; 1 shallot or small onion; 4 oz. bread crumbs (1 teacupful); 1 tablespoon chopped parsley; 1 dessertspoon fresh or dried chopped sage; beaten egg or milk to bind the forcemeat; salt and pepper; seasoned flour; beaten egg; dried white crumbs.

Put 3 to 4 tablespoons of dripping into a roasting tin. Set in a pre-heated oven (400° F. or Reg. 6) for 5 minutes. Remove, put in the pork, baste, and return to the oven. Roast for about 1¼ hours, basting frequently.

In the meantime, prepare the stuffing. Melt the butter in a small saucepan, add the onion finely chopped, cover and cook slowly until soft but not coloured. Mix with the breadcrumbs,

herbs, and seasonings and add enough egg or milk to bind. Shape
into small balls, roll in the flour, then egg and crumb. Fry in deep
fat until golden brown.

Dish the pork, pour off the fat, dust in a little flour, brown
lightly, and add enough stock to make a thickened gravy. Season
well, strain the gravy into a sauce-boat, and arrange the forcemeat balls round the pork.

Grilled Pork Chops, Barbecue Sauce
4–5 loin chops; a little oil; watercress to garnish.

BARBECUE SAUCE: 1 teaspoon flour; 1 teacup meat or potato
stock; 1 tablespoon Soy sauce; 2 tomatoes, concasséd; a dash of
Worcester sauce; seasoning.

Trim the chops, removing any surplus fat and brush the surface
with oil. Heat the grill thoroughly. Grill the chops 5 to 7 minutes
on each side, brushing the meat from time to time with oil to
keep it moist. Leave the chops on the grid to keep warm while
preparing the sauce.

Skim the fat from the grill pan, turning the last dessertspoonful
or so with any sediment into a small saucepan, scraping out the
griller pan well. Stir in the flour and cook very gently for 1 or 2
minutes. Remove from the heat and blend in the potato stock,
sauces, and seasoning. Return to the fire, stir until boiling, then
add the tomatoes. Simmer 1 minute. Spoon a little over the
bottom of the serving-dish, arrange the chops down the centre,
and garnish with 'bouquets' of watercress. Hand the remaining
sauce separately.

Loin of Pork with Prunes
2 lb. loin of pork with the crackling; butter and two tablespoons of
orange juice for roasting; a sprig of rosemary; 12–18 good prunes
soaked in red wine barely to cover; blanched almonds; anchovy
fillets.

GRAVY: 1 glass white wine; ¼ pint jellied stock; kneaded butter.

Rub the pork well with butter. Set to roast with the orange

juice and rosemary in a hot oven (400° F. or Reg. 6) for about
1 to 1½ hours. Cover first with paper, and when the fat begins to
run remove it and baste frequently until brown and crisp.

In the meantime simmer the prunes until tender in the wine
until it has evaporated. Take out and stone and stuff each prune
with an almond round which an anchovy fillet has been rolled.
Arrange the prunes on a buttered fireproof plate and cover with
thickly buttered paper or foil. Ten minutes before serving place
in the oven to heat. Dish the pork; pour off the fat from the tin,
add the wine and stock. Reduce a little, season and thicken with
kneaded butter, and reboil. Strain into a gravy boat, first spooning
a little round the pork. Garnish with the prunes and serve very hot.

If there is no crackling on the pork some of the prunes may be
inserted into the meat before roasting. To do this make a split
in the thick part of the meat from the underside and insert the
prune. Fasten the joint with poultry pins and roll first in seasoned
flour and then in beaten egg and browned crumbs. Heat dripping
in the tin and baste the joint before putting in the oven.

Loin of Pork Alsacienne

2½ lb. loin of pork; dripping; 1 onion stuck with a clove; pared
rind and juice of ½ lemon; 1 wineglass cider; ½ gill cream;
arrowroot.

CABBAGE: 1 small drum-head cabbage or 1 tin sauerkraut, or 1 lb.
if bought loose; 1 oz. butter; 1 onion; 4 dessert apples; 1 lemon;
2 hard-boiled eggs; chopped parsley.

Brown the pork all over in hot dripping. Pour off any surplus fat
and add the onion, rind and juice of the lemon, and the cider.
Add salt and pepper. Cover and simmer gently until the pork is
well cooked – about 1¼ hours.

In the meantime prepare the cabbage. Shred it finely and
blanch; drain well. Melt the butter in a stewpan, add the onion,
cover and cook for a few minutes; draw aside. Peel and quarter the
apples, cut away the peel and pith from the lemon, and cut the
flesh into segments. Arrange the apple quarters rounded side
downwards on the bottom of the pan with the onions. Put the

cabbage on top with the lemon and plenty of salt and pepper. Cover with a thickly buttered paper and the lid and cook gently until tender – about 45 to 50 minutes.

Take up the pork, strain the gravy, and skim. Thicken with a level teaspoon of arrowroot and add the cream. Boil up. Slice the pork, arrange on a serving-dish and spoon over the gravy. Turn out the cabbage on to a hot dish, scatter the top thickly with chopped parsley and garnish with quarters of hard-boiled egg.

Pain de Porc Farci

3–4 fillets according to size; 1 glass white wine; 2 oz. butter for roasting; ¼ pint jellied stock; 1 glass sherry for the gravy; 2 Cox's apples.

FARCE: 6 oz. minced veal or pork; ½ lb. sausage meat; 4 oz. liver; 4 oz. cooked ham; 2–3 tablespoons fresh breadcrumbs; 1 tablespoon chopped herbs and parsley; grated rind and juice of ½ lemon; 1 beaten egg.

Split the pork fillets two-thirds of the way through lengthways and beat them flat between two pieces of oiled paper; a cutlet bat is best to use for this. Alternatively the bottom of a heavy frying-pan makes a good substitute.

Prepare the farce. Mince the liver and ham and combine with the other ingredients; season well. Layer this farce between the pork fillets, shaping them to form a loaf. Sew up round the sides with a trussing needle and fine string, or fasten with poultry pins. Spread over the butter and add the wine. Roast in a hot oven for about 1 to 1¼ hours, basting frequently (400° F. or Reg. 6). When well browned, take up, remove the trussing strings, and set on a hot serving-dish. Make a gravy from the juices in a pan using the stock and sherry. Spoon a little over and round the pork and garnish the dish with fried apple rings. Serve with spinach à la crème (see page 362).

Pork Fillets Sauté Hongroise

2–3 pork fillets, according to size; 1 oz. clarified butter; 2 shallots; 1 level dessertspoon paprika; 1 level dessertspoon flour; 1 glass sherry; ¼ pint jellied stock; 1 tin 'champignons de Paris' or 2–3 oz. button mushrooms; ½ gill cream.

Chop the shallots, cut the fillets into nice-sized pieces. Sauté quickly in the butter, add the shallots and paprika, and cook slowly for 2 to 3 minutes. Stir in the flour, add the sherry and stock, and bring to the boil. Simmer gently 30 to 40 minutes. Add the 'champignons' drained from the liquor, or, if fresh, sauté in butter for 3 to 4 minutes. Pour in the cream, adjust the seasoning, and serve with boiled rice or a purée of potatoes.

BACON AND HAMS

Bacon and hams are sold smoked or unsmoked, the latter known as 'green'.

The best cuts for boiling bacon as small joints are:

SLIPPER

Weighs about 1½ lb. and is lean.

PRIME COLLAR

The whole cut is about 6 lb., but pieces can be cut from it. A mixture of fat and lean.

GAMMON HOCK

This cut weighs from 3½ to 4½ lb. and is sold boned and rolled. It is therefore best eaten cold rather than hot. A mixture of fat and lean.

CORNER GAMMON

About 4 lb. in weight and a very lean cut.

MIDDLE GAMMON

One of the best cuts and weighs 4½ to 5 lb. Lean. For a larger joint, use a half or a whole gammon.

TO PREPARE

Soak small joints in cold water to cover for 1 hour, and larger pieces for 4 to 5 hours. Whole gammon or ham is best soaked overnight.

After soaking, put the joint into fresh cold water, to cover, with an onion and carrot and a large bouquet garni. Simmer for the given time and, if eating it cold, cool completely in the liquid before taking out and skinning. Roll the fat in browned crumbs before serving. You can if you like hand a Madeira sauce separately. If the joint is sliced before serving, coat the slices with the sauce.

Bacon may also be finished by baking as follows: three-parts boil the bacon until the skin can be easily stripped off, then drain and cover the skinned surface with this mixture:

4–5 tablespoons Demerara sugar; the grated rind and juice of 1 orange; a good pinch of ground mace.

Stud with cloves and baste with ½ pint cider. Bake in a moderate oven until the sugar is brown and crisp, basting occasionally. Time to allow – 40 minutes to 1 hour, according to size.

Times for cooking and boiling

For pieces under 1 lb., allow	45 minutes.
For pieces between 1 to 2 lb., allow	1 to 1½ hours.
For pieces over 3lb., allow	30 minutes to the lb.

OFFAL

All meat in this category should be eaten as fresh as possible, and in certain instances it is well soaked and blanched before cooking to whiten and take away any strong flavour.

KIDNEYS

Lambs' Kidneys

These may be grilled or sautéd, and are skinned before cooking. For grilling, split open and thread a skewer through them to keep flat. Be careful not to overcook as they become hard and dry.

Veal Kidneys

Used principally for a sauté or ragout, in which case they are cut across into thick slices after skinning; or they may be braised whole.

Pigs' Kidneys

These are rather strong in flavour and so may be soaked for an hour or two before cooking. They can be grilled but are more suitable for a sauté or ragout.

Ox Kidney

Used with steak for a pie or pudding or as a stew. As the kidney is also strong in flavour, it may be soaked before stewing.

LIVER

Calf's Liver

This is considered the best in flavour and texture and is also the most expensive.

Lamb's Liver

This is a little stronger in flavour but is very good if really fresh.

Both these livers may be sliced and fried but avoid over-cooking as, like kidneys, the meat will be hard and dry. When fried the slices should be a delicate pink inside. Liver can also be braised as a piece.

Pig's Liver

Rather strong in flavour but particularly suitable for pâtés and terrines.

Ox Liver

This is a cheap and rather coarse cut and strong in flavour. It is best stewed.

SWEETBREADS

These are the pancreas and thymus glands, the former being the largest. Calves' sweetbreads are the finest and may be cooked in a variety of ways. A pair, or two pieces, should be allowed per person. Nowadays sweetbreads are sold by weight, 3 or 4 pieces to the lb. Lambs' sweetbreads are delicate in flavour; treat and cook as for calves'. Being smaller they are especially suitable for vol-au-vents and bouchées, as are the sweetbreads of the thymus gland. Sweetbreads must be soaked and blanched before cooking.

BRAINS

Brains are sold by the set and may be either calf's or lamb's. It is essential that they should be very fresh and they are best cooked immediately they are bought. Allow two sets of calves' brains for 3 people and 1 set of lamb's per person. Brains are best served simply *au beurre noir*, or crumbed and fried in butter. Like sweetbreads they must be soaked and blanched before cooking.

HEARTS

Lambs' hearts are the best and the most tender. They should be stuffed and braised very slowly until quite soft.

HEAD

Calf's head is an excellent dish, especially when eaten cold, *à la vinaigrette*. Hot, it may be boiled and served with a sauce verte (see page 376) or braised with a good brown gravy. The meat is tender and gelatinous. A half head, according to size, is usually enough for four and should contain a portion of the tongue. Pig's head is used for brawn, half again being enough for 4 to 6 people.

FEET

Calf's feet give a strong, gelatinous stock and are especially useful when making aspics and consommés. A stock made from them forms the base of the lemon jelly known as Calf's Foot Jelly. Trotters, or pig's feet, are also gelatinous and may be cooked with the head for brawn. As a dish they can be first boiled, then boned, stuffed, and grilled with a mustard sauce.

OXTAIL

Excellent as a stew and for soups. These are bought ready cut into pieces. Choose one that has an equal proportion of meat and bone. A medium-sized tail is usually enough for four.

TONGUES

Ox Tongues

These range from $3\frac{1}{2}$ to 6 lb. in weight and are usually salted. They should be simmered until very tender when they are skinned and pressed for eating cold (see page 308). Special tongue presses (also for brawn) can be bought. Tongue is also served hot with an appropriate sauce such as Madeira or raisin. To carve, cut downwards in $\frac{1}{4}$-inch slices, starting at the tip. When cold, the tongue is sliced thinly across the top of the round.

Calves' Tongues

These are specially good, being very delicate in both flavour and texture. They can be salted and served cold or hot as for ox tongues, or unsalted, braised, and served with various sauces and garnishes. The weight ranges from $\frac{3}{4}$ lb. to $1\frac{1}{2}$ lb. Two of medium size will serve 3 people.

Lambs' Tongues

These are much smaller, about 6 to 8 oz. each, and one is allowed per person. They are cooked and skinned as for the other tongues, and when fresh are usually braised. Salted, they can be pressed after cooking and eaten cold.

TRIPE

Tripe is the lining of an ox's stomach. It is nearly always sold 'dressed', i.e. ready blanched and half-cooked. Further cooking-time may vary from 2 to 3 hours; the tripe must be very tender when finished. The classic ways of cooking are in milk with onions or braised with a clear brown gravy.

*

Sauté of Kidneys Turbigo

12–18 'pickling' onions; ¼ lb. button mushrooms; 5 lambs' kidneys; 2 oz. butter; ¼ lb. chipolata sausages; 1 dessertspoon flour; 1 teaspoon tomato purée; 1 tablespoon sherry; 1½ gills brown stock; 1 bayleaf; salt and pepper.

2 slices stale bread for croûtes; chopped parsley.

Blanch the onions and drain; quarter the mushrooms and set aside. Skin the kidneys, cut in half lengthways. Heat a sauté or deep frying-pan, drop in the butter, and, when it is foaming, put in the kidneys and sauté briskly until nicely brown. Lift out and put in the chipolatas, lower the heat and brown also. Take them out, add the onions and mushrooms, shake over a brisk heat 2 to 3 minutes, then draw aside. Stir in the flour, purée, sherry, and stock and bring to the boil; season. Slice the sausages diagonally into 2 or 3 pieces and add to the pan with the bayleaf and kidneys. Cover and simmer gently 20 to 25 minutes. In the meantime prepare the croûtes, by cutting the bread into triangular pieces and frying in a little hot oil until golden brown. Dish the kidneys, surround with the croûtes, and sprinkle with parsley.

Ragoût of Kidneys with Red Wine

8 lambs' kidneys; 1 large onion; 1 large carrot; 6–8 oz. flat mushrooms; 1½ oz. butter; 1 tablespoon flour; 1 teaspoon tomato purée; 2 glasses red wine; 1½ gills good stock; bouquet garni.

TO FINISH: browned crumbs; 1 tablespoon butter; chopped parsley.

Skin and split the kidneys in two. Slice the onion and carrot thinly, trim and peel the mushrooms, and leave whole. Brown the kidneys quickly in the hot butter in a stewpan. Add the onion and carrot and fry until turning colour; stir in the flour and after a minute or two the purée. Boil the wine until reduced by about a quarter and add with the stock. Bring to the boil, replace the kidneys, and add the bouquet. Cover and simmer gently for 20 minutes in the oven. Remove the bouquet and turn into a china casserole. Lay the mushrooms on top, stalk side uppermost, sprinkle well with the crumbs and dot with the butter. Return to the oven uncovered for a further 15 minutes or until the top is nicely browned. Sprinkle with chopped parsley. Serve with potatoes 'Normande'. Ox or pig kidneys may be used for this dish, but allow longer time for cooking.

Kidneys in Potatoes (a supper dish)

5 large even-sized potatoes; 5 thin rashers unsmoked streaky bacon, No. 4 cut; 5 lambs' kidneys; sherry (optional); butter.

Scrub the potatoes, roll in salt, and bake until soft for about 1 to 1½ hours. Remove the rind and rust from the rashers and flatten out. Skin the kidneys and wrap each in a rasher of bacon. Cut the tops off the potatoes and scoop out enough of the pulp to make room for the kidney. Season the insides with pepper and a touch of French mustard; add a nut of butter. Put in the kidneys, sprinkle with sherry, and replace the tops. Return to the oven for a further 20 minutes or until the kidneys are nicely cooked. After 10 minutes the tops can be taken off and the bacon allowed to brown. Serve hot in a napkin.

Veal Kidneys Robert

3–4 veal kidneys, according to size; 2 oz. butter; 1 dessertspoon flour; 1 wineglass white wine or stock; 1 large teaspoon mixed English mustard; 1 teaspoon chopped parsley; a good squeeze of lemon juice; salt and pepper.

GARNISH: French beans and new potatoes 'château' (see page 359).

Skin the kidneys and leave whole. Melt half the butter in a deep frying-pan or sauté pan, put in the kidneys and cook briskly, seasoning with salt and pepper until lightly brown on all sides. Reduce the heat and continue to cook gently on top of the stove or in the oven for 7 to 10 minutes with the lid on the pan, then take out, slice, and keep hot. Add the flour to the pan, then the wine or stock, and boil up well. Draw aside; add the mustard and the rest of the butter in small pieces. Finish with the lemon juice, parsley, and seasoning. Add the kidneys without their juice, which may coagulate the sauce. Bring slowly to boiling-point. Serve at once, garnished with the beans and potatoes.

Calf's Liver with Orange

PILAFF: 1 oz. butter; 1 onion; 5 oz. long-grained rice; ¾–1 pint stock; 1 oz. grated cheese.

GARNISH: 1 orange; ½ oz. butter.

LIVER: 1 onion; 2 cloves garlic; 2–3 tablespoons flour; salt, pepper, dry mustard, and cayenne; 6–8 slices calf's liver; 2 oz. butter; 1 glass red wine and the same of good stock; 1 dessert-spoon chopped parsley and thyme.

Prepare the pilaff (see page 111), and set to cook; slice the orange thinly, keeping on the rind, and set aside.

Chop the onion finely and crush the garlic. Add a good pinch of each of the spices to the flour and roll the liver in this. Fry the slices quickly, until brown, in half the butter; take out and arrange in a hot dish; keep warm. Add the rest of the butter to the frying-pan, put in the onion and garlic, and cook slowly until golden. Add the wine, reduce to half over strong heat, then add the stock and herbs. Boil for 1 minute, then spoon over the dish. Wipe out the pan, drop in the butter for the garnish, dust with sugar, and add the sliced orange. Brown quickly on both sides and arrange round the liver. Take up the pilaff and finish with the butter and cheese; serve with the liver.

Liver Sauté à la Basque

¾–1 lb. liver; 1–2 aubergines; 3 onions; 1 lb. ripe tomatoes; a clove of garlic; oil and butter for frying; a little stock; chopped parsley.

Slice the aubergine and degorge; slice the onions thinly, blanch and drain. Skin and slice the tomatoes, crush the garlic. Slice the liver and roll in seasoned flour.

Heat a large frying-pan, add 3 to 4 tablespoons of oil and when hot fry the aubergine slices until brown on both sides. Take out and keep hot. Add a little extra oil to the pan if necessary and fry the onions until golden brown and crisp. Take out with a slice and keep hot. Add a good nut of butter to the pan and fry the liver quickly on both sides until brown. Dish *en couronne* with the slices of liver and aubergine alternating. De-glaze the pan with a little stock, add the garlic, boil up, and strain over the liver. Fill the centre with the tomatoes passed through butter and scatter over the onions and chopped parsley.

Petits Pains de Foie (Liver Creams)

PANADE: 1½ oz. butter; 1½ oz. flour; 1½ gills flavoured milk (as for a Béchamel, page 369).

¾ lb. calf's liver; 3 thin slices lean ham; 2 small eggs; ½–¾ pint Madeira sauce; 1 oz. button mushrooms; 1 tablespoon of cream.

First prepare the panade. Make up as for a Béchamel and leave till cold. Well butter some small dariole moulds and stamp out a round of ham to fit the bottom. Alternatively butter a ring mould and dust out with browned crumbs.

Mince the liver, beat in the panade, pass through a sieve. Add the eggs, one at a time, and finish with the cream. Season well with salt, pepper, and French mustard. Fill the mixture into the moulds and poach gently in a bain-marie in the oven for 15 to 20 minutes or until firm to the touch. Slice the mushrooms thinly and shred the trimmings of the ham. Add to the Madeira sauce and simmer for 5 minutes.

Take out the creams and leave for 3 or 4 minutes before turning out. Pour a little of the sauce on to the serving dish, turn out the creams, and serve. Hand the rest of the sauce separately.

Sweetbreads Poulette

2 pairs calves' sweetbreads (1–1½ lb.); onion; carrot; bouquet garni; veal stock.

POULETTE SAUCE: $1\frac{1}{4}$ oz. butter; 1 oz. flour; scant $\frac{3}{4}$ pint stock in which the sweetbreads were cooked; 1–2 egg yolks; good $\frac{1}{2}$ gill of cream; squeeze of lemon juice; 1 dessertspoon chopped parsley.

GARNISH: 1 cucumber; 1 shallot finely chopped; 1 oz. butter; chopped mint; potatoes Château (page 359).

Blanch the sweetbreads, drain and trim, removing any ducts or skin, and press between two plates. Put them into a pan with the sliced onion, carrot, and bouquet. Cover with the stock. Water may be used but the stock will give a better sauce. Simmer 45 to 50 minutes. Drain off and measure $\frac{1}{2}$ to $\frac{3}{4}$ pint of the stock. Make the roux for the sauce, pour on the stock, and stir until boiling. Cook till syrupy in consistency. Draw aside, add the egg yolks and cream mixed together. Thicken over the fire without boiling and finish with the lemon juice and parsley. Cut the sweetbreads into thick slices, reshape, and dish. Coat with the sauce. If lambs' breads are used, put them into the sauce before dishing. Garnish with the cucumber and potatoes. For the cucumber – peel, quarter lengthwise, cut into short lengths, and blanch. Drain. Melt the butter in a pan, add the shallot, and after a minute or two the cucumber. Season, cover, and cook 5 to 6 minutes. Finish with the mint.

Sweetbread Flan with Red Wine and Prunes

1–2 pairs calves' sweetbreads or 1 lb. 'throat' or lamb's sweetbreads; 1 oz. butter; 1 doz. button onions; 6–8 French plums or good prunes, previously soaked; $\frac{1}{2}$ oz. flour; 1 wineglass red wine; $\frac{1}{2}-\frac{3}{4}$ pint strong veal stock; 1 bayleaf; chopped parsley.

PASTRY: 6 oz. plain flour; large pinch of salt; 4 oz. shortening; 1 egg yolk; water to mix.

Blanch and drain the sweetbreads, trim and press between two plates. Blanch the onions. Heat a stewpan, drop in the butter, and, when it is foaming, lay in the breads. Sauté on both sides till golden brown. Remove, add the onions, and, when the colour is turning, the plums. Shake over the fire for another few minutes. Remove, add the flour, and colour slowly. Add the wine and stock, and bring to the boil. Replace the breads, onions, plums, and bayleaf and add more stock if necessary so as to barely cover the breads. Cover and braise in the oven for 40 to 50 minutes. The stock must be well reduced and the sweetbreads have a glazed appearance. Take up and slice each into 3 or 4 pieces and replace in the pan.

In the meantime make up the pastry; line into a 7-inch flan ring and bake blind. Fill with the sweetbreads and sprinkle with chopped parsley.

Sweetbreads Florentine
2–3 pairs calves' sweetbreads (1½ lb.); 1 oz. butter; 4 oz. mushrooms.

SPINACH 'EN BRANCHE': 1½–2 lb. (See page 362.)

POTATOES DUCHESSE: 1 lb. potatoes; ½ oz. butter; 1 egg yolk; a little nutmeg.

MORNAY SAUCE: ½ pint milk; 1 slice onion and carrot; bouquet garni; ¾ oz. butter; ¾ oz. flour; 1 oz. grated cheese.

Soak the sweetbreads in salted water for 2 or 3 hours or overnight. Drain. Cover with cold water and bring to the boil. Refresh and press between two plates. Sauté slowly in butter for 15 to 20 minutes with the mushrooms but do not allow to colour.

In the meantime, prepare the spinach, potatoes, and Mornay sauce. Dish the spinach, arrange the sweetbreads on the top. Pipe the potatoes round the edge using an 8-cut vegetable rose pipe and brush with beaten egg. Coat the sweetbreads with the Mornay sauce. Sprinkle a little extra grated cheese mixed with a spoonful of browned crumbs and brown in a quick oven for 7 to 10 minutes.

Ris de Veau Soubise
2–3 pairs calves' sweetbreads, according to size; 1 onion; 1 carrot; 1 clove garlic; a pinch of chopped or dried thyme; 1 bayleaf; 1½ oz. butter; 1 glass white wine; 1 glass good veal or chicken stock.

VELOUTÉ SAUCE: ½ oz. butter; scant ½ oz. flour; stock from the breads; 4 tablespoons onion purée made with 3 large Spanish onions, sliced, blanched, cooked until tender in stock, then drained and puréed; 1 tablespoon thick cream.

TO FINISH: 2 oz. button mushrooms; 2 oz. cooked ham; grated Gruyère cheese.

Parboil the sweetbreads for 10 minutes or so in salted water, drain, refresh, and trim. Press between two plates until cold. Chop the onion, carrot, and garlic finely. Melt the butter in a sauté pan, lay in the sweetbreads, and sauté for 5 minutes on each side. Lift out carefully and put in the vegetables. Cover and cook for 3 to 4 minutes, then replace the breads with the thyme, bay-leaf, wine, and stock. Season, cover, and simmer for 15 minutes or until tender. In the meantime, slice and cook the mushrooms in a nut of butter and shred the ham. Dish the sweetbreads in a fire-proof dish and strain off the liquid. Make the sauce using the stock and finish with the onion purée and cream. Scatter the mush-rooms and ham on to the sweetbreads, coat with the sauce, and sprinkle well with the Gruyère cheese. Brown in a hot oven for 7 to 10 minutes. Serve with a purée of potatoes or boiled rice.

Cervelles (Brains) au Beurre Noir

2–3 sets calves' brains; court bouillon (see page 123); 2–3 oz. fresh butter; 1 large tablespoon each chopped gherkins, capers, and parsley; 3 tablespoons wine vinegar.

Well wash and soak the brains for 2 or 3 hours in salted water. Put them into a boiling court bouillon and poach for 20 to 25 minutes. Drain carefully, cut into thick slices, and arrange in a hot dish. Season with salt and pepper from the mill. Keep warm. Heat a small frying-pan, drop in the butter, and cook to a dark noisette; quickly add the rest of the ingredients and spoon over the brains. Serve with plainly boiled potatoes.

Langues d'Agneau (Lambs' Tongues) Véronique

6 lambs' tongues; 1 onion; 1 carrot; bouquet garni; salt; pepper-corns.

FOR BRAISING: Mirepoix – 2 onions; 2 carrots; 1 small turnip; $\frac{1}{2}$–$\frac{3}{4}$ pint good stock; bouquet garni; 2–3 bacon rashers.

SAUCE ESPAGNOLE: 1 oz. butter; 2 shallots; 1 carrot; 1 small piece turnip; few mushroom peelings; $\frac{3}{4}$ oz. flour; 1 small teaspoon tomato purée; 1 pint good stock; 1 glass sherry.

GARNISH: 6 oz. peeled white grapes; 1 oz. shredded almonds.

Blanch and refresh the tongues, then simmer with water to cover and the vegetables, bouquet, and peppercorns for about $1\frac{1}{2}$ hours. Plunge into cold water and skin. Have the mirepoix ready. Put the bacon on the bottom of a casserole, add the mirepoix, cover, and sweat for 6 to 7 minutes. Moisten with the stock; add the bouquet, cover and braise gently for half an hour, or until very tender, basting from time to time.

In the meantime prepare the sauce. Dice the vegetables and brown in the butter; add the flour and brown this also. Add the chopped mushroom peelings, purée, and stock, and then the bouquet and simmer for 35 to 40 minutes. Strain and return to the rinsed-out pan with the sherry. Continue simmering until syrupy in consistency, then add the grapes and almonds. Split the tongues in two, arrange in a serving-dish, and spoon over the sauce. Serve with a mousseline of potatoes (see page 357).

Chapter 7

POULTRY AND GAME

POULTRY

UNDER this general heading come the domestic birds bred especially for the table, namely chicken, turkey, duck, goose, and guinea-fowl. They fall into two distinct groups, those with webbed feet and those without. The webbed-footed birds have succulent flesh with a good protective layer of fat immediately under the skin and should always be served with an accompaniment that contrasts in flavour and counteracts the richness of the meat. The other birds lack this natural fat and consequently where the method of cooking demands great heat, e.g. with grilling and roasting, care must be taken to protect the flesh by careful basting and barding.

CHICKEN

Now that chickens are produced at a reasonable price they provide great variety in planning meals as they lend themselves to many ways of cooking and blend with a wide selection of flavours. As a general rule they have little if any fat, and because of this the French method (see page 264) of roasting poultry is superior to any other. Here butter is the fat used, and a little stock is added to the roasting-pan. This assures that the bird cooks at a lower temperature than if dripping were used; the flesh remains more succulent and the butter produces a very fine flavour, cooking down to a rich brown glaze at the bottom of the roasting-tin and providing the basis of a good gravy.

BUYING: To check if a bird is young and suitable for roasting watch the following points: the scales on the legs should be only slightly overlapping and in the male bird the spurs hardly developed. The comb and the wattle should be small and soft. The tip of the breast-bone should be pliable, in fact only gristle and not bone at all.

The 'dressed weight' of a bird is the weight after plucking and drawing, but includes the giblets (neck, heart, liver, and gizzard) after cleaning. In the case of a fresh chicken it will include the legs and the feet, too – of great value in preparing a jellied stock.

Many stores stock frozen birds only, and here the dressed weight is clearly marked, also with the information as to whether they are roasters or boilers. To get the best results the birds must be allowed to thaw slowly, preferably overnight in the refrigerator or in a cool larder. Never put near heat to hurry the process as this only results in dry and tasteless flesh, but if there is really some urgency, thaw under a running *cold* tap.

When choosing a recipe check the dressed weight of the bird. A bird 1 to $1\frac{1}{4}$ lb. and 4 to 6 weeks old is known as a poussin and is sufficient only for one portion and may be roasted or grilled.

$1\frac{3}{4}$ to 2 lb. and 8 to 10 weeks old is known as a double poussin and will serve two. It may be grilled, spit-roasted, or pot-roasted.

2 to $2\frac{1}{2}$ lb. and 3 months old is known as a broiler, is the perfect size for a sauté and will feed 4. For 6 people, two broilers should be provided.

3 lb. and over and up to one year old is known as roasting chicken. Over one year, if the hen has been laying, it is classed as a boiling fowl.

Cockerels are killed at six months unless caponized, when they are fed well and grow to a fine size, developing quite a lot of fat; but the meat remains tender and they are still suitable for roasting. Capons weigh from 4 to 8 lb. A poularde is a hen bird treated in the same way.

Boiling fowls require long, slow cooking to make them really tender and palatable. They should be covered with cold water, brought slowly to the boil, and then, after skimming, seasoning and vegetables should be added to improve the flavour. The heat is then reduced and cooking continued for at least 2 hours. A pressure cooker can, however, be useful in cutting down the cooking time, but a second and slower cooking is advisable to introduce some extra flavour, seasoning, or sauce.

TO CARVE A CHICKEN: In the kitchen:

1. Place the bird on a board, the neck end facing you, and hold firmly with a carving-fork down through the back of the bird.

2. Cut the skin around the leg, place the knife against the carcass, and press gently outwards. This will expose the joint; cut through this and slip the point of the knife under the back to release the oyster with the thigh. If the chicken is large this joint can now be divided in two, not through the hock joint but just above to give a small portion of thigh meat with the drum stick.

3. Now place the knife opposite the point where the breast and wishbone meet and cut parallel to the wishbone. This will sever the wing with a good slice of breast and the knife will automatically find the joint.

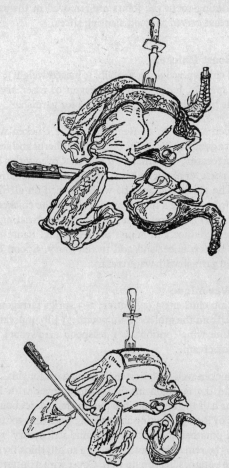

4. Remove similar pieces from the other side of the chicken.

5. Cut off the wishbone or 'merrythought', keeping the knife against the carcass.

6. Cut the breast in portions, in half, or in three depending on the size of the bird.

In the dining-room the joints are removed in the same way and the breast carved in good slanting slices.

*

French Roast Chicken

1 roasting chicken weighing 3–3¾ lb. (plucked weight); 1½–2 oz. butter; a sprig of herbs such as tarragon or rosemary; ½ pint stock made from the giblets; watercress for garnish.

Set the oven at 400° F. or Reg. 6. Rub the chicken well with butter, put a good nut inside the bird with the herbs and seasoning, and set in a roasting-tin with half the stock. Cover with a buttered paper and roast for about an hour, basting and turning from time to time. The chicken should be well browned on all sides and a frozen bird will take a little longer. Take up the chicken, carve, and keep hot. Tip the remaining stock into the roasting-tin and boil up well; reduce and adjust the seasoning. Sauté the liver in a little butter, slice, and add to the gravy. Spoon over the chicken and garnish with watercress.

Chicken Véronique

3 lb. roasting chicken; 3 oz. butter; 2–3 sprigs tarragon; ½ pint stock made from the giblets; 1 lb. potatoes; ¼ lb. muscat grapes; 1 glass white wine (optional); 1 teaspoon arrowroot; 2 table-spoons thick cream.

Rub the chicken well with butter allowing 2 oz. for this. Put salt, pepper, and the tarragon inside the bird, cover with buttered paper, pour half the bouillon into the tin, and roast about 1 hour (at 400° F. or Reg. 6), basting and turning from time to time.

Peel the potatoes and cut into julienne strips; dry well in a cloth. Rub the remaining butter round a small, thick frying-pan. Press in the potatoes, seasoning well. Cover with a buttered paper and a lid and cook slowly on top of the stove or in the oven for about 40 minutes.

Meanwhile peel and pip the grapes; squeeze over a few drops of lemon juice and keep covered.

Take up the chicken, carve, and keep hot. Strain off the juices into a small saucepan, deglaze the roasting-tin with the wine, and allow to reduce by half, then add it to the pan with the remaining stock. Bring to the boil and adjust the seasoning, then thicken with the arrowroot mixed with a little water. Turn out the 'paillasson' of potatoes, and arrange the chicken on it. Add the cream to the gravy, and the grapes at the last moment, and serve over the chicken.

Chicken Parisienne

3 lb. roasting chicken; 1–2 oz. butter; a bunch of herbs; $\frac{1}{4}$–$\frac{1}{2}$ pint strong stock made from the giblets.

MUSHROOM SAUCE: 1 oz. butter; 2 shallots; $\frac{3}{4}$ lb. firm button mushrooms; 2 tablespoons brandy; $\frac{1}{2}$ pint double cream.

Season inside the chicken with salt and pepper, put in the herbs and a good nut of the butter. Set in a roasting-tin, pour round $\frac{1}{4}$ pint of the stock. Cook in a moderately hot oven (400° F. or Reg. 6) for about 1 hour, basting and turning from time to time.

In the meantime prepare the sauce. Melt the butter, add the shallots, finely chopped, cover, and cook for 2 to 3 minutes until soft. Add the sliced or chopped mushrooms and continue cooking for 3 minutes, then pour on the brandy and reduce. Put the cream in a separate pan and boil until thick, then pour on to the mushrooms and season to taste.

Take up the chicken, carve and arrange in a deep serving-dish. Deglaze the roasting-tin with any remaining stock and boil down to one tablespoonful. Strain this through double muslin or a tammy strainer into the mushroom sauce. Pour the sauce over the chicken and serve.

Chicken with Mushrooms

3 lb. roasting chicken; $\frac{1}{2}$ lemon; 1 oz. butter; 1 clove garlic; 1 glass sherry; $\frac{1}{2}$ lb. button mushrooms; Béchamel sauce made with $\frac{3}{4}$ oz. butter, $\frac{3}{4}$ oz. flour and $1\frac{1}{2}$ gills milk infused with a slice of onion, carrot, and bouquet garni; $\frac{1}{2}$ gill single cream.

Truss the chicken, season inside the bird, then rub well with the lemon. Drop the butter into a large pan, and when it is foaming put in the chicken, the garlic, crushed with salt, and the sherry. Cover tightly and cook slowly for about 45 to 50 minutes. Turn from time to time and five minutes before the end of cooking time add the mushrooms and continue simmering.

Meantime prepare the Béchamel sauce. Take up the chicken, carve, and arrange in the serving-dish. Tip the sauce into the pan, bring to the boil, and simmer for 2 to 3 minutes; add the cream, adjust the seasoning, and spoon over the chicken.

Chicken Vichy

1 3-lb. roasting chicken; 2 oz. butter; 2 tablespoons sherry; 2 carrots; 2 onions; 1 glass red wine; ¼ pint stock; bouquet garni; 1 teaspoon tomato purée; kneaded butter.

¾ lb. small or 1 bunch new carrots; ½ oz. butter; 2 tablespoons white wine; 1 teaspoon lemon juice; 3 tablespoons cream; 1 tablespoon chopped parsley.

Brown the chicken all over in the butter in a large pan or iron casserole. Flame with the sherry, then take out the chicken. Slice the vegetables and add to the pan, cover, and sweat for 5 or 6 minutes. Replace the chicken, then add the wine, stock, bouquet, and purée. Bring to the boil, cover, and cook either in a moderate oven or on a low heat for 40 to 45 minutes. Turn and baste the bird occasionally.

In the meantime peel the carrots, and quarter or leave whole. Melt the butter in a pan, add the wine, lemon juice, 2 tablespoons of water, salt, pepper, and the carrots. Cover the pan with grease-proof paper and the lid and cook slowly until soft. Draw aside, cool a little, add the chopped parsley and the cream.

Take up the chicken; joint and arrange in the serving-dish. Strain off the gravy and thicken lightly with the kneaded butter. Adjust the seasoning and spoon over the chicken. Arrange the carrots at each end of the dish and serve.

Paprika Chicken

3 lb. roasting chicken; 1 onion; 1 lb. tomatoes or 1 medium-sized

tin of tomatoes; 1 oz. butter; 1 level dessertspoon paprika pepper; 1 glass white wine; 2 caps tinned pimento; bouquet garni.

CREAM SAUCE: $\frac{3}{4}$ oz. butter; $\frac{3}{4}$ oz. flour; $\frac{1}{4}$ pint single cream or top milk.

Slice the onion finely and if using fresh tomatoes wipe over, cut in half, and squeeze away the seeds.

Brown the chicken lightly all over in the hot butter, remove, add the paprika and, in half a minute, the wine. When reduced put in the onion, and after a few minutes add the tomatoes and pimento. Replace the chicken, add the bouquet, and salt to taste; cover and simmer for 45 minutes.

Take up and carve the chicken, and keep warm. Rub the contents of the pan through a strainer. Have the cream sauce ready and stir the purée into it. Reboil, adjust the seasoning, and spoon over the chicken. Serve with cooked nouilles or pasta shells tossed in a little boiled cream or sour cream.

Chicken Napolitana

3–3$\frac{1}{2}$ lb. roasting chicken; 2 rashers bacon; 1 onion; 1 carrot; bouquet garni; $\frac{1}{2}$ gill chicken stock; $\frac{1}{2}$ lb. spaghetti or nouille; 1 oz. butter.

MORNAY SAUCE made with 1 oz. butter, $\frac{3}{4}$ oz. flour, $\frac{1}{2}$ pint milk, 2 oz. grated cheese, and $\frac{1}{2}$ gill cream.

Lay the bacon at the bottom of a deep pan. Sit the chicken on top and surround with the sliced vegetables and herbs. Cover the pan and set on a slow heat for 10 to 15 minutes, then moisten with the stock, season lightly, and continue cooking until tender – that is for about an hour.

In the meantime cook the spaghetti, drain and refresh; toss in the butter with salt and freshly ground black pepper to taste.

Prepare the sauce using two-thirds of the cheese and finish with the cream. Carve the chicken, arrange on top of the spaghetti on a hot dish, and spoon over the sauce. Sprinkle with the rest of the cheese and brown lightly under the grill.

Poussins Citronés aux Fines Herbes

2 'double' poussins; 2 oz. butter; lemon rind and juice; salt and pepper; $\frac{1}{4}$ pint strong veal or chicken stock; 1 tablespoon chopped mixed herbs; parsley, chives, and mint; watercress to garnish.

Heat a large pan, drop in a good ounce of butter, and when it is foaming put in the chickens with the pared rind of half a lemon and the juice of one with salt and pepper. Cover the pan at once and cook on a slow to moderate fire or in the oven for 20 to 30 minutes. Take up, split the chickens, trim away the backbones, and arrange in a fireproof dish. Strain the juices from the pan, add the stock and herbs. Thicken with a very little kneaded butter or 1 level teaspoon arrowroot mixed with stock. Boil up well, adjust the seasoning, and set aside.

Sprinkle the chickens with a little lemon juice or rub the surface with a cut lemon. Sprinkle well with salt and sugar and a dusting of freshly ground pepper and paprika. Spoon over some melted butter. Five to 6 minutes before serving put under a moderate grill so that the surface becomes brown and crisp. Pour round the gravy and garnish with watercress.

Poulet au Riz

$3\frac{1}{2}$ lb. chicken; 1 onion; 1 carrot; stick of celery in season; bouquet garni; seasoning; water to cover.

PILAFF: 1 medium onion; $1\frac{1}{2}$ oz. butter; 6 oz. rice; 1 pint chicken stock.

SAUCE: 1 oz. butter; $\frac{3}{4}$ oz. flour; $\frac{1}{2}$ pint strong chicken stock; 1 egg yolk; 1 tablespoon cream.

Simmer the chicken in the water with the vegetables, herbs, and seasoning until tender. Allow approximately 1 hour for a roasting bird and 2 to $2\frac{1}{2}$ hours for a large boiling fowl. In the meantime prepare the pilaff; chop the onion finely and put in a pan with 1 oz. of the butter and cook slowly until soft but not coloured. Add the rice, fry about 1 minute or until the grains look clear, then tip on the stock and seasoning to taste. Bring to the boil, cover the pan, and set in a moderate oven until the rice is tender and the stock absorbed – about 18 to 20 minutes. Dot the remaining ½ oz. butter over the surface of the rice and leave until ready to serve. Take up the chicken and set the stock on fierce heat to reduce and strengthen in flavour. Melt the butter for the sauce, blend in the flour, and cook gently until straw-coloured; pour on the stock and stir until boiling. Boil rapidly for 3 to 4 minutes then add the egg yolk and cream liaison and reheat carefully. Adjust the seasoning and add a squeeze of lemon.

Remove the skin from the chicken, carve, and arrange in a serving-dish. Spoon over the sauce. Fork the butter into the rice and arrange at each end of the dish.

Chicken Toscana
3 lb. roasting chicken; 1 onion; 1 carrot; bouquet garni; ¾ pint water; seasoning; 4 oz. mushrooms; 1 small cucumber; 1 level dessertspoon arrowroot; 2 egg yolks; ¾ gill cream; 1 tablespoon snipped chives.

Simmer the chicken gently in the water with the vegetables, herbs, and seasoning until tender – about 45 to 50 minutes.

In the meantime chop the mushrooms finely, peel the cucumber, cut in quarters lengthwise, and then into 2-inch pieces; blanch and drain well. Strain the stock from the chicken into another pan and reduce to ½ pint. Add the mushrooms and simmer for 3 minutes.

Take up the chicken, carve into neat joints, and arrange in the serving-dish. Slake the arrowroot with a little stock, add to the pan, and stir until boiling. Adjust the seasoning, thicken with the liaison of egg yolk and cream; add the chives and well-drained cucumber. Spoon over the chicken and serve at once.

Chicken en cocotte Bonne Femme
3 lb. chicken; 1 thick rasher streaky bacon weighing 2 oz.; 2 oz. firm mushrooms; 12 button or spring onions; 1½ oz. butter or ham fat; 1 oz. flour; 1 pint chicken stock; bouquet garni; 2 potatoes.

Remove the rind and rust from the bacon, cut into lardons and blanch. Quarter the mushrooms and leave the onions whole. Melt the fat in a casserole and brown the chicken slowly on all sides over gentle heat; remove from the pan, cut into joints, and keep warm. Add the bacon, mushrooms, and onions to the pan and brown well. Dust in the flour and cook for 2 to 3 minutes until straw-coloured. Pour on the stock, season, and stir until boiling. Replace the chicken and add the bouquet. Cover the pan and cook in a moderate oven (350° F. or Reg. 4) for about an hour.

Fifteen minutes before dishing, add the potatoes, cut in large olive shapes, and continue cooking until tender. Dust with chopped parsley and serve.

Coq au Vin

3–3½ lb. roasting chicken; 2 oz. butter; ¼ lb. gammon rasher; ¼ lb. button onions; ½ bottle Burgundy or ¼ bottle and ¼ pint good chicken stock; 2 cloves garlic; bouquet garni; kneaded butter; sliced French roll for croûtes; chopped parsley.

Cut the bacon in lardons and blanch in cold water with the onions. Drain well. Brown the chicken slowly in the butter; remove and keep warm. Add the onions and bacon to the pan, and while these are browning joint the chicken and replace in the pan. Flame with the wine; add the garlic crushed with salt, the herbs, and seasoning. Cover the pan and cook very slowly for about an hour. This may be done on top of the stove or in the oven. When the chicken is tender, remove the 'bouquet'. Thicken slightly with kneaded butter and adjust the seasoning. Brown the bread croûtes in butter or oil. Dish the chicken. Surround with the croûtes and dust with chopped parsley.

Curried Chicken

1 roasting chicken; 1 tablespoon oil; 2 oz. butter; 4 shallots or 1 medium onion; 1 tablespoon curry powder; 1 teaspoon curry paste; 1 tablespoon flour; ¾ pint stock; 1 clove garlic; 1 dessert-spoon redcurrant jelly or the juice of ½ lemon and a dessertspoon sugar; ¼ pint nut milk (made with 1 large tablespoon ground almonds or desiccated coconut infused in 1 teacup boiling water for 1 hour and strained well before using).

Divide the chicken into neat joints and fry to a good golden brown in the oil and $\frac{1}{2}$ oz. of the butter; remove and keep warm. Melt the remaining fat, add the chopped onions, and cook gently until just turning colour. Add the curry powder and paste and continue cooking for 3 to 4 minutes more. Stir in the flour and cook again for one minute. Pour in the liquid gradually, add the garlic, crushed with salt, adjust the seasoning, and simmer for 20 minutes. Replace the chicken in the pan, cover tightly, and continue cooking in a slow oven or on top of the stove until tender – about 45 minutes.

Arrange the chicken in a serving-dish, add the almond or coconut milk to the curry sauce together with the sour-sweet (i.e. the lemon and sugar or redcurrant jelly), and simmer another minute or two. Add a coffeecupful of cream, reheat carefully, and spoon over the chicken. Serve plainly boiled rice and fresh chutney separately. Cucumber Raita and Dahl should be served as accompaniments.

FRESH CHUTNEY: 1 apple; 1 onion; 3 tomatoes; 3 stalks celery; 1 tablespoon chopped mint; 1 tablespoon grated horseradish; 1 clove garlic; 1 cap pimento; 1 oz. sugar; 2 tablespoons vinegar.

Peel and grate the apple and onion; skin the tomatoes, squeeze away the seeds, and chop and crush the garlic with 1 teaspoon of salt. Chop the celery and pimento and place all the ingredients in a saucepan. Bring to the boil; serve hot or cold.

CUCUMBER RAITA: 1 cucumber; 1 cupful thick sour milk or yoghourt; salt and pepper.

Peel and grate the cucumber, salt lightly. Leave $\frac{1}{4}$ hour. Strain off the liquid and mix with the sour milk and a little pepper. Serve.

DAHL: Soak a teacupful of Egyptian lentils in cold water for 1 hour. Strain. Put the lentils in a pan with a small onion chopped finely, a dessertspoonful of curry powder, and 1 pint good stock. Cover the pan and leave the mixture to boil $\frac{1}{2}$ hour. Then add a little salt and continue cooking until the lentils are quite dissolved and are about the consistency of thick pea soup.

Spatchcock Chicken

4 poussins or 2 'double' poussins; lemon; salt; pepper; 2–4 oz. butter.

SAUCE: 2 shallots; 1 glass sherry; ½ gill stock; ¼ teaspoon tomato purée and French mustard; Worcester sauce; cayenne.

FOR SERVING: watercress; fingers of lemon; straw potatoes.

Cut the poussins down the back, lay flat on a board and bat well. Cut away the backbone and run a small skewer through the legs to hold them in position and to keep the bird flat; season both sides with lemon, salt, and pepper and leave 10 to 15 minutes before grilling.

Brush the birds with melted butter and grill very gently, first on the skin side and then on the underside. Allow 10 minutes on each side and keep the birds moist with melted butter through- out the cooking time. Take up the chicken, remove the skewers, and place in a hot serving-dish.

Strain off the butter from the grill pan into a small saucepan, add the finely chopped shallots, and cook slowly until golden. Pour on the sherry and stock and boil up well. Stir in the tomato purée, mustard, a few drops of Worcester sauce, and a pinch of cayenne. Garnish the chicken with watercress and fingers of lemon and hand the potatoes and sauce separately.

Devilled Grilled Poussins with Simla Rice

DRY DEVIL MIXTURE: 1 dessertspoon salt; 1 dessertspoon sugar; 1 level teaspoon each ground pepper, ground ginger, and mustard; ½ teaspoon curry powder.

2 'double' poussins; 2 oz. butter; 2 tablespoons tomato chutney; 1 tablespoon mushroom ketchup; 1 tablespoon Worcester sauce; 1 tablespoon Soy sauce; 1 tablespoon fruit sauce such as plum, gooseberry, or A.1.; a dash of tabasco.

Split the poussins in half and cut away the back and rib bones. Mix the dry devil ingredients together and rub well into the sur- face of the birds. Leave for at least 1 hour.

Melt the butter in a small saucepan, brush the poussins with plenty of butter, and grill slowly until brown and crisp – about 10 minutes on each side. Then remove the grid from the grill pan and place the birds at the bottom. Mix all the sauces together in the pan with the remaining butter, heat gently, and then spoon over the chicken. Continue cooking under the grill, basting continually with the sauce. Take up the chicken, arrange in a serving-dish. Dilute the sauce in the pan with a little stock or potato water and spoon over the top. Garnish with watercress and hand a dish of Simla rice separately.

SIMLA RICE: 6 oz. long-grained rice; $1\frac{1}{2}$–2 oz. butter; 1 medium onion; about a level teaspoon turmeric.

Cook the rice in plenty of boiling salted water until tender, turn into a colander, and refresh with a jug of hot water. Allow to drain thoroughly.

Melt the butter, add the onion finely sliced, and cook slowly until golden brown. Stir in the turmeric, allow to cook for about 2 minutes, and then fork in the rice. Toss over the heat and season with salt and pepper to taste.

A sauté of chicken should be made with a bird weighing $2\frac{1}{2}$ lb. dressed weight, and this will feed four people. If, however, the dish is to feed six it is better to use two slightly smaller birds than one larger one. Exactly the same rules apply for the cooking of a chicken sauté as those given for meat on page 198. The chicken is cut in five pieces in the following way:

1. Cut the skin between the leg and breast with a good knife and remove the leg and thigh in one large piece, cutting through the carcass to take the 'oyster' with this joint.

2. Place the knife opposite the top of the breast-bone, cut through the wishbone taking a good section of the breast meat with the wing bone.

3. Cut two joints from the other side of the chicken in the same way.

4. Detach the breast in one piece with scissors.

5. The backbone can be put into the sauté pan with the liquid called for in the recipe to give extra flavour, or used to make stock.

Chicken Sauté Normande

2½ lb. roasting chicken; 1½ oz. butter, clarified; 1 shallot; a small
wineglass of Calvados, dry cider, or sherry; 1 level tablespoon
flour; ¼ pint strong chicken stock; bouquet garni; 2–3 tablespoons
cream; 2 dessert apples; ½ oz. butter.

Cut the chicken in five pieces (see page 273). Put the butter
and chicken, skin side down, in a sauté pan and brown slowly and
well. Turn, add the finely chopped shallot to the pan, continue
cooking 2 to 3 minutes then flame with the Calvados. Blend in
the flour and stock, season with salt and pepper; add the herbs
and stir until boiling. Cover the pan and simmer gently for about
20 minutes. Take up the chicken, trim the joints if necessary,
and arrange in the serving-dish. Add the cream to the pan, boil
up well, adjust the seasoning, strain and spoon over the chicken.
Garnish with slices of apple fried golden brown in the butter.
Dust with chopped parsley and serve.

Chicken Sauté Alsacienne

2½ lb. roasting chicken; 1 tablespoon oil; 1 oz. butter; 1½ glasses
Alsatian white wine; ½ gill strong chicken stock; 1 teaspoon
arrowroot; 1 small tin foie gras (2½ oz.); 3 tablespoons cream.

Joint the chicken. Heat the oil in a sauté pan, drop in the butter,
and when it is foaming put in the chicken skin side down. The
pan should be only just large enough to hold the pieces of
chicken. Season the chicken with salt and freshly ground black
pepper and cook gently for 15 to 20 minutes, turning as the joints
colour. Moisten with half the wine, cover the pan, and continue
to cook very gently until tender.

Dish the chicken, trimming the joints if necessary, and keep
hot. Tip the remaining wine and the stock into the pan, add the
slaked arrowroot, bring to the boil, and strain. Rub the foie gras
through a small strainer and add to the sauce with the cream.
Reheat carefully and spoon over the chicken.

Chicken Sauté Parmesan

2½ lb. roasting chicken; 1 tablespoon oil; 1 oz. butter; salt and pepper; $\frac{1}{2}$ gill strong chicken stock; Béchamel sauce made with $\frac{1}{2}$ oz. flour, $\frac{3}{4}$ oz. butter, and $\frac{1}{2}$ pint milk; 2 oz. grated Parmesan cheese; 2 egg yolks; 2 tablespoons cream; 1 tablespoon brown crumbs.

Joint the chicken. Heat the oil in a sauté pan, drop in the butter, and when it is foaming put in the chicken at once, skin side down, and colour lightly. Turn, season with salt and pepper, and pour in the stock. Cover the pan and cook gently for 20 to 30 minutes. In the meantime prepare the sauce. Cover with a buttery paper to prevent a skin forming and set aside. Sprinkle one tablespoon of the cheese on the bottom of a fireproof dish, arrange the chicken on this, trimming the joints if necessary, and keep warm. Add the Béchamel to the juices in the sauté pan and boil up; stir in all but one tablespoon of the cheese and when melted thicken with the egg yolks and cream. Spoon the sauce over the chicken and dust with the remaining cheese and breadcrumbs. Set in a hot oven to brown.

Chicken Sauté Espagnole

$2\frac{1}{2}$ lb. roasting chicken; 1–2 tablespoons oil; 1 onion; 1 clove garlic; 1 glass sherry; 1 level tablespoon flour; 4 large ripe tomatoes, concassed; 1 teaspoon tomato purée; $\frac{1}{4}$ pint strong chicken stock.

Joint the chicken. Heat the oil in a sauté pan, brown the chicken on all sides, remove and keep warm. Chop the onion and garlic very finely. Add to the pan and cook slowly until soft then tip on the sherry and allow to reduce to nothing. Blend in the flour, add the prepared tomatoes, purée, and stock, and stir until boiling. Put the pieces of chicken back in the pan, add salt and pepper to taste, cover with a lid, and simmer gently until tender – about 20 to 25 minutes.

Dish the chicken, trimming the joints if necessary, and pass the sauce through a conical strainer. Spoon over the chicken and serve dusted with chopped parsley.

NOTE: This dish may be garnished with halved tomatoes filled with sautéd mushrooms and spring onions.

Chicken Sauté Chasseur

2½ lb. roasting chicken; 1 tablespoon oil; 2 oz. butter; 3 oz. button mushrooms; 2 shallots; ½ oz. flour; 2 tablespoons brandy; 1 glass white wine; 1 dessertspoon tomato purée; 1½ gills jellied stock; 1 teaspoon chopped tarragon and chervil; 1 teaspoon chopped parsley.

Heart-shaped croûtons to garnish.

Joint the chicken. Heat the oil in a sauté pan, drop in half the butter and when foaming put in the legs and cook gently for 5 to 6 minutes, then place the wings and breast in the pan and continue to sauté slowly until golden brown on all sides. Remove the joints as they are ready, cover and keep warm.

Meantime wash and slice the mushrooms; chop the shallots finely. Drop the extra oz. of butter into the pan, add the mushrooms, and cook until golden; then add the shallots and continue to cook for 2 to 3 minutes. Blend in the flour and, after 1 minute, the brandy, white wine, tomato purée, and stock. Stir until boiling, season with pepper and the herbs, and return the chicken to the pan. Simmer until the chicken is tender, for about 10 to 15 minutes. Serve dusted with chopped parsley and the croûtons round.

Chicken Sauté Bourguignonne

2½ lb. roasting chicken; 1 tablespoon oil; 2 oz. butter; 3 oz. rasher unsmoked streaky bacon; 3 oz. button mushrooms; 1 tablespoon brandy; 2 glasses Burgundy; ½ pint demi-glace sauce (see page 373); 4 slices small French roll for croûtes.

Joint the chicken and colour in the oil and half the butter as directed in the preceding recipe, then flame with the brandy and wine and allow to reduce by half. Cover the pan and leave to simmer very gently for 10 to 15 minutes.

In the meantime cut the bacon into lardons, blanch, and drain; wash and dry the mushrooms and quarter if large. Melt the remaining butter in a small frying-pan and cook the bacon and mushrooms until golden. Drain and keep warm. Fry the croûtes in the same pan. Tip the sauce on to the chicken and simmer uncovered for 2 to 3 minutes, then add the bacon and mushrooms and adjust the seasoning. Arrange the joints in a hot serving-dish, trimming if necessary. Spoon over the sauce and garnish, and surround with the croûtes.

Suprêmes de Volaille Villeroy

6 'supremes' of chicken (see page 480); 6 rounds of buttered paper.

DUXELLES FARCE: 1 shallot; ½ oz. butter; 6 oz. mushrooms; 2 tablespoons fresh crumbs; 2–3 oz. raw minced chicken taken from the leg; 1 egg white; about ½ gill thick cream.

SAUCE SUPREME: 1 oz. butter; ¾ oz. (scant) flour; ½ pint strong chicken stock; ¼ pint single cream or creamy milk; 2 egg yolks; squeeze of lemon; nut of butter for finishing.

First prepare the duxelles. Chop and soften the shallot in the butter, add the finely chopped mushrooms, and cook for 2 to 3 minutes to evaporate any moisture. Stir in the crumbs and turn on to a plate to cool. Beat the egg white into the minced chicken by degrees, add salt and then the cream. Work in the mushroom mixture and adjust the seasoning. Slit the supremes at intervals, pipe in the farce, and set each one in a round of buttered paper. Sprinkle with a little white wine and cook *en papillote* (see Red Mullet en Papillote, page 138), for about 40 minutes.

In the meantime prepare the sauce. Make a roux, add the stock, stir until boiling and add the liaison. Reheat carefully, then add the lemon juice, adjust the seasoning, and finish with the butter. Serve the supremes coated with the sauce either in a border of potatoes duchesse or with a little boiled rice.

Chicken Croquettes

½ lb. cooked chicken meat; Bechamel sauce made with 1½ oz. butter, 1½ oz. flour, and 1½ gills flavoured milk; ½ oz. butter; 1 oz. mushrooms; 1 egg yolk.

Seasoned flour, beaten egg, and dry white crumbs for coating.

FOR SERVING: fried parsley and tomato or Hollandaise sauce.

Dice the chicken or pass through the coarse blade of a mincer. Melt the ½ oz. butter in a small sauté pan, add the finely chopped mushrooms, and simmer a few minutes. Add the chicken, Béchamel sauce, and the egg yolk. Mix well and reduce over a quick fire till the mixture leaves the sides of the pan. Turn out to cool.

Shape into croquettes on a floured board, brush with beaten egg, and roll in the crumbs. Fry in smoking-hot deep fat until golden brown. Drain well and serve garnished with fried parsley, the sauce handed separately.

Chicken Kromeskies

½ lb. cooked chicken meat; Béchamel sauce made with 1½ oz. butter; 1½ oz. flour; 1½ gills flavoured milk; ½ oz. butter; 1 oz. mushrooms; 1 egg yolk; 4 rashers streaky bacon; fritter batter (see page 401).

FOR SERVING: fried parsley and tomato sauce.

Dice the chicken meat and make up the mixture as directed in the preceding recipe and leave to cool.

Remove the rind and rust from the bacon, cut each rasher in half, and then stroke to twice its length with the blade of a heavy knife. Divide the chicken mixture into eight equal portions, shape into 'croquettes' on a floured board, and wrap each in a piece of bacon. Dip in fritter batter and fry in deep fat until golden brown. Drain well and serve garnished with fried parsley. Hand the tomato sauce separately.

Chicken Pancakes

PANCAKE BATTER: 4 oz. flour; 1 tablespoon salad oil or melted butter; 1 whole egg; 1 yolk of egg; ½ pint milk.

FILLING: 1 oz. butter; 2 oz. mushrooms; ¾ oz. flour; 1 gill stock; ½ lb. cooked chicken meat; 1 hard-boiled egg; 1 teaspoon chopped parsley; 1 tablespoon cream.

TO FINISH: 1 oz. melted butter; 1 tablespoon grated cheese.

Make up the pancake batter as directed on page 400. Leave to stand in a cool place while preparing the filling.

Melt the butter in a pan, finely chop the mushrooms, and add to the butter with salt and pepper. Cover the pan with a lid and cook slowly for 3 to 4 minutes. Remove and stir in the flour, then the stock. Bring to the boil over the fire, add the shredded chicken meat, chopped hard-boiled egg, parsley, and cream. Keep warm.

Fry about a dozen pancakes. Put a spoonful of the filling in the middle of each, fold over, and arrange them overlapping down a buttered dish for serving. Sprinkle over with a little extra melted butter and scatter over cheese. Brown under the grill.

Chicken Pie Romaine

½ lb. rough puff/flaky or puff pastry; shredded meat of 1 cooked chicken; 1 oz. flour; ½–¾ pint good chicken or veal stock; 2–3 tablespoons cream; 1–2 green peppers according to size; 2 oz. button mushrooms.

Prepare the pastry and set aside. Shred the peppers and blanch 2 or 3 minutes in boiling salted water; drain. Wipe and wash the mushrooms, cut in quarters, and sauté in ½ oz. butter for 2 or 3 minutes; then set aside. Melt the butter for the sauce, add the flour, and cook slowly until straw-coloured. Tip on the stock, stir until boiling, add the cream, and cook rapidly until of syrupy consistency. Draw aside, add the shredded chicken, peppers, and mushrooms; allow to cool. Turn into a pie plate or pie dish, cover with the pastry, decorate, brush with beaten egg, and bake in a quick oven for 25 to 35 minutes. Serve hot.

TURKEY

Turkeys are now available throughout the year and much has been done to produce small, broad-breasted birds in the hope of tempting people to use them for occasions other than Christmas.

Fresh turkeys are generally sold plucked, but the weight includes the head and inside, unless 'dressed weight' is specified, and then like frozen birds they will be plucked and drawn and the lower part of the legs removed. A 9-lb. frozen or dressed turkey is equivalent to a 12-lb. clean-plucked bird and will serve eight people. Frozen turkeys must be allowed to defrost naturally and slowly in their polythene bags before cooking, and this will take from 36 to 48 hours. Defrosted birds can be kept for a day or two in the refrigerator but must never be refrozen.

The most popular method of cooking is roasting and one or two stuffings are usually made to add flavour, chestnut and sausage for the carcass, and celery, apple, and walnut for the breast. For a large bird, say 14 lb., they may be cooked separately. The classic accompaniments to roast turkey are thickened gravy, bread or cranberry sauce, and vegetables in season. Turkeys can be French roasted in the same way as chicken, or because of their size be wrapped in greaseproof paper or foil and cooked very slowly over a long period.

Times for cooking

French roasting
Birds under 14 lb. – 15 minutes to the lb. and 15 minutes over.
Birds over 14 lb. – 10 minutes to the lb. and 10 minutes over.

Keep the bird covered with greaseproof paper or foil throughout the cooking time, and turn and baste occasionally. Snip the trussing string holding the legs in position after the first hour.

Slow roasting
Birds under 14 lb. – 20 minutes to the lb. and 30 minutes over.
Birds over 14 lb. – 15–18 minutes to the lb. and 15 minutes over.

Rub the turkey generously with butter and wrap in greaseproof paper or foil, removing this 35 to 45 minutes before the end of cooking time to brown the bird well. Cook at 325° F. or Reg. 3.

Before dishing, test to see if the bird is done by piercing the thickest part of the thigh and drumstick with a skewer. If any liquid runs it should be quite clear.

Always allow 20 to 30 minutes for dishing, making the gravy, finishing the sauce, etc., and if during this time the turkey is covered with a clean cloth wrung out in hot water it will be easier to carve when sent to the table.

*

Chestnut and Sausage Stuffing

1 lb. chestnuts; 1 pint veal stock; 1 stick celery; 1 large onion; 2 oz. butter; ½ lb. pork sausage meat; 1 teacup fresh breadcrumbs.

Remove the shell from the nuts with a sharp knife, then blanch and peel off the inner skin. Place the chestnuts in a saucepan, with the stock to cover, the chopped celery, and seasoning. Cook until the chestnuts are quite tender and all the stock has been absorbed; tip into a bowl to cool. In the meantime chop the onion finely, cook in the butter until soft, and when cool add to the sausage meat. Work in the chestnuts and enough breadcrumbs to bind.

Celery, Apple, and Walnut Stuffing

2 onions; 2 oz. butter; 8 oz. fresh breadcrumbs; 1 small head celery; 2 dessert apples; 4 oz. chopped walnuts; ½ teaspoon mixed dried herbs; 1 tablespoon chopped parsley; seasoning; about 3 tablespoons cream.

Chop the onions finely and cook in the butter until soft but not coloured. Mix the breadcrumbs, chopped celery, diced apple, walnuts, and herbs together, add the cooked onions, and season to taste. Bind with the cream.

Rice and Giblet Stuffing

2 onions; 1 oz. butter; liver, heart, and gizzard of the turkey (4 oz. in all); 4 oz. cooked rice; 1 dessertspoon chopped parsley; 2 oz. stoned raisins; 1 small egg.

Chop the onion finely and cook until soft in the butter, then add the diced giblets and fry 3 to 4 minutes. Mix with the rice, herbs, and raisins and bind with the egg. Season with salt and freshly ground black pepper.

GUINEA FOWL

A native bird of West Africa, it is in season throughout the year. Many years ago it was known as turkey in this country. The meat

is white like chicken but the flavour a little like pheasant. The
bird needs careful cooking as it tends to be dry, but any recipe
given for chicken can be used and the following is particularly
good.

*

Guinea Fowl en cocotte

1 2½–3-lb. guinea fowl; 2 oz. butter; 6 small onions; ½ pint single
cream; seasoning; juice of ½ lemon; 1 tablespoon cranberry conserve or blackcurrant jelly.

Truss the bird neatly, put in a deep pan with the butter, and brown
slowly but well on all sides.

In the meantime blanch the onions, drain, and add to the casserole with the bird and colour also; pour over the cream, season
with salt and finely ground black pepper, cover, and cook very
gently for 50 to 60 minutes. Baste with the cream during the cooking time. Take up the bird and keep warm; add the lemon juice
and conserve to the pan and stir until melted. Adjust the seasoning
and thicken if necessary. Carve the bird, arrange in the serving-
dish, and spoon over the sauce.

DUCK

Duck are in season throughout the year but are at their best
during June and early July. The young birds should be roasted
and the classic accompaniments are sage and onion stuffing,
apple sauce, new potatoes, and green peas. Choose a bird with a
plump breast and remember that a duck will feed fewer people
than a chicken of the same weight. The breast is very shallow and a
3 to 3½-lb. bird will feed only four people. Allow 15 minutes to
the lb. for cooking time and 15 minutes over.

*

Canard à l'Orange

1 duck; 1 oz. butter; ¼ pint stock; 3 oranges; ¾ pint demi-glace
sauce (see page 373); 1 glass red wine; 1–2 tablespoons redcurrant
jelly; watercress to garnish.

Place the thinly pared rind of 1 orange in the bird with a good nut of butter and seasoning. Smear the remaining butter over the breast; truss and place the bird in a roasting-tin with the stock. Roast in a moderate oven, basting and turning from time to time.

In the meantime prepare the sauce and cut the orange into segments without pith or membrane. Dish the duck. Tip off the fat from the roasting-tin, leaving the sediment behind, and add the wine and any juice from the oranges and boil up well. Strain into the sauce, add the redcurrant jelly, and simmer to a syrupy consistency. Adjust the seasoning. Spoon a little sauce over the duck, garnish it with watercress at one end and with the orange sections at the other, and hand the remaining sauce separately.

Caneton aux Cerises

1 duckling with giblets; ¼ pint stock; ½ gill red wine.

SAUCE: 1 oz. butter; mirepoix of 1 oz. each onion and shallot; ¾ oz. flour; ¾ pint stock; 1 tablespoon chopped mushroom stalks; ¾ gill red wine; salt and pepper.

ACCOMPANIMENT: 1 lb. cherries – red, preferably Morellos; ¾ gill port wine; 2 tablespoons castor sugar; 1 orange; 4 tablespoons redcurrant jelly.

Set the duck in a roasting-tin with the giblets and stock but reserve the wine and the liver. Roast in a moderate oven for 40 to 60 minutes according to size.

In the meantime prepare the sauce and the cherries. Brown the mirepoix in the butter, add the flour and brown also; add all the remaining ingredients and simmer for 30 to 40 minutes. Strain and reserve the vegetables.

Stone the cherries and place in a casserole with the sugar and a pinch of powdered cinnamon. Cover and cook slowly for five minutes. Remove from the heat and allow to cool. In another pan, reduce the wine by half, adding the grated rind and juice of the orange, also the juice from the cherries. Then add the redcurrant jelly and when it has all melted add to the cherries.

Carve the bird and arrange in a serving-dish. Pound the carcass and raw liver with the reserved wine and vegetables, bring to the boil, strain, and add the liquor to the sauce. Spoon the sauce over the duck and serve the cherries separately.

Caneton aux Navets

1 duckling; 1 oz. butter; 1 lemon; ¼ pint stock; 1 glass white wine; ½ pint demi-glace sauce.

GARNISH: 1 lb. small new turnips; ½ lb. small onions; 1 oz. butter; 1 level tablespoon castor sugar.

Place the thinly pared rind of the lemon in the bird with a good nut of butter and seasoning. Smear the remaining butter over the breast; truss and place the bird in a roasting-tin with the stock. Roast in a moderate oven, basting and turning from time to time. Prepare the sauce in the meantime.

Blanch the turnips and place in a shallow saucepan or casserole with the melted butter and castor sugar. Cook over a gentle heat, shaking the pan from time to time until the turnips are tender and the sugar has caramelized. Then add the onions, also blanched, and continue cooking a few minutes.

Dish the duck, skim off the fat, add the wine and juice of ½ a lemon to the roasting-tin, and boil up well. Strain into the sauce and reduce rapidly to the desired consistency. Spoon a little sauce over the duck, garnish with the turnips and onions, and hand the remaining sauce separately.

Braised Duckling with Olives

1 duckling; 1 oz. butter; 1 glass port; ½ pint demi-glace sauce; bouquet garni containing a good strip of lemon rind; 1 doz. large green olives.

Brown the duck in the butter in a deep casserole and when nicely coloured on all sides tip off the fat; moisten with the wine, allow to reduce by half, and then add the herbs and sauce. Cover and cook very gently until tender – about 45 minutes. In the meantime 'turn' the olives and blanch in boiling water for 5 minutes; drain and leave soaking in cold water for half an hour, then drain again. Take up the duck, skim the sauce thoroughly, add the olives, reheat, and adjust the seasoning. Spoon over the duck and serve very hot.

GOOSE

In season from September to February but at their very best around Christmas. In this country they are usually roasted and the classic accompaniments are the same as for duck. A bird up to 6 months old is known as a gosling or green goose. When choosing an older bird make sure that the legs are soft and yellow and still have some down on them. A goose very quickly 'runs to fat' and for its size and weight has little meat as, like the duck, the breast is shallow. A 10-lb. goose will feed only eight people.

*

Roast Goose with Prune and Apple Stuffing
1 young goose weighing 10–12 lb.; 1½ tablespoons salt; ½ teaspoon white pepper; 20 prunes; 6 apples.

Soak the prunes in water or red wine and then remove the stones; peel and quarter the apples.

Rub the goose inside and out with the salt and pepper and stuff with the apples and prunes. Truss and sew up. Cover the breast with a little fat and roast in a moderate oven about 2½ hours. When almost done, baste with 2 to 3 tablespoons of cold water to crisp the skin. Take up the bird, pour off the fat, and brown 1 tablespoon flour in the sediment; tip on ½ pint stock made from the giblets, season, and boil up well. Strain the gravy, pour a little round the goose, and hand the remainder separately. Serve with browned potatoes and braised red cabbage.

Roast Goose with Potato Stuffing
1 young goose; seasoning; 1 oz. butter; 1 teaspoon mustard; ½ teaspoon salt; a pinch cayenne pepper; 1 glass port wine.

POTATO STUFFING: 2 onions; 1 lb. potatoes; 1 teaspoon dried sage; 3 oz. butter or thick cream; salt and pepper.

First prepare the stuffing. Chop the onions finely and cover with cold water; cook until tender and drain well. Boil the potatoes, drain and dry thoroughly over gentle heat, then mash until smooth; work in the butter and onions and season to taste. Fill the body of the goose with the stuffing, truss and sew firmly at each end. Mix the butter with the made mustard, salt and cayenne and spread over the breast of the bird. Set in a roasting-tin and cook in a moderate oven for about $2\frac{1}{2}$ hours, basting and turning from time to time. When almost done, tip off the fat, pour over the port, and continue cooking until the skin is crisp.

GAME

Under this heading come the wild birds and animals: black game, capercaillie, grouse, hare, partridge, pheasant, pigeon, quail, rabbit, snipe, teal, venison, widgeon, wild duck, and woodcock.

Unlike poultry, which is now in season throughout the year, game is protected by law (with the exception of pigeon and rabbit) and has a closed season during which period the birds may not be shot or sold.

It is necessary to hang game and the length of time allowed is very much a case for personal taste, but even when 'high' meat is not appreciated a short time for hanging is essential if the flesh is to be tender and have flavour, particularly important as young game birds are roasted quickly and served slightly underdone. Time for hanging will also depend on the weather and the condition of the birds if badly shot. In warm or thundery weather game ripens more quickly. Handle game to be hung as little as possible; hang by the beak, unplucked and undrawn, in a cool, airy room or outhouse and keep protected from flies. When the bird is ready the tail feathers are easy to pull. Old birds are hung in exactly same way, allowing perhaps a little longer time to make quite sure that the meat is tender, but the cooking method must be quite different. Birds bought from a shop are normally already hung. Gentle heat over a long period is necessary to break down the tissue (a process started by hanging) and to soften the tough sinews found in old birds. Pot-roasting, braising, and casserole cooking are suitable.

Young birds can be identified in the following way. The legs should be smooth and pliable; the feet supple and easily broken; and in the male bird the spurs are short and rounded. The feathers on the breast and under the wing are soft and downy and the long wing feathers quite pointed; on an older bird these become rounded.

As roasting is considered by many to be the finest way of cooking game, a general recipe with the classic accompaniments follows but the season and approximate time for hanging and cooking is given under each bird.

*

Roast Game

1 young game bird; 1–2 slices of fat bacon or barding fat; 2 oz. butter or bacon fat.

ACCOMPANIMENTS: clear gravy; fried crumbs; watercress to garnish; game chips; green salad (see page 349); bread sauce.

Set the oven at 400° F. or Reg. 6.

Wipe the bird inside and out with a damp cloth but do not wash. Place a nut of butter worked with seasoning and a squeeze of lemon inside the bird and then truss with fine string or linen thread if the bird is small. Avoid using skewers unless very fine as these can cause the loss of natural juices during cooking. Put on the giblets with water to cover and vegetables to flavour, season lightly, and simmer for 30 to 40 minutes. Heat the butter or bacon fat in a roasting-tin and put in the game bird when the butter is foaming or when the bacon fat is smoking. Baste frequently and turn during cooking time. Five minutes before dishing remove the barding bacon, baste and dredge with flour. Baste again and return to the oven to 'froth' the breast.

Take up the bird, remove the trussing string, and keep hot while preparing the gravy. Tip off the fat from the roasting-tin but leave any sediment; 'dry' the pan with the lightest dusting of flour and tip on the stock from the giblets. Boil up, reduce well, season carefully, and strain. The gravy should be well flavoured, a good brown colour, and quite clear. Place the bird on a hot

serving-dish and garnish with watercress. (Small birds are
frequently served on a croûte of fried bread or toast.) Hand the
gravy and accompaniments separately.

FRIED CRUMBS: 4 heaped tablespoons fine breadcrumbs; 1 oz.
clarified or unsalted butter.

Heat the butter in a small frying-pan and when it is foaming put in
the crumbs and stir until golden brown. Serve in a small gratin
dish.

BLACK GAME

In season 20 August to 10 December. Larger than grouse; one
will feed 3 to 4 people. Hang 6 to 7 days, and, as the flesh is
inclined to be dry, roast for 45 to 60 minutes with a good nut of
butter inside. Serve on buttered toast with the usual accompaniments for roast game.

CAPERCAILLIE OR CAPERCAILZIE

Of the same family as grouse and is in season at the same time.
Hang for at least 6 to 7 days or the flesh will be tough and lack
flavour. Roast for 45 to 50 minutes and serve with the usual
accompaniments.

GROUSE

In season 12 August to 10 December. The best of the game
birds. Hang 6 to 7 days, although if very young 3 to 4 days
would be enough. Roast unless the bird is old.

Grouse en cocotte

2 old grouse; 1 oz. butter or dripping; 2 carrots; 2 onions; 1
turnip; 1 stick celery; ½–¾ pint jellied stock; bouquet garni;
1 glass red wine; 1 dessertspoon redcurrant or rowan jelly.

Melt the butter in a stewpan, wipe the grouse, and brown slowly on all sides. Remove from the pan and keep warm. Cut the vegetables into small dice, add to the pan, cover, and cook slowly until they absorb the fat and begin to take colour. Replace the grouse on top of the vegetables, season with salt and pepper, add the herbs, and pour over enough stock to cover the vegetables. Flame the wine in a small saucepan and pour over the grouse. Cover the pan tightly and cook on top of the stove for 40 minutes, then continue cooking in a moderate oven for 20 to 30 minutes. Baste 2 or 3 times while cooking. Take up the grouse, split it in half, cut away the backbone, and arrange in the serving-dish. Strain the liquid from the pan and reduce until syrupy; adjust the seasoning and add the redcurrant jelly. Stir until melted and spoon over the grouse. Garnish with glazed onions.

HARE

In season from early autumn to 28 January. They can be hung up to 10 or even 14 days in cold weather and are secured by the back legs to allow the blood to drain and collect in the thorax; this is used to thicken the gravy in many recipes. The flesh of the hare is close and dry and is greatly improved if marinaded before cooking. An English hare is considered to be finer than the Scotch or blue hare and will feed 8 to 10 people. Only a very young hare should be roasted whole. It is more usual these days to roast the back or saddle only and to use the legs and 'wings' for jugging.

*

Saddle of Hare Vigneronne

1 saddle of hare; a piece of barding bacon; 2 onions; 1 carrot; 2 cloves garlic; 1 tablespoon brandy; 2 glasses sherry; bouquet garni; ¾ gill good stock; ¼ gill cream; 2 tablespoons blood from the hare; 1½ oz. butter; 20–30 good grapes.

Trim the saddle and put into a china dish. Cover and surround with the sliced vegetables, chopped garlic, and herbs; pour over the brandy and sherry and leave to marinade several hours, overnight if possible.

Take up the saddle, wipe and cover with the barding bacon. Strain the marinade, put the vegetables at the bottom of a fire-proof dish, set the hare on the top, and cook in a moderate oven for ½ hour. Pour over the liquid from the marinade, baste well, cover the dish, and continue cooking for about 30 to 40 minutes. Take up the saddle and keep hot. Pour the stock into the pan and boil up well; add the cream and reduce a little. Stir in the butter in small pieces and the blood. Strain into a small pan, add the grapes, and heat carefully without boiling. Put the saddle on a serving-dish, surround with the grapes, and spoon over the sauce.

Sauté of Hare with Chestnut Purée

1 hare with blood (use the back and part of the hind legs only – the remainder can be jugged).

MARINADE: 2 glasses red wine; 1 large bouquet garni; 1 sliced onion and carrot; 6–8 peppercorns; 1 dessertspoon wine vinegar; 1 tablespoon olive oil.

FOR THE SAUTÉ: 1 medium onion finely chopped; 2 oz. butter; 1 scant ounce flour; the strained marinade from the hare; 1½ gills to ½ pint strong jellied stock; 1 dessertspoon redcurrant jelly; 4 oz. button mushrooms; 4 oz. chipolata sausages.

Joint the hare. Put all the ingredients for the marinade into a saucepan and bring to the boil. When quite cold pour over the joints of hare and leave 2 to 3 days before cooking.

Wipe the hare and brown slowly in the hot butter, remove and brown the sausages and quartered mushrooms also. Add the onion and after a few minutes the flour; allow to colour, then add the strained marinade, stock, and jelly. Bring to the boil, season, and replace the hare. Simmer for 40 to 50 minutes. Then draw aside and add the blood mixed with a teaspoonful of arrowroot. Bring to boiling-point, then dish and serve with:

Chestnut 'au gratin'

1 tin unsweetened chestnut purée; ¼ pint Béchamel made with 1 oz. butter, 1 oz. flour, and ¼ pint flavoured milk; 1 large egg; brown crumbs; grated cheese and melted butter to finish.

Have the sauce ready and beat it into the purée. Season very well and beat in the yolk, adding a little creamy milk if necessary. Whip the white, fold in, and turn into a buttered gratin dish. Sprinkle well with crumbs, cheese, and melted butter. Brown in a quick oven for 15 to 20 minutes.

Jugged Hare

Legs and 'wings' of hare, or 1 hare jointed with the blood; 1 tablespoon good dripping or ham fat; 2 onions; 2 carrots; 1 stick celery; bouquet garni; approximately 1½ pints stock or water; 1 tablespoon redcurrant jelly; small glass port wine; forcemeat balls.

Wipe the pieces of hare and reserve the blood. Brown in the hot dripping in a stewpan; remove and keep warm. Slice the vegetables, add to the pan, cover, and cook slowly for 6 to 7 minutes; then replace the hare, add the seasoning and stock, cover the pan, and braise gently in the oven for 2 or 3 hours or until quite tender. Remove the joints and place in a deep casserole for serving. Strain the stock and measure – there should be ¾ pint. Return to the pan with the jelly and port, simmer 5 minutes, and adjust the seasoning. Draw aside and add the blood. Reheat, stirring well, but do not allow to boil. Strain the sauce over the hare, cover, and set the casserole in a slow oven for 15 to 20 minutes. Send to the table with forcemeat balls arranged on top or if preferred served separately.

PARTRIDGE

There are two varieties of partridge shot in this country – the grey partridge and the red-legged or 'Frenchman'. They are in season from 1 September to 1 February; the young grey birds should be hung for 3 to 4 days as they have a very subtle flavour of their own and are best roasted, but an older bird or the 'Frenchman', which needs extra time and care in cooking, should be hung for 6 or 7 days.

*

Partridge au Chou

2 partridges; 1 oz. butter, clarified; 2 shallots; 1 glass white wine;
½ pint jellied stock; bouquet garni containing a stick of celery;
2 even-sized carrots.

1 Dutch white cabbage; 1 large onion; 1 oz. butter; 1 glass white
wine; 6 oz. salt and belly pork.

Brown the birds on all sides in the butter, add the finely chopped
shallots to the pan, and allow to brown; tip on the wine and
reduce to nothing.

Pour the stock into the pan, add seasoning and herbs and the
carrots whole. Cover and cook very gently for about an hour. Cut
the cabbage in half, remove the core, and shred finely. Slice the
onion and put in a stewpan with the butter, cover and cook until
soft but not coloured. Add the cabbage and stir over gentle heat
10 minutes, then add the wine and seasoning. Cover with a
buttered paper and a lid and cook gently for about 30 to 40
minutes. In the meantime simmer the pork for 30 minutes, then
remove the rind, cut the meat in julienne strips, add it to the
cabbage, and continue cooking for 10 to 15 minutes.

Take up the partridges, carve and arrange in a serving-dish.
Cut the carrots into thin rounds and use as garnish. Strain the
liquid in the pan, reduce to a glaze, and spoon over the partridges.
Dish the cabbage and serve separately.

Partridge Bourguignon

2 plump partridges; 1 oz. butter; 2 glasses Burgundy; ½ pint good
jellied stock; 1 teaspoon tomato purée; bouquet garni; 4 oz.
rasher unsmoked streaky bacon; 4 oz. button mushrooms; 2 doz.
pickling onions; 1 oz. butter; kneaded butter made with 1 oz.
butter and ½ oz. flour.

Drop 1 oz. butter in a heavy casserole and when foaming put in
the partridges and colour slowly on all sides. Season with salt
and pepper and add the herbs. Flame just one glass of the wine,
pour over the birds, and add the stock and tomato purée. Cover
with paper and lid and place in a moderate oven to cook. In the
meantime remove the rust and rind from the bacon, cut into

lardons, and blanch to remove the saltpetre; wash the mushrooms in salt water, drain, and cut into quarters. Blanch the small onions. Melt the 1 oz. butter in a frying-pan, put in the bacon and onions, and cook until taking colour; then add the mushrooms and continue cooking for 2 or 3 minutes.

When the partridges have had 40 minutes' cooking, add the bacon, mushrooms, and onions and continue cooking until all are tender (about 10 or 15 minutes). Take up the partridges, carve and arrange in a serving-dish, and keep warm. Flame the remaining glass of wine, add to the juices in the pan, and then thicken with the kneaded butter. Spoon the sauce and garnish over the birds.

Partridge aux Olives Noires
2 partridges; 2 oz. butter; 2 shallots; 4 oz. gammon rasher; 4 oz. black olives; 1 glass red wine; 1 teaspoon tomato purée; ½ pint demi-glace sauce.

Roast the birds (first covering the breasts with fat bacon) in a fairly hot oven for 20 to 25 minutes, using two-thirds of the butter. In the meantime melt the remaining butter in a small sauté pan; add the finely chopped shallot and the bacon cut in strips and blanched. Cook slowly until golden brown, then add the stoned olives. After two minutes tip on the wine, reduce by half, and then add the purée and sauce. Simmer together a few minutes. Split the partridges, trim away the backbone, arrange on a hot dish, and spoon over the sauce.

PHEASANT

In season 1 October to 1 February and should be hung for 6 to 7 days. The cock bird is larger than the hen but the hen is fatter and the flesh more succulent. A good pheasant will serve four or five people as there is plenty of breast-meat. Roast the young birds and pot-roast or casserole the older birds.

*

Pheasant Flamande
1 good pheasant; 1 carrot; 1 onion; 1½ oz. fresh butter; larding

bacon; ¼ pint good stock; 6 heads chicory; 1 oz. butter; juice of
one lemon; 2–3 tablespoons water.

Cover the pheasant with a piece of larding bacon. Heat a large
pan or casserole, drop in the butter, and, while it is still foaming,
put in the pheasant. Put the onion and carrot cut in quarters
around. Cover and cook on a brisk to moderate heat for 5 minutes,
then cook on the side of the fire until the bird is almost cooked,
turning it over from time to time.

Meanwhile trim and wash the chicory. Lay it in a casserole in
which the butter has been melted. Season well with freshly ground
pepper and salt. Add the lemon juice and water; cover. Cook
in a moderate oven until the liquid has evaporated and the chicory
is tender.

Take up the pheasant, remove the bacon. Deglaze the pan with
the stock, and strain. Arrange the chicory in a deep dish, carve the
pheasant, and put on top; pour over the gravy and put back in the
oven for 7 to 8 minutes before serving.

Pheasant Normande

1 plump pheasant; 1 oz. clarified butter; 2 shallots; 1 glass
Calvados; 2 Cox's apples; ¼ pint jellied stock; bouquet garni; ¼
pint thick cream.

Brown the pheasant on all sides in the butter, add the finely
chopped shallots to the pan, and cook until golden. Flame with
the Calvados and reduce by half. Tip on the stock, add the peeled,
cored, and sliced apples, seasonings, and bouquet, and bring
to the boil. Cover tightly and cook gently for about 50 minutes.
Take up the pheasant, carve, and arrange in the serving-dish.

Pass the contents of the casserole through a fine sieve or nylon
strainer and return to the rinsed pan. Thicken lightly with a very
little slaked arrowroot. Boil the cream, add to the sauce, adjust
the seasoning, and spoon over the pheasant. Serve with a julienne
of celery and potato.

JULIENNE OF CELERY AND POTATO
1 shallot, chopped; 2–3 even-sized potatoes; 1 head celery; 1 oz.
butter.

Cut the potatoes and celery into julienne strips. Heat the butter in a sauté pan, add the celery and shallot, and shake over the heat for 4 to 5 minutes. Add the potatoes, season, cover the pan, and continue to cook on the stove-top or in the oven until the vegetables are tender.

Pheasant Périgord

1 plump pheasant; 1–2 oz. butter; ¼ pint jellied stock; 2 glasses sherry; ½ pint demi-glace sauce; 1 truffle for garnish or 2 oz. small button mushrooms.

FARCE: 1 shallot; 1 oz. butter; 6 oz. minced veal; 4 oz. calf's liver, minced; 1 2–3 oz. tin pâté de foie; 2–3 tablespoons fresh breadcrumbs; 1 dessertspoon chopped herbs and parsley; 1 tablespoon brandy; a little beaten egg.

First prepare the farce. Cook the shallot in the butter until soft and allow to cool. Mix the veal, liver, and pâté together, add the breadcrumbs, herbs, and brandy, and season to taste. Add the prepared shallot and enough beaten egg to bind. Bone out the pheasant, season and spread with the farce, sew up or secure with poultry pins, reshape and truss firmly, set in a roasting-tin, rub the bird well with butter, and pour round the stock and 1 glass of the sherry. Roast for about 1½ hours at 400° F. or Reg. 6, basting and turning during the cooking.

Meanwhile prepare the demi-glace sauce. Take up the pheasant and keep warm. Tip off the fat from the roasting-tin and deglaze with the remaining glass of sherry, scraping the sides of the pan well. Strain it into the sauce. Carve the pheasant and arrange it in the serving-dish. Add the truffle cut into slices to the sauce and spoon over the pheasant. If using mushrooms in place of the truffle, these should be sliced and cooked in a nut of butter and a squeeze of lemon.

PIGEON

There is no closed season for pigeon but they are at their best from March to October. They should be cooked very fresh from 12 to

24 hours after killing. Their flesh is particularly delicate and butter should be used for browning or roasting. 20 to 25 minutes will be ample time for French roasting a young bird.

*

Pigeon with Raisins

2–4 pigeons, depending on size; 1–2 oz. butter; 6 small onions; ½–¾ pint clear beef stock; 2 oz. stoned raisins; ¼ pint water; kneaded butter made with 1 oz. butter and ½ oz. flour.

Brown the pigeons very slowly on all sides in the butter, remove, and keep warm while browning the onions. Return to the pan, pour over the stock, season, and bring to the boil; cover and cook in a very moderate oven for 1 hour.

Meanwhile clean the raisins and leave to soak in the water.

After the pigeons have been cooking 40 minutes, baste them well and add the raisins and water to the pan. Continue cooking until tender, then dish. Split the pigeons in half, cut away the backbones, and arrange in a serving-dish. Thicken the gravy with the kneaded butter, adjust the seasoning, and spoon over the birds.

Pigeon Italienne

2–4 pigeons; 2 oz. butter; 1 shallot; ¾ pint tomato sauce (see page 378); 1 doz. button onions; 2 oz. button mushrooms.

Brown the pigeons slowly in half the butter, remove from the pan, and cut each one in two, cutting away the backbone, and keep warm. Add the finely chopped shallot to the pan and cook until soft, then dust in 1 teaspoon flour and colour carefully. Tip on the tomato sauce, well flavoured with garlic, and stir until boiling. Replace the pigeons, cover tightly, and cook in a slow oven for about an hour. Meanwhile blanch the onions, drain, and return to the pan with ½ oz. butter and ½ teaspoon castor sugar and cook over gentle heat until brown. Slice the mushrooms and cook for 2 or 3 minutes in a small covered pan with the remaining ½ oz. butter, seasoning, and a squeeze of lemon.

Dish the pigeons, add the onions and mushrooms to the sauce, and spoon over. Serve with nouilles tossed in butter or a little boiled cream.

Pigeons Allemand

3 pigeons; bacon rashers; croûtes of bread.

FORCEMEAT: 1 oz. butter; 1 tablespoon finely chopped onion; 1 tablespoon finely chopped mushroom; the chopped livers and giblets of the pigeons; 1 tablespoon finely chopped parsley; 3–4 tablespoons fresh white crumbs; 1 yolk of egg; seasoning.

FOR BRAISING: 1 large onion; 1–2 carrots; 1 stick celery; 1 dessertspoon oil; $\frac{1}{2}$ oz. butter; 1 glass sherry; $\frac{1}{2}$–$\frac{3}{4}$ pint good stock; bouquet garni; $\frac{1}{2}$ oz. kneaded butter.

Bone out the pigeons, leaving in the leg bones. Prepare the forcemeat by softening the onion in butter, add the mushroom and giblets, and cook briskly for a few minutes. Draw aside. Add the parsley and crumbs and, when thoroughly mixed, the yolk and seasoning, adding a spoonful of stock if necessary. Fill into the pigeons, truss them neatly, and cover each with a piece of bacon.

Slice the vegetables. Heat the oil and butter in a stewpan, put in the vegetables, cover, and allow to cook gently for 5 to 6 minutes; then draw aside, lay the pigeons on the vegetables, and flame with the sherry; pour round the stock and add the bouquet. Put the pan into the oven uncovered and braise for 45 to 50 minutes, basting occasionally. Meanwhile fry the croûtes. Take up the pigeons, cut in two, and arrange on the croûtes in a hot dish. Strain the liquor from the pan, add the kneaded butter to thicken slightly, boil rapidly for a few minutes, then coat over the pigeons. Serve with fruit compote such as cranberry, mirabelle plum, or cherry.

Salmis of Pigeons

4 pigeons; $1\frac{1}{2}$ oz. butter; $\frac{1}{2}$ teacup stock; 1 oz. diced carrot, onion, and celery (mirepoix); $1\frac{1}{2}$ oz. butter; 1 oz. flour; bouquet garni; sprig of thyme; 4–5 parsley stalks; $\frac{3}{4}$ pint stock; $\frac{1}{2}$ teaspoon tomato purée; 2 glasses red wine; $\frac{1}{4}$ lb. mushrooms; croûtes of bread.

Roast the pigeons lightly in a hot oven with the butter and stock for about 15 minutes. Meanwhile melt 1 oz. butter, add the mirepoix, and cook slowly until soft but not coloured. Then add the remainder of the butter and flour and allow to cook to a good brown. Draw aside, add the stock, purée, and bouquet, season lightly, and simmer, skimming occasionally, for 20 minutes.

Cut the breasts from the pigeons, split them in two, and place them in a casserole. Chop or pound the carcasses, add the wine, and turn into a saucepan. Strain the sauce and add the vegetables to the carcasses. Allow this to boil rapidly for a few minutes, then strain back again into the sauce, pressing well to extract all the juice. Simmer the sauce for about 20 minutes or until syrupy consistency. Adjust the seasoning.

Pour half the sauce over the pigeons in the casserole; set on a gentle heat or in the oven for about 10 to 15 minutes. Meantime sauté the mushrooms and fry the croûtes. Add the mushrooms with the remaining sauce to the salmis, and continue cooking for a further seven minutes. Garnish with the croûtes and serve.

QUAIL

A small game-bird that is eaten quite fresh, the day after being killed. The breast is usually covered with vine leaves and then wrapped in a thin rasher of bacon. Roast for just 15 minutes, basting with butter. Serve on a croûte of fried or toasted bread.

RABBIT

In season early autumn to February, although it can be bought throughout the year as there is no restriction on its sale. Imported rabbit and Ostend (tame) rabbit are available at all times. Rabbit must be paunched immediately it is killed and eaten within 1 to 3 days.

*

Fricassée of Rabbit
1 rabbit; 1 onion; 6 peppercorns; salt; bouquet garni.

SAUCE: 1½ oz. butter; ¼ lb. button mushrooms; 1 oz. flour; ½ pint liquid from the rabbit; ¼ pint single cream or top milk; lemon juice; 1 teaspoon chopped parsley.

GARNISH: croûtes of fried bread and bacon rolls.

Soak the rabbit in salted water for 12 hours to whiten the flesh. Cut into joints and blanch to remove any strong flavour. Place the rabbit in a pan with warm water barely to cover, bring to the boil, and skim well; add the onion, seasoning, and herbs, cover and simmer gently for about an hour or until the meat is tender. Strain off ½ pint of the rabbit liquor for the sauce and keep the rabbit warm. Melt ½ oz. of the butter, add the mushrooms, halved (or quartered if large), and cook for 2 to 3 minutes. Add the rest of the butter and, when melted, stir in the flour. Cook for a further 2 minutes, then blend in the stock and creamy milk and stir until boiling. Simmer for a few minutes and adjust the seasoning, then add the lemon juice and parsley. Place the rabbit in a serving-dish, spoon over the sauce, and garnish with the fried croûtes and grilled bacon rolls.

Rabbit Moutardé

1 good rabbit (about 1½ lb.); 4 oz. green streaky bacon or pickled pork in the piece; 1 oz. ham fat, butter, or dripping; 6 medium-sized onions, quartered; scant 1 oz. flour; 1–1¼ pints stock; salt; freshly ground black pepper; 1 dessertspoon French mustard; bouquet garni; ½ gill cream; 1 dessertspoon chopped parsley.

Joint the rabbit and soak overnight in salted water with a dash of vinegar in it. Drain, rinse, and dry the pieces well. Remove the rind from the bacon, cut into large dice, and blanch. Drain and set aside. Heat the fat in a heavy stewpan, lightly brown the pieces of rabbit, remove, then add the bacon and onions. Fry, shaking and stirring occasionally until nicely coloured. Draw aside, blend in the flour and stock, and stir until boiling. Put in the pieces of rabbit with the herbs, very little salt, pepper, and the mustard. Cover the pan tightly and simmer for about an hour until the rabbit is very tender. Dish the rabbit, remove the herbs, and reduce the sauce if necessary over a brisk fire. Add the cream and parsley. Spoon over the rabbit and serve very hot. Hand a lentil purée separately.

LENTIL PURÉE: ¾ pint Egyptian lentils; 1 onion stuck with a clove; 1 carrot cut in thick rounds; bouquet garni; 3–4 tablespoons good stock; 2 oz. butter.

Wash the lentils very thoroughly and put to soak in tepid water for 2 hours. Put into a pan, cover with plenty of water, add a little salt, the onion, carrot, and herbs, and bring very slowly to the boil. Simmer until the lentils can be crushed between the fingers and thumb, then rub through a sieve. Return to the rinsed-out pan and stir briskly over heat. Add the stock to lighten the purée, remove from the heat, and beat in the butter and a little pepper.

Rabbit Flamande

1 rabbit; 1 tablespoon dripping; 3 oz. salted belly pork; 4 onions; ½–¾ pint mild ale; seasoning; 2 lumps sugar; 2–3 slices from a French roll; French mustard.

Soak the rabbit overnight as directed in the previous recipe. Simmer the pork for 20 minutes, then drain and cut into lardons. Wash and dry the rabbit well and cut into joints. Heat the dripping in a casserole, add the pork and sliced onions, and brown slowly and well; remove from the pan and colour the rabbit on all sides, then tip off any excess fat. Put the onions and pork back on top of the rabbit, season well, and add the sugar. Cover with the slices of bread, spread generously with French mustard, and pour in the ale to come up to the level of the bread. Cover tightly and cook in a moderate oven for about 2 hours or until very tender. Remove the lid from the pan for the last 15 minutes of cooking time to brown and crisp the bread.

Rabbit Sauté Chasseur

1 young rabbit; 1 dessertspoon oil; 1 oz. butter; 2 shallots; ¾ oz. flour; 1 glass white wine; ½ pint good stock; 1 teaspoon tomato purée; bouquet garni; 2 oz. mushrooms.

GARNISH: croûtes of fried bread.

Joint and soak the rabbit in the usual way, then drain and dry thoroughly. Heat the oil in a sauté pan, drop in the butter, and, when it is foaming, put in the rabbit and colour nicely on all sides. Add the chopped shallots to the pan, cook for 2 to 3 minutes, then dust in the flour and allow to colour. Pour on the white wine, stock, and tomato purée, blend until smooth, add seasoning and the herbs, and bring to the boil. Cover the pan and simmer gently for about an hour. Meanwhile slice the mushrooms if buttons, or chop finely if flat, and add these to the pan 20 minutes before serving. Garnish with the croûtes of fried bread and dust with chopped parsley.

SNIPE

These small birds, like woodcock, are dressed without being drawn. The head is skinned and the long beak is used as a skewer to hold the legs in position. They are served rather underdone and should, as the old cooks say, 'just fly through the kitchen'. Brush them well with melted butter, bard with fat bacon, set on a piece of toast to catch the juices from the trail, and cook for about 15 minutes. Baste frequently with butter. Serve with watercress and a good gravy. They are in season from 1 September to 28 February and should be hung for 3 to 4 days.

TEAL

One of the smaller wild ducks, in season 1 September to 28 February but at their best before Christmas. Hang for only 1 to 3 days and allow one bird per person. Roast for 20 to 25 minutes and serve with watercress and quarters of lemon or an orange salad or bigarade sauce (see page 374).

WIDGEON

A wild duck larger than the teal, in season at the same time but at its best in October and November. Hang for 1 to 3 days and one bird will serve two people. Roast 35 minutes. Accompaniments are the same as for teal.

WILD DUCK

In season from 1 September to 28 February, but really best during November and December. Hang for 1 to 3 days and allow one bird for two people. Roast 35 minutes and serve with watercress, a good gravy, and orange salad or a bigarade sauce (see page 374).

*

Spiced Wild Duck
2 wild duck; 2–3 oz. butter; ½ teaspoon ground ginger; bouquet garni; 1 clove garlic; 1 glass port wine; juice of 1 orange; 2 croûtes of bread.

GARNISH: 10 small dessert apples; 3–4 tablespoons redcurrant jelly; 2 tablespoons wine vinegar.

Brown the birds lightly in the butter in a deep casserole, season with salt and freshly ground black pepper, add the ginger, bouquet, and finely chopped garlic; cover and cook for about 50 to 60 minutes, basting from time to time.

Meanwhile peel and core the apples and bake in the oven in the remaining butter until golden brown. Melt the redcurrant jelly in the vinegar and keep warm.

Carve the ducks by splitting in half and removing the backbone and set each duck on a croûte of fried bread. Place the apples round the dish and coat each one with a spoonful of the jelly. Skim the fat from the juices in the pan, add the port and orange juice, and boil up well. Adjust the seasoning and strain into a sauce-boat for serving.

VENISON

Venison is the meat of the red, roe, and fallow deer. It is in season from late June until January. The buck venison is considered the finest and is in season only from late June until late September,

but the doe venison remains in season through November and
December. The meat is very similar to mutton, but not having the
same natural protective layer of fat it lacks flavour and so it is
usual to marinade venison for a few days in a mixture of oil, wine,
spices, herbs, and seasonings. The marinade may be used in the
cooking or added to the accompanying sauce. Hang for 8 to 10
days, keep wiped free of moisture every day, and protect from
flies.

*

Braised Venison with Celery Hearts

2–2½ lb. venison from haunch or loin; dripping or oil; sliced
vegetables for braising; onion, carrot, celery; large bouquet of
herbs including the pared rind of an orange; ½ pint stock; juice
of the orange; 1 tablespoon redcurrant jelly; 1 oz. kneaded
butter.

MARINADE: 2 glasses red wine; 2–3 tablespoons oil; 1 onion,
sliced; 1 dessertspoon juniper berries; 1 teaspoon allspice; 1 bayleaf; a bunch of parsley stalks.

BRAISED CELERY: 2 large heads of celery (see page 343).

Trim the venison and tie up neatly. Lay in a deep dish. Combine
the ingredients for the marinade, bring up to the boil, and when
cold pour over the meat. Leave 2 or 3 days, turning occasionally.
To braise, wipe the meat and brown quickly all over in hot
dripping or oil and butter mixed. Remove and put in the sliced
vegetables. Cover the pan and cook gently 5 or 6 minutes. Lay
the meat on the top; add the herbs, marinade, and stock. Cover
and braise gently in the oven for 1½ to 2 hours or until tender.
Baste occasionally.

When the venison is tender, take up, carve, and arrange in the
serving-dish. Strain off the gravy, reduce a little, and add the
orange juice and jelly. When dissolved, thicken with the kneaded
butter and reboil. Spoon a little over the venison and arrange
round the braised celery hearts. Serve the rest of the sauce
separately.

Fillets of Venison Poivrade

1½–2 lb. fillet of venison cut into small thick steaks; red wine; heart-shaped croûtes from stale bread; 2–3 oz. raisins; 1 oz. salted cashew nuts.

SAUCE POIVRADE: 3 tablespoons oil; 1 tablespoon each diced carrot, onion, and celery; 1 tablespoon flour; a few mushroom peelings; 1 teaspoon tomato purée; 1 pint good bone stock; 1 large glass red wine; bouquet garni; 3 tablespoons wine vinegar.

Sprinkle the steaks with a little red wine and salad oil; set aside.

Meanwhile prepare the sauce. Dice the vegetables finely; heat the oil, add them, and allow barely to colour. Dust in the flour and cook slowly to a russet brown. Add the peelings, purée, ¾ pint of the stock, and the wine. Bring to the boil and simmer for 30 minutes. Add the rest of the stock in two parts, bringing the sauce to the boil between each addition and skimming well. Continue to simmer a further 15 to 20 minutes, then strain. Rinse out the pan, add the vinegar, and reduce to half. Add the sauce, reboil, and finish with a nut of butter. Set aside.

Brown the croûtes in hot butter, take out and keep warm. Sauté the steaks for 3½ to 4 minutes on each side and dish them *en couronne* with a croûte between each steak. Add the raisins to the pan, shake up over brisk heat, add the nuts, and turn into the centre of the dish. Serve the sauce separately.

Chapter 8

THE COLD TABLE

In this chapter will be found dishes that were once served from the side-table to supplement a lunch or dinner: such things as galantines, cold tongue or pies, and the like. Nowadays these form part of a cold luncheon or buffet, together with others rather more elaborate which are especially suitable for entertaining.

ASPIC

Aspic plays a large part in cold-table work and, when properly made, is a pleasant adjunct to the dish. Good stock, whether meat, chicken, or fish, is essential for aspic and must be well flavoured and seasoned before clarifying. The flavour too will be improved if the stock is a good jelly, and this also enables the gelatine to be reduced in quantity. Again, if the stock is reasonably clear this helps the process of clarifying.

Aspic jelly may, if wished, be lightly acidulated with a few drops of vinegar or lemon juice to taste, though this depends somewhat on the dish. In most cases, however, the wine is enough to give the jelly a pleasant 'bite'. Aspic will keep for several days after making, especially if stored in a jug. Once set, run a little cold water over the top to prevent the jelly drying and losing flavour. Pour off the water before use.

Aspic is used in the following ways:

1. For glazing, i.e. brushing or spooning the cool jelly over the foods to be coated. The jelly must be on the point of setting, cool and thick without being lumpy, and, if too set, should be melted and then cooled again before use. As a rule two or three coats are necessary, allowing the jelly to set between each. A little ice is of help when doing this.

2. For lining both small and large moulds to be decorated and filled with a mousse or cream of some sort. Nowadays this type of work is only done for formal entertaining, but it is useful to know how. Ordinarily the moulds are filled as Prawns in Aspic (see page 25). In this case (and, for example, when setting fruit or jelly for turning out) care must be taken not to have the pieces of fish or fruit too large as the weight of these will tend to split the jelly when it is turned out.

To line large or small moulds with jelly, first choose a plain mould such as a charlotte or dariole mould. Chill thoroughly and pour in a small quantity of cool aspic. Turn the mould continually on ice until there is an even layer of aspic both on the bottom and sides of the mould. Add more cool aspic if necessary, paying particular attention to the sides of the mould. Now decorate suitably with sprays of tarragon or chervil, truffle, mushroom, cucumber rind, etc., first dipping the decoration into cool aspic before arranging on the bottom and sides of the mould or moulds. When set, line again with cool aspic. To make the decoration stand out more distinctively the moulds may then be coated with aspic cream – $\frac{1}{4}$ pint aspic, 1 teaspoon gelatine, and $\frac{1}{2}$ gill thick cream.

First dissolve the gelatine in the aspic before adding the cream. After lining and decorating, the moulds are filled with a mousse of some kind, e.g. lobster, chicken, or salmon.

3. For decoration. The most usual form is chopped aspic. Turn the set jelly on to a piece of well-damped greaseproof paper and chop, but not too finely. Tilt the paper from time to time to turn the jelly without touching it with the hands. Spoon it on to the dish or use a forcing-bag and pipe to decorate. For a galantine or whole bird, aspic croûtons are sometimes used. These are small triangles or crescents cut from an inch-thick piece of set jelly and then placed round the edge of the dish.

Any dish or food either set in or decorated with aspic looks best on a silver or stainless-steel dish. Polish it well before using and run a film of aspic over the bottom. Let it set before arranging the food on the dish.

Bought aspic is perfectly suitable for brushing over cold chicken or game but for fish or anything delicate in flavour it is best to make the aspic with the appropriate stock.

*

Aspic Jelly
1¾ pints good stock, meat, chicken, or fish, well skimmed and free from grease; ½ gill each dry white wine and sherry; 2 oz. gelatine; 2 egg whites.

First choose a large pan, preferably of thick enamel and big enough so that the liquid only fills it by about a third. Scald it out with boiling water and scald also a large whisk and teacloth. Wring the latter dry, double it, and spread it over a bowl. Now turn the cold stock into the pan and add the wines to the gelatine. Whisk the whites to a light froth, add to the pan, set on gentle heat, and whisk backwards, i.e. from left to right, so that the whites are well whisked into the liquid. When just hot, add the gelatine mixture and continue to whisk as before until the liquid reaches boiling-point. Take out the whisk and allow the contents of the pan to boil up. Draw carefully aside and leave to settle for 4 to 5 minutes. Repeat this process twice more without stirring, bringing the liquid rapidly to the boil each time. After the third time,

and when the pan has been left to settle well, pour the contents on
to the cloth all at once. Lift up the cloth carefully and set over
another clean bowl; pour what liquid has come through into the
first bowl over the 'filter', i.e. the egg white, on the cloth. This
process may be repeated once more, when the aspic should be
crystal clear. If this is not so then the stock was at fault or the
whisking imperfectly carried out.

To Cook and Press a Tongue

1 ox tongue, salted and weighing 4–6 lb.; a plateful of roughly-
cut-up root vegetables; a large bouquet garni; a few peppercorns.

Wash the tongue and place in a large pan. Cover well with cold
water and bring slowly to the boil. Skim well, add the vegetables,
herbs, and peppercorns, and simmer until the bones at the root of
the tongue are easily pulled out (after about 3 hours). Cool in the
liquid, then take out the tongue, skin, and trim away some of the
root, removing the bones. Curl the tongue round and put into a
large cake tin; cover with a plate to fit just inside the tin with a
heavy weight on the top. Leave until next day before turning out.
Serve with Cumberland Sauce.

CUMBERLAND SAUCE

2 large tablespoons redcurrant jelly; 1 glass port or red wine;
juice of 1 orange; juice of $\frac{1}{2}$ lemon; about 1 teaspoon shredded
orange rind, blanched.

Heat the jelly until dissolved, then stir in the rest of the ingredients.
Serve cold.

Brawn

$\frac{1}{2}$ pig's head, salted, from the butcher; 1 lb. shin of beef; 1 large
onion; 6–8 peppercorns; a large bouquet garni or a teaspoon of
mixed dried herbs.

Wash the head and put into a large pan with the beef, the whole
onion, peppercorns, and herbs. Cover with cold water, bring to

the boil, cover and simmer gently until the bones can be easily pulled out and the beef is very tender (after about 3 hours). Take out the onion and lift out the head and beef. Remove all the bones and cut or pull both the pork and beef into small pieces. Add enough of the liquid to moisten well and turn into a brawn mould or cake tin. If the latter is used, put a plate to fit on top of the brawn with a 2-lb. weight on it. Leave until the next day before turning out. Cut into thin slices and serve with the following dressing:

2–3 tablespoons of wine vinegar; 1 large teaspoon mixed mustard; 3 tablespoons oil; 2 tablespoons brown sugar.

Combine these ingredients and season to taste with salt and pepper.

Galantine of Veal
3 lb. breast of veal boned.

STUFFING: 6 oz. pork sausage meat; 6 oz. ham or tongue; 2 chopped shallots softened in butter; a few pistachio nuts; chopped herbs; salt, pepper; 1 whole beaten egg.

FOR BRAISING: 1 oz. butter; 2 large onions; 2 large carrots; ½ pint stock; bouquet garni; seasoning.

MEAT GLAZE.

First prepare the stuffing. Mince the ham or tongue and mix with the sausage meat, shallot, pistachio nuts, herbs, and seasoning. Bind with the beaten egg. Spread the stuffing over the veal, roll, and sew up with a trussing-needle and fine string. Melt the butter, add the prepared veal, and brown lightly on all sides; remove and keep warm. Add the vegetables, cover, and cook slowly until just coloured. Replace the veal on the vegetables, add the stock, seasoning, and herbs, cover, bring to the boil, and then cook in the oven for about 2 hours. Baste frequently. When cold remove string and brush well with the glaze. Slice and arrange on a serving-dish. Garnish with various salads: tomato, cucumber, bean, etc.

Terrine of Pork Fillet

3 pork fillets; larding bacon or rashers of streaky.

FARCE: ½ lb. flat dark mushrooms; 1 medium-sized onion; 1 dessertspoon chopped mixed herbs (thyme, sage, and parsley); 3 oz. breadcrumbs; 10 oz. pig's liver; 5 oz. streaky bacon; about ½ oz. blanched halved pistachios.

Slit the fillets to flatten, and bat them out. Slice the larding bacon thinly and line a loaf tin with it. Set aside. Now chop the mushrooms and cook to a paste with the finely chopped onion and herbs in a nut of butter. Cool. Mince the liver and bacon, combine with the mushroom mixture, and add the pistachios. Lay a piece of pork fillet in the bottom of the tin and cover with a layer of farce. Lay another piece on the top and cover again with farce. Continue in this way until the tin is full and there are about 4 or 5 layers of fillet and farce. Cover with foil or greaseproof paper, set in a bain-marie, and cook in the oven (325–350° F. or Reg. 3 to 4) for about 1 to 1½ hours. Take out, put an even weight on the top, and leave until next day. Then turn out, cut into slices, and dish garnished with watercress.

Pigeon, Beefsteak, and Mushroom Pie

3 pigeons; 2 lb. shin of beef; 1 oz. butter; 2 pints stock or water; 6 oz. mushrooms.

½ lb. puff pastry; ½ pint aspic jelly well flavoured with sherry.

Brown the pigeons slowly in butter in a pan or cocotte. Take out and split in two. Cut the beef into 1-inch squares and put into the pan with the pigeons and stock, cover, and cook slowly for 2 to 2½ hours. Cut the breast meat from the pigeons, discard the carcasses, add the aspic, and leave it all to get cold.

Wash the mushrooms (cut in quarters if large) and place in a pie dish with the cooked meats and liquid. Cover with the puff pastry, decorate suitably, brush with beaten egg, and bake in a hot oven (Reg. 7 or 425° F.), to cook the pastry, for about 20 minutes.

Serve cold, filling the dish with more aspic if necessary.

Steak Flan

RICH SHORT CRUST: 8 oz. plain flour; 3 oz. butter; 2 oz. shortening; 1 small beaten egg; 1 to 2 tablespoons water.

ASPIC JELLY: 1¾ pints good jellied stock; 1½ oz. gelatine; ½ gill each sherry and white wine; 2 egg whites.

FILLING: 1 lb. fillet beef; ½ lb. ripe tomatoes; ¼ lb. or 1 small packet frozen whole French beans; 2 tablespoons grated horse-radish; ¼ pint lightly whipped cream; 2 eggs hard-boiled and sliced; salt, pepper, mustard.

Make the pastry. Roll out and line into a fluted flan ring. Bake blind.

Make the aspic by putting the stock into a scalded enamel pan with the gelatine softened in the wines. Add the whites whipped to a froth, then whisk over the heat until boiling. Draw aside for 2 to 3 minutes, then boil up once more and leave for 4 to 5 minutes. Then pour through a scalded cloth. Set aside.

Have ready the fillet roasted for about 20 to 30 minutes. Slice when cold, and cut into shreds. Scald, quarter, and pip the tomatoes; cook the beans. Combine the cream, horseradish, and eggs. Season well. Set aside.

Fill a sandwich tin ¾ inch deep with the aspic. When set arrange the beef, beans, and tomatoes in the tin and fill up with cool aspic. Leave to set. Spread the horseradish cream on the bottom of the flan case. Dip the bottom and sides of the tin into hot water for a second or two, then turn out on to the flan.

Beef Salad Strogonoff

2 lb. boned sirloin of beef; 12 oz. button mushrooms; 1 cup thick sour cream; 18–24 olives; 3 large onions (Spanish for preference); quarters of lemon.

Roast the beef with a little butter and white wine for about 25 to 30 minutes, basting well. Allow to get completely cold.

Slice a third of the mushrooms and cook in a dessertspoon of water and a squeeze of lemon juice. Cook the remaining mushrooms whole in the same way for 4 to 5 minutes. Turn half the

olives and shred the rest. Slice the beef and shred neatly. Turn into
a bowl, season well with pepper from the mill, and add the sliced
mushrooms and shredded olives. Stir in the sour cream and adjust
seasoning.

Have ready the onions thinly sliced and blanched for 5 minutes.
Drain. Toss up with a little French dressing. Dish the beef and
garnish with the onion, whole olives, lemon quarters, and the
mushrooms also mixed with French dressing and a little sour
cream.

Chicken Tourtière

RICH SHORTCRUST PASTRY: ¾ lb. flour; ½ lb. butter; 2 oz.
shortening; 1 egg yolk; water to mix.

FILLING: 3-lb. roasting chicken; 4 oz. boiled rice; 1 bunch spring
onions; 4 hard-boiled eggs; 1 egg; 1 lemon.

Make up the pastry and leave in the refrigerator while preparing
the filling.

Cut the breast meat from the chicken, remove the skin, divide
the suprêmes, and set on one side. Mince the remaining flesh of
the chicken and mix with the rice, grated lemon rind and juice,
finely chopped spring onions, and 2 hard-boiled eggs. Season and
bind with a little beaten egg.

Line a deep flan ring or cake tin which has a loose bottom with
the pastry, prick the bottom, and then cover with about half the
rice mixture. Arrange the suprêmes on the top and then fill
between with the remaining eggs cut in quarters and the rice
mixture shaped into large marbles. Cover with pastry and
decorate. Brush with beaten egg and bake in a moderate oven for
1 to 1½ hours. When cold fill up with aspic jelly.

Vitello Tonnato

2½ lb. loin of veal (boned); 1 tablespoon oil; 1 glass Vermouth;
bunch of herbs.

MOUSSE: 1 tin tuna fish (5 oz.); 1 oz. butter; ¼ pint Béchamel sauce
made with ½ oz. butter and ½ oz. flour; ½ gill cream.

GARNISH: 1 tin artichoke hearts; $\frac{1}{2}$ lb. tomatoes; aspic jelly.

Tie the meat neatly, brown on all sides in the hot oil, and pour over the Vermouth. Season with salt and pepper and the herbs, cover tightly, and cook in the oven 1 to $1\frac{1}{4}$ hours. Allow to cool in the liquid.

Meantime pound the tunny fish with the butter, work in the cold sauce, seasoning, and a little tomato purée. Half-whip the cream and fold into the mixture. (See page 406 for how to half-whip cream.)

Cut the veal in thick, even slices, spread between each slice with the tunny mousse, and reshape the joint. Put in the refrigerator until quite firm, then brush with aspic jelly on the point of setting. Set on a serving-dish and surround with the artichoke hearts and a good tomato salad.

Jellied Ham Bourguignonne
2–2$\frac{1}{2}$ lb. mild sweet cured or unsmoked lean bacon.

JELLY: 2$\frac{1}{2}$ pints firm jellied veal stock; $\frac{1}{4}$ bottle dry white wine; 1 dessertspoon tarragon vinegar; 2 egg whites; 2 large tablespoons chopped parsley.

Simmer the bacon until tender and leave to cool in the liquid. Add the wine to the jelly with the vinegar and clarify with the egg whites. Strain through a scalded cloth and leave to cool. Take out the bacon, skin, slice rather thickly, and cut into shreds. Turn into a glass bowl for serving and press lightly on to the bottom of it (the meat should come about half-way up the sides). Moisten with the cool jelly and leave to set. Add the parsley to the rest of the jelly and, when on the point of setting, pour carefully into the bowl. Leave several hours before serving.

If the stock is not a firm jelly, a small quantity of gelatine – say about a level dessertspoon – can be added before clarifying. The finished jelly, however, should only just be set in the bowl. Cooked ham may be used in place of the bacon if wished, but the slices should be fairly thick.

313

Cornets de Jambon

12 thin slices of ham, 12 button mushrooms or 12 thin slices of truffle; 1 bunch watercress for garnish.

ASPIC JELLY.

MOUSSE: 4 oz. pâté de foie and 1 oz. minced ham trimmings; ¼ pint Béchamel sauce made with 1 oz. flour and 1 oz. butter; ½ oz. butter; 1 tablespoon sherry; ½ teaspoon French mustard; ½ gill cream partially whipped.

Trim the slices of ham and line into cornet moulds. Mince the trimmings and pound with the pâté, butter, and cold Béchamel sauce. Season with the sherry, French mustard, salt, and freshly ground black pepper and then fold in the cream.

Fill the ham cornets with this mousse, using a bag and pipe, and decorate the top with the mushrooms, previously cooked in a little water and lemon juice, or else top with a slice of truffle. Turn out the moulds and brush each cornet with aspic jelly and, when set, place on a bed of vegetable salad (beans, carrots, potatoes) bound with mayonnaise collée (see page 154). Alternatively arrange on chopped aspic and garnish with watercress.

Chicken Mayonnaise
1 large roasting chicken or boiling fowl.

MAYONNAISE: 2–3 egg yolks; ½ pint olive oil; vinegar or lemon juice to taste; salt; pepper; a little dry mustard.

RICE SALAD: 6 oz. rice; 3 large ripe tomatoes; 4 tablespoons diced carrots; 4 tablespoons green peas; ½ cucumber diced; French dressing; watercress to garnish.

Simmer the chicken until tender (allowing 50 minutes for a roaster and about 2 hours for a boiler) in water to cover, with a bouquet garni, seasoning, and an onion and carrot to flavour. Cool in the liquid, and set aside.

Boil the rice, rinse with hot water, and drain well. In the meantime prepare the mayonnaise. Cook the carrots and peas, drain, and refresh them. Salt the cucumber lightly and scald and peel the tomatoes. Quarter, take out the seeds, and cut the flesh into shreds.

Mix the rice with the peas, carrots, cucumber, and tomatoes, moisten with French dressing, and season well. Set aside. Drain the chicken well, remove the skin, and slice off the meat. Cut this into coarse shreds and moisten with a third of the mayonnaise diluted with a little boiling water. Arrange the chicken at one end of the serving-dish and coat with the rest of the mayonnaise. Pile the rice salad at the other end of the dish. Garnish with bouquets of watercress.

Chicken Bangkok
2 2½-lb. roasting chickens; seasoning; bouquet garni; herbs for flavouring; 1 onion; 1 carrot; 2–3 oz. butter; ¼ teaspoon ground ginger; large pinch turmeric; pinch cayenne; 2 tablespoons mango chutney; squeeze of lemon juice; 1 clove garlic.

Cover the chickens with water, add the seasoning, herbs, and vegetables, and poach carefully until tender – about 40 minutes. Allow to cool in the liquid. Cream the butter, work in the spices and chutney, and season with the pepper, lemon juice, and garlic crushed with salt. Joint the chickens, arrange on a flat fireproof platter and cover generously with the spiced butter. Leave in the refrigerator until quite firm. Grill the chicken until the skin is well browned. Allow to cool and serve garnished with watercress. Hand these accompaniments separately.

Spiced Apricots
¾ lb. apricots; ¼ pint water; small glass white wine; 2 tablespoons wine vinegar; 2-inch stick cinnamon; 6 peppercorns; 1 clove; 4 tablespoons granulated sugar.

Halve the apricots and remove the stones. Place the water, wine, vinegar, spices, and sugar in a stewpan and dissolve over gentle heat, put in the apricots, and poach slowly until tender – about 15 minutes. Remove the apricots carefully with a draining-spoon and lay in a shallow bowl. Reduce the syrup by boiling hard until thick. Strain over the apricots and chill well before serving.

Fresh or tinned pineapple may be used in place of apricots.

Sweet and Sour Cucumber
1 cucumber; salt; 1 tablespoon castor sugar; 1 tablespoon wine vinegar; lemon juice; chopped mint.

Peel the cucumber, split in half lengthways, and then cut in slices, sprinkle with salt, cover with a plate, and set in the refrigerator for half an hour. Meanwhile mix the sugar and vinegar together and add lemon juice and pepper from the mill to taste. Drain off any liquid from the cucumber. Add the dressing to the cucumber with a little chopped mint.

Savoury Rice
4 oz. boiled rice (see page 110); 2 oz. picked prawns; 1 green pepper; 1 oz. shredded almonds; French dressing.

Shred, blanch, and refresh the pepper; blanch the almonds and cut into needle-like shreds. Mix these ingredients with the rice and prawns and moisten with French dressing coloured with paprika. To make the almonds tender and juicy soak in boiling water for half an hour before shredding.

Chicken with Tunny Fish

3–3½ lb. roasting chicken; 1 onion stuck with a clove; 1 carrot; 1 stick celery; 1 glass white wine; ½ pint water; bouquet garni; 7 oz. tin tunny fish; ¼–½ pint mayonnaise; ¼ pint cream; lemon juice.

FOR SERVING: 6 oz. boiled and drained rice; French dressing; paprika; tomato and celery salad.

Put the chicken with the vegetables, wine, water, and herbs in a large pan. Season with salt and pepper and add the tunny fish. Cover and simmer until tender, turning the bird occasionally, for about 1 hour. Allow the chicken to cool in the liquid. Meantime moisten the rice with French dressing well seasoned with paprika and arrange this on the serving-dish.

Take up the chicken, remove the skin, and cut into neat joints. Set these on the rice. Remove the vegetables and herbs from the pan and strain the tunny from the liquid. Pound or work in a blender until smooth. Mix the tunny purée into the mayonnaise, sharpen with lemon juice, and fold in the lightly whipped cream. Dilute with a little of the cooking liquid if necessary. Spoon this sauce over the chicken and garnish with a tomato and celery salad.

Chicken Mousse Italienne

3 lb. roasting chicken; 2½ pints water; 1 onion; 1 carrot; salt; peppercorns; bouquet garni.

BÉCHAMEL SAUCE: ½ pint milk; slice of onion; small bouquet garni; 3–4 peppercorns; 1½ oz. butter; 1¼ oz. flour.

¼ lb. well-creamed butter; ¼ pint cream, partially whipped; ¼ lb. lean ham; ¼ lb. ox tongue; 1 glass sherry; 1 oz. gelatine; ½ lb. tomatoes to garnish.

Simmer the chicken for 50 minutes in the water with the vegetables, seasoning, and herbs to flavour, then leave in the liquid to
cool. Meanwhile prepare the sauce and let it get cold.

Strain off the chicken stock, adjust the seasoning, and pour
into a scalded pan. Add the gelatine, sherry, and egg whites
whipped to a froth, and clarify. Remove all the skin and bone
from the chicken and pass the meat twice through the mincer;
place in a bowl, pound well, and add the sauce by degrees
with plenty of seasoning. Fold in the butter and whipped
cream.

Put one-third of the chicken mousse in a large Pyrex soufflé
dish and spoon over a thin layer of the cool chicken jelly. When set,
arrange half the shredded ham and tongue on top and cover this
with another layer of jelly. When set, spread on the second and
third portions of mousse, layering them with the remaining ham
and tongue. Garnish with sliced tomato and a layer of aspic.
Serve in the dish with salads to accompany.

Poussins en Gelée

5 poussins; 3 oz. butter; seasoning; $\frac{1}{4}$ pint strong jellied stock.

STUFFING: 1 lb. chestnuts; 1 small onion; good stock; $\frac{1}{2}$ lb. ham;
$\frac{1}{4}$ lb. tongue; aspic jelly; watercress or celery tops.

Rub the birds all over with butter, season inside, set in a roasting-
tin with the stock, and roast for about 30 minutes in a quick oven,
basting frequently. In the meantime prepare the stuffing. Skin
the chestnuts and cook in stock to cover with the finely chopped
onion and seasoning. When the chestnuts are tender and broken
and the stock has been absorbed, turn into a bowl and allow to
cool. Finely chop the ham and tongue, mix with the chestnuts.
Take up the chicken, cut in two, and remove the backbone. Tip
any juices in the pan into the stuffing, mix well, and adjust the
seasoning. While the chickens are still warm, fill each half with
the stuffing, reshape each bird, and set on the serving-dish. When
cold, brush with aspic jelly and garnish with watercress or celery
tops.

Chaudfroid of Chicken

1 large roasting chicken; flavouring vegetables; bouquet garni for poaching.

CHAUDFROID SAUCE: ¾ pint Béchamel sauce made with 1¼ oz. butter, 1¼ oz. flour, and ¾ pint flavoured milk; ¾ gill aspic; ¼ oz. (1 rounded teaspoon) gelatine; 2 tablespoons thick cream.

TO FINISH: 1½ to 2 pints chicken aspic jelly; 2 oz. button mushrooms or sprays of chervil or tarragon for decoration; watercress.

Poach the chicken until tender with water to cover and the vegetables and herbs to flavour. Cool in the liquid.

Meantime prepare the Béchamel and when cool add the gelatine dissolved in the aspic. Adjust the seasoning and stir in the cream. Tammy the sauce into a bowl, press a piece of damped greaseproof paper down on to the surface to prevent a skin forming, cover with a plate, and set aside. Drain the chicken (the aspic can be made from the stock if wished), joint neatly, remove the skin, and set the joints on a wire rack with a tray underneath. Coat each with the chaudfroid when on the point of setting. Give another coat if necessary when the first one has set, though if the sauce is thick enough in the first instance one coat is usually sufficient. When quite set, decorate each joint with the thinly sliced mushrooms previously cooked in a tablespoon or two of water with a squeeze of lemon juice. Dry the slices well before arranging them on the sauce; alternatively use a spray of the herbs. Spoon over a little cool aspic, making sure that the joints are well coated. Leave for an hour or two. Meanwhile put the rest of the aspic to set for chopping. To dish, arrange the joints on a bed of chopped aspic and garnish with bouquets of watercress.

TAMMYING is a process used for fine flour sauce to give an epecially smooth texture and glossy appearance. To tammy, cover bowl with a teacloth or a doubled piece of butter muslin. Pour the sauce into this, gather up the ends, folding the sides of the muslin over the sauce, then twist or wring the sauce through the cloth or muslin.

Roast Stuffed Turkey en Gelée

8 lb. turkey; butter; a little stock and sherry for roasting.

HAM MOUSSE: 2 lb. ham; ½ lb. pâté de foie; ½ lb. butter; ½ pint
Béchamel sauce made with 1½ oz. butter and 1½ oz. flour; ¼ pint
cream.

GARNISH: aspic jelly and truffle.

French roast the turkey (as for chicken, page 264) with the butter,
stock, and sherry for 2 hours and allow to cool. Prepare the aspic
jelly and ham mousse. Mince the ham twice and then pound in a
mortar with the pâté de foie, creamed butter, and cold sauce.
Season well and fold in the half-whipped cream. Carefully
remove the supremes of the turkey and then cut away the breast-
bone with the scissors. Fill the carcass with the mousse, shaping it
carefully. Cut the supremes into slices and place on the mousse,
leaving an open space down the centre. Arrange the sliced truffle
along the breast and baste or brush the bird with the cold aspic
jelly. Leave to set. Serve on a large flat dish, garnish with chopped
aspic or aspic croûtons.

This recipe can also be used for a capon.

Jellied Duck with Orange

1 duck; seasoning; a little butter; 3 large oranges; 2 cans consommé; 1 lemon; 1 oz. gelatine; 1 bunch watercress.

Season the duck inside, cover the breast with butter, and roast
in a moderate oven (400° F. or Reg. 6) until tender. Cool.
Joint the duck, remove the bone, and cut into neat portions.
Sprinkle with salt, cover, and chill well.

Meanwhile remove the rind from 1 orange with a potato peeler
and leave to infuse in the juice of the lemon. Cut away the pith
and inner membrane from all three oranges, remove the sections,
and arrange at the bottom of a pie plate or shallow cake tin. Chill.
Soak the gelatine in 2 tablespoons of cold water, strain on the
orange-flavoured lemon juice, and dissolve over gentle heat. Stir
this into the strained consommé and adjust the seasoning.

Pour ¼ inch of this jelly over the orange sections and leave to set. Garnish the centre with watercress, place the pieces of duck on the top, and spoon over the rest of the aspic. Set in a cool place. To serve, turn out on to a round serving-platter and hand a watercress salad separately.

Pheasant Turinois

1 pheasant; oil for browning; onion, carrot, and celery for flavouring; 1 glass sherry; ½ gill strong stock, and the same of aspic if available; 1½ lb. good chestnuts; ½ gill whipped cream; 1–2 sticks shredded celery.

Brown the pheasant carefully, leave in the pot, and add the flavouring vegetables. After a few minutes flame with the sherry and add the stock. Season, cover, and simmer for 40 to 50 minutes. Cool in the liquid, then remove the pheasant. Strain the liquid and take off any fat. Mix with the aspic and set aside.

In the meantime peel and cook the chestnuts in stock. When tender push through a sieve, season, and moisten with a little of the liquid. When cold combine with the cream and a little finely shredded celery. Spoon this purée down a serving-dish, carve the pheasant, and arrange the slices on the top. When the gravy is on the point of setting, brush over the pheasant. Serve with a celery, apple, and tomato salad.

PÂTÉS

A pâté can vary from the smooth minced and pounded mixture of livers usually called Pâté Maison to the coarse texture of a Pâté de Campagne. They have several things in common: the 'meat' must be well seasoned and a combination of lean and fat; they must be tightly sealed so that they cook in their own juices, no extra liquid being added save perhaps a little brandy to add flavour and help preserve the pâté. If a mixture of meats have been used, they are pressed after cooking to make for ease in slicing.

Pâtés make an excellent first course. Sliced and served on individual plates, they are accompanied by freshly made toast and pats of unsalted butter, but the more substantial types such as a Terrine Maison or a Pâté en Croûte are more suitable for the cold table.

Pâté Maison

8 oz. chicken liver; 4 oz. butter; 1 medium onion; 1 small bouquet garni; 1 clove garlic; seasoning; 1 tablespoon brandy.

Chop the onion and garlic finely and soften in 1 oz. of the butter until just turning colour. Add the liver, herbs, and seasoning and fry together for about 3 minutes. Cool, then chop very finely or mince if the quantity is large. (This could be done in the liquidizer.) Pass through a fine sieve and work in the remaining butter, well creamed. Add the brandy, then fill into a china pot; smooth over the top and cover with a layer of clarified butter.

Danish Pâté

¾ lb. pig's liver; ¼ lb. very fat bacon; ½ pint creamy milk; slice of onion; 6 peppercorns; 1 bayleaf; 1 oz. butter; ¾ oz. flour; 3 rashers streaky bacon; a pinch of ground mace; 5 boned anchovies or 1 teaspoon anchovy essence.

First prepare the sauce: bring the milk slowly to the boil with the onion, peppercorns, and bayleaf. Melt the butter, add the flour away from the fire, and strain on the flavoured milk. Blend well, add salt, then stir until boiling and turn on to a plate to cool.

Spread the rashers of streaky bacon out on a board and line into a pie dish or shallow tin.

Pass the liver and fat bacon through the mincer twice or work in the blender, and then rub through a fine wire sieve. Put the mixture into a bowl and mix in the sauce by degrees, adding the mace and anchovy essence or pounded anchovies. Adjust the seasoning and fill into the prepared dish or tin. Cover with a buttered paper and set in a tin of water. Cook in a moderate oven (350 °F. or Reg. 4) until firm to the touch (about 1 hour). Leave until the next day before turning out.

Pâté de Campagne

1 lb. minced pork; 1 lb. minced veal; ½ lb. minced ham or bacon; 6 oz. minced pork fat; ½ lb. pig's liver; 2 cloves garlic; salt; pepper; allspice; 1 glass brandy or sherry; slices of fat, unsmoked bacon; bayleaf; lard or clarified butter.

Combine the minced meats and fat; remove all skin and ducts from the liver, pass through a mincer or blender and add to the mixture. Season with freshly ground black pepper and allspice, crush the garlic with salt, and add with the brandy. Line a terrine with the fat bacon. Press in the farce, place a bayleaf on the top, and then the lid. Seal down with a flour-and-water paste and cook in a bain-marie for about 1½ hours in a moderate oven. Press lightly until cold, then run a little melted lard or clarified butter over the top

Bacon Pâté

12 oz. 'green', or unsmoked long back bacon rashers (No. 4 cut); 1lb. minced veal or pork; 1 small onion, finely choppeds 6 oz. fresh white crumbs; 2 chopped hard boiled eggs; 2 beaten eggs; salt; pepper; ground mace.

Line a loaf tin with 4 or 5 of the rashers. Put aside another 6 or 8 and mince the remainder. Add to the veal with the onion, crumb;

and the chopped hard-boiled eggs. Bind the beaten eggs and when thoroughly mixed, press a layer into the tin and damp your hand with cold water to smooth it down nicely. Spread 3 or 4 rashers on this to form a layer, then again press in another good layer of the meat. Again layer with the rest of the bacon and fill up with the veal mixture. Smooth over and cover with a piece of foil or a double sheet of greaseproof paper. Set the tin in a roasting-tin filled with hot water and put into a moderate to slow oven (325 – 350 ° F. or Reg. 3 to 4) for about 1¼ to 1½ hours. Remove and press lightly until cold. To serve, turn out and cut in slices.

Terrine Maison

6 rashers streaky bacon; ½ lb. pig's liver; 1 small onion; 1 clove of garlic; ½ lb. sausage meat; ½ lb. minced fat pork; 2 chopped hard-boiled eggs; 1 teaspoon chopped herbs; ½ lb. veal or game; seasoning; bayleaf.

Take a small earthenware terrine. Line across the bottom and sides with bacon. Mince the liver with the onion and garlic and add to the sausage meat and pork. Season well, add the chopped eggs and herbs, and put a layer of this farce on the bottom of the terrine.

Cut the veal or game into fine strips; arrange this in layers with the rest of the farce until the terrine is full. The top layer must be of farce and the bayleaf should be placed on top. Put the lid on and seal round the edge with a paste of flour and water. Stand in a roasting-tin full of water and cook in a moderate oven for 1 to 1½ hours. Take out, remove the lid and put a weight on the top (of not more than 2 lb.). Leave until the next day, then fill up the sides of the terrine with good jellied stock. Leave until quite set and then turn out.

Terrine of Hare 'en croûte'

PASTRY: 1 lb. flour; 3 oz. lard; 4¼ oz. butter; 2 eggs; salt.

Sift the flour on to a pastry board or slab, make a well in the centre, and in this place the other ingredients. Work the lard, butter, eggs, and salt together and then draw in the flour. Knead until smooth and leave in a cool place for half an hour before shaping.

FILLING: 1 young hare; 1 lb. minced pork; ¼ lb. very fat bacon; salt; pepper; brandy; jellied stock for finishing.

Remove the liver and the blood from the hare and set on one side. Cut the flesh from the thighs and the back, remove the tendons, and cut into neat fillets. Chop or mince the remaining meat with the liver and mix with the pork and blood. Season with salt and pepper and a little ground allspice and moisten with 2 or 3 table-spoons of brandy. Cut the fat bacon into long thin strips. Cut off one third of the pastry and keep on one side for the top and decoration. Roll out the remaining pastry and line into a large raised pie mould.

Put a good layer of the 'farce' in the bottom and press down well. Arrange the fillets of hare on top, divided by the strips of bacon and then another layer of farce. Continue in this way until the pie is full and press again.

Cover with a layer of pastry and decorate with small rounds or crescents of the pastry made with a fluted cutter. Brush with beaten egg and make a small hole in the top, inserting a small 'chimney' of paper to allow the steam to escape.

Bake in a moderately hot oven (400° F. or Reg. 6) for about 1¼ hours. Cover with a damp greaseproof paper when the pastry is nicely brown. When the pie has cooled, fill with jellied stock made from the bones of the hare with vegetables, herbs, season-ing, and white wine to flavour. Allow a scant ounce of gelatine to one pint of stock.

Raised Pie
10 oz. flour; 1 egg; 1 teaspoon salt; 5 oz. butter; 4 tablespoons water.

Sift the flour on to a marble slab or formica table top, make a depression in the middle, add the salt, very cold water, butter, and egg. Melt the salt in the liquid, mix in the butter, and then gradually work in the flour. Knead the paste till smooth and put away in a cold place for 2 hours. Line a pie mould and fill with the prepared mixture:

¾ lb. lean veal or game; ¾ lb. sausage meat; 6 rashers bacon; 2 hard-boiled eggs; 1 teaspoon chopped herbs; 1 bayleaf; ¾ lb. liver; 1 small onion; clove of garlic; salt; pepper.

Line the bottom and sides of the pie with the bacon; mince the liver, onion, and garlic and mix with the sausage meat. Season well, add the chopped eggs and the herbs, and put a layer on top of the bacon. Cut the veal or game into strips, put in a layer, then another layer of farce until the pie is full. Put on the cover, neaten, and decorate. Cook 1½ hours at least in a moderately hot oven.

Chapter 9

VEGETABLES AND SALADS

ARTICHOKES – GLOBE OR GREEN

THESE are the buds of a large and handsome plant flowering in the middle to late summer in England. However, owing to imports from other countries the season has been greatly extended and artichokes are now in the shops from April to November.

PREPARATION AND COOKING: Well wash the artichokes in salted water. Trim the sharp points of the leaves square with the scissors and cut off any stalk to level the base. Artichokes are served as a separate course either as a first course or as a 'dressed' vegetable or entremets served after the main course.

327

To cook, boil them in salted water for 45 minutes or until a leaf can be pulled out easily. Drain well and serve

    1. hot, with a sauce-boat of melted butter; or
    2. cold, with a vinaigrette sauce.

When serving in this way pull out the centre leaves and carefully scrape out the 'choke', making sure that every particle is removed. The 'choke' lies on top of the 'fond' or bottom, which is the most prized part of the artichoke. Now pour in a little vinaigrette and leave to marinade before serving with extra dressing.

Finger bowls should be provided for formal entertaining when artichokes are served in either of these ways. Artichokes may be stuffed for a more substantial dish, as in the recipe for Artichokes Barigoule.

*

Artichokes Barigoule

5–6 artichokes; 3 oz. cooked ham; 3 oz. cooked tongue; 1 medium-sized onion; 1 oz. butter; 8 oz. mushrooms; 5 tablespoons fresh white crumbs; 1 dessertspoon mixed chopped herbs; fat or streaky bacon.

SAUCE: 1 onion; 1 clove garlic; 1 oz. butter; 1 dessertspoon flour; 1 dessertspoon tomato purée; $\frac{1}{2}$ lb. tomatoes; a bayleaf; $\frac{1}{2}$ pint stock.

Trim the artichokes and boil them until a leaf can be pulled out easily. Drain and refresh. Pull out the centre leaves and remove the choke, then set aside.

Prepare the sauce. Chop the onion and garlic, soften in butter, add the flour, purée, tomatoes cut in half and squeezed to remove the pips, and the bayleaf. Season and moisten with the stock. Cover and simmer to a pulp.

Meanwhile prepare the stuffing. Chop the mushrooms, ham, and tongue and set aside. Melt the butter, add the finely chopped onion, cook until soft, then add the mushrooms and continue cooking for 5 or 6 minutes. Draw aside, stir in the ham, tongue, crumbs, and herbs, and season to taste. Fill the stuffing into the artichokes, wrap and cover each in bacon, and set in a deep

VEGETABLES AND SALADS

casserole. Strain the sauce and pour just enough round the artichokes to moisten nicely. Cover the whole with a thickly buttered
paper and the lid. Braise in a slow to moderate oven 30 to 40
minutes. Take up and arrange the artichokes on a serving-dish.
Add the rest of the sauce to the pan, boil up, finish with a ½ oz. of
butter, and strain round the dish. Dust the whole with chopped
parsley.

JERUSALEM ARTICHOKES

These are a different family and grow underground. The season
is from late October until March, and they are one of the best of
the winter vegetables.

PREPARATION AND COOKING: Peel the artichokes and keep in
water with a slice of lemon or a dash of vinegar. Boil for approximately 7 to 8 minutes. (They may alternatively be boiled and
peeled afterwards.) Toss in butter and parsley before serving.
Artichokes are good roasted or sautéd to accompany roast lamb,
or simmered in milk after peeling and the liquid used for a
Béchamel or Mornay sauce.

*

Artichokes Velouté
1½ lb. artichokes; 8 small onions; ½ pint water; 2 tomatoes; 1 oz.
butter; 1 oz. flour; ½ pint milk; 1 teaspoon chopped parsley.

Trim the artichokes and cut in pieces the size of a walnut. Blanch
the onions for 5 minutes, drain, and put into a saucepan with the
artichokes, water, and half the milk. Add half a bayleaf and salt
and cover the pan. Simmer for 20 to 30 minutes. Peel the tomatoes,
squeeze them gently to remove the seeds, and cut in slices. Melt
the butter in a saucepan, add the flour off the fire, then strain on
half a pint of the liquor from the artichokes, reboil, add the
remaining milk, adjust the seasoning, and simmer for a few
minutes. Drain the artichokes, return to the pan, pour over the
sauce, add the tomatoes and some chopped parsley, and allow to
simmer a minute or two before serving.

Sauté of Artichokes, Onions, and Walnuts

1 lb. Jerusalem artichokes; ½ lb. pickling onions; 2 oz. shelled walnuts; 1½ oz. butter; 1 teaspoon castor sugar; seasoning.

Trim the artichokes and cut into even-sized pieces. Blanch for 5 minutes, then drain well. Blanch the onions, drain, and return to the pan with the butter and sugar and shake over gentle heat until taking colour; add the artichokes and walnuts, season with salt and freshly ground black pepper, and continue cooking until the artichokes are tender.

ASPARAGUS

Generally served as a separate course, usually as an entremets rather than a first course. The season for English asparagus is from mid May to the end of June. Early asparagus from France arrives at the end of February.

PREPARATION AND COOKING: Cut off the bottom of the stalks, scrape or peel the white part, wash well, and tie in bundles. Boil in plenty of salted water with the lid off the pan, for 12 to 15 minutes or until just tender. Drain well and dish on a napkin and serve with melted butter or a Hollandaise sauce; or if to be eaten cold, with a vinaigrette. As asparagus, like globe artichokes, is eaten with the fingers, finger bowls are an asset.

AUBERGINES OR EGG PLANTS

Imported from France from July to November and from the Canaries during the winter months, though more expensive.

PREPARATION AND COOKING: Aubergines are not as a rule peeled. If they are to be cooked as an accompaniment they are cut in diagonal slices, or, as a main dish, split and stuffed. In either event, they are scored, lightly salted after cutting, and left for half an hour. This process is to *dégorger* and takes away any strong flavour; in that respect it is akin to blanching. Aubergines can also be wrapped in oiled paper and baked until soft (about

45 minutes). The flesh is then scooped out, mixed with a French dressing, and used as an hors d'œuvre.

*

Aubergine with Tomatoes

2–3 aubergines, according to size; salad or olive oil; 2 large onions; ¾ lb. ripe tomatoes; 1 tablespoon mixed chopped herbs; browned crumbs; 1 small tin anchovy fillets; butter; grated Parmesan cheese.

Split the aubergines in two, score round the edge and across, salt, and leave for half an hour. Wipe dry. Sauté rather slowly in the oil, then scoop out the pulp with a spoon leaving the skins intact. Slice the onions thinly, add to the pan, and cook until turning colour. Meanwhile skin and concassé the tomatoes, split the anchovy fillets in two, and soak in a little milk to soften. Chop the pulp from the aubergines and add to the pan with the tomatoes. Simmer for a few minutes. Set the skins on a baking-sheet, fill with the mixture, and arrange a lattice of anchovy fillets over the top of each. Dust with Parmesan cheese and brown in a quick oven for 10 to 15 minutes.

Ratatouille

2 aubergines; 2 courgettes; ½ lb. tomatoes; 1–2 green peppers; 1 onion; 2 cloves garlic; 2–3 tablespoons oil; seasoning.

Slice and degorge the aubergines and courgettes. Skin the tomatoes, squeeze away the seeds, and cut in rough slices. Halve the peppers, remove the core and seeds, and shred finely. Slice the onion and chop the garlic. Heat the oil in a sauté pan, add the onion and garlic, and cook for 2 to 3 minutes. Wipe any moisture from the aubergines and courgettes, drop in the pan, and fry a further 2 to 3 minutes on each side, adding extra oil if necessary. Season, add the tomatoes and peppers, cover the pan, and cook gently for at least 1 hour.

If preferred the mixture can be turned into a casserole after

the initial frying and the cooking finished in a moderate oven.
See also meat chapter, page 213.

BROAD BEANS

In season from the middle of June to late July. Broad beans, like
most summer vegetables, should be eaten while young. At their
best the podded beans are about the size of large peas; over this
size their 'jackets' must be taken off after cooking and before
they are served.

Broad beans may be served with a good knob of butter and
some chopped savory, or mixed with a poulette sauce (see page
371).

FRENCH BEANS

These are generally considered the best and are in season from
May to August, though imports from Madeira are available much
earlier. A variety known as 'wire' beans are the true 'haricots
verts', narrow and of a brilliant dark green, but these are hard to
find and appear only in the late summer.

RUNNER BEANS

Should be picked before they are allowed to get too long. Eaten
like this they are tender and juicy. The season is July to
September.

PREPARATION AND COOKING: For French beans, top and tail
and run a knife or peeler down the sides to take off the string.
Leave whole or snap in half before plunging in boiling, salted
water. Cook for 15 to 20 minutes, then drain and toss up with
butter.

For runner beans, slice thinly after trimming and cook in
the same way.

*

French Beans with Onion

1–1½ lb. French or 'wire' beans; 1½ oz. butter; 1 onion; salt;
pepper.

Prepare and boil the beans. When cooked, drain them well;
chop the onion finely, rinse out the pan, heat the butter in it,
and add the onion. Fry slowly until brown, and season well. Dish
the beans and spoon the onion and butter over.

BEETROOT

In season from early July throughout the winter. During the
summer months, until September when the crop is lifted and
stored, small or baby beets are pulled to thin the rows and sold in
bunches. They may be bought raw or cooked, but have more
flavour when freshly boiled. They are delicious cooked whole and
served hot or cold.

PREPARATION AND COOKING: Care must be taken not to cut or
damage the skin in any way as this causes the beetroot to 'bleed'
and lose colour. For this reason 1 to 2 inches of the top should be
left on until the beetroot is cooked. Beetroots are boiled or
wrapped in paper and baked until the skin, when rubbed, will
slip off easily – an indication that the beetroot are cooked.

*

Sweet and Sour Beetroot

(As an accompaniment to roast beef and pork)
2 large cooked beetroots; 1 oz. butter; 1 teaspoon salt; 2–3 tablespoons vinegar; 2 tablespoons sugar.

Chop or mince the beetroots, put into a pan with the other
ingredients. Set on moderate heat and stir until thoroughly
hot. Pepper well, adding more salt if necessary to give a sharp
and piquante taste. Serve very hot.

Beetroot Salad

If possible use freshly cooked beetroots. Cut in wafer-thin slices and marinade in the chosen dressing while still warm. The dressing may be a French one or spiced as follows:

1 teaspoon dill or caraway seeds; ½ teacup boiling water; 2 tablespoons wine vinegar; 1 teaspoon salt; 1 dessertspoon sugar; pepper from the mill.

Bruise and crush the seeds well, pour over the boiling water, leave to infuse for half an hour. Strain, add the vinegar, salt, and sugar. Spoon over the beetroot and finish with a good grinding of pepper. Leave for some hours before serving.

For BROCCOLI, see under Cauliflower, page 340.

BRUSSELS SPROUTS

At their best during the winter months when the first touch of frost has been on them. Unfortunately sprouts sold in the shops often resemble small cabbages; ideally they should not be larger than a walnut in size, sometimes smaller, and be sweet and nutty in taste. For the garden the red Brussels sprout is well worth growing and turns dark green when cooked.

PREPARATION AND COOKING: Trim off the stalk, so removing the bottom leaves. If the sprouts are small there is no need to make a cross-cut on the bottom; this spoils the shape of the sprout. Wash well in salted water. Sprouts frequently suffer from over-cooking. Cook for 7 to 8 minutes at the most in boiling, salted water and drain while still firm. Return to the pan with a good knob of butter, salt and pepper and simmer for a few minutes.

*

Sprouts with Cheese

1–1½ lb. small sprouts; ½ oz. butter.

SAUCE: 1 oz. butter; 1 oz. flour; ½ pint milk and water mixed; 1½ oz. grated cheese; salt; pepper; French mustard.

Boil sprouts until tender, drain well, and return to the pan. Shake over the heat with the butter for a few minutes, then draw aside. Meanwhile prepare the sauce as usual and simmer for a minute or two, then beat in the cheese off the heat and season well. Pour the sauce over the sprouts, shake the pan gently to mix well together, and if necessary reheat without boiling. Serve with a grill or roast.

'Pain de Choux'

A good way of using over-large sprouts or sprout tops.

1½–2 lb. sprouts; 1 teacup of fresh white crumbs; ½ teacup hot milk; 1½ oz. butter; salt, pepper, a pinch of ground mace or nutmeg; 1 egg yolk.

TO FINISH: ½ pint Béchamel or Mornay sauce, or browned crumbs.

Trim sprouts, boil, drain, and press well until dry. Pass through a Mouli sieve. Add the milk to the crumbs and set aside. Put the purée into the pan and add the butter in small pieces. Stir over the heat, seasoning well. When the purée leaves the side of the pan, draw aside and beat in the soaked crumbs and yolk. Well butter a small cake tin and dust out with the browned crumbs. Fill with the mixture, tie round a buttered paper, set in a roasting-tin half filled with water (a bain-marie), and cook in a moderate oven for 40 minutes or until firm to the touch. Leave for a few minutes before turning out. Coat with either of the sauces if not using the crumbs.

CABBAGE

There are several varieties of cabbage in season at different times of the year, and it is helpful to know what kind should be used for each way of cooking. Winter cabbages such as January King are good for boiling, braising, or stuffing; Savoys, on the other hand, are better plainly boiled, or, if plentiful, with the hearts boiled whole and coated with a cream sauce. The drum-head or Dutch cabbage, a hard white variety and also a winter cabbage, is excellent stewed in butter and is the cabbage for cole-slaw or salad. Red cabbage is in season from early November to

March. It is best known as a pickle but cooked is also the classic accompaniment for braised game or pork.

Cabbage, especially from the garden, needs little boiling time. For plain boiling 10 to 12 minutes should be ample; the tender green spring cabbage, for example, in season from May to August, will take only 6 to 8 minutes and is best quartered before boiling; then drain and finish cooking in butter with chopped herbs or parsley. Cabbage is plunged into plenty of boiling, salted water for blanching or cooking.

*

Creamed Cabbage

1 green cabbage, 1½–2 lb. in weight; ½–1 oz. butter; salt; pepper; a pinch of ground mace or nutmeg; ¼ pint Béchamel sauce made from ½ oz. butter, ½ oz. flour, and ¼ pint flavoured milk.

Quarter the cabbage, first removing any coarse outside leaves. Trim away the hard stalk and cut the cabbage into shreds. Boil until tender and drain thoroughly. In the meantime make the Béchamel. Return the cabbage to the pan with the butter, shake over the heat to drive off any moisture, add the Béchamel, and season well. If wished, finish with a spoonful of cream. Turn into a dish and serve.

As a variation the top may be well sprinkled with grated cheese and the dish browned in a quick oven.

Buttered Cabbage

1 cabbage, 1½–2 lb.; 1–2 oz. butter; 1 small onion stuck with a clove; salt; freshly ground black pepper; sugar.

Trim the cabbage, cut in four, and wash thoroughly. Cut away the hard stalk and then shred the cabbage. Place it in a large pan of fast-boiling water and boil for 1 minute only. Strain, refresh, and drain well. Turn into a well-buttered casserole with the onion, the rest of the butter, seasoning, and a pinch of sugar. Cover with greaseproof paper and the lid and cook in the bottom of a moderate oven (350° F. or Reg. 3 to 4) until tender (about 1 hour). Take out the onion before serving in the dish.

Cabbage 'Alsacienne'

1 small drumhead or Dutch cabbage (1½–2 lb.); 1 onion; 1 small head celery; 1 oz. butter; 1 wineglass white wine or the same of stock; 1 teaspoon vinegar or a squeeze of lemon juice; 1 tablespoon chopped parsley.

Shred the cabbage finely, blanch in boiling, salted water for 1 to 2 minutes, and drain well. Melt the butter in a shallow pan, slice, and add the onion and celery. Cook for a few minutes, add the cabbage and liquid. Season well. Cover and cook gently for 15 to 20 minutes or until barely tender. Add the chopped parsley just before serving.

This type of cabbage will also cook well without blanching. After shredding, put into a deep frying or shallow stewpan with 1 to 2 oz. butter, salt, and pepper. Cook gently with a lid on the pan for 5 or 6 minutes. Moisten with 3 to 4 tablespoons stock or water and continue to cook for 4 to 5 minutes. The cabbage should be lightly crisp. (See also Pork Alsacienne, page 245.)

Braised Cabbage with Chestnuts

1 lb. chestnuts weighed when peeled (about 1½ lb. unpeeled); 1 medium green cabbage (1½–2 lb.); 2 onions; 2 carrots; 2–3 sticks celery; 1–2 oz. butter; bouquet garni; good stock; 4–6 rashers bacon, cut in half; chopped parsley.

Cover the chestnuts with stock, add a nut of butter and salt and pepper, and simmer gently until barely tender. Meanwhile trim and blanch the cabbage; slice the vegetables and sweat in a little of the butter. Set the cabbage on the vegetables and separate the leaves a little. Add the chestnuts, fitting them down between the leaves, and pour round about ¼ pint of stock. Cover with a thickly buttered paper and the lid. Braise in a moderate oven for 50 minutes to 1 hour, basting occasionally. Dish the cabbage carefully, reduce the stock to a glaze, and spoon over the dish. Grill or fry the bacon, garnish the cabbage with this, and dust with chopped parsley.

Dolmas 'Maigre'

STUFFING: 8 oz. mushrooms; 1 oz. butter; a handful of small spring onions or 1 medium-sized sliced onion; 4 tablespoons cooked rice; 2 hard-boiled eggs chopped.

1 cabbage; stock; tomato sauce; chopped parsley.

Wash and slice the mushrooms and cook in the butter with the finely sliced onion. Mix all the ingredients in a bowl and season well with salt and freshly ground black pepper.

Trim the cabbage, blanch it whole for two or three minutes, drain well, then carefully detach the leaves, removing any hard stalk. Put a small tablespoon of the filling on each leaf and roll up like a parcel to form a sausage. Roll them lightly in flour and arrange in criss-cross layers in a thick stewpan or casserole. Barely cover with stock. Bring carefully to the boil, season, and simmer for 20 to 30 minutes. Meanwhile prepare a good, rather thin tomato sauce (see page 378). Lift the dolmas into a fireproof dish, draining well from the liquor, spoon over the tomato sauce, and set in the oven for another 20 to 30 minutes. Serve with a good dusting of freshly chopped parsley over the dish.

Red Cabbage with Apple

1 medium-sized red cabbage (1½–2 lb.); 1 onion; 1 oz. butter; 2 cooking apples; 2–3 tablespoons wine vinegar and the same of water; 1 tablespoon sugar; salt; pepper; kneaded butter.

Quarter the cabbage, cut out the stalk, and shred the cabbage finely. Blanch and drain. Slice the onion, soften in a large stewpan with the butter, peel, quarter, core, and slice the apples before adding them. Cook for a few minutes. Turn out on to a plate. Add the cabbage to the pan, layering with the apple mixture and sprinkling with the vinegar, water, sugar, and seasoning. Cover with a thickly buttered paper and the lid and cook in a slow to moderate oven for about 1½ hours or until very tender. Stir from time to time and moisten with a little extra water or stock if necessary. Bind with the kneaded butter. Adjust the seasoning and serve.

CARROTS

In season from late June to March, though supplemented by imports from Holland.

PREPARATION AND COOKING: Peel with the swivel type of peeler which takes off a very thin layer of skin. For baby or freshly pulled carrots, scrape lightly and leave on about $\frac{1}{2}$ inch of the green top; keep whole or quarter lengthways according to size. For large carrots slice thinly into rounds.

Carrots are best plainly boiled with water barely to cover, a pinch of sugar, and a nut of butter. The water is allowed to evaporate completely, leaving the carrots lightly glazed. Finish with a little extra butter and chopped parsley. Carrots may also be served in a Poulette Sauce (see page 371).

CAULIFLOWER AND BROCCOLI

Cauliflower and broccoli are very alike but are in season at different times of the year – broccoli from March to June, or earlier when imported from abroad, and cauliflower from the summer to late autumn.

PREPARATION AND COOKING: One or two outside leaves are taken off when the bottom of the stalk is trimmed, otherwise the green leaves are left on and the cauliflower left soaking in cold water for half an hour or so. Alternatively, the cauliflower can be broken off into sprigs, not more than 5 or 6, and reshaped after boiling. This ensures that it is absolutely clean and gives an even distribution of stalk. Cauliflowers are boiled (for about 20 minutes) and drained before finishing in various ways.

*

Cauliflower with Almonds
1 large cauliflower; $1\frac{1}{2}$ oz. whole almonds; 1 cupful fresh white crumbs; 1 clove garlic, optional; 1 good ounce butter.

Break the cauliflower into large sprigs, taking the stalk and some of the green. Boil until tender and strain carefully. Well butter a pudding basin and arrange the sprigs in this, stalks to the centre. Press lightly with a small plate and keep warm.

Blanch the almonds, shred and soak for half an hour in a little water. Drain well. Fry with the crumbs in the butter until golden brown. Season well, adding the garlic. Turn out the cauliflower carefully and scatter the crumb mixture over it.

Cauliflower Italienne

1 large cauliflower; 1 lb. tomatoes; 10 green olives; 2 cloves of garlic; 1 large onion; 1 tablespoon chopped parsley; 1 pint Béchamel made with 2 oz. butter, 1½ oz. flour, and 1 pint flavoured milk; 2 oz. grated Gruyère cheese; 1 oz. butter; salt and pepper.

Cook the cauliflower in boiling, salted water for 10 to 12 minutes (it should then be a little firm) and drain well. Concassé the tomatoes, stone and chop the olives.

Finely chop the onion and garlic, cook in the butter until soft but not coloured, and then mix in the chopped parsley. Prepare the Béchamel sauce.

Arrange the cauliflower in a buttered gratin dish, spoon over the tomatoes and olives, followed by the onion and parsley mixture. Season. Coat with the Béchamel sauce, sprinkle with the cheese and melted butter, and brown in a hot oven.

Pain de Choufleur (Cream of Cauliflower)

1 large or 2 small cauliflower or broccoli; 1 bayleaf; 1½ gills Béchamel sauce made from 1 oz. butter, 1 oz. flour, and 1½ gills flavoured milk; 2 small eggs; 1 tablespoon of cream; salt, pepper and ground mace; a handful of good spinach leaves.

½ pint sauce Mornay (see page 369).

Break the cauliflower into sprigs, using some of the green and all of the stalk. Cook until tender in boiling, salted water with the bayleaf, then drain well. Remove the bayleaf and rub through a Mouli sieve. Weigh the purée, which should be about 1 lb. Make the

Béchamel sauce and allow to cool. Dip the spinach leaves into boiling water for a minute or two. Well butter a deep sandwich or shallow cake tin, line this with the leaves, laying the outside of the leaf against the tin. Add the purée to the sauce, beating well; season well with salt, pepper, and mace. Beat in the eggs and add the cream. Fill into the mould, cover with buttered paper, and cook in a bain-marie in a slow to moderate oven for 20 to 30 minutes or until firm to the touch. Turn out and pour round it a thinnish Mornay sauce.

CELERIAC

A root celery looking something like a turnip. It comes into season in late November until the end of February. A useful all-purpose vegetable and is equally good cooked or in a salad.

PREPARATION AND COOKING: First peel, then quarter, and cut again into eight pieces if using as a cooked vegetable. Keep in acidulated water (that is water with vinegar or lemon juice added) before serving in any of the following ways:

1. Boil 10 to 15 minutes, then drain and toss in butter and chopped parsley.

2. Coat with a Mornay sauce after boiling and brown in the oven.

3. As croquettes – flour, egg, and crumb the pieces after they have been cooked and fry in shallow or deep fat.

For a purée, see page 357.

*

Celeriac and Tomato Salad

1 root celeriac; 1 lb. tomatoes; 1 shallot; 1 dessertspoon chopped parsley; French dressing made with a little additional French mustard.

Peel the celeriac, cut into thin slices and then across into fine strips. Blanch in boiling, salted water for half a minute, then drain and refresh. Scald and peel the tomatoes, quarter, seed, and shred them. Chop the shallot finely, add to the celeriac with the tomatoes and parsley and moisten with the dressing. Toss up together and serve.

If the celeriac is cut very finely the blanching can be dispensed with.

Salad Belle Hélène

1 large root celeriac; 1 cooked beetroot; 1 oz. walnut kernels; ½ pint mayonnaise.

Peel and cut the celeriac into medium-sized julienne shreds. Cook until barely tender and then drain. Peel and slice the beetroot, not too thinly, and stamp into crescents with a fluted cutter. Chop the walnuts coarsely. Mix 2 or 3 tablespoons of the mayonnaise with the celeriac and pile up in the serving-dish. Thin the rest of the mayonnaise slightly with a little boiling water and coat over the celeriac. Surround with the crescents of beetroot and scatter over the walnuts.

CELERY

English celery is at its best from late October to January and, like sprouts, should have a touch of frost to be crisp and tender. Celery is equally good raw or cooked, particularly if braised.

PREPARATION AND COOKING: Trim off a little of the root, break off the stalks, and cut or shred if for a salad. Save the solid part of the root for flavouring. When braising the whole hearts are used.

*

Celery and Walnut Julienne
(To serve with roast chicken, cutlets, etc.)

1 head celery; 1 oz. butter; 1 lemon; 4 tablespoons stock; 1½ oz. walnut kernels; chopped parsley.

Wash and cut the celery in neat match-like strips, blanch in salted water, and drain and dry well. Chop the onion and cook slowly in the butter until soft but not coloured, then add the celery and stock. Season with salt and pepper and cook gently until barely tender. Break up the nuts and add, together with the juice of the lemon, and shake up over the heat for a minute or two. Dust with chopped parsley and serve.

See also page 294 for Julienne of Celery and Potato.

Braised Celery
3 large heads of celery; 1 large onion; 1 large carrot; 1 oz. butter; bouquet garni; about ½ pint jellied brown stock.

Wash and trim the celery taking off one or two of the outside stems. Split in two, blanch for a few minutes in boiling, salted water, then drain well. Cut the onion and carrot in small dice; sweat them in the butter in a stewpan, put in the celery cut across in half if the stems are too long, and pour round the stock. Add seasoning and the bouquet, cover and braise in the oven until tender (about 1 to 1½ hours). Baste well from time to time. When cooked the liquid should be well reduced and the celery nicely glazed. More stock may be added if necessary during the cooking. Dish the celery carefully and strain over the gravy.

CHICORY

Imported largely from Belgium as *endives*. It is in season from early November to March. (Confusingly, our 'endive' is known as *chicorée frisée* in France and is a salad green.) Chicory or endive is one of the 'blanched' vegetables like seakale and celery and is equally useful as a cooked vegetable or salad.

PREPARATION AND COOKING: Trim the bottom of each head of chicory and take off one or two of the outside leaves if necessary. Wash and wipe dry. Slice the head into thick diagonal pieces with a stainless-steel knife if for a salad. Leave whole for a cooked vegetable. Contrary to the usual practice it is better not to blanch but to cook straight away in the minimum of liquid. The chicory is then tender, succulent, and not bitter.

*

Stewed Chicory

1–1½ lb. chicory (5–6 heads); 1 oz. butter; salt; pepper; juice of ½ a lemon (a dessertspoon); scant ½ teacup water; chopped parsley.

Prepare the chicory. Rub the butter over the bottom of a stewpan or enamelled casserole and well butter a piece of greaseproof paper. Lay the chicory in the pan, season well with salt and pepper from the mill, and pour over the lemon juice and water. Tuck the buttered paper well down over the chicory and cover the pan closely. Cook slowly on the stove-top or in the oven for 45 minutes to 1 hour or until the chicory is tender. Serve with the juice from the pan spooned over and dusted well with chopped parsley.

Chicory and Orange Salad

1 lb. chicory; 3 oranges; 2 large carrots; French dressing (see page 381).

Prepare the chicory. Cut the peel, pith, and skin from the oranges with a sharp knife, then cut between the sections and remove any pips. Shred the red part of the carrot into fine needle-like strips. Mix all the ingredients in the salad bowl and toss in the French dressing.

COURGETTES OR ZUCCHINI

'Baby marrows' 4 to 5 inches long. In season from France from May (and later from England) until October.

PREPARATION AND COOKING: Do not peel but wipe and leave whole. Blanch for 1 to 2 minutes in boiling water. Drain and add an ounce of butter to the pan with salt and pepper and a dessertspoon of chopped mixed herbs. Cover and cook slowly until tender (about 15 to 20 minutes).

Courgettes are delicious as a salad, and in this case cook in a little olive oil in place of butter. When cool, dress with a vinaigrette or tomato dressing (see pages 381 and 29). If the courgettes are large, cut in thick diagonal slices before cooking.

*

Courgettes 'Provençales'

4–6 courgettes, according to size; 3–4 tablespoons salad oil; 2–3 shallots or 1 small onion; 1 lb. tomatoes; 4 oz. grated cheese.

Wipe the courgettes and cut into thick slices. Chop the shallots finely; peel and slice the tomatoes. Sauté the courgettes in the hot oil until just coloured (about 6 to 8 minutes). Take out, add the shallots and, after a minute, the tomatoes. Cook for 2 to 3 minutes and season. Arrange the courgettes and tomatoes in layers in a fireproof dish, scattering the cheese between each layer and finishing with the tomatoes. Make sure the dish is well filled. Bake in a moderate oven for 45 minutes.

CUCUMBERS

Cucumbers are now obtainable nearly all the year round, though they are cheapest from May to September. Outdoor or Ridge cucumbers are plentiful in late July to September and are best for pickles and chutneys.

PREPARATION AND COOKING: Peel the cucumber with a peeler unless the skin is very tender, in which case leave it on. For a salad, slice the cucumber as thinly as possible, salt lightly, and press between two plates with a weight on top. Leave for half an hour. Tip off any liquid, then finish with the appropriate dressing. Alternatively, peel the cucumber, quartered lengthways, cut across into small chunks, and salt lightly. To cook, blanch in boiling water for 2 to 3 minutes then drain and return to the pan with a little butter, salt, and pepper. Cover and cook 4 to 5 minutes or until tender.

*

Cucumber and Chive Salad

1 cucumber; a small bunch of chives; salt; a teaspoon of sugar; a dessertspoon of tarragon vinegar; 1 small cupful of cream; 2 tablespoons oil; pepper.

Prepare the cucumber as for a salad (see above). Mix the sugar and vinegar together, stir in the cream, and add the oil by degrees; then season with the pepper. Arrange the drained cucumber in a shallow dish, spoon over the dressing, and scatter the chives, cut finely with scissors, over the top.

FLORENTINE FENNEL (FINOCCHIO)

A white bulbous stem imported from France and Italy in early spring. Tasting strongly of aniseed, it is delicious as a cooked vegetable or raw in a salad.

*

Fennel Meunière

2–3 heads of fennel; 2 oz. butter; juice of $\frac{1}{2}$ lemon; salt; pepper; chopped parsley.

Trim and cut the fennel into quarters. Cook in boiling, salted water until barely tender (about 10 to 15 minutes), then drain well. Arrange in the serving-dish. Melt the butter, cook to a noisette, add the lemon juice, salt, pepper, and a dessertspoon of chopped parsley. Pour at once over the fennel and serve very hot.

Fennel and Lemon Salad

1 large head of fennel; 1 thin-skinned lemon; 1 dessertspoon chopped parsley.

CREAM DRESSING: 1 tablespoon lemon juice; 2 tablespoons oil; 2 tablespoons cream; 1 dessertspoon sugar; salt and pepper to taste.

Slice the fennel thinly, blanch for 1 minute in boiling water, drain, and refresh. Pare the rind from half the lemon and cut into very fine shreds, blanch well and drain. Cut away the pith from the lemon and slice out the flesh. Cut into pieces and mix with the fennel and parsley. Combine the ingredients for the dressing and mix into the salad. Serve.

LAMBS LETTUCE OR CORN SALAD (MÂCHE)

A winter salad with a daisy-like leaf. Its chief merit is that it comes into season when there is little else to use as a salad green. Lambs lettuce is easy to grow and even a severe frost does it no harm.

PREPARATION: Wash the little plants very well to remove any grit and dry thoroughly before tossing in a French dressing. By itself, lambs lettuce is a little dull, but it is excellent mixed with sliced beetroot.

LEEKS

In season from late October throughout the winter.

PREPARATION AND COOKING: Leeks have to be very well washed to get out every particle of grit. To be certain this is done, make a cross-cut 2 inches down in the green part of the leek after trimming off the root and some of the top. Hold the leek under the running tap, flicking back the cut leaves to wash away the grit.

Tie in bundles to boil in salted water, uncovered, until tender (about 12 to 15 minutes). Drain thoroughly and serve with a little melted or noisette butter poured over them. Leeks may also be braised in a little stock and butter and basted well during the process.

Young leeks, especially 'thinnings' from the garden about the size of a pencil, are delicious in a salad. These should be boiled, dipped in cold water, and then well drained. They can then be marinaded in a vinaigrette dressing (see page 381) or coated with mayonnaise. Alternatively the leeks can be cut across into inch lengths, cooked and drained as before and mixed with quartered hard-boiled eggs and prawns and bound with mayonnaise.

*

Leek Pie

½ lb. quantity flaky pastry.

8 leeks; 8 oz. unsmoked bacon or salt pork; ½–¾ pint stock; 2 eggs; ½ gill cream.

Clean and slice the leeks across into 1-inch pieces, blanch and drain. Cut the bacon into dice and blanch also. If using pork, cook until just tender. Put the leeks and bacon into a pan, cover with the stock, add seasoning, and simmer for 10 to 15 minutes. Lift out the leeks and bacon into a pie plate; beat the eggs; add the cream, and stir into the juice in the pan. Pour this over the leeks and cool. Roll out the pastry, cover the pie, and decorate to taste. Bake in a hot oven until golden brown (about 35 minutes). Serve hot or cold.

LETTUCE

Lettuce is in the shops throughout the year, though the proper season for those grown out of doors is from May to September. Forced lettuce, though a pleasant and tender green, has little flavour compared with the other. There are three main varieties of lettuce:

1. *Cabbage*, or round lettuce, first in season;
2. *Cos*, from mid June to late August;
3. *Webbs*, or iceberg lettuce, a curly-leaved variety, in season from July to September.

Cos is a firm lettuce and so is best for braising. Braise with a mirepoix and baste with good veal or chicken stock. Cos will always keep crisp in hot weather, as will the iceberg variety.

To prepare, wash well and dry thoroughly. A salad basket is best for this. The leaves are then pulled apart and put into the salad bowl ready for dressing. If the lettuce has lost its crispness, put into a polythene bag or in the salad drawer of the refrigerator for a little while. Lettuce is principally a salad green and mixes well with watercress, sliced cucumber, and chopped fresh herbs.

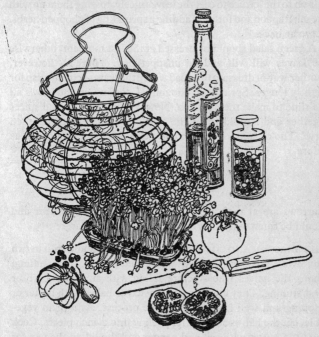

Green Salad

Take any of the above varieties of lettuce, making sure the leaves are crisp and thoroughly dry. If only a delicate flavour of garlic is wanted peel a clove and rub it well round the salad bowl.

For a stronger flavour, crush with a little salt and add to the dressing. For a French dressing, take 1 tablespoon of wine vinegar, red or white; salt, pepper from the mill, a good pinch of sugar, and 3 to 4 tablespoons of olive oil. Mix in this order and when the dressing thickens taste for seasoning. More salt should be added if the dressing is sharp yet oily. Sprinkle just enough of this on to the lettuce to coat the leaves nicely, tossing them up with the salad spoon and fork and adding a sprinkling of chopped herbs. Serve at once.

A green salad should be dressed at the last moment, otherwise the leaves will wilt and be unappetizing. There is, however, another way of dressing the salad where the leaves remain crisp for slightly longer. Sprinkle in enough oil, tossing up the leaves all the time to make them glisten. Now mix the vinegar and spices together and sprinkle over the bowl. Stir once or twice, then serve. The oil and vinegar should be in the same proportion as before.

MARROWS

Marrows are at their best from early July to September and should be eaten when they are young and not too large.

PREPARATION AND COOKING: Peel the marrow and split in two lengthwise, scoop out the seeds with a metal spoon. If for stuffing, blanch the halves whole before filling with any good herb or meat stuffing. They are then pot-roasted or baked with butter or dripping and well basted during the process. As a plain vegetable, cut the halves across after peeling into 2-inch pieces. Cook in a little butter with salt and pepper and the lid on the pan for about 7 minutes or until tender. Finish with chopped herbs or parsley.

*

Marrow Hongroise

1 marrow; 3–4 tablespoons olive oil; 2 shallots; 1 teaspoon or more of paprika; salt; pepper; sugar; a good pinch of dill seeds; 2–3 tablespoons wine vinegar; kneaded butter.

Peel the marrow, scoop out the seeds, and cut into match-like strips or very thin slices. Chop the shallots finely. Heat the oil, using a sauté or deep frying-pan. Add the shallots and cook slowly until soft but not coloured. Put in the marrow with the paprika and salt and pepper. Sauté for 4 or 5 minutes, then add the dill seeds and vinegar. Dust with sugar and simmer for about 5 or 6 minutes. Adjust the seasoning and thicken if wished with a little kneaded butter. Serve hot as an accompaniment.

Marrow cooked in this way is good cold, in which case do not thicken.

MUSHROOMS

Forced mushrooms are in season all the year round, though at times more plentiful and so slightly cheaper than at others.

Field mushrooms are in season from July to September.

There are three grades of forced mushrooms:
1. *Buttons*, the most expensive;
2. *Cups* or 'select'; and
3. *Flats* or 'open'.

PREPARATION AND COOKING: As a rule button mushrooms are not peeled, merely washed or wiped before cooking. The others, if the skin seems tough, are peeled and the stalks cut level with the caps. These trimmings are kept for flavouring. If, however the mushrooms are to be chopped they are not peeled but washed and dried before chopping.

*

Duxelles

A use for the stalks and peelings or when flat mushrooms are cheap and plentiful. Wash the mushrooms, squeeze lightly, and chop finely. Put a nut of butter, or ½ oz., to ½ lb. more of mushrooms into a shallow pan. Add the mushrooms, season well, and cook quickly until most of the liquid has evaporated and the mushrooms form a moist but firm paste. This can now be used straight away but to keep for flavouring turn into small pots and press down well. If to keep for longer than a few days, run a little clarified butter over the top.

Mushrooms Gratinés en Coquilles

¾–1 lb. 'cup' mushrooms; 4 tablespoons fresh breadcrumbs; 1 oz. melted butter; 2 egg yolks; 2–3 tablespoons cream; 1 heaped dessertspoon each of finely chopped parsley and chives; 1 clove garlic crushed with salt; seasoning.

Mornay sauce; grated cheese; browned crumbs; melted butter.

Wash and peel the mushrooms, remove the stalks, and set aside 3 to 4 for each person. Chop the stalks and peelings and any remaining mushrooms. Add the crumbs and bind with the butter, yolks, and cream. Mix in the herbs, garlic, and seasoning. Fill the mushroom cups with this mixture, arrange in buttered scallop shells, coat with Mornay sauce, and sprinkle with cheese, crumbs, and melted butter. Bake in a moderate oven 12 to 15 minutes.

ONIONS

A vegetable that plays some part in almost every savoury dish. It has, however, an indigestible quality but this is mitigated by blanching.

Besides the ordinary onion available all the year round there are one or two other varieties:

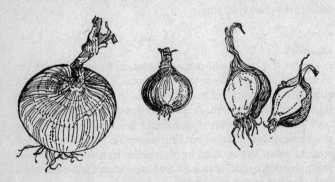

1 *Spanish* – very large onions which are ideal for boiling, brais-

ing, or for fried onion rings. Especially mild in flavour and are to be had from late autumn onwards.

2. *Pickling or button onions* – a small round brown onion used for a garnish or hors d'œuvres.

3. *Shallots* – a little larger than a pickling onion, oval in shape with a red-brown skin. They are particularly mild and delicate in flavour and so are much used for sauces and sautés.

PREPARATION AND COOKING: When peeling an onion, cut off the top and root with a sharp knife, then with a small vegetable knife peel off the first and second skin or until the onion is completely white. In doing this take care that the under-skin is not broken in any way as this releases the oil which brings tears and not only spoils the shape of the onion but may cause it to disintegrate during cooking. For button onions, scald them for 1 to 2 minutes in boiling water, then plunge into cold water. The skin is then easily removed.

All onions, if to be cooked whole or otherwise than for flavouring, must be blanched, i.e. put into cold water and brought to the boil. The water is then drained off and the onions are ready for further cooking. For boiled onions the blanching process can be carried out two or three times to make the onions thoroughly digestible.

To braise onions, see celery, page 343. Here they may be dusted with castor sugar during the last half-hour or so to caramelize the top. Once the sugar has started to brown continue to baste with the stock.

*

Glazed Onions

As a garnish take ½ lb. button onions or shallots, for a vegetable allow 1 lb. for four people. Peel carefully, put into a pan, cover with cold water, bring to the boil, and drain. Return to the pan and while still hot add salt, pepper, and 1 teaspoon of sugar with ½ oz. butter to 1 lb. onions. Cover and cook on a slow heat for 7 to 10 minutes or until the onions are tender and coated with a sticky brown glaze.

Onions à la Grecque
(for an hors d'œuvre or salad)

$\frac{1}{2}$–$\frac{3}{4}$ lb. button onions; 2 glasses white wine; 3 tablespoons olive oil; $\frac{1}{2}$ lb. ripe tomatoes; salt; pepper; 1 teaspoon each fennel and coriander seeds.

Peel the onions very carefully, blanch for 7 minutes, drain, and return to the pan. Concassé the tomatoes and add with the wine, oil, and spices. Cover and simmer for 40 minutes, when the onions should be very tender but whole. Lift them out carefully into an hors d'œuvre dish. Strain the liquid over them and serve very cold.

Onion Ragout
1 lb. small or button onions; 2 oz. butter; 1 glass white wine; 1 glass stock; 1 small tin tomatoes; salt; pepper; a small piece of cinnamon stick; 1 bayleaf; 1 clove or a pinch of ground cloves.

Blanch the onions; brown them in the butter in a stewpan, then add the wine and stock. Rub the tomatoes through a strainer and add with the seasoning and spices. Cover and simmer until the onions are tender (about 20 to 30 minutes). Adjust the seasoning and serve hot with a grill or roast.

PEAS

In season from early June to the end of August. The younger they are eaten the better, especially if they are cooked in the English way – plainly boiled with a sprig of mint and finished with a good lump of butter. Older peas, however, have their uses in soups and purées. The following recipes are two classic ways of cooking peas.

*

Petits Pois à la Française
1 pint young green peas, when shelled; 1 Cos lettuce; $\frac{1}{2}$ teacup cold water; 1–2 oz. butter; 6 small spring onions; 1 teaspoon sugar; bouquet of parsley stalks and a sprig of savory.

Put the peas into a pan with the lettuce cut in four lengthwise, the onions, sugar, bouquet, and 1 oz. of the butter. Pour in the cold water. Bring to the boil over steady heat and cook fairly fast for 25 minutes with a deep plate on top of the pan filled with cold water. As the peas cook, renew the water in the plate as it evaporates or comes to the boil. Two minutes before serving, take out the bouquet and lift out the lettuce and the onions. Take the pan off the heat and add the butter, shaking well. Serve in a hot dish with the lettuce arranged round the peas.

Petits Pois à la Flamande

1 pint young green peas, when shelled; 2 oz. butter; bouquet of parsley; 6–8 baby carrots; salt; pepper.

Scrape the carrots leaving on the green top. Cook them separately with just enough water to cover, salt, pepper, and 1 oz. butter. Boil fairly fast for 15 minutes, then add the peas and the bouquet and cook still fairly fast for 25 minutes. The liquid should disappear at the same time that the vegetables are cooked.

PEPPERS

Peppers are imported from the same countries and at the same time as aubergines. They may be both green and red, this depending on the stage at which they were picked, the green ones being a little milder in flavour. Pimentos are the same but the name is usually applied to the tinned red pepper.

PREPARATION AND COOKING: Peppers may be stuffed, shredded for a salad, or used as a garnish. To prepare, either cut off the tops or split in two and take out the core and seeds. Be particularly careful to remove all the seeds, as they are very hot. They should then be blanched (see page 476). Red peppers can be grilled until the skin cracks and turns brown, almost black. It is then carefully peeled off and the peppers quartered or cut in pieces.

*

Pepperoni

2 green and 2 red peppers; 1 medium onion; 1 clove garlic; 1 oz. butter.

Cut the peppers in two, remove the core and seeds, and slice finely. Slice the onion and crush the garlic with salt. Melt the butter in a stewpan, add the onion and garlic, and cook slowly until soft but not coloured. Add the peppers and seasoning and cook until just tender.

Stuffed Green Peppers

5 large green peppers; 1½ oz. butter; 1 onion; 1 clove garlic; 2 oz. mushrooms; 4 oz. long-grained rice; ¾ pint stock; 4 oz. cooked ham; ½–¾ pint tomato sauce.

Cut the tops off the peppers, scoop out the seeds and core. Blanch, refresh, and set aside. Chop the onion finely, crush the garlic with a little salt, and slice the mushrooms. Soften the onion in 1 oz. of the butter, add the garlic and mushrooms and, after 2 minutes' cooking, the rice. Fry for a minute, add the stock, and bring to the boil. Season, cover, and put into a moderate oven for 15 to 20 minutes or until the rice is tender and the stock absorbed. Shred the ham and fork it into the rice with the rest of the butter. Fill this pilaff into the peppers, pack them into a well-buttered, deep, fireproof dish, and spoon over the tomato sauce. Cover with a lid or buttered paper and cook in a moderate oven for 40 to 50 minutes. Serve in the dish.

POTATOES

English new potatoes are in season from early June, though imported ones are in the shops from Christmas onwards. 'Old' potatoes are at their best in the autumn when the main crop is gathered. Of the many varieties of potatoes grown, the floury type is best for the majority of dishes; a waxy potato is more suitable for salads.

PREPARATION AND COOKING: As a general rule new potatoes are cooked in boiling, salted water with a sprig of mint after scraping; old potatoes are put into cold water and brought to the boil. They may be peeled first or boiled in their skins and peeled afterwards. If the potatoes are inclined to break when only partly cooked, drain off after 10 minutes' boiling, put a piece of muslin or cloth on top, cover the pan, set on a low heat, and finish by steaming.

*

Puréed and Mousseline Potatoes

After boiling, drain and dry the potatoes thoroughly. Crush well or put through a Mouli sieve – this if the potatoes are to be piped. To 1½ lb. of potatoes, usually enough for four people, beat in by degrees with a wooden spoon up to ½ pint or more of boiling milk with a good nut of butter and salt and pepper. The amount of milk depends on whether the potatoes are for a purée or mousseline. For the latter, the consistency should be that of lightly whipped cream. To keep hot without spoiling, level the surface of the purée in the pan and cover with 2 to 3 tablespoons of the hot milk. Put on the lid and leave in a warm place for half an hour or longer. Before dishing beat up together.

Potatoes in their Jackets

Choose large, even-sized potatoes, scrub them well, and roll in salt. Bake in a moderately hot oven (370° F. or Reg. 4 to 5) for about 1½ hours or until the potato will give when pressed.

Make a cross-cut on the top and squeeze the potato to enlarge the cut. Put a pat of parsley or plain butter in the centre of each, and serve at once in a napkin.

Roast Potatoes

Choose even-sized potatoes, peel, and boil for about 7 to 10 minutes. Drain and scratch well along and across each potato to roughen the surface. Have ready a roasting-tin with about ½ inch of smoking hot dripping or oil, put in the potatoes, and baste at once. Roast in a hot oven for about 30 to 40 minutes or until golden brown and crisp, turning and basting well from time to time. Drain on a piece of kitchen paper and salt lightly before serving.

When cooking a joint in the oven the potatoes can be put to roast round the meat if wished.

Potatoes Maître d'Hôtel

1½ lb. even-sized potatoes; 2 oz. butter; 1 chopped shallot; 2 tablespoons chopped parsley; salt and pepper.

Scrub the potatoes and boil or steam in their skins until tender but firm. Drain, dry, peel, slice thickly, and arrange in a hot dish. Keep warm.

Just before serving, melt the butter in a small pan, add the shallot, cover, and cook slowly for 2 or 3 minutes. Draw aside, add parsley and plenty of salt and pepper; spoon over the potatoes.

Sauté Potatoes

1½ lb. potatoes; 2 tablespoons oil; 1 oz. butter; 1 dessertspoon chopped parsley.

Scrub the potatoes and boil in their skins. Drain when tender, peel and slice. Heat a frying-pan, put in the oil and, when hot, the butter. Slide in all the potatoes at once. Add seasoning and sauté, turning the contents of the pan occasionally until golden brown and crisp. Draw aside, adjust the seasoning, and add the parsley. Turn into a hot dish for serving.

Potatoes Lyonnaise

Add one sliced onion, fried golden brown, to sauté potatoes.

Potatoes Normande

1–1½ lb. potatoes; 1 oz. butter; ½ pint milk; seasoning.

Cut the potatoes in thin slices and arrange overlapping in a well-buttered, fireproof dish. Season between layers with salt and freshly ground black pepper, pour over the milk and cover with the remaining butter cut into small pieces. Bake in a moderately hot oven (380 to 400° F. or Reg. 5 to 6) for about 50 to 60 minutes.

Potatoes Savoyarde

1–1½ lb. potatoes; 1–2 cloves garlic; 2–3 oz. Gruyère cheese, grated; a good ½ pint stock; butter; seasoning.

Slice the potatoes, lay them in a well-buttered fireproof dish with the crushed garlic and cheese in layers with plenty of seasoning. Pour in the stock and bake in a moderately hot oven (380 to 400° F. or Reg. 5 to 6) for 45 minutes or until tender.

Potatoes Boulangère

2 onions; 1½ lb. potatoes; 1–2 oz. good dripping; ¾ pint stock.

Slice the onions, blanch, and drain. Slice the potatoes thinly. Rub a fireproof dish thickly with half of the dripping and put in the onions and potatoes in layers, seasoning well. The last layer should be of potatoes neatly arranged. Dot the top with the rest of the dripping and pour in the stock at the side. Bake for 50 minutes to 1 hour or until brown.

Do not put the potatoes in water after slicing as this will take away some of the starch which is necessary to give a creamy consistency to the dish.

Potato Mayonnaise

Choose a waxy potato or a special salad potato such as 'Kipfler'. 1½ lb. potatoes; ⅓–¾ gill well-seasoned French dressing flavoured with shallot and garlic; ½ pint mayonnaise.

Scrub and boil the potatoes in their skins. Peel and slice while hot. Moisten with French dressing. When cold, mix with about a third of the mayonnaise. Dilute the remainder with a tablespoon of boiling water. Dish the potatoes and coat with mayonnaise. The salad may be decorated with sliced pickled walnut or gherkins.

Château Potatoes

1 lb. old or baby new potatoes; 1–2 oz. butter; pepper and salt.

Peel the potatoes, cut into quarters lengthways, and trim off the sharp edges with a potato peeler. If the potatoes are new, scrape and leave whole. Wash and dry thoroughly. Melt the butter in a shallow pan, add the potatoes, and sauté over moderate heat, shaking the pan occasionally, until a golden brown. Season lightly, cover the pan, and put into the oven to finish cooking for about

10 to 12 minutes. If more convenient, the potatoes may be browned in a frying-pan and then turned with their butter into a cake tin. This is then covered with a lid or plate and finished in the oven as before.

Potatoes Anna
1 lb. potatoes; 1–2 oz. butter.

Peel the potatoes, cut into thin rounds and dry well in a cloth. Rub half the butter round a small, thick frying-pan. Arrange the potatoes in neat, overlapping circles, seasoning well between each layer and adding the remaining butter in small pieces. Cover with a buttered paper and a lid and cook slowly for about 20 to 30 minutes. Put the pan in a moderate oven for another 10 minutes before turning out.

When making this, or a similar type of potato dish (e.g. Savoyarde), arrange the potatoes in the dish directly after slicing. If left in water they lose starch and so do not give a creamy consistency to the liquid they are cooked in or hold together if they are cooked in butter.

Potato Croquettes
1 lb. potatoes; a nut of butter; 1 egg yolk; about 2 tablespoons hot milk; beaten egg and dried white crumbs for coating.

Cook the potatoes in boiling, salted water until tender; drain and dry. Pass quickly through a wire sieve or potato ricer and then return to the pan. Beat in the butter, egg yolk, hot milk, and salt and pepper to taste. Divide the mixture into small rounds or cork-shaped pieces, roll in seasoned flour, brush with beaten egg, and roll in dried white crumbs. Fry in smoking hot deep fat until golden brown.

NOTE: If shallow-fried, it is important to have sufficient fat to cover the croquettes completely or they will burst in frying.

PURPLE-SPROUTING BROCCOLI

In season early April to May. Small purple heads like a cauliflower. Calabresse, very like purple-sprouting broccoli but with a greenish white flower, is also in season at about the same time and is prepared and cooked in the same way.

PREPARATION AND COOKING: Trim the stalk lightly, leaving on most of the green leaves. Wash and tie in bundles. Boil gently with the lid off the pan for 12 to 15 minutes. When tender, lift out carefully, drain on a cloth or muslin and lay on a hot dish. Pour over a little melted butter. For a separate course or dressed vegetable serve with Hollandaise Sauce (see page 376).

SALSIFY

A tap-rooted winter vegetable with a delicate flavour. There are two varieties, the white salsify and the black scorzenora, so called because of the black skin. Of the two this is considered the finest.

PREPARATION AND COOKING: Scrape or peel the salsify. Wash and scrub the scorzenora well. Boil in salted water until tender (about 30 to 35 minutes), drain, peel off the skin from the scorzenora, and return to the pan with about 1 oz. of butter, and salt and pepper. Reheat and serve. Butter the salsify in the same way.

This vegetable is more usually served as a dressed vegetable (that is as an entremets or separate course) with Hollandaise Sauce to accompany.

SEAKALE

Like chicory, a blanched vegetable and in season during the winter. Seakale is something of a delicacy and is also served as a dressed vegetable or separate course with melted butter or Hollandaise Sauce.

PREPARATION AND COOKING: Wash and remove the little black root, tie in bundles, and boil for about 45 minutes or until just tender. Drain well and serve on a napkin.

SORREL

A summer vegetable and one which has to be garden grown or gathered wild in the fields as it is rarely found in the shops. It is the classic accompaniment to a fricandeau (see page 234) and makes a delicious soup. Wash and boil as for spinach.

SPINACH

Generally obtainable all the year round unless the weather is very severe. There are three varieties:

1. Summer spinach;
2. Winter or Perpetual spinach; and
3. Spinach beet – a hardy variety though not a true spinach.

As spinach cooks down very much, between 2 and 3 lb. should be allowed for four.

PREPARATION AND COOKING: Spinach must be very thoroughly washed in several waters once the stalks have been picked off. Put into a large pan of boiling, salted water and boil uncovered for 7 to 8 minutes, pushing the spinach well down. Drain and press very well either in the colander or between two plates.

*

Spinach 'en branche'
Return to the pan with ½ to 1 oz. butter, salt and pepper, and reheat.

Spinach à la Crème
2–3 lb. spinach; 1 oz. butter; ¼ pint Béchamel sauce or ½ gill double cream; salt; pepper; a pinch of ground mace or nutmeg.

Boil the spinach, drain, press, and pass through a Mouli sieve. Heat the butter to a *noisette*, stir in the spinach, increase the heat, and cook until all the surplus moisture has been driven off. Then add the sauce or cream and season well.

Pain d'Épinards

2 lb. spinach; ½ pint Béchamel sauce made with 1 oz. butter, 1 oz.
flour, and ½ pint flavoured milk; 2 eggs; 1 tablespoon cream; salt;
pepper; nutmeg.

Boil the spinach, drain and press between two plates. Sieve,
return to the pan with a nut of melted butter, and dry off a little
over the heat. Prepare the sauce, add to the spinach, and draw
aside. Beat in the eggs and cream and season well. Turn into a
well-buttered ring or plain mould. Cover with a buttered paper
and stand in a tin of hot water. Cook in oven Reg. 4 for about
50 minutes or until firm to the touch. Remove and leave for a
few minutes before turning out. Fill the centre with sautéd
mushrooms and hand a cream sauce separately if wished.

Spinach Soufflé

4 large tablespoons of cooked, sieved, or chopped spinach (from
about 1–1½ lb.); 1½ oz. butter; 1 heaped tablespoon flour; ¼ pint
creamy milk; salt; pepper; mace or nutmeg; 1 oz. grated cheese;
3 egg yolks; 4 egg whites; browned crumbs.

Dry off the spinach if necessary in a nut of the butter. Turn
out. Melt the rest of the butter in the pan, stir in the flour,
pour on the milk, and stir until boiling. Draw aside, add the
spinach, and season well. Beat in the cheese and egg yolks. Prepare a size-2 soufflé case. Whip the whites stiffly, cut and fold into
the mixture, turn into the prepared case, dust the top with
browned crumbs and bake in a moderately hot oven (380° F. or
Reg. 5) for 25 minutes.

SWEET CORN

Grown in England and also imported. In season from August to
late September. Sweet corn should be eaten when young and
tender with the grains a greeny white in colour. Older, it is best
stripped from the cob for soup or fritters.

PREPARATION AND COOKING: For corn on the cob, cut off any

bottom stalk and strip away the leaves. If young and green boil for 5 minutes, otherwise 15 or 20 minutes, before draining and serving with melted butter. Serve as a separate course. After boiling the cobs can be wrapped round with thin rashers of streaky bacon and grilled until the bacon is crisp. Corn on the cob is eaten with the fingers and finger bowls are again an asset.

The kernels of sweet corn are good in a salad with shredded ham as hors d'œuvre.

*

Sweet Corn Fritters
4 large tablespoons kernels – fresh, tinned, or frozen; 1 cup fresh white crumbs; 2 eggs; 1 tablespoon thick cream; salt; pepper; $\frac{1}{2}$ teaspoon baking powder; oil and butter for frying.

Cook the kernels until just tender; drain and dry over the heat with a nut of butter. Turn into a bowl. When cool, stir in the crumbs. Separate the yolks and whites, work the yolks with the cream and add to the corn. Season well and add the baking powder. Whip the whites stiffly and fold into the mixture. Heat about $\frac{1}{2}$ gill oil, add 1 oz. butter, and fry the mixture in dessertspoons, turning when brown on one side. Drain on kitchen paper and serve with a tomato sauce or as an accompaniment to chicken or veal.

TOMATOES

Though tomatoes are available all the year round they are more expensive during the winter months. English tomatoes are in season from mid June to September, when they are at their best and cheapest.

PREPARATION AND COOKING: Tomatoes need little preparation beyond peeling and, in certain circumstances, squeezing out the seeds. To skin, pour boiling water over them, count twelve, and pour off the water. Replace with cold water, then peel. To remove the seeds cut out the stalk with the point of a small knife and scoop out the seeds with the handle of a teaspoon. The tomatoes are then ready to be chopped (concassés) or sliced. Alternatively quarter the tomatoes, cut away the stalk, and flick out the seeds. These quarters are used whole or shredded in salads, sauces, and sautés.

*

Tomatoes Duxelles

6 large, even-sized tomatoes; 6 oz. flat mushrooms; 2 shallots; $1\frac{1}{2}$ oz. butter; 3 tablespoons breadcrumbs; 1 tablespoon mixed chopped herbs – parsley, lemon thyme, or basil; 1 egg yolk; 3 rounds stale bread; garlic butter.

Slice off the tops from the flower end of the tomatoes and carefully scoop out the seeds. Strain the juice. Set aside. Choose six even-sized mushrooms, peel and stalk; chop these trimmings with the remaining mushrooms and chop the shallots. Heat 1 oz. of the butter in a sauté or frying-pan, cook the whole mushrooms quickly in this, take them out, and set aside. Add the chopped mushrooms (duxelles) with the shallots to the pan and cook slowly for 5 or 6 minutes, then increase the heat to drive off any surplus moisture. Draw aside, stir in the crumbs, herbs, and egg yolk. Season well. Fill into the tomatoes and top each with a mushroom. Toast the bread; stamp out into six rounds or cut in squares. Spread these with the garlic butter, set a tomato on each, cover with a buttered paper, and cook in a moderate oven for 10 minutes. Serve very hot as a savoury or luncheon dish.

Tomatoes Provençale

$\frac{1}{2}$ lb. potatoes; 1 lb. ripe tomatoes; 3 large onions; 4 tablespoons olive oil; lemon thyme and tarragon; nutmeg; browned crumbs.

Boil the potatoes with their skins on. Meanwhile, scald, peel, and slice the tomatoes and cut the onions into thin rings. Heat the oil in a frying-pan and brown the onions in this. Put a spoonful or two of the oil from the pan into a fireproof dish with half the tomatoes; scatter over about a third of the onions with salt, pepper, grated nutmeg, and a little coarsely chopped thyme and tarragon. Peel and slice the potatoes thinly and arrange on top with a little more onion, seasoning and herbs. Finish with the rest of the tomatoes, spoon over the remaining onion and oil from the pan, and sprinkle with the crumbs. Bake in a moderate oven for 20 to 30 minutes. Serve hot to accompany a grill or roast.

Tomato Salad

1 lb. sound ripe tomatoes; 1 small lemon; 1 medium-sized onion; chopped basil or parsley.

DRESSING: lemon juice; oil; salt; sugar; pepper.

Scald and peel the tomatoes, slice them thinly roundways, and arrange in a dish. Salt lightly and grate over the rind of the lemon. Slice the onion thinly, blanch, and drain. Prepare the dressing with 1 tablespoon of the lemon juice and 3 of oil; salt, sugar, and pepper to taste. Scatter the onion over the dish and spoon on the dressing. Leave for an hour before serving.

WATERCRESS

At its best in late spring and throughout the summer. Used mostly for salads and garnishing but also good cooked in soups or in butter (see Eggs Cressonière, page 65).

PREPARATION: If the cress is good, leave in the bundle for washing. Swish well in the water and shake dry. Cut off as much of the stalks as is necessary but do not throw them away – use them for a soup or snip with the scissors into a green salad or for a watercress butter.

Chapter 10

SAUCES, SAVOURY AND SWEET

THE making of a good sauce is a comparatively simple matter once you have learnt and remembered the basic principles. These are few and easy to grasp.

LIAISONS

All sauces and many soups have a liaison of some kind which binds the liquid together and can at the same time enrich it.

*

Roux
The first and most important liaison is a *roux*, a mixture of butter and flour where the butter should weigh slightly more than the flour. This gives a soft roux blending smoothly with the liquid.

PENGUIN CORDON BLEU COOKERY

There are three kinds of roux – white, 'blond', and brown. Melt the butter gently, then stir in the flour off the heat, and this gives a white roux. To finish the sauce, pour on the liquid, which should be cold or just warm if the roux is hot, or warm if the roux is cold. This makes the blending with the liquid an easy matter and gives a smooth texture to the sauce.

Brown roux is described on page 372 and 'blond' roux on page 371, under the sections of sauces for which they are used.

Kneaded Butter (Beurre Manié)

A liaison used to thicken sauces, ragouts, and sautés where the quantity of liquid is unknown. Take almost twice as much butter as flour, e.g. 1 rounded tablespoon of butter to 1 level tablespoon of flour. Work together on a plate into a paste. Add this in small pieces to the contents of the pan off the heat. Stir, or, if adding to a ragout or sauté, shake the pan gently, avoiding any possibility of breaking the meat. The butter melts and draws the flour into the liquid. Reboil, and, if not thick enough, repeat the process.

Egg Yolks and Cream

This liaison is for finishing sauces, especially veloutés, and for cream soups. Work the yolks and cream together and pour in about half a cupful of the hot sauce by degrees so that the eggs can cook gradually, then return, also by degrees, to the main bulk of the sauce. Reheat, stirring continually, but do not boil.

Arrowroot or Potato Fécule

This liaison is used mostly for soups and ragouts. Mix either of these starches with 2 to 3 tablespoons of cold water before adding to the near-boiling liquid off the heat. Bring to the boil and after a few seconds draw aside. Do not continue to cook as the liquid may thin again. This type of liaison must be used sparingly – a tea-spoon to a level dessertspoon is generally ample.

FLOUR SAUCES

The flour sauces are perhaps the most familiar and the most used. Béchamel is one of these and forms the base of several other sauces.

*

Béchamel (basic recipe)

½ pint milk; a slice of onion; 6 peppercorns; a blade of mace; a bayleaf.

ROUX: ¾ oz. butter, good weight; ¾ oz. flour; salt; pepper.

Add the onion and spices to the milk, cover the pan, and set on a low heat to infuse for 5 to 7 minutes. Do not allow to boil. Pour off and wipe out the pan. Make a white roux, strain on a good third of the milk, blend, and add the remainder. When thoroughly mixed, season lightly, return to the heat, and stir continually until boiling. Boil for 1 or 2 minutes, then adjust the seasoning. These quantities give a consistency for coating vegetables, fish, and eggs. A sauce to accompany a dish is slightly thinner (that is with a higher proportion of liquid), and is termed a 'flowing' sauce.

The following sauces have this coating Béchamel as their base:

Mornay

Here the flavouring of the milk may be omitted and the quantities for the roux reduced to ½ oz. each butter and flour. Make as for the Béchamel and beat in 1½ oz. grated cheese for ½ pint of sauce by degrees. This will give a glossy sauce. Adjust the seasoning, adding plenty of pepper. See Eggs Mornay (page 61); also for fish, vegetables, and chicken dishes.

Soubise

½ pint Béchamel, made with 1 oz. butter, 1 oz. flour (scant weight), and ½ pint milk; 2–3 large onions; 1 oz. butter; and 2–3 tablespoons cream.

Prepare the Béchamel and set aside. Slice or chop the onions, blanch, drain well, and soften in the butter without colouring. Rub through a nylon sieve or strainer. Beat this purée into the Béchamel, reheat, and add the cream. See Eggs Soubise (page 64); also for fish, veal, and lamb dishes.

Aurore

½ pint Béchamel; ½ gill strong fresh tomato pulp made with ½ lb.
tomatoes; 1 shallot; 1 bayleaf; ½ oz. butter; 2–3 tablespoons cream.

Make the Béchamel and set aside. Wipe the tomatoes, squeeze
to remove the seeds, cut up, and put into a pan with the chopped
shallot, bayleaf, and butter. Cook to a pulp and sieve. Beat this
into the sauce, add the cream, and adjust the seasoning. See
Eggs Aurore (page 62); also for fish, vegetables, and meat.
(For Egg Sauce, see page 123).

There is also a second method of making a Béchamel sauce,
one which is particularly delicate in flavour. This is used for
vegetables or eggs or where a finer sauce is wanted.

Béchamel (long method)

MIREPOIX: 1 small onion; 1 small carrot; 1 half stick of celery;
1 oz. butter.

1 oz. butter; 1 oz. flour for the roux; 1 pint milk; a small bouquet
garni; grated nutmeg; salt and pepper.

Cut the vegetables in fine dice, melt the butter in a thick and
roomy saucepan, put in the mirepoix, and press a piece of paper
down on the top. Cover the pan and cook slowly for 5 to 7 minutes
without colouring. Then turn the contents of the pan on to a plate.
Make a white roux with the butter and flour in the pan and set
aside. Bring the milk to the boil, pour on to the roux, whisking
well, then add salt, pepper, and a little nutmeg. Stir until boiling
and add the mirepoix. Set on low heat to simmer very gently
for 40 minutes with the pan half covered, stirring occasionally;
then run the sauce through a strainer, pressing the vegetables
lightly to extract the juice. Return to a clean pan for reheating.

This sauce is often used coated over a mixture of vegetables in
season, cooked and finished in butter, and arranged in bouquets in
a hot dish. It is good also coated over poached or soft-boiled eggs.

Velouté Sauce

Another of the flour sauces, but made on a blond roux and with a
white stock – fish, vegetable, or meat – in place of milk.

$\frac{3}{4}$ oz. butter; $\frac{3}{4}$ oz. flour; $1\frac{1}{2}$ gills good stock (any of the above) well strained and free from grease; $\frac{1}{2}$ gill creamy milk; salt; pepper; a few drops of lemon juice.

LIAISON: 1 egg yolk; 2 tablespoons cream.

Melt the butter, add the flour, and cook on a slow heat for 1 or 2 minutes or until a pale straw colour (blond roux). Draw aside. Pour on the stock, blend, return to the heat, and stir until thickening. Season and add the milk. Bring to the boil and cook for several minutes or until syrupy in consistency. Draw aside, add the lemon juice, and serve; or finish with a liaison according to the recipe being followed.

Poulette

$\frac{1}{2}$ pint velouté sauce; $\frac{1}{2}$ teaspoon lemon juice; 1 large teaspoon chopped parsley.

Prepare the sauce and finish with an egg and cream liaison (page 368) and the additional lemon juice and parsley. Use for vegetables and certain meat dishes, e.g. calf's head.

Suprême

A rich chicken-flavoured sauce for coating a suprême of chicken, or meat cream (veal, ham, or chicken), and has a rich liaison.

$1\frac{1}{4}$ oz. butter; 1 oz. flour; $\frac{1}{2}$ pint strong chicken stock; $\frac{1}{4}$ pint cream; 3 egg yolks.

Make a blond roux with the butter and flour, pour on the stock, blend and stir over the heat until boiling. Season, draw aside, and add the liaison of egg yolks and cream.

Mushroom or Sauce Duxelles

2 oz. cup or flat mushrooms; 1 shallot; $1\frac{1}{4}$ oz. butter; 1 oz. flour; $\frac{1}{2}$ pint veal or chicken stock; 2 tablespoons cream; salt; pepper; 1 teaspoon chopped mixed herbs or parsley.

Wash the mushrooms and chop them finely. Chop the shallot.

Melt half the butter in a saucepan, add the shallot and, after a minute, the mushrooms. Cook for 3 or 4 minutes, draw aside, add the rest of the butter, and stir in the flour. Season, pour on the stock, blend, then stir until boiling. Boil for 1 to 2 minutes and add the cream and herbs. Simmer for half a minute, then serve over fish, meat, or eggs.

Parsley Sauce (for boiled chicken, fish, or eggs)
1 large handful fresh parsley; $\frac{1}{2}$ pint velouté sauce made with the appropriate stock.

Pick the stalks from the parsley, wash well, and plunge into boiling salted water. Boil uncovered for 5 to 7 minutes, then drain and press well. Rub through a strainer. Make the velouté sauce (see page 370) and beat in the purée (there should be about a teaspoonful). Finish with a little cream if wished in place of the egg yolk.

Brown Roux
This is the basis of the third and last of the basic flour sauces. The flour is cooked in the fat until a rich brown before adding the liquid. As a rule, vegetables are first cooked in the fat before adding the flour for a brown sauce, though for a demi-glace – literally a half-glaze and a finer sauce altogether – no vegetables are called for. For both sauces a good bone stock is used; that for a brown sauce can be a mixed stock, while that for a demi-glace must be a jellied bone and beef stock such as is made for a consommé. A brown sauce (also rather confusingly called a demi-glace sometimes) is the one most frequently used nowadays owing to the difficulty of making this special stock. However, if carefully made with a clear bone stock a brown sauce passes well for a demi-glace. Bone stock is emphasized, as without this the proper semi-clear, 'sticky' consistency of the sauce cannot be obtained; in fact, the better the stock the better the flavour and consistency of the sauce.

TO DÉPOUILLER A SAUCE: *Dépouiller* means literally to skin, i.e. to skin off the scum or fat which rises to the surface during the simmering of the sauce. This is helped by the addition of a small quantity of cold stock to the sauce, usually about $\frac{1}{2}$ to $\frac{3}{4}$ gill reserved from the total amount of liquid called for in the recipe, e.g. one pint. This reserved stock is added in two or three parts and the sauce allowed to reboil before skimming thoroughly. This process is done towards the end of the simmering time and is made simpler by tilting the pan up slightly with an old metal spoon or lid. The fat will then rise to the surface on one side and can be easily skimmed off with a metal spoon. When the *dépouillement* is completed, and the sauce is of the right consistency, the whole is strained into a clean pan for finishing according to the recipe.

If properly done, *dépouillement* clears the sauce and gives it a glossy appearance.

*

Brown Sauce or Demi-Glace

3 tablespoons oil; 1 small carrot; 1 small or half onion; 1 small stick celery; 1 tablespoon flour; 1 pint brown bone stock; a few mushroom peelings; 1 teaspoon tomato purée; bouquet garni.

Cut the vegetables in fine dice; heat a shallow saucepan or small stewpan. Put in the oil and add the vegetables. Cook on a low heat until the vegetables are barely coloured, then stir in the flour and continue to cook slowly, stirring occasionally with a metal spoon (a wooden spoon might burn and cannot scrape the pan so well) until a good russet brown. Draw aside, add $\frac{3}{4}$ pint of the stock and the rest of the ingredients. Bring to the boil, half cover with the lid, and simmer for 25 minutes. Then *dépouillé* the sauce with the reserved stock, strain, season lightly, and use for any of the sauces given below.

Sauce Chasseur (for grills, entrées, and roasts)

$\frac{1}{2}$ pint demi-glace sauce; $\frac{1}{2}$ oz. butter; 1 shallot; 2 oz. button mushrooms; 1 glass white wine; 1 dessertspoon tomato purée.

Have ready the demi-glace. Chop the shallot finely, soften in the butter without colouring. Slice and add the mushrooms, shake over the heat until just turning colour, then pour in the wine and reduce to half. Add the purée and the sauce; simmer for 2 or 3 minutes then serve.

Sauce Madère (for grills, steaks, and cutlets)
This calls for especially good stock when making the demi-glace and extra stock allowed for the *dépouillement*, which should be carried out more thoroughly than usual.

½ pint strong 'clear' demi-glace; 1 sherry glassful of Madeira.

Heat the demi-glace, correct the seasoning, add the Madeira, and serve.

Sauce Bigarade (for duck and rich game)
½ pint demi-glace; 2 shallots; a nut of butter; 1 glass red wine; a small bayleaf; rind and juice of 1 orange; 1 teaspoon red-currant jelly.

Chop the shallots finely and soften in the butter in a small sauce-pan. Add the wine and bayleaf. Reduce gently by about a third. Add, with the juice and half the pared rind of the orange, to the demi-glace. Simmer for 5 to 7 minutes. In the meantime shred the remaining rind thinly, blanch for 5 minutes, and drain. Strain the sauce and return to the pan with the shredded rind and jelly. Bring slowly to the boil, stirring frequently to dissolve the jelly. To be correct, this sauce should have a small bitter or Seville orange in place of a sweet one. If, however, the latter has to be used, sharpen the sauce with a few drops of lemon juice.

Sauce Bordelaise – see page 209.

Sauce Poivrade (or Piquante)
This is a sharp sauce used for devils and grills. A simpler version will be found under miscellaneous sauces, page 378.

½ pint demi-glace; 1 large tablespoon tarragon vinegar; 1 large teaspoon capers; 1 teaspoon chopped herbs and parsley; 1 tea-spoon tomato purée.

Reduce the vinegar down to a teaspoonful, add to the demi-glace with the rest of the ingredients, bring to the boil, and serve.

Sauce Blanche or Butter Sauce

This sauce calls for care in making. It is excellent for serving with vegetables and fish as an alternative to Hollandaise. It also forms the base of other sauces.

For ½ pint take: 2 oz. fresh butter; ½ oz. flour; 1½ gills water; a pinch of salt and pepper; a few drops lemon juice.

Choose a saucepan that will hold at least double the quantity of sauce so that there is plenty of room to beat vigorously without spilling. Take a good half ounce of the butter, melt it gently in the pan, and stir in the flour off the heat. Do not cook but work well with a wooden spatula to a smooth paste. Now boil the water and when bubbling pour it on to the paste, still off the heat, in a steady stream, beating well with a sauce whisk until smooth and free from lumps. Add the salt, pepper, and lemon juice and the rest of the butter in small pieces, whisking just enough to mix into the sauce. Pour at once into a sauce-boat and serve. If, however, the sauce has to be kept hot, stand the pan in a bain-marie and add the lemon juice just before serving.

NOTE: It is important that a Sauce Blanche is not boiled at any time as this gives an unpleasant gluey taste. The flour will be cooked if the water is really boiling when it is poured on.

Sauce Batarde

Add a liaison of 1 or 2 egg yolks to the Sauce Blanche before the addition of the butter.

Mustard Sauce (for grilled herrings, mackerel, and boiled fish)
To the above quantities of Sauce Blanche, take 1 dessertspoon of good French mustard.

Add the mustard to the sauce with the butter. This sauce can also be made on a velouté base; whisk the mustard into the sauce at the last moment and do not boil once it has been added.

Caper Sauce (for boiled mutton, grilled or boiled fish)
To the same quantity of Sauce Blanche add 1 tablespoon of

French capers and a heaped teaspoon of chopped parsley just before serving. This sauce can also be made on a velouté base.

Sauce Verte (Green Sauce) (for salmon, trout, or grilled mackerel)

2 handfuls spinach; 3–4 sprays each tarragon and chervil; a ¼ cucumber.

½ pint Sauce Blanche; liaison of 2 egg yolks and 2 tablespoons cream.

Boil the spinach and herbs for 5 or 6 minutes; drain, press, and pass through a fine wire strainer. Peel the cucumber and cut into fine dice, blanch in boiling water for half a minute, then drain.

Prepare the sauce, whisk in the liaison before the butter, and finish the sauce with the purée (about 1 tablespoon). Reheat the sauce carefully if necessary, but on no account boil. Just before serving stir in the cucumber.

Another method of preparing this sauce is described on page 380.

Sauce Hollandaise (for salmon, asparagus, vegetables, entrées, and fish dishes)

3 tablespoons wine vinegar; 6 peppercorns; ½ bayleaf; a blade of mace; 2 egg yolks; 3–4 oz. fresh butter.

Place the vinegar, peppercorns, bayleaf, and blade of mace in a small saucepan and reduce to a dessertspoonful; set aside. Work the butter until slightly soft. Cream the egg yolks in a small bowl with a nut of the butter and a small pinch of salt. Strain on the vinegar, set the bowl in a bain-marie on a gentle heat, and stir the mixture, until thick, with a sauce whisk or wooden spatula. Add the rest of the butter in small pieces about the size of a hazelnut, stirring continually. When all the butter has been added, season delicately and, if the sauce is too sharp, add a little more butter. It should be lightly piquante, barely holding its shape, and lukewarm rather than hot. For a sauce to accompany a dish it may be diluted slightly with a spoonful or two of cream.

NOTE: The water in the bain-marie should be lukewarm to begin with, gradually increasing till very hot, about 170 to 180° F., but on no account to boiling-point. If the sauce is thickening too quickly, remove the bowl from the bain-marie and continue to add the butter off the heat.

Sauce Béarnaise

This sauce is similar to a Hollandaise but much thicker and slightly sharper in taste. It is served with fillet steaks, shellfish, and the richer kinds of fish when grilled.

4 tablespoons wine vinegar; 1 shallot; 1 bayleaf; 1 blade of mace; 6 peppercorns; 2 large egg yolks; 4 oz. fresh butter; 1 heaped teaspoon of chopped mixed tarragon, chervil, and parsley; salt; pepper; half a teaspoon meat glaze.

Reduce the vinegar with the spices to 1 tablespoon. Strain on to the yolks worked with a nut of the softened butter and thicken in a bain-marie, adding the rest of the butter until the sauce is the consistency of whipped cream. Add the herbs, seasoning, and meat glaze. In default of the glaze, the jellied gravy underneath a bowl of beef dripping makes a good substitute.

Sauce Mousseline (for asparagus, salmon, cutlets, etc.)

3 egg yolks; small pinch of salt and of ground white pepper; juice of $\frac{1}{2}$ a lemon; 3–4 oz. fresh butter; 2–3 tablespoons lightly whipped cream.

Work the yolks, seasoning, and a small nut of the butter in a basin and cream until thick. Add the lemon juice, stand in a bain-marie, and whisk until mousse-like. Add the softened butter in small pieces, about the size of a hazelnut, whisking all the time. Just before serving, fold in the cream and adjust the seasoning.

Sauce Maltaise (for asparagus, fried sole, scampi, etc.)

Make as for Sauce Mousseline, but use the grated rind and juice of half a blood orange in place of the lemon juice.

MISCELLANEOUS SAUCES

Tomato Sauce

½ oz. butter; ½ oz. flour; 1½ gills stock; bouquet garni; a pinch of pepper, salt and sugar; 1 lb. tomatoes or 1½ cups tinned tomatoes; a nut of butter to garnish.

Melt the butter in a saucepan, add the flour, mix, and pour on the stock; bring to the boil. Cut the tomatoes in two, squeeze to remove the seeds, and add them to the pan with the bouquet garni, pepper, salt, sugar, and the juice strained from the tomato seeds. Cover and simmer for half an hour. Pour through a strainer, pressing well to extract the juice. Adjust the seasoning and reheat. Beat in the nut of butter before serving.

Sauce Piquante

¾ oz. butter; ½ oz. flour; 1 onion; 2 tomatoes; few mushroom peelings; 1 teaspoonful tarragon vinegar; 1 teaspoon chopped parsley; 1 teaspoon tomato purée; bouquet garni; ½ pint well flavoured stock; salt; pepper; sugar.

Melt the butter, slice and add the onion, and brown lightly. Stir in the flour and allow to brown. Squeeze the tomatoes and slice roughly, adding the mushroom peelings, bouquet garni, stock, and vinegar. Season, bring to the boil, and simmer gently for 20 to 30 minutes. Strain and return to the pan, adding a pinch of sugar and adjusting the seasoning.

Mint Sauce

1 large handful mint leaves; 1 tablespoon castor sugar; 2 table-spoons boiling water; 3 tablespoons wine vinegar; a pinch of salt.

Wash and dry the mint leaves; chop them finely or pound in a mortar until smooth with a little of the sugar. Turn into a bowl, and add the boiling water. This will 'set' the colour. Stir in the sugar, vinegar, and salt. Taste and add more sugar or vinegar if necessary. The sauce should be bright green and thick in consistency.

Orange Mint Sauce

A large handful of mint leaves; 1 level tablespoon castor sugar;
1 or more lumps of sugar; 1 heaped teaspoon redcurrant jelly;
1 orange; 2 tablespoons boiling water; 2–3 tablespoons wine
vinegar.

Strip the sprigs then bruise and pound the leaves in a mortar
until fine, or work in a blender; again they may be chopped finely,
but the former methods are better. Add the castor sugar. Rub
lumps of sugar over the orange rind until soaked with the oil and
add to the mint with the jelly. Pour on the boiling water. Add the
strained juice of the orange and the vinegar and a little more sugar
to taste.

Apple Sauce

1 lb. cooking apples; thinly pared rind of ½ lemon; 2–3 tablespoons water; 1 dessertspoon sugar; ½ oz. butter.

Peel and core the apples and place in a saucepan with the lemon
rind and water. Cover tightly and cook until soft and pulpy. Stir
in the butter and sugar and serve hot.

Horseradish Sauce

2 heaped tablespoons fresh-grated horseradish; ½ teaspoon mustard; salt; pepper; sugar; 1 dessertspoon vinegar; ¼ pint
cream.

Mix the vinegar, seasonings, and horseradish together. Whip
the cream lightly and mix carefully with the other ingredients.
Adjust the seasoning to taste.

Mayonnaise

3 egg yolks; salt; pepper; a little French mustard; ½ pint olive
oil; 1–2 tablespoons wine vinegar.

Cream the yolks well in a basin adding two large pinches of salt and one pinch of pepper and the mustard. When thick, add two tablespoons of the oil very slowly, dripping it in from the point of the spoon. If the sauce becomes too thick dilute with a few drops of vinegar. Now add the rest of the oil a little more quickly, beating well all the time. Add the vinegar to taste and when the sauce becomes too solid. Adjust the seasoning. A good mayonnaise should be made with a fairly high proportion of egg yolks to oil, though the sauce will thicken perfectly well with 3 yolks to a pint of oil. With the additional yolks the flavour and texture of the sauce is better.

Mayonnaise as a basic sauce may be flavoured with tomato and pimento for serving with shellfish (see Lobster Cordon Bleu, page 176) and for a Sauce Verte for salmon, trout, eggs, and so on. For serving as an accompanying sauce, thin with a tablepoon of boiling water or tomato juice.

Sauce Verte (second method)

½ pint mayonnaise; a good handful of green herbs consisting of watercress, parsley, and spinach leaves; 2 fillets of anchovy; cream.

Prepare the mayonnaise. Boil the herbs for 5 or 6 minutes in salted water and when tender drain and rub through a strainer with the anchovies. Add this purée to the mayonnaise with a tablespoon of boiling water. Finish with a tablespoon of cream if wished.

Sauce Tartare (for fried or grilled fish)

2 hard-boiled eggs; 1 raw egg yolk; salt; pepper; ½ pint oil; 1 tablespoon vinegar; 1 teaspoon each chopped parsley and snipped chives; 1 teaspoon chopped capers or gherkin.

Split the hard-boiled eggs, take out the yolks, and rub them through a strainer into a bowl. Add the raw yolk and work well together with the seasoning. Add the oil as for a mayonnaise and dilute with the vinegar when necessary. Finish with the herbs and

capers and if wished add the shredded hard-boiled white of
1 egg.

Curry Cream Dressing – see Eggs à l'Indienne, page 87.

Tarragon Cream Dressing (for fruit salads, or fruit such as
pears, plums, or peaches, served with meat)
1 large egg; 2 tablespoons castor sugar; 3 tablespoons tarragon
vinegar; $\frac{3}{4}$ gill cream.

Beat the egg with the sugar until well mixed. Add the vinegar and
stir in a bain-marie until thick (the mixture should look like lemon
curd). Take off the heat and leave until cold. Whip the cream
lightly and fold into the dressing.

French Dressing
1 large tablespoon white- or red-wine vinegar; a small $\frac{1}{2}$ teaspoonful French mustard; 2 pinches salt; pepper from the mill;
a small clove or less of garlic; 3–4 tablespoons olive oil.

Put the vinegar into a small bowl with the mustard. Chop and
crush the garlic with the salt to a cream and add to the vinegar
with the pepper. Mix well and add the oil. When the dressing has
thickened, taste and adjust the seasoning. Half to one teaspoonful
of castor sugar may be added at this stage if the vinegar is sharp.
If the dressing is sharp and yet oily to taste, add more salt as this
will 'cut' the oil.

Vinaigrette Dressing (1)
To the above quantity of French dressing add 1 tablespoon mixed
chopped herbs (thyme, parsley, and chives). If wished, a teaspoonful of chopped capers may also be added.

Vinaigrette Dressing (2)
2 tablespoons wine or tarragon vinegar; 1 teaspoon lemon juice;
5–6 tablespoons olive oil; 1 dessertspoon each chopped parsley
and chives; 1 shallot; 2 soft-boiled eggs ($3\frac{1}{2}$ minutes boiling).

Work the vinegar, oil, and seasonings together as for a French dressing. Spoon out the soft yolks from the eggs and add to the dressing with the chopped shallot and herbs. Finish with the chopped whites.

Chapter 11

PASTRIES AND PUDDINGS

PASTRIES

FOR good pastry-making the following points should be remembered; they apply most particularly to all types of short pastry, suet crust, flaky, and puff pastries:

1. Work in a cool, airy room, planning to make pastry before the kitchen gets warm and steamy from other cooking.

2. Keep a board specially for the purpose. A piece of marble or slate shelf is ideal, but today's formica table-tops can be used if the surface is cool.

3. Use fresh fine plain flour and firm but not hard fat and ice-cold water for mixing.

4. Handle the fat and flour lightly but firmly with cool hands.

5. Make sure the correct amount of water is added as the amount will vary a little with the quality of the flour. Too dry a mixture will make the pastry difficult to handle – it will crack when rolled out, crumble after baking, and be dry to eat; too wet a mixture will shrink and lose shape during baking and be tough and hard to eat.

6. Oven temperatures are important. They are given under the various recipes but a pastry oven is a hot one varying from 375° F. or Reg. 5 for a sweet short pastry to 425 to 450° F. or Reg. 7 to 8 for the rich flaky and puff pastries.

*

Shortcrust Pastry

½ lb. plain flour; 4–6 oz. butter, margarine, lard, or shortening (one of the commercially prepared fats), or a mixture of any two; 3–4 tablespoons cold water.

Sift the flour with a pinch of salt into a mixing-bowl, cut the fat into the flour with a round-bladed knife, and as soon as the pieces are well coated with flour rub in with the fingertips until the mixture looks like breadcrumbs. Make a well in the centre, add the water, reserving about a tablespoon, and mix quickly with a knife. Press together with the fingers, adding the extra water if necessary to give a firm dough. Turn on to a floured board, knead lightly until smooth, then chill for 15 to 20 minutes before using. Bake in a moderately hot oven (380 to 400° F. or Reg. 5 to 6). The time will depend on thickness, filling, size, and so on, and will be given in individual recipes.

Rich Shortcrust Pastry

½ lb. plain flour; 6 oz. butter; 1 dessertspoon castor sugar; 1 egg yolk; about 1½ tablespoons cold water.

Sift the flour with a pinch of salt; drop in the butter and cut it into the flour until the small pieces are well coated, then rub them in using the fingertips until the mixture resembles fine breadcrumbs. Stir in the sugar; mix the egg yolk and water together, tip into the fat and flour, and mix quickly to a firm dough. Turn on to a floured board and knead lightly until smooth. Chill for 15 to 20 minutes before using and bake in a moderately hot oven (380° F. or Reg. 5).

Cheese Pastry

6 oz. plain flour; salt, pepper, a pinch of cayenne; 4 oz. butter or margarine; 4 oz. finely grated cheese (half Cheddar and half Parmesan); 1 egg yolk; 1 tablespoon water.

Sift the flour with the seasonings into a mixing-bowl, drop in the butter, and cut into the flour with a round-bladed knife. When the pieces of butter are well coated with flour, rub them in with the fingertips until the mixture looks like breadcrumbs; do not over-rub, particularly in warm weather, or the pastry will be heavy. Add the cheese and stir in with the knife. Mix the egg yolk and water, tip into the dry ingredients, and mix quickly to a firm dough. Turn on to a floured board and knead lightly until smooth. Chill for half an hour before rolling out and cook on baking-tins lined with greaseproof paper in a moderately hot oven (375° F. or Reg. 5).

American Pie Pastry

½ lb. self-raising flour; 5 oz. lard or shortening; 2 tablespoons cold water.

Place the lard or shortening in the pastry bowl, add a good pinch of salt and the water, and cream the ingredients together. Sift the flour over the softened fat and, using a round-bladed knife, cut the fat into the flour and mix to a rough paste. Chill for 30 minutes. Turn on to a floured board, knead lightly, and then use for fruit pies.

Suetcrust Pastry

½ lb. self-raising flour; 4–5 oz. suet; about ¾ gill of cold water to mix.

Sift the flour with a pinch of salt into a mixing-bowl. If using fresh butcher's suet, remove any skin and chop finely using a little of the measured flour to prevent it sticking. Stir the suet into the flour and mix to a firm dough with the cold water. Turn on to a floured board, knead lightly until smooth, then roll out and use at once.

NOTE: For a particularly light crust 1 oz. of the flour can be omitted and replaced by the same quantity of fresh white crumbs.

Hot-water Crust

¾ lb. plain flour; 5 oz. good English lard; ¼ pint milk or water.

Warm the flour and sieve into a mixing-bowl with salt and pepper and make a well in the middle. Heat the lard with the milk or water and when boiling tip quickly into the flour and mix until smooth with a wooden spoon. Use at once. Have the filling for raised pies ready before the pastry is mixed and keep the pastry not being worked in a warm basin covered with a cloth.

French Pie Pastry or Pâte à Pâté

10 oz. plain flour; 1 level teaspoon salt; 4 tablespoons cold water; 5 oz. butter or margarine; 1 egg.

Sift the flour on to a pastry board or slab; make a well in the centre and in this place the salt and water. Dissolve the salt in the water, work in the butter and egg, then gradually draw in the flour. Knead the paste until smooth, then chill for 1 to 2 hours before using.

Flaky Pastry

This is a traditional English farmhouse pastry and should be made with good lard and butter – nothing else will give quite the same result.

½ lb. plain flour; 3 oz. butter; 3 oz. lard; about ½–¾ gill cold water to mix.

Sift the flour with a pinch of salt into a mixing-bowl, rub in half the butter, and mix to a firm but pliable dough with the water. Turn on to a lightly floured board, knead until smooth and roll to an oblong. *Cover the top two thirds of the pastry with half the lard and cut in small pieces, fold in three, seal the edges and give a half turn to bring the sealed ends in front of you.* Roll again to an oblong and repeat from * to * twice, using first the butter and then the lard. Chill for 10 to 15 minutes, then roll out, fold once more, then use as required. Bake in a hot oven (425° F. or Reg. 7.)

Rough Puff Pastry (1)

½ lb. plain flour; 6 oz. butter or firm margarine; about ¼ pint ice-cold water to mix.

Sift the flour with a pinch of salt into a mixing-bowl. Cut the butter in even-sized pieces about the size of walnuts and drop into the flour; mix quickly with the water and turn on to a lightly floured board. *Roll to an oblong, fold in three and give a half-turn to bring the open edges in front of you.* Repeat from * to * twice to give the pastry three turns in all. Chill for 10 minutes and give an extra roll and fold if it looks at all streaky, then use as required. Bake in a hot oven (425° F. or Reg. 7).

Rough Puff Pastry (2)

½ lb. plain flour; 6 oz. butter or firm margarine; about ¼ pint ice-cold water to mix.

Sift the flour with a pinch of salt into a mixing-bowl. Take 1 oz. of the butter and rub it into the flour. Mix to a firm but pliable dough with the water, knead lightly until smooth, then set in a cool place for 10 to 15 minutes. Place the remaining butter between two pieces of greaseproof paper and beat to a flat cake with the rolling-pin. The butter should be the same consistency as the dough. Roll out the dough to a rectangle, place the butter in the middle, fold like a parcel, and turn over. *Roll out to an oblong, fold in three and give a half-turn to bring the open edge towards you.* Repeat from * to * twice to give the pastry three turns in all. Chill for 10 minutes, then roll out and use as required. Bake in a hot oven (425° F. or Reg. 7).

Puff Pastry

½ lb. plain flour; ½ lb. butter; about ¼ pint ice-cold water; a
squeeze of lemon juice.

Sift the flour with a pinch of salt into a mixing-bowl, rub in
a piece of the butter about the size of a walnut, and mix to a firm
dough with the water and lemon. Knead until smooth and leave in
a cool place 15 minutes. Place the butter between two pieces of
paper and beat it with the rolling-pin two or three times to make a
flat pliable cake; dust lightly with flour. Roll out the dough to a
rectangle, place the butter in the middle, fold like a parcel,
and turn over. *Roll to an oblong, fold in three, and give a half-
turn to bring the open edge in front of you.* Repeat from * to *.
Wrap in greaseproof paper or a teacloth and leave in a cool place
for 10 to 15 minutes. Continue in this way until the pastry has had
six rollings or 'turns'. If, at the end of the sixth turn, the pastry
looks at all streaky, give one extra turn but never more or it will
not rise to its full capacity. Chill for 10 minutes after shaping and
before baking in a hot oven (425° F. or Reg. 7).

SHAPING A VOL-AU-VENT CASE

Roll out the puff pastry to about ½ inch thick and cut into a
large round, 8 inches in diameter, with a bevelled edge. Turn

the pastry over and brush the top with beaten egg. (The pastry is now slightly larger at the top than the bottom. This is to ensure that the vol-au-vent rises with straight sides.) Mark a round in the centre, cutting through the pastry only the slightest fraction of an inch. Decorate the vol-au-vent with the back of a knife, marking the centre in a lattice and the outside rim in chevrons. Chill for 10 minutes then bake on a damp baking-sheet for 35 to 40 minutes at 400° F. or Reg. 6. Remove the centre circle of pastry and carefully scoop away any soft uncooked paste underneath; return to the oven to dry for 2 or 3 minutes. The shell is now ready for filling.

SHAPING BOUCHÉE CASES

Roll out the puff pastry to barely ¼ inch thick and stamp into 3-inch rounds with a fluted cutter. Brush with beaten egg, mark the centre very lightly with a 1-inch cutter, and place on a damp baking tray. Chill for 10 minutes, then bake in a hot oven until brown and crisp (425° F. or Reg. 7) for 10 to 15 minutes. Remove the centre of each bouchée, scoop away any soft paste from the inside, and fill as required. ½ lb. puff pastry will make 9 bouchée cases of entrée size and may be filled with shrimps, prawns, sweetbreads, or chicken mixed with a creamy Béchamel sauce.

COCKTAIL-SIZED BOUCHÉES

Roll the puff pastry very thin (about ⅛ inch thick) and cut with a 1½-inch plain or fluted cutter. Brush with beaten egg and mark the centre in the same way as for the larger bouchée. Chill for 10 minutes and bake in a hot oven (425° F. or Reg. 7) until brown and crisp (about 8 to 10 minutes). In rolling, cutting, and baking in this way the small bouchée will shrink in diameter but rise quite straight. If the pastry is any thicker it will rise and topple over in baking.

*

French Flan Pastry or Pâte Sucrée
4 oz. plain flour; 2 oz. butter; 2 oz. castor sugar; 2 egg yolks; 2 drops of vanilla essence.

Sift the flour with a pinch of salt on to the pastry board or slab, make a small well in the centre, and in this place the other ingredients. Using the fingertips of one hand work only the butter, sugar, and yolks together, then quickly draw in the flour and knead lightly until smooth. Wrap in a polythene bag or teacloth and chill for 1 hour before using. Bake at 375° F. or Reg. 5 to a pale biscuit colour. On no account should this pastry be brown; this would mean the sugar had caramelized and the flavour would be spoilt.

Almond Pastry or Pâte Frolle

6 oz. plain flour; 3 oz. ground almonds; 4 oz. butter; 3 oz. castor sugar; 1 egg; 1 egg yolk; 2 drops vanilla or almond essence, or the grated rind of ½ a lemon.

Sift the flour with a pinch of salt on to a pastry board or slab; make a small well in the centre and sprinkle the almonds on the flour. Place the butter, sugar, eggs, and flavouring in the middle of the flour and work these ingredients together with the fingertips of one hand. When blended, draw in the flour and almonds and knead lightly until smooth. Wrap and chill for 1 hour before using. Bake in a moderate oven (375° F. or Reg. 5) to a pale biscuit colour.

Bavarian Apple Strudel

PASTRY: 6 oz. flour; 4 oz. butter; 2 level tablespoons castor sugar; 3 tablespoons milk.

FILLING: 1½ lb. cooking apples; 2 oz. sultanas; 2–3 tablespoons sugar; ½ teaspoon mixed spice; 2 tablespoons fresh breadcrumbs.

Prepare the pastry as shortcrust using the milk to mix and set in a cool place. Peel, core, and slice the apples thinly, mix with the sugar, spice, and crumbs. Roll the pastry to an oblong and place on a baking-tin. Spread the filling down the centre half and fold the sides over gently so the filling shows. Brush with milk and bake in a moderate oven (400° F. or Reg. 6) for about 20 to 30 minutes. Serve dusted with icing sugar and cut into thick slices.

Farmhouse Treacle Tart

FLAKY PASTRY (as on page 386).

FILLING: I teacupful golden syrup; $1\frac{1}{2}$ teacups fresh bread-crumbs; juice and grated rind of $\frac{1}{2}$ a lemon.

Prepare the pastry and chill well. Mix all the ingredients for the filling together using a whole lemon if very small. Roll out the pastry and cut in two; roll one piece rather thinner than the other and line into a square or oblong tin. Spread over the syrup mixture. Place the second piece of pastry over, seal the edges well, 'knock up', and flute. Bake in a hot oven for 30 to 40 minutes. Just before it is finished, remove from the oven and brush with a little beaten egg white. Dust at once with castor sugar and return to the oven for 2 or 3 minutes to frost the top. Leave to cool somewhat, then cut into squares for serving.

Tarte aux Pommes Ménagère

PÂTE SUCRÉE (as on page 389).

I lb. apples; 3 heaped tablespoons apricot jam; a squeeze of lemon.

Prepare the pastry and chill for I hour. Line a 7-inch flan ring with the pastry and prick the bottom lightly. Peel and quarter the apples, remove the core, and slice thinly. Arrange the slices over-lapping in circles to fill the flan; dust the top layer only with a little sugar, and bake in a moderate oven (375° F. or Reg. 5) for 20 to 30 minutes.

Meanwhile heat the jam with the lemon until thoroughly melted, then strain. If home-made jam is used, a little water may be necessary. When the flan is cooked, remove the ring and brush the top and sides with the glaze.

Tarte aux Pommes Grillée

PÂTE SUCRÉE: 6 oz. flour; 3 oz. butter; 3 oz. castor sugar; 3 egg yolks.

FILLING: 2 lb. apples; $\frac{1}{2}$ oz. butter; 2 tablespoons marmalade; sugar to taste.

TO FINISH: beaten egg; castor sugar.

Make up the pastry (see page 390) and leave to chill. Wipe, quarter, and core the apples. Rub the butter over the bottom of a heavy stewpan, slice the apples into the pan, cover with a paper and lid, and cook slowly to a pulp. Rub through a strainer. Return the apple purée to the pan, add the marmalade and sugar, and cook until thick. Turn out and leave to cool. Roll out two-thirds of the pastry and line into a 7-inch flan ring; prick the bottom lightly and fill with the apple mixture. Roll out the remaining pastry into an oblong and cut in narrow strips. Arrange these in a lattice over the top of the flan. Brush the flan with beaten egg, dust with castor sugar, and bake in a moderate oven (375° F. or Reg. 5) for about 30 minutes.

Tarte aux Poires Provençale

PÂTE SUCRÉE (as on page 389).

3–4 ripe dessert pears; apricot glaze or jelly.

FILLING: 4 oz. butter; 4 oz. castor sugar; 2 eggs; 4 oz. ground almonds; 1 oz. flour; almond essence or Kirsch to flavour.

Prepare the pastry and leave to chill. Meanwhile peel, halve, and core the pears and poach in a sugar syrup until tender and transparent. Allow to cool and then drain.

Prepare the filling. Soften the butter with a wooden spoon, add the sugar, and cream together until light and fluffy; beat in the eggs gradually and then stir in the almonds, flour, and flavourings.

Line a 7- or 8-inch flan ring or sandwich tin with the pastry. Prick the bottom and fill with the almond mixture. Bake in a moderate oven (380° F. or Reg. 5) for about 30 minutes. When cool brush with hot apricot glaze, leave to set, and then arrange the pears over the top. Brush again with the apricot glaze and decorate with whipped cream or finely chopped pistachio nuts.

Tarte aux Fruits

PÂTE SUCRÉE: (as on page 389).

1 lb. fresh fruit, such as apricots or plums, or bottled or tinned fruit.

GLAZE: ½ pint juice from the fruit after poaching or the drained syrup from the bottled or tinned; 1 heaped tablespoon apricot jam; 2 teaspoons arrowroot.

Prepare the pastry and chill 1 hour. Line a 7-inch flan ring and bake blind. To do this, prick the bottom of the flan with a fork, line the pastry with greaseproof paper, and fill with dried beans, rice, or crusts of bread. Bake for about 10 to 12 minutes in a moderate oven (375° F. or Reg. 5) then remove the beans and paper and the flan ring and return the pastry to the oven to finish cooking for about 5 minutes. Lift on to a wire rack to cool. Poach the fruit if fresh is being used, or drain well if it is canned, and arrange in the flan case. Melt the jam in the fruit juice, mix the arrowroot with a little of the juice, and add to the pan. Stir over heat and boil for 1 to 2 minutes until clear. Brush or spoon this glaze over the fruit to fill the flan.

Tartelettes aux Fruits

PÂTE SUCRÉE (as on page 389).

Fresh fruit in season – peaches, grapes, cherries; apricot or red-currant jelly glaze depending on the colour of the fruit.

Make up the pastry and chill until firm. Roll out thinly and lay the sheet of pastry over 4 or 5 tartlet tins. Press the pastry down into the tins with a small ball of the paste and when well lined roll the rest off with the rolling-pin. Chill before lining with small pieces of greaseproof paper and filling with beans or rice. Bake blind in a moderately hot oven (380° F. or Reg. 5) for 8 to 10 minutes. After 7 minutes take out the paper and beans and return the tartlets to the oven to finish baking. Carefully remove the pastry cases from the tins and when cool brush them out with hot glaze. When set fill with the chosen fruit. If using grapes, pip them and do not peel. Brush well with the glaze.

Tarte aux Pommes à l'Orange

PÂTE SUCRÉE: 6 oz. flour; 3 oz. butter; 3 oz. castor sugar; 3 egg yolks.

FILLING: 2 lb. cooking apples; granulated sugar; grated rind of 2 oranges.

TO FINISH: 2 seedless oranges; apricot glaze.

Prepare the pastry, chill, and then line a 7- or 8-inch flan ring and bake blind as in the preceding recipe.

Meanwhile prepare the filling: wipe, quarter, and core the apples, slice into a buttered pan, cover lightly, and cook to a pulp. Sieve and return to the pan with the orange rind and 2 to 3 tablespoons of sugar. Cook until thick, turn out, and cool.

To finish, turn this purée into the flan and smooth over the top. Cut away the peel and pith from the oranges, slice into rounds, arrange them on top of the flan, and brush with apricot glaze.

Tarte aux Abricots Bourdaloue

PÂTE SUCRÉE (as on page 389).

1 lb. fresh apricots; ½ pint water; 5 oz. granulated sugar.

BOURDALOUE CREAM: ½ pint milk; 2 egg yolks; 1 egg white; 2 oz. sugar; 1¼ oz. flour and cornflour mixed; 1 tablespoon ground almonds; 1–2 tablespoons cream.

Make up the flan pastry and chill well. Halve the apricots and poach in the syrup made from the sugar and water. Prepare the Bourdaloue cream. Scald the milk, cream the yolks with a spoonful of the sugar until light, then work in the flours. Tip on the scalded milk, return to the pan, and stir over gentle heat until boiling. (If this is done too quickly the cream will be lumpy when cold.) Add the ground almonds, turn out, and cool. Whisk the remaining sugar and egg white together until stiff, then stir it into the mixture with a little whipped cream. Line a 7-inch flan ring, bake blind, and when cold fill with the Bourdaloue cream. Drain the apricots very well and arrange over the cream. Boil the apricot syrup until very thick, allow to cool, and then brush it over the fruit just before serving the flan.

Tartelettes Cœur à la Crème

PÂTE SUCRÉE (as on page 389).

2–4 oz. 'Petit Suisse' cream cheese; castor sugar; 2–3 table-spoons cream; small ripe strawberries; ½ lb. red-currant jelly.

Line tartlet tins with the pastry, prick, and bake blind for 8 to 10 minutes in a moderate oven (375° F. or Reg. 5).

Rub the cream cheese through a small strainer, add sugar to taste, and beat in the fresh cream. When the pastry cases are cold, fill with the cream and cover with the strawberries. Beat the redcurrant jelly until quite smooth, strain into a saucepan, and heat without stirring until melted and clear. Brush this glaze over the strawberries.

Danish Strawberry Cake

4 oz. flour; 3 oz. butter; 1¼ oz. icing sugar; 1 egg yolk; a few drops of vanilla; strawberries; 2–3 tablespoons redcurrant jelly glaze; cream.

Sift the flour on to a board or marble slab; make a well in the centre, put in the butter, icing sugar, egg yolks, and vanilla. Work up together to a smooth paste. Set in a cool place for ½ hour; roll or pat out to a round ¼ inch thick, prick all over, and bake in a moderate oven for 20 minutes.

When cool, cover with strawberries, brush over with a thick redcurrant glaze, and decorate with rosettes of whipped cream.

Galette Normande

PASTRY: ½ lb. flour; 5 oz. butter; 2½ oz. icing sugar; 2 egg yolks; a few drops vanilla essence.

FILLING: 2 lb. cooking apples; ½ oz. butter; ½ lemon; sugar to sweeten.

TO FINISH: glacé icing; 1 tablespoon redcurrant jelly.

Make up the pastry as described in the previous recipe. Divide into 3 equal portions and chill for ½ hour. In the meantime pre-pare the filling. Wipe the apples, cut in four, and remove the core. Rub the butter over the bottom of a thick stewpan, put in the sliced apples, add the grated lemon rind and juice, cover with paper and lid, and cook gently until soft and pulpy. Rub through a wire or nylon strainer. Return the apple purée to the pan, add sugar to taste, and stir over brisk heat until thick and clear. Allow to cool.

Roll out the pastry into equal-sized rounds about 8 inches in diameter and bake in a moderate oven (375° F. or Reg. 5) to a pale golden colour (about 15 minutes). Do not allow to brown. When the pastry is cold, fill and sandwich with the 'apple marmalade'. Cover the top with a thin layer of glacé icing and marble with the redcurrant jelly.

Lintzer Torte

8 oz. plain flour; 4 oz. butter; 4 oz. castor sugar; 1 whole egg; 1 yolk; 2 oz. almonds, ground without blanching; cinnamon and grated lemon rind to flavour.

1 lb. fresh raspberries brought to the boil and cooked rapidly for 2 to 3 minutes with sugar to sweeten.

Sift the flour with a pinch of salt and the cinnamon and make a well in the centre. Place in this the butter, sugar, egg, and lemon rind and sprinkle the almonds on the flour. Work the ingredients together and leave in a cool place for ½ hour.

Roll out the pastry to between ¼ and ½ an inch thick and line into a flan ring. Fill with the cold raspberry mixture and put a lattice of the pastry across the top. Bake in a moderate oven for 20 to 30 minutes. Allow to cool, and then brush with a redcurrant or raspberry glaze.

Almond Fruit Flan

ALMOND PASTRY: 6 oz. flour; 2½ oz. ground almonds; 3 oz. sugar; 3 oz. butter; 2 egg yolks; vanilla or Kirsch to flavour.

A mixture of fresh fruit in season such as pears, grapes, pine-apple, bananas, strawberries, grapes, greengages, etc.

APRICOT GLAZE (as on page 457).

Sift the flour on to a board or slab. Make a well in the centre, put in the sugar, butter, yolks, and flavouring, and sprinkle the almonds on the flour. Work up together and chill for 1 hour. Roll out the pastry, line into an 8-inch flan ring, and bake blind.

While the flan is still warm, brush out with apricot glaze and leave until cold and set. This will prevent the juices from the fruit spoiling the pastry.

Prepare the various fruits and arrange in the prepared flan case. Brush again with the hot glaze. Serve with a bowl of whipped cream.

Tarte aux Pruneaux

PASTRY: 6 oz. flour; 3 oz. butter; 3 oz. castor sugar; 2 oz. ground almonds; 1 whole egg; 1 yolk; a drop of vanilla.

CREME PATISSIÈRE: 2 oz. castor sugar; 1 egg; 1 yolk; $\frac{3}{4}$ oz. flour; $\frac{1}{2}$ oz. cornflour; $\frac{1}{2}$–$\frac{3}{4}$ pint milk; Grand Marnier.

$\frac{3}{4}$–1 lb. good prunes; red wine; almond paste made with 3 oz. ground almonds, 1$\frac{1}{2}$ oz. castor sugar, egg-white to bind, and Grand Marnier to flavour.

Redcurrant jelly.

Soak the prunes overnight in enough wine to cover, then simmer in the wine until tender. Cool and stone. Mix the almond paste in the order given and stuff into the prunes; set aside.

Make up the pastry, line into a fluted or plain flan ring, and bake blind.

Prepare the crème patissière. Break the yolks into a bowl and cream with a third of the sugar and the flours, diluting with a little of the milk. Scald the remainder, pour on, blend, and return to the pan. Stir until boiling, draw aside, and cool. Whip one white, add the rest of the sugar, and whip until stiff. Fold into the cream and flavour with the liqueur. Fill into the flan case.

Arrange the prunes on top. Make a glaze from the redcurrant jelly and the wine from the prunes, strain, and when cool coat lightly over the flan.

Salambos à l'Orange

CHOUX PASTRY: 3$\frac{3}{4}$ oz. plain flour; 1$\frac{1}{2}$ gills water; 2$\frac{1}{2}$ oz. butter; 3 eggs.

CARAMEL TOPPING: 3 oz. castor sugar.

FILLING: ¼ pint cream; 1 orange; 4–6 lumps of sugar.

Prepare the choux pastry as directed on page 400 and using a forcing bag and plain éclair pipe shape the mixture into balls the size of a pullet's egg on a lightly greased baking tin. Bake until crisp in a moderate oven (400° F. or Reg. 6) about 25–30 minutes.

NOTE: Choux pastry is best when baked in a rising temperature, so have the oven set at 375° F. or Reg. 6 when the pasty is put in.

When cold prepare the topping.

Place the castor sugar in a small heavy pan and cook slowly to a rich brown colour and then dip in each petit chou. Rub the sugar over the orange to remove all the zest and then pound with a little of the juice to give a rich syrup. A little rum or brandy can be added if liked. Whip the cream and add the orange syrup to flavour.

Split each caramel-topped chou and fill with the orange-flavoured cream.

Profiteroles au Chocolat

CHOUX PASTRY: 3¾ oz. plain flour; 3 oz. butter; 1½ gills water; 3 eggs,

CHOCOLATE CREAM: 1 whole egg; 1 egg yolk; 2 oz. castor sugar; ¾ oz. flour; ½ oz. cornflour; ½ pint milk; 2–3 oz. chocolate.

CHOCOLATE SAUCE: see page 420.

Prepare the choux pastry and pipe out or put in teaspoons on a lightly greased baking tin. Bake on a moderate oven 15–20 minutes until firm to the touch. Put on a rack to cool.

Meantime prepare the cream filling. Separate the egg; cream the two yolks and sugar together until light, add the flour and a little of the cold milk to make a smooth paste. Melt the chocolate in the remainder of the milk, pour it on the egg mixture, blend and return to the pan. Stir over gentle heat until the mixture boils. Whip the egg white until stiff, turn a little of the boiling cream into a bowl and fold in the white. Return this to the pan and stir carefully for 2 or 3 minutes over heat to set the egg white.

Fill the profiteroles with the chocolate cream. Pile up in a serving dish and pour over the chocolate sauce just before serving.

Strudel Pastry

10 oz. fine plain white flour; salt; 1 egg; ¼ pint luke-warm water.

Sift the flour with salt into a mixing-bowl, beat the egg until frothy, add the warm water, and tip on to the flour. Mix quickly until smooth, then turn the dough on to a pastry board and beat thoroughly until elastic. This beating is done by taking the dough in the hand and throwing it down on the board until it is smooth and shiny and leaves the hand quite clean. Put in a clean, floured basin, cover, and leave in a warm place for about 15 minutes. Roll the pastry on a floured board to a good-sized rectangle, then lay on a floured cloth and leave till elastic (about 5 to 10 minutes). Pull the strudel pastry gently from all sides till it is as thin as paper. It is then brushed copiously with melted butter, covered with the filling, and rolled up ready for baking in a moderately hot oven (400° F. or Reg. 6) for about ½ hour.

Strudel Filling

APPLE: 1 lb. apples; 1 oz. each currants and sultanas; sugar and spice to taste; 2 tablespoons brown crumbs.

Peel, core, and slice the apples very thinly, mix with the dried friut, sugar, spice, and crumbs,

CREAM CHEESE STRUDEL: 2 oz. butter; grated rind 1 lemon; 2 oz. castor sugar; 12 oz. curd or cream cheese; 2½ oz. sultanas or raisins soaked 1–2 hours in juice; ½ lemon; 1 heaped teaspoon flour; 2 egg yolks or 1 whole egg.

Cream the butter with the lemon rind, add the sugar and beat until light. Sieve the curd or cream cheese and work into the butter and sugar with the fruit and flour. Beat in the egg.

NOTE: A cream cheese strudel is good served with a cherry compote and in this case the sultanas and raisins can be omitted.

HOT PUDDINGS

Beignets Soufflés

CHOUX PASTRY: 3¾ oz. plain flour; 3 oz. butter; 1½ gills water; 3 eggs.

APRICOT-JAM SAUCE: 2 heaped tablespoons apricot jam; 1½ gills water; grated rind and juice of 1 lemon; 1 teaspoon arrowroot.

Prepare the choux pastry. Sift the flour with a pinch of salt on to a sheet of stiff paper. Place the butter and water in a pan over gentle heat. When the butter has melted bring the water to the boil, draw aside, and immediately tip in all the flour. Beat until smooth and the mixture leaves the side of the pan. Leave to cool. Whisk the eggs lightly and add by degrees to the mixture, beating thoroughly. If the eggs are exceptionally large it is wise to keep back one white, adding it only if necessary. The finished paste should be smooth and shiny and hold its shape.

Heat a deep fat bath until the fat is just under haze point (370° F.) and drop in the choux paste in teaspoonsful. As the fritters begin to swell, raise the temperature of the fat a little and cook until golden brown on all sides. Drain well, toss in castor sugar, and serve with a sharp sauce handed separately.

To make the sauce, place the jam, water, lemon rind, and juice in a saucepan over a gentle heat and bring slowly to the boil. Thicken with the arrowroot mixed with a little cold water and boil until clear. Strain and use.

Pancake Batter

4 oz. plain flour; 1 egg; 1 egg yolk; ½ pint milk; 1 tablespoon melted butter or oil.

Sift the flour with a good pinch of salt into a mixing bowl, make a well in the centre and drop in the whole egg and extra egg yolk. Start adding the milk to the egg and draw in the flour very gradually. When half the milk has been added, beat well and add the butter or oil. Whisk in the rest of the milk, cover, and keep in a cool place for ½ hour before using.

Heat a heavy 6-inch frying-pan. Grease very lightly with oil or clarified butter and put a good tablespoon of batter in the middle; roll the pan to coat the surface evenly, then keep over brisk heat until the pancake is brown on the underside. Loosen around the edge with a palette knife and toss or turn over and brown the other side. Slide the pancake on to a wire cake rack. As the pancakes are made, stack them one on top of the other and, if being fried several hours before they are needed, wrap in a clean teacloth until wanted. To reheat, place overlapping on a lightly buttered baking-tin, brush with a little melted butter, and slip into a quick oven to heat through (400° F. or Reg. 6) for about 7 to 8 minutes. The pancakes are then ready for stuffing according to the recipe, or may be served with sugar and lemon.

Fritter Batter (1)

4 oz. plain flour; 2 egg yolks; 1 tablespoon oil; ¼ pint milk; 1 egg white.

Sift the flour with a pinch of salt, make a well in the centre, and drop in the egg yolks and the oil. Mix to a smooth batter with the milk and beat well. Cover and stand in a cool place for ½ hour. Whisk the egg white until stiff and fold into the batter just before using.

Fritter Batter (2)

4 oz. plain flour; a small 'nut' of yeast, about ¼ oz.; 1 tablespoon oil; 1 teacup warm water; 1 egg white (optional).

Sift the flour with a pinch of salt. Soften the yeast in the warm water and mix into the flour with the oil; beat well. Cover and leave in a warm place for about 20 to 30 minutes. Whisk the egg-white and fold into the batter just before using.

Crêpes aux Cerises

Pancake batter (see page 400); 1 dessertspoon Kirsch.

½ lb. black cherries; 2 tablespoons castor sugar; 2 tablespoons Kirsch; ½ gill thick cream; 2 tablespoons shredded browned almonds.

Prepare the pancake batter, adding the dessertspoon of Kirsch with the milk; cover and leave to stand in the usual way.

Stone the cherries, dust with the sugar, pour over the Kirsch, cover, and leave to stand ½ hour.

Fry the pancakes paper-thin; put a spoonful of cherries on each, roll up, and lay on a baking-tin. Dust well with castor sugar and put in a quick oven for 3 to 4 minutes. Place in a hot serving-dish, pour over the cream, and scatter over the nuts.

Crêpes Pralinées

PANCAKE BATTER (see page 400).

PRALINE BUTTER: 2 oz. unsalted butter; 1½ oz. castor sugar; 2 tablespoons praline powder; rum to flavour.

Prepare the batter and while it is standing prepare first the praline powder and then the butter.

PRALINE POWDER: 2 oz. almonds, unblanched; 2 oz. castor sugar, good weight.

Put together into a pan. Set on low heat until the sugar melts. When turning a pale golden brown, stir with a metal spoon and continue cooking until a good nut brown. Turn on to an oiled tin or plate; leave until hard, then crush into coarse powder or pound to a paste.

Cream the butter, beat in the sugar by degrees, and, when white and whipped-looking, mix in the praline and flavour well with rum.

Fry the number of pancakes required, spread the inside of each with the praline butter, and roll up like a cigar. Heat for a moment in a quick oven, then serve at once. These are good with Pêches Flambées, a rich fruit compote such as blackcurrant or morello cherries, or kissel.

Crêpes Suzette

BATTER: 3 oz. plain flour; 1 egg; 1 egg yolk; 1½ gills creamy milk; 1 tablespoon melted butter; 1 tablespoon brandy.

ORANGE BUTTER: 3 oz. unsalted butter; ½ dozen lumps sugar; 2 oranges; 1 tablespoon or more Cointreau, Curaçao, or Grand Marnier.

TO FLAME: 1 glass brandy or any of the above liqueurs.

Make up the batter in the usual way, adding the brandy with the melted butter, and leave to stand for ½ hour. Cream the butter. Rub the loaf sugar over the orange rind until soaked with the orange zest and oil. Crush the sugar and add to the butter, working in the liqueur and a little orange juice.

Fry the pancakes paper thin, stack one on top of the other, cover, and leave until wanted. Spread the butter over each pancake, fold in three, and arrange overlapping down a fireproof dish. Put in a quick oven for 6 to 7 minutes. Heat the brandy and liqueur together, set light to it, and pour flaming over the dish as it comes from the oven.

Scalloped Apples

1–1½ lb. good flavoured apples; brown or white sugar to taste; 1 large lemon; 1–2 oz. candied fruits; thin bread and butter; whites of 1 or 2 eggs; 2 oz. castor sugar to each white.

Peel, quarter, and core the apples. Cut into slices and arrange in a buttered soufflé case or pie dish in layers with the sugar, the grated rind of the lemon, and the lemon flesh cut into segments. Have ready the candied fruits, cut in slices and blanched to soften. Lay these on the top and, when the dish is full, cover with a piece of buttered paper. Put into a moderate oven (375° F. or Reg. 5) until the apple is soft. Take out, cover the top with small squares of bread and butter, and put back to brown delicately.

Whip the whites until stiff, whisk in 2 teaspoons of the measured sugar for one minute, and then fold in the remainder very carefully. Pile this meringue over the pudding. Dredge with castor sugar, leave for a few minutes, then brown lightly in a cool oven (280 to 300° F. or Reg. 1).

Baked Vanilla Soufflé

9 oz. creamy milk; 3 oz. granulated sugar; ½ vanilla pod or ½ teaspoon essence; ¾ oz. flour; ¾ oz. butter; 3 egg yolks; 4 egg whites; 1 tablespoon icing sugar.

Choose a large saucepan which will hold the mixture when the beaten egg whites are added. Set aside 3 tablespoons of the milk, put the remainder into the pan, and bring to the boil; draw away from the heat and add the sugar and vanilla. Cover the pan tightly and leave to infuse for 15 minutes, stirring occasionally to dissolve the sugar. Mix the flour with the cold milk, remove the vanilla pod from the hot milk, and add the flour mixture by degrees. Stir over gentle heat until boiling and allow to boil for 5 seconds only. Remove from the heat, cover the surface of the sauce with the butter cut in small pieces, put the lid on the pan, and leave for 10 to 15 minutes.

Meanwhile set the oven at 380° F. or Reg. 5, and prepare a size-1 soufflé case by buttering the inside and dusting with icing or castor sugar. Tie a band of buttered greaseproof paper round the dish to stand 1½ inches above the top. Mix the butter into the sauce and beat in the egg yolks one at a time. Whisk the egg whites until stiff, but not dry, add one tablespoon to the mixture, and stir in to soften; then add the remainder, and cut and fold it in most carefully. Turn into the prepared soufflé case, smooth the top with a palette knife, make a few cuts round the sides, and put at once into the oven. Bake for about 18 to 20 minutes, then carefully open the oven door, draw the oven shelf forward, and dust the top of the soufflé with the icing sugar. Replace and continue cooking a few minutes to colour the top. Remove the paper and serve at once.

Baked Orange Soufflé

9 oz. creamy milk; 3 oz. loaf sugar; 2 oranges; ¾ oz. flour; ¾ oz.

butter; 3 egg yolks; 1 liqueur glass Grand Marnier or Curaçao (optional); 4 egg whites; 1 tablespoon icing sugar.

Set aside 3 tablespoons of the milk, put the remainder into a saucepan, and bring to the boil. Meanwhile wipe the oranges and then rub the loaf sugar over the rind to remove all the zest. Add the sugar to the milk, cover the pan, and leave on one side to infuse for about 15 minutes. Mix the cold milk with the flour and continue as instructed in the Vanilla Soufflé recipe (page 404), adding the liqueur after the egg yolks. Bake and serve in the same way.

Baked Chocolate Soufflé
3 oz. plain block chocolate; 1 tablespoon water; 9 oz. creamy milk; 3 oz. granulated sugar; 2–3 drops vanilla essence; ¾ oz. butter; ¾ oz. fécule or arrowroot and flour mixed; 3 egg yolks; 4 egg whites; 1 tablespoon icing sugar.

Grate the chocolate, put it into a saucepan with water over very gentle heat, and stir until melted and quite smooth. Reserve 3 tablespoons of the milk to mix with the fécule and stir the rest into the chocolate. Bring the chocolate-flavoured milk to the boil, draw away from the heat, add the sugar and vanilla, cover the pan, and leave to infuse for 15 minutes. Stir the mixture of cold milk and fécule into the chocolate milk and continue as directed in the Vanilla Soufflé recipe (page 404). Bake and serve in the same way.

Steamed Chocolate Soufflé
1½ oz. butter; 1½ oz. flour; 2 oz. unsweetened chocolate; ½ pint milk; 1½ oz. castor sugar; 2 eggs.

Melt the butter in a large saucepan, remove from the heat, and blend in the flour. Cut the chocolate into small pieces and dissolve slowly in the milk; bring to the boil, pour on to the butter and flour, and blend until smooth. Return the pan to the fire, stir continuously until boiling, and then beat in the sugar. Butter a 1-pint charlotte mould, dust with castor sugar, and have ready a steamer full of boiling water. Now beat one whole egg and one egg yolk into the mixture, then whisk the egg white until stiff and fold in carefully. Turn the mixture into the prepared tin, cover with a buttered greaseproof paper, and steam gently until set (about 25 to 30 minutes). Turn on to a hot dish and serve with a hot chocolate or sabayon sauce.

COLD PUDDINGS

Under this section you will find puddings as simple and easy to prepare as creamed rice and custards as well as the more elaborate cold soufflés and mousses.

In many of these recipes you are directed to 'half-whip' the cream; this means that the cream, when lifted on the whisk, will leave a trail and will not be nearly stiff enough to pipe or hold its shape. In this way the cream can be folded into a mixture with no danger of it turning to butter and it will give the characteristic spongy texture to a mousse or soufflé.

As custard puddings and those set with gelatine sometimes prove troublesome the following points should be remembered:

1. When a custard or egg-and-milk mixture is being cooked it will curdle if made too hot. For the very cautious this cooking may be done in a double boiler, but there is no reason why an ordinary saucepan should not be used if the mixture is stirred briskly the whole time. Have a good-sized mixing-bowl on the kitchen table, then, if by chance the custard gets too hot and shows signs of curdling, it can be tipped immediately into the cold bowl and whisked well. This will check the cooking at once and generally rectify matters.

2. Gelatine, whether leaf or powdered, should be soaked in the water or the liquid named in the recipe before being dissolved over heat. DO NOT STIR the gelatine while soaking but leave it to absorb the liquid undisturbed. In this way all the gelatine will be melted when put over heat. If adding the dissolved gelatine to a cold mixture, such as a soufflé or mousse which has been stirred on ice, get the gelatine as hot as possible without letting it boil and then it will not set in threads before you have had a chance to mix it in.

3. Wait until mixtures with gelatine are setting creamily before pouring them into a mould or soufflé case. They must be stirred carefully until this point is reached or they will have an uneven texture, firm at the bottom and soft and fluffy at the top.

4. If egg whites are to be added to any set cream, do not start to whisk them until every other ingredient has been added. Whisk them by hand with a balloon whisk to get the best result.

*

Creamed Rice

3 tablespoons Carolina rice; vanilla pod or vanilla essence; 1 pint milk; $1\frac{1}{2}$ oz. castor sugar; $\frac{1}{4}$ pint cream.

Wash the rice in several waters, then cook slowly in the milk with the vanilla pod until soft and creamy. Add the sugar, turn into a bowl to cool, and remove the vanilla pod; if using vanilla essence add it at this stage. When the rice is quite cold, fold in the lightly whipped cream. Serve with a fruit sauce or compote.

Crème Caramel

3 oz. loaf sugar; $\frac{3}{4}$ gill water; 2 eggs and 2 yolks; 1 pint milk; 1 oz. sugar; $\frac{1}{2}$ teaspoon vanilla essence.

Dissolve the loaf sugar in the water and boil without stirring until a rich brown colour. Pour at once into a dry, hot mould, coat all over, and leave until cold and set.

Beat the eggs and pour on the milk heated with the sugar. Add the essence and when cool strain the mixture into the prepared mould and cover with a greased paper. Cook in a bain-marie till set (375° F., or Reg. 5). For time and method see following recipe. When quite cold turn out and surround with a little additional crushed caramel.

Crème Margot

4 oz. granulated or loaf sugar; $\frac{1}{4}$ pint water; $\frac{3}{4}$ pint milk; 2 eggs; 2 egg yolks; 1 oz. castor sugar.

TO FINISH: $\frac{1}{2}$ gill cream; $\frac{1}{2}$ lb. strawberries.

Put the granulated sugar with half the water in a small heavy saucepan, over very gentle heat. When dissolved increase the heat and boil rapidly to a rich brown caramel. Cover the hand with which you are holding the pan (to avoid being burnt!). Pour on the remaining water and stir until smooth. Warm the milk to blood heat, add the caramel, and leave to melt. Meanwhile beat the eggs and yolks with the sugar until light, then pour on the warm caramel-flavoured milk. Strain into a soufflé case or charlotte tin, cover with a double thickness of greaseproof paper, and set in a roasting-tin. Pour in enough hand-hot water to come nearly to the top of the mould and set in a moderate oven (375° F. or Reg. 5) until firm (about 45 minutes). Leave to cool a little before turning out. Serve masked with cream and surrounded with sliced strawberries or a fresh strawberry sauce.

Bavarois with Meringues

BAVAROIS: 5 lumps sugar; 1 orange; ¾ pint milk; 3 egg yolks; 1½ tablespoons castor sugar; 1 level dessertspoon gelatine (scant ½ oz.); 3 tablespoons water; ¼ pint cream.

MERINGUES: 1 egg white; 2 oz. castor sugar.

First prepare the meringues. Whisk the egg white until stiff, add 1 teaspoon of the sugar, and continue beating for ten seconds; then fold in the rest. Pipe this mixture into tiny meringues on Bakewell paper, using a ¼-inch plain pipe. Dry in a slow oven (260° F. or Reg. ½) for about 40 minutes. Peel off the paper and leave to cool.

Rub the loaf sugar over the rind of the orange to remove all the zest and then dissolve in the milk over a gentle heat. Cream the egg yolks and castor sugar together until thick and light, then pour on the milk. Return to the pan and thicken the custard without boiling, stirring continually. Strain into a bowl and allow to cool. Have the gelatine soaked in the water, then dissolve over gentle heat. Add to the custard. Stir over ice until the mixture thickens, then fold in just 2 to 3 tablespoons of half-whipped cream and pour at once into a lightly oiled plain mould.

When set, turn out and mask with the rest of the whipped

cream and cover with the little meringues. Dust with grated chocolate and serve with either chocolate or melba sauce.

Coffee Parfait

½ pint milk; 1 oz. coffee beans; 3 egg yolks; 1½ oz. castor sugar; 1 level dessertspoon gelatine (scant ½ oz.); ½ gill water; ½ pint cream.

TO FINISH: ¼ pint cream; coffee dragées.

Scald the milk with the coffee beans to give a good flavour. Cream the egg yolks with the sugar until light, strain on the milk. Return to the pan and stir over a gentle heat until thick, then strain into a bowl and leave to cool. Dissolve the gelatine in the water and half-whip the cream. Add the gelatine to the custard, fold in the cream, and when it is on the point of setting pour into a lightly oiled mould. To serve, turn out, mask with whipped cream, and decorate with rosettes of cream and coffee dragées.

Crème Brûlée

4 egg yolks; 1 level tablespoon castor sugar; 1 pint cream; 1 vanilla pod, split, or a few drops of essence; castor sugar.

Mix the yolks well with the sugar. Put the cream and vanilla pod together into a double saucepan. Cover and bring up to scalding-point, then remove the pod and pour on to the yolks, blending well. At this stage, if the pod is not available, add the essence. Return to the pan and thicken very carefully over the heat, stirring constantly. On no account allow it to reach boiling-point – scalding-point (about 185° F.) should be enough. Strain into a pie or gratin dish. It is advisable to slip the dish into a gentle oven to 'skin' the top – do not allow to colour in any way. Allow to stand for several hours or preferably overnight. Heat the grill and dust the surface of the cream with castor sugar so that it presents a uniformly white appearance, but avoid getting too thick a layer. Push the dish at once gently under the grill. Allow the sugar to melt and take colour, then remove from the heat and stand in a cold place for 2 or 3 hours before serving. It is usual to serve this with a dish of fruit as it is a little rich on its own, although delicious.

Sugared Fruit

Take any soft fruit in season, for example raspberries, redcurrants, blackcurrants, or strawberries, either as a mixture or by themselves. Prepare the fruit and fill into a glass or china bowl in layers with icing or castor sugar. Cover the top with a plate and chill thoroughly in the refrigerator for an hour or two before serving.

Fresh Fruit Salad

¼ lb. lump or granulated sugar; ½ gill (½ teacup) water; 3 or 4 different kinds of dessert fruit according to season – pears, bananas, grapes, oranges, for example.

First prepare the syrup by dissolving the sugar in the water over a gentle heat and then boil rapidly for 1 minute. Pour off and allow to get cold.

Prepare the fruit, slicing the peel and pith away from the oranges and cutting the flesh away from the membranes. Peel and pip the grapes; slice the bananas and peel and slice the pears. (Always leave fruit liable to discolour till last.) Pour over the syrup, mix carefully, and turn into a glass bowl for serving. Chill and, if wished, sprinkle with a liqueur before serving.

NOTE: When making a fresh-fruit salad the syrup must be really thick, for as the fruit stands the juice will run out and so thin down the syrup.

Orange Compote

Syrup, made from 1 lb. loaf sugar and ½ pint water; 8 good oranges.

Dissolve the sugar slowly in the water, bring to the boil, and cook for 1 minute without stirring. Allow to cool immediately. Peel the oranges, cutting away all the pith, skin, and membrane, and slice into thin rounds. Arrange in a glass bowl, pour over the syrup, and chill thoroughly before serving.

Apricot Moscovite (using dried fruit)

5 oz. dried apricots; ½ pint milk; 3 egg yolks; 3 oz. castor sugar; scant ½ oz. gelatine (1 level dessertspoon); juice of ½ lemon; ¼ pint cream; sugar syrup for the sauce, made with ¼ pint water and 3 oz. granulated sugar.

Wash the apricots and soak overnight in twice their volume of water. Stew gently with the soaking liquid and a strip of lemon rind to flavour. When tender, rub through a fine sieve or strainer; allow to cool. Scald the milk, cream the yolks with the sugar, pour on the milk, blend, then return to the pan. Thicken over the heat without boiling, strain, and cool. Dissolve the gelatine in the lemon juice and 2 or 3 tablespoons of cold water and add to the custard.

Measure 1½ gills of the apricot purée; lightly whip the cream and add the purée to this. Cool the custard and when on the point of setting fold in the apricot cream. Turn at once into an oiled mould and leave to set. Thin the remaining apricot purée with the sugar syrup and chill well. To serve, turn the Moscovite on to a dish and pour round the sauce. Decorate with extra cream if liked.

Apricot Moscovite (using fresh fruit)

½ lb. apricots poached till tender in syrup made with ½ pint water and 5 oz. granulated sugar; ½ pint milk; 3 egg yolks; 2 oz. castor sugar; scant ½ oz. gelatine; ¼ pint cream; Kirsch to flavour (optional).

Scald the milk, cream the yolks with the sugar, pour on the milk, blend, then return to the pan. Thicken over the heat without boiling, strain, and cool. Dissolve the gelatine in ½ gill of the apricot juice over heat and add to the custard. Take half the apricots from the syrup and rub them through a fine sieve. Half-whip the cream and add the purée to this. Cool the custard. When on the point of setting, fold in the apricot cream and flavour with the Kirsch. Turn at once into an oiled mould to set. Rub the remaining apricots through a fine strainer, chill and flavour with Kirsch. If it is wished, a few blanched apricot kernels may be added to the sauce. To serve, turn on to a platter and pour round the fresh apricot sauce.

Apricot Charlotte

1 lb. apricots; syrup for poaching made with 1½ gills water and 4 oz. granulated sugar; 2 tablespoons castor sugar; ¾ oz. gelatine; ¾ gill water; ½ pint cream.

TO FINISH: 'Langues de Chats' or Boudoir biscuits or Biscuits Alsaciens; ¼ pint cream.

Poach the halved apricots in the light syrup and when tender drain, reserve 4 to 6 for decoration, and rub the remainder through a fine sieve or strainer. Measure ½ pint of the purée and stir in ¼ pint of the apricot syrup and the castor sugar. Dissolve the gelatine in the water and add to the apricot mixture. Half-whip the cream and fold into the purée, stir until thickening, then pour into a lightly oiled 7-inch cake tin and leave in a cool place to set. To serve, turn out, spread the sides with whipped cream, and arrange the biscuits around the sides. Decorate the top with the reserved apricot halves and rosettes of piped cream.

Charlotte Mexicaine

1 pint milk; 2 oz. coffee beans; 4–6 oz. plain block chocolate; 2 oz. sugar; 6 egg yolks; ½ oz. gelatine; ½ gill water; 1½ gills cream; 1 egg white.

TO FINISH: 'Langues de Chat' or Biscuits Alsaciens; ¼ pint cream.

Scald the coffee beans in the milk to flavour, and strain. Break the chocolate and put into a pan with a little of the milk; dissolve very slowly, then add the remaining milk and stir until smooth. Cream the egg yolks and sugar until light and tip on the milk. Return to the pan and cook until the custard coats the back of the spoon; DO NOT BOIL. Strain into a bowl to cool. Melt the gelatine in the water, add to the mixture and stir until it begins to thicken. Lightly whip the cream and whisk the egg white until stiff but not dry and fold both into the custard. Turn into a lightly oiled soufflé case or 7-inch cake tin and leave to set. To serve, turn out and spread the side of the charlotte with cream.

Arrange the biscuits around, overlapping each one. Decorate the top with rosettes of cream and grated chocolate or coffee dragées.

Cold Chocolate Soufflé

¾ pint milk; 3 oz. plain block chocolate; 3 eggs; 2 oz. castor sugar; ½ oz. gelatine; ½ gill water or black coffee; ¼ pint cream.

Put a ¼ pint of the milk into a pan with the chocolate and dissolve over very gentle heat. Whisk in the remaining milk and bring to blood heat. Separate the yolks from the whites, cream them with the sugar until thick and light, and pour on the flavoured milk. Blend and return to the pan. Stir over the fire until thick; DO NOT BOIL. Strain into a pan and cool. Dissolve the gelatine in the water or coffee over heat, then add to the custard. When cool, stand the pan in a bowl of ice and stir until on the point of setting. Take off the ice and quickly fold in half the cream, partly whipped, and the stiffly whipped egg whites. Do not whip these until just before setting the custard on ice. Turn at once into a 5½–6-inch prepared soufflé case and leave to set. When set, remove the paper and decorate with the rest of the cream.

Soufflé Monte Cristo

¾ pint milk; vanilla pod or essence; 4 egg yolks; 3 oz. castor sugar; ½ oz. gelatine; ½ gill water; ¼ pint cream; 3 egg whites; 2 oz. chocolate caraque (see page 448); 4 large almond macaroons or 6 oz. ratafias; fruit juice, rum, or liqueur.

DECORATION: ½ gill cream.

Prepare a 6-inch or No. 2 soufflé case in the normal way and set a lightly oiled 1-lb. jam jar in the middle. A cube or two of ice dropped in the jam jar will hold it in position and help the soufflé to set more quickly.

Scald the milk with the vanilla pod. Separate the eggs and cream the yolks with the sugar until light, then tip on the milk. Return to the pan and cook until the custard coats the back of the spoon. Strain and cool. If using vanilla essence add it at this stage. Dissolve the gelatine in the water and stir into the custard. Stand the mixture on ice and stir until on the point of thickening, then quickly fold in the half-whipped cream and stiffly whisked egg whites. Pour the mixture into the prepared soufflé case, layering it with the caraque. Leave in a cool place to set. Meanwhile break the macaroons or ratafias in small pieces and sprinkle with the fruit juice, rum, or liqueur. When the soufflé is set, remove the jam jar carefully and fill the cavity immediately with the macaroons. Decorate the top with whipped cream and caraque.

Cold Lemon Soufflé

3 large eggs; $\frac{1}{2}$ lb. castor sugar; $2\frac{1}{2}$ lemons; $\frac{1}{2}$ pint cream; $\frac{1}{2}$ oz. gelatine; $\frac{1}{2}$ gill water.

TO FINISH: a little extra cream; 2 tablespoons browned ground almonds or ratafia crumbs.

Prepare a 6-inch or No. 2 soufflé case. Separate the eggs and place the yolks, sugar, grated lemon rind, and strained juice in a basin and whisk over gentle heat until thick and mousse-like. Remove from the heat and continue whisking until the bowl is cold.

NOTE: If using an electric beater with a fixed head, whisk the yolks, sugar, and rind until thick, then heat the lemon juice, add, and continue whisking 'to the ribbon'.

Half-whip the cream and fold into the mixture. Dissolve the gelatine in the water over heat and stir into the mixture. Whisk the egg-whites until stiff but not dry; set the soufflé mixture on ice and fold in the egg whites. As the mixture begins to thicken, turn at once into the prepared case and put in a cool place to set. When firm, remove the paper, press the nuts or crumbs gently round the sides, and decorate the top with rosettes of cream.

Cold Raspberry Soufflé

1 lb. fresh raspberries; 4 eggs; 4 oz. castor sugar; $\frac{1}{4}$ pint cream; scant $\frac{1}{2}$ oz. gelatine (1 level dessertspoon); $\frac{1}{2}$ gill water.

TO FINISH: $\frac{1}{4}$ pint cream; pistachio nuts.

Reserve 8 of the best raspberries for decoration and rub the rest through a nylon sieve or strainer – it should give $1\frac{1}{2}$ gills to a $\frac{1}{2}$-pint of purée. Prepare a 6-inch or No. 2 size soufflé case. Separate the eggs and place the yolks in a basin with the sugar and raspberry purée and whisk over gentle heat until thick and mousse-like. Remove from the heat and continue whisking until the bowl is quite cold.

NOTE: When using an electric beater no heat is necessary.

Half-whip the cream and fold into the mixture. Dissolve the gelatine in the water over heat, add to the mixture, stand over ice, and stir until it begins to thicken. Whisk the egg whites until stiff but not dry, fold into the soufflé, and turn into the prepared case. Leave in a cool place to set. When firm, remove the paper and decorate the top with rosettes of cream, raspberries, and pistachio nuts.

Caramel Mousse

6 oz. loaf or granulated sugar; $\frac{1}{2}$ gill water; 2 egg yolks; 3 whole eggs; 2 oz. castor sugar; $\frac{1}{4}$ pint cream; scant $\frac{1}{2}$ oz. gelatine; juice of 1 lemon.

First prepare the caramel. Put the loaf sugar in a heavy pan with a little water and when dissolved cook steadily to a rich brown caramel. Cover the hand holding the saucepan and add the $\frac{1}{2}$ gill of cold water. Stir until all the caramel is melted and pour into a bowl to cool. Put the egg yolks and whole eggs in a basin with the sugar and whisk over gentle heat until very thick and mousse-like. Remove from the heat and continue whisking until the mixture is quite cold. Lightly whip half the cream, add to the mixture with the cold caramel, and set the bowl on ice. Make up the lemon juice to a $\frac{1}{2}$ gill with water, if necessary, and dissolve the gelatine in this over heat. Stir into the mousse and as the mixture begins to thicken pour into a lightly oiled ring mould and leave in a cool place to set. Turn out the mousse and mask with the remaining cream. In summer-time the centre may be filled with fresh raspberries or strawberries.

Tangerine or Orange Mousse

Make in the same way as caramel mousse, substituting a good

¼ pint fresh tangerine or orange juice in place of the caramel. Add the grated rind of 3 tangerines or 2 oranges. A tangerine mousse is good with a compote of chestnuts and an orange mousse can be set in a chocolate case made in the following way:

Chocolate Case

3 oz. plain block chocolate; 1 large (7 or 8 inch) paper case used for baking cases.

Melt the chocolate on a plate over a saucepan of hot water. Do not let it get too hot or it will lose its gloss. Spread or brush the melted chocolate on the inside of the paper case to give an even coating. Set in a cool place to harden. Peel away the paper very carefully and use the chocolate case to hold a mousse or soufflé mixture.

Mousse au Chocolat à l'Orange (Chocolate and Orange Mousse)

6 oz. plain block chocolate; ½ gill water; 3 eggs; 2 egg yolks; 2½ oz. castor sugar; ¼ oz. (1 teaspoon) gelatine; juice of 1 orange; ½ gill cream.

TO FINISH: 2 tablespoons ground hazelnuts; thinly sliced candied orange peel; a little whipped cream.

Melt the chocolate with the water to form a thick cream. Whisk the eggs, egg yolks, and sugar together in a basin over hot water until thick. Remove from the heat and continue to whisk until the bowl is cold, then add the chocolate. Dissolve the gelatine in the orange juice over heat and add to the mousse. Stir until thickening, then fold in the partially whipped cream. Turn at once into a prepared soufflé case or glass bowl. When set, decorate with the ground nuts, candied peel, and cream.

Mousse au Chocolat Basque

6 oz. good block chocolate; a small coffee-cupful of water or black coffee; ½ oz. butter; rum or vanilla; 3 eggs.

Break the chocolate and cook to a thick cream with the water or coffee and flavouring. Draw off the fire and beat in the butter and the yolks of the eggs one by one. Whisk the egg whites until stiff and stir briskly into the chocolate. When thoroughly mixed, pour into small pots and leave overnight. Serve with a rosette of cream piped on the top and 'cigarettes russes' (see page 456) handed separately.

Le Turinois

2 lb. chestnuts; 5 oz. unsalted butter; 5 oz. castor sugar; ½ lb. good dessert chocolate; vanilla essence, rum, or brandy to flavour.

Put the chestnuts into a pan, cover with cold water, bring to the boil, draw off the heat. Take out the nuts one at a time and remove both the outer and inner peel and skin. Simmer the peeled nuts in water until tender with a vanilla pod, then drain and pass through a fine sieve.

Cream the butter thoroughly, add the sugar by degrees, and beat until white. Break up the chocolate and melt in a pan to a cream with about half a teacup of water. Allow to cool a little, then add to the mixture with the chestnuts. Flavour with vanilla essence, rum, or brandy. Turn into a loaf tin, lightly oiled, with the bottom lined with paper. Leave in a cool place until the next day, then turn out and serve cut in slices with a bowl of whipped cream.

NOTE: 2 lb. of chestnuts should yield a good 1½ lb. of sieved chestnuts.

Pineapple Mousse en Surprise

3 eggs; 2 yolks; 2 oz. castor sugar; ¼ pint tinned pineapple juice; ½ oz. gelatine; 1 lemon; ¼ pint cream; 2 egg whites.

FOR FINISHING: 1 medium pineapple; 1 doz. ratafias; castor sugar; Kirsch; ¼ pint cream.

Prepare a 6-inch soufflé case and set a small oiled jam jar in the centre. Place the whole eggs and yolks in a basin, add the sugar, and whisk over heat until thick. Remove from the heat and continue whisking until cold. Soften the gelatine in 2 tablespoons of cold water and then dissolve over heat in the juice of the lemon and add to the mixture with the pineapple juice. Stir over ice until thickening, then fold in the partially whipped cream and stiffly whisked egg whites. Pour into the prepared soufflé case and leave to set. Meanwhile peel and slice the pineapple and sprinkle with sugar and moisten the ratafias with a little Kirsch. When the soufflé is set, carefully remove the jam jar and *immediately* fill the middle with the macerated pineapple and ratafias. Decorate the top with whipped cream.

Vacherin Chantilly and Melba Sauce

4 egg whites; ½ lb. castor sugar; ½ pint cream; vanilla essence.

Whisk the egg whites until stiff, add one teaspoon of the measured sugar for each egg white, and continue whisking for about ½ minute. Fold in the remaining sugar with a tablespoon and fill into a piping-bag fitted with a small éclair pipe. Pipe the mixture on to two rounds of Bakewell paper about 8 or 9 inches in diameter and bake in a cool oven (300° F. or Reg. 1) for about 50 to 60 minutes until lightly coloured and quite dry. Remove to a wire cooling tray, peel off the paper, and leave to cool. Whip the cream lightly, add ½ teaspoon castor sugar and 1 or 2 drops of vanilla essence, and continue whisking until it will hold its shape. Sandwich the two rounds with half the cream, dust the top with icing sugar, and pipe the remaining cream in rosettes round the outside edge. Serve the Melba Sauce separately.

Melba Sauce

½ lb. raspberries; 3–4 heaped tablespoons sifted icing sugar.

Rub the raspberries through a nylon sieve or strainer and beat the icing sugar into the purée a little at a time, adding enough to thicken the purée.

Vacherin Chantilly aux Fruits

Prepare the meringue in the same way as directed in the previous recipe and sandwich with cream and fresh fruit in season, such as strawberries, peaches, pineapple, or a mixture such as bananas, grapes, and clementines.

Coffee Meringue Cake

4 egg whites; ½ lb. castor sugar.

BUTTER CREAM: 4 oz. sugar; ½ gill water; 4 egg yolks; ¼ lb. unsalted butter; coffee essence.

DECORATION: finely chopped brown almonds; coffee dragées.

Have ready three baking-sheets lined with Bakewell paper. Set the oven at Reg. ½ to 1 or 280 to 300° F. Prepare the meringue in the same way as for Vacherin and spread or pipe the mixture into thin rounds, 8 or 9 inches in diameter, on the prepared baking-tins. Bake until dry and crisp (about 50 to 60 minutes).

Meanwhile prepare the butter cream. Dissolve the sugar in the water, boil to the thread (that is, until it is sticky), and pour on to the egg yolks. Whisk until thick. Cream the butter and beat in the egg mousse by degrees. Flavour with the coffee essence.

When the meringue rounds are quite cold spread with the butter cream and shape into a cake. Spread the top and sides with the same cream and cover with the browned almonds. Decorate with the dragées.

NOTE: This cake must be made 24 hours before serving. It keeps well in an airtight tin.

Hazelnut Meringue Cake

4 egg whites; 9 oz. castor sugar; vanilla essence; ½ teaspoon vinegar; 4½ oz. browned ground hazelnuts; ¼ pint cream; icing sugar and raspberries to finish.

Prepare two 8-inch sandwich tins by rubbing the sides with butter and dusting with flour and lining the bottom with a disc of Bakewell paper. Set the oven at 375° F. or Reg. 5. Whisk the egg whites until stiff, then gradually beat in the castor sugar. Continue beating until very stiff, adding the vanilla and vinegar. Lastly fold in the prepared nuts. Fill into the prepared tins and bake for about 30 to 40 minutes. When cool fill with whipped cream, dust the top with icing sugar, and hand raspberries in a Melba sauce separately.

Hazelnut Meringue Cake with Apricot Cream

4 egg whites; 9 oz. castor sugar; vanilla essence; ½ teaspoon

vinegar; 4½ oz. browned ground hazelnuts; 4 oz. dried apricots; ½ lemon; ¼ pint water; 4 oz. granulated sugar; ¼ pint cream.

Prepare and bake the hazelnut meringue in the same way as in the previous recipe.

Have ready the apricots soaked overnight, then stew gently in their liquid with a strip of lemon rind to flavour; when tender, rub through a fine sieve or strainer. Allow to cool. Dissolve the sugar in the water, add the lemon juice, and boil for 3 minutes. Whip the cream, sweeten, and mix in a little of the apricot purée, and fill into the cake. Dust the top with icing sugar. Dilute the remaining apricot purée with the sugar syrup and serve this sauce separately.

Gâteau Ganache

The foundation of this cake is made with the same hazelnut meringue mixture used in the previous recipe. It is filled with chocolate-flavoured cream and served with chocolate sauce.

¼ pint cream; 6 oz. good dessert or bitter chocolate; 4 oz. granulated sugar; ½ pint water.

Break up the chocolate, put into a pan with a little of the water, and melt very slowly. Tip on the rest of the water, add the sugar, and when dissolved allow to simmer with the lid off for 10 to 15 minutes. Pour off and allow to cool. Now whip the cream and fold in 2 to 3 tablespoons of the chocolate sauce. Spread this on one round, cover with the other, and put a light weight on the top. Cover and leave overnight in the refrigerator. Next day decorate the top with rosettes of whipped cream. Serve with the chocolate sauce.

Meringue Baskets

4 egg whites; 8½ oz. icing sugar; vanilla essence.

Rice paper or Bakewell paper for baking.

Set the oven at 280 to 300° F. or Reg. 1 and have ready a pan half-full of gently simmering water.

Whisk the egg whites and sugar together in a basin over the hot water until the mixture is very thick and will hold its shape.

Flavour with 2 or 3 drops of vanilla essence and fill into a bag fitted with an 8-cut vegetable rose pipe. Shape into small baskets on the paper and cook until set and crisp on the outside (about 45

minutes). Serve filled with either whipped cream or whole strawberries coated with a little melted red-currant jelly before being put in the baskets.

Tangerine Sabayon

4 tangerines; 8–10 lumps of sugar; 4 egg yolks; 4 tablespoons granulated sugar; 4 tablespoons water; ½ pint cream; 4 ripe dessert pears, preferably Comice; 4 bananas.

First prepare a tangerine syrup by rubbing the zest from the tangerines with the loaf sugar, then squeezing and straining the juice. Crush the sugar, pour on ¼ gill (2½ tablespoons) of the juice, and stir until the sugar dissolves. Melt the granulated sugar in the water, then boil steadily until the syrup will form a thread when pulled between the finger and thumb. Pour gradually on to the egg yolks and then whisk over heat until thick. Set the bowl on ice and continue beating until quite cold. Pour in the tangerine syrup and keep until wanted. Prepare the fruit and moisten with a little tangerine juice or liqueur such as Grand Marnier; cover and chill well. When ready to serve, whip the cream, fold in the sabayon, and pour over the fruit.

Poires au Vin Rouge

5–6 small ripe dessert pears; ¼ pint water; ¼ pint claret or burgundy; 5 oz. loaf sugar; strip of lemon rind; small piece of stick cinnamon; 1 level teaspoon arrowroot; 1 oz. shredded almonds.

Place the sugar in a pan with the wine, water, and flavourings and dissolve slowly. Increase the heat and boil for 1 minute. Peel the pears, leaving the stalks on but removing the 'eye' from the bottom, and place at once in the prepared syrup. The pears should sit in the syrup, and to hold them in position cut a disc of greaseproof paper the size of the stewpan and make a small hole for the stalk of each pear. Cover the pan with the lid and poach the pears in a moderate oven until tender, but allow at least 20 to 30 minutes, even if the pears are ripe, or they will discolour around the core on standing. Remove the pears, strain the syrup, check the quantity, and reduce if necessary to ½ pint. Mix the arrowroot with a little water, add to the syrup, and stir until boiling; cook until quite clear. Arrange the pears in a serving-dish, spoon over the wine sauce, and scatter the toasted almonds on top. Serve cold with a bowl of whipped cream handed separately.

Fruit Suédoise

1½ lb. fresh apricots or red South African plums; ½ pint water; 4 oz. granulated sugar; ½ oz. gelatine; a few blanched almonds.

Halve the apricots or plums and poach them carefully in a syrup prepared from the sugar and water. Even if the fruit is very ripe it must be cooked for at least 15 minutes to get the best flavour. Drain the fruit and keep a few of the best caps on one side. Rub the rest through a nylon sieve or strainer. Measure ¾ pint of the syrup, pour ½ pint into the fruit purée, dissolve the gelatine in the remaining ¼ pint over a gentle heat, and mix together. Put half a blanched almond into each reserved half-apricot or plum and arrange on the bottom of a charlotte or cake tin. When the purée is on the point of setting, pour carefully into the tin and leave in a cool place to set. Turn out and pour round a Crème à la Vanille (see following recipe) or decorate with whipped cream.

Crème à la Vanille

½ pint milk; ½ vanilla pod; 2 large or 3 small egg yolks; 1 level teaspoon arrowroot; 1½ oz. castor sugar.

Scald the milk with the vanilla pod, cover, and leave to infuse for 2 or 3 minutes. Using a wooden spoon, cream the egg yolks with the arrowroot and sugar until thick and light, then tip on the flavoured milk. Return to the saucepan and stir continuously over a gentle heat until the mixture coats the back of the spoon. Strain into a bowl and allow to cool.

Apples Bristol

4–5 dessert apples (Cox's Pippin is the best); 2–3 large oranges; ¾ pint water; 6 oz. granulated sugar.

CARAMEL: 3 oz. granulated loaf sugar; ½ teacup water.

Place the sugar and water in a pan, dissolve over gentle heat, then boil rapidly for 1 minute. Peel the apples, quarter, and core them. Put at once into the syrup, cover the pan, and simmer for 10 to 15 minutes until they are tender, then draw the pan aside and leave covered until cold. Pare the rind from half an orange and cut it into fine shreds. Simmer for 5 or 6 minutes then drain and rinse with cold water. Cut the peel and pith from the oranges, then slice into rounds or cut the flesh into sections if preferred. Set aside.

To make the caramel, dissolve the sugar in the water, then boil rapidly to a rich brown. Pour on to an oiled tin to set. Crush into fairly small pieces.

To dish, lift the apples carefully into a glass dish or china bowl. Arrange the oranges on top and spoon over a little of the syrup. Scatter the caramel and orange peel over and serve chilled.

Gooseberry Fool

2 lb. gooseberries; 3–4 heads of elderflowers; ½–¾ pint water; castor sugar; ¼ pint thick custard; ½ pint double cream.

Top and tail the gooseberries, wash, and put them into a pan with the water. Tie the elderflowers in a small piece of muslin, add to the pan, and cover. Simmer until the fruit is soft, then take out the elderflowers, drain off the juice, and reserve.

Rub the fruit through a nylon sieve or pass through a fine mouli. Measure this purée, which should give about a pint, sweeten to taste, and set aside until quite cold. Have ready the custard which should be cold and smooth (proportions 1 level dessertspoon of custard powder to ¼ pint milk) and mix this into the purée. Half-whip the cream and fold it in, leaving the fool slightly 'marbled' with the cream. Serve in glasses or in a bowl with sponge fingers or a crisp biscuit.

If a tart- or rich-flavoured fruit such as black- or redcurrants are used, thicken the fruit when cooked with a little arrowroot or potato fécule. This makes for a smoother texture and flavour. Canned or bottled fruit also needs to be thickened so that some of the juice can also be used with the purée.

Apple Mousse Gatinaise (to serve 6)

2 lb. Cox's orange pippins; 1 oz. butter; 3 tablespoons water; 3 oz. honey; 1 level dessertspoon gelatine; ½ pint cream; ½ teaspoon vanilla essence; toasted walnut kernels.

Peel, core, and chop the apples. Melt the butter in a shallow pan, put in the apples and water, cover, and set on a low heat until soft. Remove the lid and cook quickly, stirring frequently until a firm purée, draw aside, and add the honey and the gelatine previously soaked in 3 tablespoons of cold water. Stir until honey and gelatine are dissolved, then turn out and allow to cool.

Whip the cream until firm and fold into the apple mixture with the vanilla essence and a little castor sugar (if necessary).

Pile the mixture in a glass bowl and chill for 2 hours. Sprinkle the crushed walnut kernels over the top before serving.

Pear Fresco (to serve 6)

6 ripe dessert pears; 2–3 tablespoons brandy or liqueur (optional); ¾ pint milk; 1 vanilla pod; 3 egg yolks; 2 egg whites; 3 oz. castor sugar; 1 oz. cornflour; ¾ oz. flour; ½ pint cream; a few browned hazel nuts or flaked almonds.

Scald ½ pint milk with the vanilla pod, cover, and leave to infuse. Cream the egg yolks with half the sugar until thick and light, add the flours, and thin down with the remaining ¼ pint milk. Strain on the flavoured milk, return to the saucepan, and stir over gentle heat until boiling. Cook a few minutes, then turn into a basin, cover with a wet greaseproof paper to prevent a skin forming, and leave to cool. Whip the egg whites until stiff, add the reserved sugar, and continue whisking to a thick meringue. Beat this mixture into cold vanilla custard. Whip the cream lightly and fold into the custard.

Peel the pears, cut in even slices, and sprinkle with the liqueur. Layer the cream and the pears in a deep bowl, cover, and chill well. Just before serving scatter the nuts over.

Fraises Escoffier (to serve 6)

2 lb. strawberries; 2 oranges; 2 oz. loaf sugar; ½ gill brandy or Grand Marnier.

Hull the strawberries and place in a deep bowl. Wipe the oranges and then rub the lump sugar over the fruit to remove all the zest. Place the sugar now saturated with the oil from the oranges in a small bowl or mortar. Squeeze the juice from the oranges and strain over the sugar. Crush the sugar in the orange juice, add the brandy, and stir until dissolved.

Pour this syrup over the strawberries, cover, and leave soaking at least one hour. Serve the strawberries well chilled with cream handed separately.

Pêches Carmen (to serve 6)

8 ripe peaches; 1½ lb. raspberries; 2–3 oz. icing sugar; 2 table-spoons Kirsch (optional).

Rub the raspberries through a nylon strainer or hair sieve then work the icing sugar into the purée by degrees. Flavour with kirsch if liked. Peel the peaches, put at once into a glass bowl, and spoon over the raspberry purée. Chill before serving.

Chartreuse au Citron

LEMON JELLY: 1½ pints water; 1¾ oz. gelatine; 7 oz. loaf sugar; thinly pared rind of 3 lemons; 1½ gills lemon juice; 2-inch stick of cinnamon; whites and shells of 2 eggs; ½ gill sherry.

8 oz. black grapes.

First prepare the jelly by adding about ¼ pint of the water to the gelatine and set aside to soak. In the meantime scald both pan and whisk. Pour into the pan the rest of the water, add the sugar, and set on a low heat to dissolve with the lemon rind, juice, and cinnamon. Now add the gelatine and stir until all is melted. Then add the whites, whisked to a froth, the lightly crushed egg-shells, washed, and the sherry. Whisk and allow to boil up. Draw aside, leave for a minute or two, then repeat twice more. Leave to settle, then pour through a scalded jelly-bag or cloth. Immediately a small quantity of jelly is through, take it up and pour it back again on the top of what is in the cloth.

When cool run a little into a ring mould. When almost set arrange the grapes, pipped, on the surface, set these in a little jelly, and then fill up the mould with cool jelly. Leave to set. Turn out and fill the centre with chopped jelly. Decorate with whipped cream.

Griestorte

3 eggs; 4 oz. castor sugar; rind and juice of $\frac{1}{2}$ lemon; 2 oz. fine semolina; $\frac{1}{2}$ oz. ground almonds.

TO FINISH: $\frac{1}{4}$ pint cream; $\frac{1}{2}$ lb. raspberries.

Separate the eggs, cream the yolks and sugar together until thick and mousse-like, then add the lemon juice and rind and continue beating to the ribbon. Stir in the semolina and ground almonds. Whisk the egg whites until quite stiff but not dry, then fold into the mixture and turn at once into an 8-inch sandwich or cake tin which has been greased, lined with a disc of greaseproof paper, greased again, and dusted with castor sugar and flour. Bake in a very moderate oven (350° F. or Reg. 4) for 30 to 40 minutes. When cool, split and fill with the whipped cream and cover the top of the cake with the raspberries.

Griestorte with Fresh Peaches or Pears

Allow two fresh peaches or pears for a cake. Peel and slice the fruit and put in the cake with the cream. Dust the top with icing sugar.

Gâteau aux Noisettes Normande

3 eggs; $4\frac{1}{2}$ oz. castor sugar; 1 tablespoon coffee essence; 3 oz. flour; $1\frac{1}{2}$ oz. ground toasted hazelnuts.

FILLING: 1 lb. dessert apples; grated rind and juice of $\frac{1}{2}$ lemon; sugar to taste; $\frac{1}{4}$ pint cream for decoration.

Prepare an 8-inch sandwich tin and set the oven at 375° F. or Reg. 5.

Whisk the eggs, sugar, and coffee essence together over a gentle heat until thick and mousse-like. Remove from the heat and continue whisking until the bowl is cold. Then fold in the flour, sifted with a pinch of salt, and the nuts. Turn into the prepared tin and bake for about 25 minutes.

Meanwhile peel, core, and slice the apples and place in a shallow pan with the lemon rind and juice. Cover and cook until soft, add the sugar to taste, and cook down to a purée. Allow to cool. Split the cake and fill with the apple mixture. Dust the top with icing sugar and decorate with whipped cream.

Gâteau aux Fraises

3 oz. plain flour; ½ teaspoon ground cinnamon; 3 eggs; 3¾ oz. castor sugar; grated rind of ½ lemon.

TO FINISH: ¼ pint cream; ¾ lb. strawberries; 4 tablespoons red-currant jelly.

Sift the flour with the cinnamon and a good pinch of salt and set on one side. Break the eggs, add the sugar gradually, and whisk over gentle heat until thick and mousse-like; then remove from the heat and continue whisking until the mixture is cold. Fold in the sifted flour and the grated lemon rind and turn into a prepared 8- or 9-inch sandwich tin and bake in a moderate oven (350° F. or Reg. 4) for 15 to 20 minutes. Turn on to a rack to cool.

Whip the cream, add a drop of vanilla essence and a little sugar to taste with a quarter of the strawberries cut in slices. Split the cake, sandwich with this mixture, and slide on to a board or serving-plate. Prepare a glaze with the red-currant jelly (see page 395, Tartelettes Cœur à la Crème) and brush over the cake. Cut the strawberries in half, arrange on the top, and brush again with the glaze.

Gâteau aux Abricots

Prepare as above, sandwiching with whipped cream flavoured

with praline. Arrange fresh apricots, poached in a sugar syrup and drained on the top, and brush with apricot glaze.

Gâteau d'Ananas

Prepare the sponge as for the strawberry gateau but omit the cinnamon and lemon rind. Fill with whipped, sweetened cream flavoured with Kirsch and about 2 to 3 tablespoons of diced pineapple. Cover the top with overlapping slices of pineapple, brush with apricot glaze, and decorate with diamonds of angelica.

Angel Cake with Strawberries

2 oz. fine white plain flour; $3\frac{1}{2}$ oz. castor sugar; 6 egg whites; pinch of salt; $\frac{3}{4}$ teaspoon cream of tartar; $2\frac{3}{4}$ oz. castor sugar; 2–3 drops of vanilla essence; $\frac{1}{2}$ pint cream; 1 lb. strawberries.

Sift the flour and the $3\frac{1}{2}$ oz. castor sugar together three times and set on one side. Place the egg-whites with the salt and cream of tartar in a deep bowl and whisk with a rotary beater until foaming. Add the second portion of sugar, 2 tablespoons at a time, and the essences, and continue whisking until the mixture will stand in peaks. Carefully fold in the sifted flour and sugar. Turn the mixture into a clean, dry, 9-inch tube cake pan, level the surface, and draw a knife through to break any air bubbles. Bake the cake in a moderate oven (375° F. or Reg. 5) for 30 to 35 minutes or until no imprint remains when a finger lightly touches the top.

When the cake is done, turn the tin upside down on a wire cake rack and leave until quite cold when the cake will fall easily from the tin. To finish, split through 2 or 3 times and fill with whipped sweetened cream and a few sliced strawberries. Mask the cake with cream and decorate with rosettes of cream and whole berries.

Austrian Curd Cake (1)

$2\frac{1}{2}$ oz. butter; 5 oz. sugar; 10 oz. curd; 2 eggs; 2 oz. ground almonds; 2 oz. raisins; 2 tablespoons semolina; rind and juice of 1 lemon.

Cream the butter, add the sugar and the curd gradually, and beat until light and creamy. Separate the eggs and beat the yolks into the mixture one at a time, then stir in the ground almonds, raisins, semolina, and lemon. Whisk the egg whites until stiff but not dry and fold quickly into the mixture. Bake in a 7-inch sandwich tin in a moderate oven (375° F. or Reg. 5) for 45 to 60 minutes. Serve dusted with icing sugar.

Austrian Curd Cake (2)

4 oz. rusks; 1 oz. butter; 5 oz. castor sugar; $\frac{3}{4}$ oz. flour; 1 lb. curd cheese; $\frac{1}{2}$ teaspoon vanilla essence; 4 eggs; $1\frac{1}{2}$ gills cream.

Crush the rusks with a rolling pin and mix with the melted butter and 2 tablespoons of the sugar. Sprinkle about one-third of this mixture at the bottom of a 9-inch cake tin. Sift the remaining sugar with the flour and a pinch of salt and mix into the curd cheese. Separate the eggs and beat the yolks into the curd mixture with the vanilla essence. Add the cream and beat again very thoroughly. Whisk the egg whites until stiff and fold into the mixture. Pour into the prepared tin and sprinkle the rest of the crumb mixture on top. Bake in a moderate oven (350° F. or Reg. 4) for about 1 hour or until the mixture is firm. Leave to cool in the cake tin.

Savarin Chantilly

$4\frac{1}{2}$ oz. flour; $\frac{1}{2}$ oz. sugar; $\frac{1}{4}$ oz. yeast; $\frac{3}{4}$ gill milk; 2 eggs; $1\frac{3}{4}$ oz. butter; a pinch of salt.

SYRUP: 4 oz. loaf sugar; $\frac{1}{4}$ pint water; 2 thinly pared strips of lemon rind or $\frac{1}{2}$ a split vanilla pod.

TO FINISH: $\frac{1}{4}$ pint cream; a little sugar and vanilla essence to taste.

Sift the flour into a warm basin, cream the yeast with the sugar until liquid; warm the milk to blood heat, add to the beaten eggs and mix with the yeast. Tip this liquid into the flour and beat vigorously with the hand for 5 minutes. Put the mixture into a freshly greased mixing-bowl, cover with a damp cloth, and set in a warm place for 45 to 60 minutes until well risen. Cream the butter until soft, work into the yeast mixture with the salt, and beat well for 5 minutes. Well butter an 8-inch savarin mould, pour in the mixture and leave to prove, again in a warm place, for 10 minutes. Bake in a moderately hot oven (400° F. or Reg. 6) until firm and golden brown (approximately 25 minutes).

Meanwhile prepare the syrup. Dissolve the sugar slowly in the water, add the lemon or vanilla and then boil rapidly for about 1 minute. Flavour with liqueur or rum. Turn the savarin carefully on to a cake rack and, while still warm, baste with the hot syrup. The savarin should be thoroughly soaked and should glisten with the syrup. Should it prove difficult to turn from the mould, spoon over a little of the syrup while it is still in the tin. Serve with the whipped, sweetened cream piled in the middle.

Savarin Montmorency

Prepare in the same way as above; flavour the syrup with Kirsch and fill the middle with a compote of black cherries lightly thickened with arrowroot. Serve the cream separately.

Savarin aux Ananas

Prepare in the same way as Savarin Chantilly and flavour the syrup with Kirsch. Have ready a fresh pineapple cut in half-circles and macerate well in sugar and Kirsch. After soaking, cut the Savarin on the bias in slices about $1\frac{1}{2}$ inches thick and place a piece of pineapple between each slice. Serve with whipped cream piled in the centre.

ICES

CREAM ICES, FRUIT ICES, AND WATER ICES

To make perfect ices an ice-cream freezer or churn is essential. In this the mixture is beaten throughout the freezing time, and results in a smooth, light, and creamy-textured ice. It is possible to make ices in the ice trays of a refrigerator turned down to maximum but the mixture must be beaten several times during the freezing. A teaspoon of gelatine melted in a little water and added to every pint of liquid will help to keep smooth an ice made in this way but it can never be compared with one made in a churn.

PREPARATION OF MIXTURE AND FREEZER:

1. Scald the ice-cream container and the dasher before use.

2. Assemble the churn complete with dasher, top, and handle and check that it is working smoothly before packing with ice and salt.

3. Pack the machine with chipped ice and salt in layers allowing 1 part of freezing salt to 6 parts of ice. Make sure that the last layer is ice and that it only comes two-thirds of the way up the container. In this way there is less danger of salt entering the mixture and so ruining it.

4. Wipe the lid of the container before removing it to pour in the mixture.

5. Make sure the mixture is quite cold and just pleasantly sweet to taste. If too sweet the ice will not freeze, and if not sweet enough it will freeze hard and rough.

6. Do not fill the churn more than two-thirds full as the mixture expands as it freezes.

7. Turn the handle of the freezer steadily and drain away any water as the ice melts and repack with ice and salt.

8. When the mixture is thick, remove the dasher and press the ice together. Place a piece of waxed or greaseproof paper under the lid and replace carefully. Repack with ice and salt if necessary, cover with a thick blanket or sack to exclude the warm air, and leave the ice to 'ripen' or 'mellow' for one hour if possible.

*

Vanilla Ice-cream

1 pint single cream; 1 vanilla pod or 1 teaspoon vanilla essence; 3 egg yolks; 2½ oz. granulated sugar; 1 coffee cup water.

Put the cream in a heavy saucepan with the vanilla pod split and scraped lightly to release a few of the seeds. Bring slowly to scalding-point (about 185° F.) and allow to cool. If using essence it is not essential to scald the cream; the vanilla can be added to the raw cream.

Put the sugar and water in a pan, dissolve over gentle heat, and then boil steadily until the syrup will form a thread when pulled between finger and thumb. Whisk the yolks in a small bowl, pour on the boiling syrup carefully, and then whisk until very thick. Strain on the cream, pour the mixture into the churn, and freeze as directed on page 431.

Vanilla ice can be served quite plain with fruit, chocolate, or butterscotch sauce.

Butterscotch Sauce

1 tablespoon golden syrup; ½ oz. butter; 2 tablespoons demerara sugar; 1 cup water; lemon.

Cook the syrup, butter, and sugar to a rich brown toffee. Add the water and a squeeze of lemon. Boil up and pour on to 1 teaspoon of custard powder previously slaked with a tablespoon of the water. Reboil if necessary.

Poires Belle Hélène

Vanilla ice-cream; ripe dessert pears poached in a vanilla syrup until clear and very tender; hot chocolate sauce.

To serve, scoop the vanilla ice-cream into a chilled glass bowl, surround with the chilled pears, and, as it is being served, pour over it the hot chocolate sauce.

Pêches Melba

Vanilla ice-cream; fresh peaches poached in a sugar syrup until tender; Melba Sauce (see page 418).

Serve the ice-cream in a chilled bowl or coupe glasses with the chilled peaches around and the Melba Sauce poured over.

Praline Ice-cream with Kissel
Vanilla ice-cream; 3 tablespoons powdered praline.

To make the praline, take an equal quantity of unblanched almonds and castor sugar and place in a small heavy saucepan over gentle heat. As the sugar melts and turns to a caramel, stir with a metal spoon until the almonds are toasted on all sides. Turn on to an oiled plate or tin. When cold and set, crush with a rolling-pin or pass through a nut-mill or mincer. Store in an airtight tin.

Prepare the vanilla ice-cream in the usual way and when frozen remove the dasher, scrape down the sides of the churn, and fold the praline into the mixture. Pack down the ice-cream, cover with a waxed paper and the lid, and leave to ripen. Serve this ice-cream with a fruit kissel.

Kissel
Kissel can be made with fresh, stewed, or bottled raspberries, cherries, or blackcurrants, either mixed or by themselves.

1¾ pints strong, well-flavoured and sweetened fruit juice; pared rind of 1 orange; 1 glass claret or burgundy; 1 level tablespoon arrowroot; strained juice of 1 orange; 3–4 tablespoons stewed fruit.

Put the juice, rind, and wine into a pan and bring slowly to the boil. Slake the arrowroot with the orange juice, take out the rind and add the arrowroot while on the boil, stirring vigorously, then remove from the fire. Add the fruit and pour into a bowl. Dust the top lightly with sugar to prevent a skin forming and serve hot or cold but not chilled.

White Coffee Ice
½ pint single cream; 2 oz. coffee beans; 1 whole egg and 1 egg yolk; 2 oz. castor sugar; ½ pint double cream.

Scald the single cream with the coffee beans and infuse until a delicate coffee flavour is obtained. Cream the egg and yolk thoroughly with the sugar until light in colour, strain on the cream, and whisk well; strain again and leave to cool. Whip the double cream very slightly and add to the coffee-flavoured custard.

Have ready the ice bucket packed with ice and salt as directed on page 431. Pour in the custard mixture and churn until thick. Scrape down the container, remove the paddle, and leave the ice-cream to ripen. This ice is good served with a hot ginger sauce.

Ginger Sauce

2 tablespoons granulated sugar; 4 tablespoons water; squeeze of lemon; 4–6 pieces of stem ginger; 2 tablespoons syrup from the jar.

Dissolve the sugar in the water and then boil steadily until thick. Add the lemon juice, sliced ginger, and syrup.

Chocolate Cream Ice

½ pint milk; 6 oz. plain block chocolate; 1 whole egg; 1 egg yolk; 2 oz. castor sugar; ½ pint double cream; ½ teaspoon vanilla essence.

Grate the chocolate and place in a saucepan with the milk over very gentle heat to dissolve. Meanwhile beat the whole egg and egg yolk with the sugar very thoroughly. When the chocolate has melted, bring just short of the boil and pour slowly on to the egg and sugar. Whisk well, strain, and cool.

Lightly whip the cream and add to the chocolate custard with the essence. Pour the mixture into the prepared ice churn and freeze until stiff. Pack down and leave to 'ripen' before serving.

Fruit Cream Ice

¾ pint sweetened fruit purée such as strawberry, raspberry, apricot, or damson; 3½ oz. granulated sugar; ¾ gill water; 3 egg yolks; ¾ pint single cream.

First prepare the fruit purée. Strawberries and raspberries are rubbed through a fine nylon strainer and sweetened with castor sugar to taste, but apricots and damsons must be cooked in a sugar syrup until tender and then puréed.

Dissolve the sugar in the water and boil steadily to the thread. Pour the hot syrup on to the egg yolks and whisk to a thick light mousse; add the cream. Stir the cold-fruit purée into the egg-and-cream mixture and pour into the prepared ice machine. Freeze until stiff, pack down, and leave to ripen.

Orange Water Ice

1 pint water; zest and juice of 1 lemon; zest and juice of 3 oranges; 6 oz. loaf sugar; ½ egg white.

Rub the zest from the lemon and oranges with the loaf sugar and place in a saucepan with the water. Dissolve very slowly, then boil steadily for 10 minutes. When quite cold, add the strained fruit juice and pour into the prepared ice churn. Freeze until the mixture is thick and slushy and then add the stiffly whisked egg white and continue to freeze until stiff.

NOTE: For lemon water ice use the zest of 2 lemons and the juice of 3.

Pineapple Water Ice

6 oz. loaf sugar; ¾ pint water; ¾ pint fresh pineapple pulp.

Dissolve the sugar in the water, then increase the heat and allow to boil steadily for 10 minutes. Allow to get quite cold. Mix with the pineapple pulp or if preferred the pulp can be squeezed to obtain the juice, but there must be ¾ pint of juice to the ¾ pint of sugar syrup. Freeze the mixture in the usual way.

Soufflé en Surprise

1 pint vanilla ice-cream; 3 ripe peaches; 2–3 tablespoons brandy or liqueur; 3 eggs; 1 dessertspoon castor sugar; 1 dessertspoon cream; 2–3 drops vanilla essence.

Have the ice-cream prepared and packed down in the churn.

Peel the peaches, slice, and leave to macerate in the brandy or liqueur with a little sugar to taste. Have ready a large soufflé case (size 0) standing in a roasting-tin well packed with chipped ice. Failing ice, rough kitchen salt can be used as an insulator around the soufflé case. Set the oven at 450° F. or Reg. 8. Separate the eggs and work the yolks with the sugar, cream, and vanilla until light. Whisk the egg whites until stiff but not dry and fold into the yolks. Put the ice-cream at the bottom of the soufflé case. Spoon the peaches over and pile the soufflé mixture on the top. Dust with icing sugar and put immediately into the oven. Bake for 5 minutes, then serve at once.

Bombe Favorite

8 half shells of meringue; ½ pint double cream; 1 or 2 table-spoons Kirsch; castor sugar.

Lightly oil a bombe mould or alternatively a 7-inch cake tin. Line the bottom of this with a disc of paper.

Break the meringue shells into 2 or 3 pieces each, whip the cream lightly, and flavour with the Kirsch and a little castor sugar. Fold in the meringue pieces and turn at once into the mould or tin. If using a bombe mould, cover the top with a piece of greaseproof paper and the lid. Rub the edge round with lard to make sure that it is watertight and bury in a bucket of ice. For a cake tin, put into a polythene bag after covering the top of the cream with the paper. Tie and seal the bag securely with Scotch Tape before putting into the ice for 2 hours. Alternatively the mould or tin may be put into a deep freeze for the same length of time. Turn out when lightly frozen and pour round a Melba sauce (see page 418).

Chapter 12

BREADS, CAKES, AND PATISSERIE

BREADS

BREAD making is a simple process once the first principle has been understood. This is that yeast, which raises the bread, is a living organism and needs warmth to make it grow. Cold, such as that of a refrigerator or deep freeze, will check the growth, while great heat, as in an oven, will kill it completely, which is why bread is baked in a hot oven once the yeast has done its work.

To grow, yeast likes moist heat, so when the dough is put to rise (especially for the sponging process) the bowl can be set on a stove rack with a pan of gently steaming water underneath. For the long rising a damp cloth may be put over the top of the bowl and the bowl itself stood in a warm, draught-free corner or in an airing cupboard.

There are three stages in bread making – sponging, rising, and proving. Sponging helps the yeast to start growing, a process which takes about 15 to 30 minutes depending on the quantity of bread or rolls being made. Rising may take anything from 1 to 3 hours or more, again depending on the quantity and the temperature. For bread an average temperature of 75° F. is the best so that the dough rises steadily. Proving is the final rising carried out after the dough has been shaped and is done at a slightly greater temperature than the long rising. The temperature for proving should not exceed 85° F. and takes approximately 20 minutes for loaves and 10 to 15 minutes for rolls and buns. The bread or rolls should then be put into the oven at once when it is clear that the dough has started to rise.

*

Household Bread (to make 3 loaves)
3 lb. plain flour; 1 tablespoon salt; 1 oz. yeast; 1 teaspoon sugar; 1½ pints warm water.

Use 3 tins, lightly greased, 9 inches by 5 inches by 3 inches.

Sift the flour with the salt into a large, warmed mixing-bowl. Cream the yeast with the sugar until liquid, add the luke-warm water, and pour it all into the middle of the flour, stirring in enough to make a thick batter, and then dust this with flour. Cover the basin with a cloth and set in a warm place for 20 to 30 minutes or until the yeast breaks through. Then draw in the rest of the flour, using first a spoon and then your hand: this process is known as sponging. When the dough leaves the sides of the bowl turn it on to a lightly floured board and knead it thoroughly until it is smooth and elastic (about 10 minutes). Put the dough in an oiled bowl, turning it over once so that the top surface is lightly greased. Cover with a damp cloth and set to rise in a warm, draught-free spot until it is double in bulk (about 1 to 1½ hours).

Turn the dough on to a floured board; cut it into 3 pieces and shape them into loaves, kneading lightly to drive out any air. Set each piece in a lightly greased tin, cover again with a cloth, and set in a warm place to prove until the sides of the

dough reach the top of the tin and the centre is well rounded –
(15 to 20 minutes). Bake in a hot oven (425 to 450° F. or Reg. 7)
for 30 to 40 minutes. When done, the bread will shrink slightly
from the sides of the tin and will sound hollow if the bottom is
tapped after being turned out.

Bread Rolls

1 lb. flour; 1 teaspoon salt; 1 oz. butter; 1 egg; ¾ oz. yeast; 1 teaspoon sugar; ½ pint warm milk and water mixed; beaten egg or
melted butter for brushing.

Sift the flour with the salt. Melt the butter, beat the egg, cream
the yeast with the sugar, and pour on the liquid. Pour all into the
centre of the flour, sponge as for bread, then knead for 5 or 6
minutes. Put in a warm place to rise for 40 to 50 minutes or until
double in bulk. Knead lightly and shape into rolls, each about the
size of a small egg (this quantity will make 18 to 20 rolls). Set on a
baking sheet, cover with a cloth, and prove for 5 to 10 minutes.
Brush with egg or melted butter and bake in a hot oven for 15 to
20 minutes.

Potato Rolls

1½ lb. flour; ½ lb. potatoes; 3 oz. butter; 1 level dessertspoon salt;
1 tablespoon sugar; 1 good ounce yeast; ¾ pint milk and water
mixed; 2 small eggs.

Peel the potatoes, boil in salted water, drain, and dry. Push
through a ricer or sieve and weigh: there should be 6 oz. Sift the
flour and rub in the butter; add the salt and potatoes. Cream the
yeast with the sugar and add to half the luke-warm liquid with
the beaten eggs. Pour into the flour, adding the rest of the liquid
to form a soft dough. Knead lightly until all stickiness has disappeared. Put into a clean, oiled bowl and turn the dough over so
that the surface is lightly oiled; cover with a cloth and leave to rise
until double in bulk. Push the dough down and shape into rolls.
Prove and bake as in the previous recipe.

This potato dough is especially light and is ideal for keeping in a
refrigerator before baking. It will last fresh for ten days or so.

Take out as much dough as and when required and set to rise until double in bulk, then make up as for rolls. If storing in a refrigerator, put the bowl covered with a lid or plate directly into the refrigerator after kneading. Push the dough down as and when necessary during the time of storing.

Milk Bread

1 lb. flour; 1 teaspoon salt; approximately ½ pint milk; 1½ oz. butter; 1 teaspoon castor sugar; 1 egg; ½ oz. yeast.

Sieve the flour and salt and warm the mixture slightly. Melt the butter, add the milk, and make it luke-warm. Cream the yeast and sugar; beat the egg and add to the yeast and sugar, with the milk. Pour into a well made in the flour. Mix to a soft dough with the hand and beat well until it is smooth and elastic. The dough may be very slack but with continued beating the mixture will become firmer. Cover with a cloth and put to rise in a warm place for 1 to 1½ hours, then shape into a twist or put in loaf tins. Place on a greased baking-sheet and prove for 15 minutes. Glaze with beaten egg mixed with a pinch of salt, and either sprinkle with poppy seeds or leave plain. Bake in a hot oven (400–425° F. or Reg. 6–7) for 40 to 45 minutes.

Brioche Loaf

DOUGH: ¾ lb. flour; 1 teaspoon salt; scant ¾ oz. yeast; 1 teaspoon sugar; small half-teacup of warm milk; 2 eggs; 2 oz. butter.

FRUIT: 4 oz. sultanas; 1 oz. currants; 1 oz. candied peel; 1 oz. glacé cherries; 1 oz. castor sugar.

Sift the flour and salt into a warm basin, cream the yeast with the sugar, and add to the milk and beaten eggs. Add all the liquid to the flour and beat thoroughly. Cream the butter and work into the paste. Cover and rise 40 minutes in a warm place.

Meanwhile prepare the fruit. Clean the currants and sultanas, chop the peel finely, and halve the cherries. Stir these into the dough with the castor sugar and turn at once into a lightly greased loaf tin. Cover with a cloth and prove for 10 to 15 minutes. Bake in a hot oven for about 50 minutes.

If a savoury loaf is wanted, omit the fruit and stir in 2 oz. grated cheese, with salt and pepper to taste, after rising. Alternatively, the loaf may be left plain.

Kougelhopf

12 oz. flour; ½ teaspoon salt; ½ oz. yeast; ½ gill warm milk; 4 oz. butter; 3 eggs; 1 oz. castor sugar; ¼ lb. raisins or currants; 2 oz. almonds.

Sift the flour and salt into a warm bowl. Dissolve the yeast in the milk, melt the butter, beat the eggs, and stir all into the flour with the sugar. Beat well, then add the cleaned fruit. Well butter a large fluted mould. Blanch and shred the almonds and press them round the sides and on the bottom of the mould. Pour in the yeast mixture, to three-quarters-fill the mould. Leave to rise until the dough is up to the top of the tin. Stand on a thick baking-sheet and bake in a moderately hot oven for about an hour. Turn out and serve when cold, plain or buttered. Leave upside-down.

Danish Pastries

12 oz. flour; good pinch of salt; 1 oz. yeast; 2 oz. castor sugar; 1 egg; good teacupful warm milk; 9 oz. butter.

Sift the flour with the salt into a mixing-bowl. Cream the yeast with the sugar until liquid, add the warm milk and 2 oz. of the butter, and stir until dissolved. Then add the beaten egg. Pour the ingredients into the flour and mix to a smooth dough. Cover the dough and leave at room temperature until double in bulk (about 1 hour). Punch down the dough, turn it on to a floured board, roll out, and cover two thirds of the dough with half the butter divided in small pieces. Fold in three and roll out as for flaky pastry; fold in three and roll again. Press on the remaining butter, fold, and leave in a cool place for 15 minutes. Roll and fold twice more and leave again for 15 minutes. Chill well before shaping. This quantity makes about 12 pastries. Danish pastries are made in traditional shapes, the best known of which are cartwheels and pinwheels, and may be filled with an almond paste, jam, or sultanas or raisins. To shape, roll out the dough when well chilled so that it is firm and easy to handle.

For CARTWHEELS, roll the dough out as thinly as possible to a large oblong, spread with a thin layer of almond filling or a good apricot jam. If using almond filling sprinkle the surface with a good handful of raisins. Roll up lengthways into a long roll and cut this into ½- to ¾-inch slices. Set these cut side down on to a greased baking-sheet, prove until double in bulk, brush the top lightly with beaten egg, sprinkle with flaked almonds, and bake in a moderately hot oven (380° F. or Reg. 5) for 25 to 30 minutes. Brush while still warm with a thin white glacé icing flavoured with vanilla.

For PINWHEELS, roll out the dough thinly and cut into 4-inch squares. Make a cut from each of the corners to within half an inch of the centre. Fold the alternate points of each square to the centre, pressing each point down firmly. Put a small teaspoonful of almond filling or jam in the centre. Prove and bake as for cartwheels. Brush with the glacé icing while still warm.

Almond Filling
2 oz. ground almonds; ½ egg beaten, or a little egg white; 2 tablespoons castor sugar.

Mix the almonds with the sugar and work in enough of the egg or egg white to make a firm paste.

Croissants
12 oz. flour; scant ½ oz. yeast; ½ teaspoon salt; 6 oz. butter; about ¼ pint warm milk and water.

Sift the flour on to a board or slab. Divide into four, take one quarter, and make a well in the centre. In this put the yeast and mix it with 2 to 3 tablespoons of warm water, enough to dissolve the yeast and make a soft dough with the flour. Have ready a saucepan of warm water; drop the ball of dough into this and set aside. Now add the salt to the rest of the flour, make a well in the centre of this, put in half the butter, and work up, adding enough warm milk and water to make a firm paste. Beat on the board or slab for about 5 or 6 minutes. Lift the yeast 'cake' from the water with your hand or a draining spoon (the 'cake' should be spongy and well risen) and mix it into the paste. When thoroughly incorporated, turn into a floured bowl, cover with a plate, and put in a refrigerator for 12 hours. Roll out the paste to a square, set the rest of the butter in the centre, and fold up like a parcel. Now give the paste three turns as for puff pastry and, if necessary, a fourth if the butter is not completely incorporated. Rest the paste between every two turns. Chill before shaping.

To shape, roll out very thinly to an oblong, divide in two lengthways, and cut each strip into triangles. Roll up each one starting from the base and seal the tip with a touch of beaten egg or cold water. Curl them to form a crescent, set on a damped baking-sheet, prove, then brush with beaten egg. Bake in a hot oven for about 25 minutes. This quantity of paste will make about 12 croissants.

Brioches

10 oz. flour; scant ½ oz. yeast; ½ teaspoon salt; 3 small eggs; 2–3 tablespoons milk; 7 oz. butter.

Sift the flour on to a board or slab; divide it into four. Make up one quarter to a soft dough with the yeast and a little warm water as in the recipe for croissants.

Drop into a pan of warm water and set aside to rise. Add the salt to the rest of the flour and mix to a paste with the beaten eggs using the milk if necessary. Beat well on the slab until thoroughly elastic. Cream the butter and work into the paste. Drain the yeast cake and mix with the paste. Turn into a floured bowl, cover with a cloth, and leave to rise for 2 to 3 hours in room temperature. When risen to the top of the bowl, push down, cover with a plate, and put into a refrigerator for 12 hours or overnight. Then knead lightly and divide into pieces the size of a small egg. Roll each into a ball and put into brioche moulds (these are fluted deep tartlet moulds). Pinch the tops well to form a little cottage loaf and set to prove. Brush with egg wash and bake in a hot oven for about 20 to 25 minutes or until very well browned. This quantity will make about a dozen.

CAKES

When setting out to make a cake, always collect and weigh all the ingredients, prepare the cake tin, and set the oven to the correct temperature before starting to mix. The cake can then be made and put into the oven without delay.

TO PREPARE DRIED FRUIT: This should be cleaned before use and may either be rubbed on a sieve, or in a strainer with a little flour, or washed. If the latter, make sure the fruit is well dried before use or it may ferment should the cake be kept for any length of time.

TO PREPARE CAKE TINS: For shallow tins it is necessary to line the bottom only. Cut a disc of greaseproof paper to fit the bottom of the tin, melt a little shortening (or salad oil may be used), and first brush the sides and bottom. Put in the paper and rebrush; dust out with flour. If making a whisked sponge, dust first with castor sugar and then flour. This gives a firm, smooth surface to the outside.

For a deeper tin, cut a strip of greaseproof paper one inch or so longer than the circumference and one inch wider than the depth of the tin; fold over a half-inch of the paper along the length and cut with scissors slantwise into the fold. When this is opened out it will fit neatly into the tin and only needs a disc at the bottom to complete the lining. Brush evenly with melted lard or salad oil, or, if the cake is very rich and fruity, this can be omitted.

*

Gingerbread

4 oz. butter; ½ lb. golden syrup; 3 oz. granulated sugar; 1 table-spoon orange marmalade; 2 small eggs; ¼ pint milk; 4 oz. self-raising flour; a pinch of salt; 1 teaspoonful of ground ginger; 1 teaspoonful mixed spices; ½ teaspoonful bicarbonate of soda; 4 oz. wholemeal flour.

Prepare an 8-inch-square tin and set the oven at 325° F. or Reg. 3.

Put the butter, syrup, sugar, and marmalade into a saucepan and heat gently until the sugar has dissolved. Allow to get almost cold, then add to the beaten eggs and milk. Sift the self-raising flour with the salt, spices, and soda and mix in the wholemeal flour. Pour the liquid into the dry ingredients and beat to a smooth batter; be careful not to over-beat but only until smooth. Turn into the cake tin and bake for 1½ hours.

Rich Ginger Cake

4 oz. butter; 4 oz. Barbados sugar; 2 eggs; 8 oz. plain flour; 10 oz. black treacle (a breakfast cupful); 2 oz. sliced preserved ginger; 2 oz. sultanas (or if preserved ginger is not liked, 4 oz. sultanas); 1 teaspoon ground ginger; 5 tablespoons milk; ½ teaspoon bicarbonate of soda.

Prepare an 8-inch cake tin and set the oven at 350° F. or Reg. 4.

Cream the butter well, add the sugar, and continue to beat until light. Sift the flour with the ground ginger and a pinch of salt. Beat in the eggs, one at a time, sprinkling each with a dessertspoon of the flour. Then stir in the treacle, sultanas, preserved ginger, and the remaining flour. Warm the milk gently and add the soda; stir at once into the mixture, and turn into the cake tin. Bake for 1½ hours. Towards the end of the baking time lower the heat if the cake is getting too brown. Cool for a little in the tin before turning out. This cake improves with keeping.

Madeira Cake

6 oz. fresh butter; grated rind of ½ lemon; pinch of ground cinnamon; 8 oz. castor sugar; 10 oz. flour; 4 large eggs; 1 heaped teaspoon baking powder; ½ gill milk; 2–3 thin slices citron peel.

Prepare a 7½-inch cake tin. Set the oven at 350 ° F. or Reg. 4.

Cream the butter thoroughly with the lemon rind and cinnamon, then add the sugar by degrees, beating until white and fluffy. Then beat in the eggs one at a time with a sprinkling of flour; cut and fold in the remainder with the baking powder and milk. Turn into the cake tin, arrange the peel on the top, and bake for about 1½ hours. Lower the heat after the first 40 minutes.

Orange Cake

2 eggs; their weight in butter, sugar, and flour; 1 level teaspoon baking powder; juice of one orange; grated rind of 1 or 2 oranges according to size.

Separate the egg yolks from the whites. Sift the flour with the baking powder and a pinch of salt. Cream the butter with half the orange rind, add the sugar, and beat again until light and fluffy. Beat in the egg yolks and fold in the flour and orange juice. Whisk the egg whites until stiff and dry and fold in very lightly. Bake in a buttered tin until set and golden brown (350 ° F. or Reg. 4) for about 30 minutes. Turn on to a wire cake tray. When cool cover with a glacé icing to which has been added the rest of the finely shredded blanched orange rind.

French Almond Cake

4 oz. butter; 5¼ oz. castor sugar; 3 oz. ground almonds; 3 eggs; 1½ oz. flour; vanilla or Kirsch.

Prepare a moule à manqué 7-inch tin or a deep sandwich tin of the same size. Cream the butter thoroughly; beat in the sugar by degrees. Add the eggs one at a time with the almonds, beating well. Fold in the flour with the flavouring. Turn into the prepared tin and bake in a moderately hot oven (350 ° F. or Reg. 4) for 45 to 50 minutes. Turn out and dust with castor sugar.

Gâteau de Savoie

2½ oz. fécule (potato flour) or 1¼ oz. each arrowroot and plain flour; 3 eggs; 5 oz. castor sugar; grated rind and juice of ½ lemon; icing sugar.

Prepare an 8½-inch sandwich tin or a 7-inch cake tin, and set the oven at 370 ° F. or Reg. 4. Sift the flours together. Separate the eggs. Cream the egg yolks and sugar with a wooden spatula until light, add the flour with the lemon juice and rind. Beat thoroughly. Whisk the egg whites to a stiff foam and fold them into the mixture. Turn it into the sandwich tin and bake in a moderate oven for about 45 minutes. When cool dust with icing sugar.

Luncheon Plum Cake

½ lb. butter; ½ lb. brown sugar; 4 eggs; ¾ lb. flour; 8 oz. each sultanas and raisins; 4 oz. glacé cherries; grated rind and juice of 1 lemon; ½ teaspoon mixed spices; 1 teaspoon bicarbonate of soda; a little milk or cider.

Prepare an 8-inch cake tin and set the oven at 350 ° F. or Reg. 4.

Cream the butter with the lemon rind, add the sugar, and beat until light. Whip the eggs and work into the mixture by degrees, sprinkling with a little flour. Then divide the rest of the flour and add the prepared fruit to one half and the soda and mixed spice to the other. Stir in the fruit and flour and lemon juice and when well incorporated add the soda and flour and enough milk or cider to make a consistency that will drop from the spoon. Turn at once into the prepared tin and bake for about 1½ hours. Lower the heat to Reg. 3 after the first hour.

Note: If you use an electric beater it is better to add the lemon rind at the same time as the juice, as finely grated rind gets stuck round the blades of an electric beater.

Rich Plum Cake (for Christmas or Birthdays)

¾ lb. butter; ¾ lb. brown sugar; 3 oz. ground almonds; 3 oz. shredded almonds; 6 oz. finely chopped candied peel; ¾ lb. currants; ¾ lb. sultanas; ½ lb. raisins; 2 oz. glacé cherries; 5 eggs; ¾ lb. flour; 1 teaspoon baking powder; 1 glass sherry.

Prepare a 9-inch cake tin and set the oven at 350 ° F. or Reg. 4.

Cream the butter thoroughly, add the sugar, and beat well. Beat in the almonds and the prepared fruit with the cherries cut in half. Separate the eggs and beat the yolks into the mixture. Sift the flour with the baking powder and whip the whites stiffly. Cut and fold them into the mixture with the flour and sherry. Add a little milk if necessary to bring the mixture to a soft consistency that will drop easily from the spoon. Turn into prepared cake tin and bake for 3 hours. Lower the heat to Reg. 3 after the first hour. The cake when cooked should shrink slightly from the sides of the tin and, if a warm steel knitting needle, inserted into the centre of the cake is clean when withdrawn, the cake is done.

Gâteau au Chocolat

2 oz. unsweetened chocolate; about $\frac{1}{2}$ gill water; 3 eggs; $4\frac{1}{2}$ oz. castor sugar; $2\frac{1}{4}$ oz. plain flour; a pinch of salt; 6 oz. butter cream (see page 457); 4–6 oz. plain block chocolate; caraque chocolate (see below); icing sugar.

Grate or slice the chocolate. Melt with the water to a thick cream and set aside to cool. Whisk the eggs and sugar together over gentle heat until thick and mousse-like, remove the bowl from the heat, and continue whisking until the bowl is cold. Sift the flour with the salt and fold into the mixture with the melted chocolate. Turn into a prepared 8–9-inch cake tin and bake in a moderate oven (370° F. or Reg. 4) about 45 to 50 minutes.

While the cake is cooking melt the plain chocolate on a plate over a pan of hot water and when quite smooth beat into the butter cream. When the cake is cool, split and fill with a thin layer of the chocolate butter cream. Reshape the cake, spread the top and sides with the same cream, and press chocolate caraque over and round. Decorate with icing sugar.

Chocolate Caraque

Break up 1 oz. plain block chocolate and melt on a plate over hot water. Do not allow the plate to get too hot. Work the melted chocolate well with a palette knife and then spread thinly on a marble slab. When *just* set 'curl off' with a thin knife.

Gâteau au Chocolat Glacé

Prepare and bake the cake as directed in the preceding recipe and make a 4-oz. butter quantity of butter cream. When the cake is cooked, split and fill with a thin layer of the butter cream and brush the top and sides with apricot glaze. Coat with glacé icing (see over) and decorate with rosettes of butter cream.

Chocolate Glacé Icing

3 oz. plain block chocolate; 4 tablespoons stock syrup or water; 8 oz. icing sugar; ½ teaspoon salad oil; 2–3 drops vanilla essence.

Cut the chocolate into small pieces and place in a saucepan with the sugar syrup or water. Dissolve over gentle heat and then bring just to the boil. Allow to cool slightly. Beat in the finely sieved icing sugar a spoonful at a time, add the oil and essence, and warm.

Gâteau au Moka

3 oz. plain flour; 1½ oz. butter; 3 eggs; 3¼ oz. castor sugar; 1 tablespoon coffee essence; 4 oz. butter cream; apricot glaze; fondant or glacé icing; coffee essence; 8–10 browned hazelnuts or almonds.

Sift the flour with a pinch of salt two or three times and warm the butter gently until soft and pourable, taking care not to get it hot and oily. Break the eggs, add the sugar and coffee essence, and whisk over gentle heat until the mixture is thick and mousse-like (to the ribbon). Remove the mixing-bowl from the heat and continue whisking until it is cold. Fold in two-thirds of the flour, then the melted butter, and lastly the remaining flour. Turn quickly into an 8-inch prepared American cake pan and bake 30 to 35 minutes in a moderate oven (370° F. or Reg. 4–5).

When cool, split and fill with a layer of coffee-flavoured butter cream. Reshape the cake and brush over the top and sides with a thin coating of hot apricot glaze. When set, ice with coffee fondant or glacé icing, pipe 8 to 10 rosettes of the butter cream round (one for each portion or slice of cake), and decorate with a browned hazelnut or split almond on each.

Gâteau au Citron

4½ oz. plain flour; 2 oz. butter; 4 eggs; 4½ oz. castor sugar; 1 lemon; lemon curd; glacé icing.

Sift the flour with a pinch of salt, and warm the butter until it is soft and pourable. Break the eggs, add the sugar and the grated rind of half the lemon, and whisk over gentle heat until

449

thick and mousse-like. Remove the bowl from the heat and continue whisking until the bowl is cold. Fold in two thirds of the flour very gently, then the melted butter, followed quickly by the remaining flour. Turn the mixture at once into an 8–9-inch prepared American cake pan and bake in a moderate oven (370° F. or Reg. 4–5) for about 30 to 35 minutes.

Meanwhile remove the remaining rind from the lemon with a potato peeler and cut into fine needle-like shreds; cook in boiling water until tender.

When the cake is cool, split and fill with lemon curd. Reshape the cake and brush with apricot glaze. Prepare a fondant or glacé icing (see page 458), add the well-drained shreds of lemon rind, and pour over the cake.

Coffee and Nut Doboz Torte

4 eggs; 6 oz. castor sugar; 5 oz. flour.

BUTTER CREAM: 3 oz. sugar; $\frac{1}{2}$ gill water; 3 egg yolks; $\frac{1}{2}$ lb. unsalted butter; 2 oz. browned hazelnuts; coffee essence.

CARAMEL: 5 oz. loaf sugar; $\frac{3}{4}$ gill water.

DECORATION: 2–3 tablespoons of browned ground hazelnuts and a few whole ones.

First prepare your baking sheets. Brush with melted lard or oil and dust lightly with flour, then mark an 8-inch circle on each, using a plate or saucepan lid as a guide.

Whisk the eggs, add the sugar gradually, and whisk over a pan of hot water until thick. Remove from the heat and continue whisking until the bowl is cold. Sift the flour with the salt and fold lightly into the mixture using a metal spoon. Divide into 5 portions and spread over each circle on the prepared tins. This can be done in rotation, but each time the baking-sheets must be wiped, regreased, and floured. Bake in a moderate oven (375° F. or Reg. 5) about 5 to 8 minutes. Trim each round with a sharp knife while still on the baking sheet and then lift on to a wire rack to cool.

Meanwhile prepare the butter cream. Dissolve the sugar in the water, boil to the thread, and pour on to the egg yolks and whisk until thick. Cream the butter and beat in the egg mousse by degrees. Keep a little of this on one side for decoration. Grind the hazelnuts, pound to a paste with the coffee essence, and then work into the butter cream.

Take one round of the cake and lay on an oiled tin ready to coat with caramel. Melt the sugar in the water over a very low heat without boiling, then increase the heat and cook rapidly to a rich brown. Pour at once over the one round of cake, and when on the point of setting mark into portions with an oiled knife and trim round the edges.

Sandwich the rounds together with the coffee-nut cream, put the caramel-covered round on the top, spread the sides with more butter cream, and press round the ground nuts. Flavour the reserved butter cream with coffee essence. Pipe rosettes on each portion and decorate with the whole nuts.

Gâteau Progrès

7 oz. castor sugar; 5½ oz. ground almonds; 5 egg whites; 2–3 drops vanilla essence; 4 oz. plain chocolate; 6 oz. butter cream; 2 oz. praline; chopped browned almonds.

Sift the sugar and ground almonds together. Whisk the egg-whites until stiff but not dry, and fold in the sugar, almonds, and vanilla essence. Divide the mixture into 5 portions and spread on to greased and floured baking-tins in 8-inch rounds. Bake in a moderate oven (350° F. or Reg. 4) for about 15 minutes.

Trim with a sharp knife while still hot and then remove to a wire rack to cool. (These nut-meringue rounds may be baked in rotation.) Cut the chocolate into small pieces and put on a plate over a pan of hot water to melt; do not allow to become too hot. Add to the butter cream. Put one large tablespoon of the chocolate butter cream on one side for decoration, crush the praline to a smooth paste, and add to the remainder.

Sandwich the meringue rounds together with the chocolate-praline butter cream, spread the top and sides with the same cream, and press finely chopped almonds round. Dredge the top with icing sugar and pipe PROGRÈS with the reserved butter cream.

PATISSERIE

Éclairs au Chocolat

Choux pastry (see page 400); pastry cream flavoured with chocolate, or fresh cream whipped, sweetened and flavoured with vanilla; chocolate fondant or glacé icing.

Fill the choux pastry into a large forcing-bag fitted with a ½-inch plain pipe, and pipe into finger-lengths on a lightly greased baking-tin. Bake in a fairly hot oven (400° F. or Reg. 6) until crisp and golden brown, about 25 minutes.

If the choux pastry is well made and thoroughly beaten the éclair will be hollow, but if, on splitting, any soft mixture remains in the centre, remove with the handle of a teaspoon.

When cool, fill with the chocolate pastry cream or fresh cream and coat the tops with the chocolate fondant or glacé icing.

Frangipane Tartlets

Trimmings of puff pastry.

FRANGIPANE: 4 oz. butter; 4 oz. castor sugar; 2 eggs; 4 oz. ground almonds; 1 oz. plain flour; orange-flower water or Kirsch to taste; apricot glaze; glacé icing; glacé cherries.

First prepare the frangipane. Soften the butter with a wooden spoon, add the sugar and beat together until light and fluffy. Beat in the eggs gradually and then stir in the almonds and flour. Flavour with the orange-flower water or Kirsch. Line deep tartlet moulds with the puff pastry, prick the bottoms, and fill with the almond frangipane mixture. Bake in a moderately hot oven (400° F. or Reg. 6) for about 15 minutes.

When cool, brush the tops with apricot glaze and place a glacé cherry in the centre of each. Coat each cake with a thin layer of white glacé icing flavoured in the same way as the frangipane.

Amandine Tartlets

PÂTE SUCRÉE (see page 389); frangipane; flaked almonds; apricot glaze; 1–2 tablespoons ground almonds.

Line tartlet moulds with the pâte sucrée, prick the bottoms, and fill with the frangipane. Scatter the flaked almonds over the top and bake for 12 to 15 minutes in a moderate oven (380° F. or Reg. 5). As soon as they are cooked, remove from the tins, brush the tops with hot apricot glaze or redcurrant jelly, and decorate the outside edge with the browned ground almonds.

Conversations

Trimmings of puff pastry; frangipane; royal icing.

Roll out the pastry very thin and line into boat-shaped moulds. Prick the bottoms and half fill with the frangipane. Damp the edges with beaten egg and cover with a layer of puff pastry; seal well. Have ready a 1-egg quantity of royal icing and add a good pinch of flour which will prevent the icing bubbling when baked. Cover the top of each cake with a thin layer of the icing and decorate with four strips of puff pastry ¼ inch wide and bake in a moderate oven (380° F. or Reg. 5) for about 25 minutes.

Mokatines

2¼ oz. plain flour; 1 oz. butter; 2 eggs; 2¼ oz. castor sugar; 4 oz. butter cream; coffee essence; fondant or glacé icing.

Prepare the cake mixture as directed in the Gâteau au Citron recipe and bake in a 6–7-inch-square tin.

When cool, split and sandwich with a thin layer of coffee-butter cream. Reshape the cake, trim and cut into 8 neat oblongs, about 2½ inches long and 1 inch wide. Brush the top and sides

with hot apricot glaze, ice with coffee-flavoured fondant, and
decorate with a piping of the coffee-butter cream.

Mille Feuilles

6 oz. puff pastry or trimmings; $\frac{1}{4}$ pint double cream; 2–3 tablespoons good raspberry jam; glacé icing.

Roll out the pastry to one large thin sheet and place on a large,
damp baking-sheet, 10 by 12 inches. Prick well and bake in a
hot oven until golden brown and crisp (7 to 10 minutes). Remove
from the oven, trim the edges, and cut the pastry into four long
strips. Turn each strip over and return to the oven for 2 or 3
minutes. Reserve the trimmings, crush with a fork or rolling pin,
and keep on one side.

When the pastry is cool, sandwich the strips together, spreading one layer with the jam and the other two with whipped cream.
Press together very gently and cover the top with a thin layer of
glacé icing. Decorate the top with the crushed trimmings.

Almond Macaroons

7 oz. castor sugar; 1 oz. granulated sugar; 4 oz. ground almonds;
$\frac{1}{2}$ oz. rice flour; 2 large or 3 small egg whites; $\frac{1}{2}$ teaspoon vanilla
essence; rice paper; split almonds.

Mix the sugars together and sift with the almonds and rice flour
into a mixing-bowl. Add the egg whites and essence and beat all
together with a wooden spoon for about 5 minutes. Scrape down
the sides of the bowl and leave to stand for 5 minutes.

Cut the rice paper into 3-inch squares and place shiny side
down on a dry baking-tin. Beat the almond mixture for a further
5 minutes, until thick and white, and then fill into a large forcing-
bag fitted with a $\frac{1}{2}$-inch éclair pipe. Shape the macaroons neatly,
place a split almond in the middle of each, and bake in a moderate
oven (350° F. or Reg. 4) for 20 to 30 minutes.

Galettes Nantaises

4 oz. plain flour; good $1\frac{1}{2}$ oz. butter; 2 oz. castor sugar; $1\frac{1}{2}$ oz.
ground almonds; salt; 2 egg yolks.

Make up the biscuit paste in the same way as pâte sucrée, working in the almonds with the flour, and chill for one hour. Roll out fairly thinly and cut with a fluted cutter about 3½ inches in diameter. Place on a lightly buttered tin and brush with beaten egg. Mark the top of each biscuit into squares with a fork and put a pinch of ground almond in the centre. Dredge with castor sugar and bake in a moderately hot oven (400° F. or Reg. 6) for 7 or 8 minutes.

Galettes Napolitaines

BISCUIT MIXTURE: 6 oz. plain flour; 2½ oz. ground almonds; 3 oz. castor sugar; 3 oz. butter; 2 egg yolks; vanilla essence or Kirsch to flavour.

TOPPING: 3½ oz. icing sugar; 1 egg white; a large pinch flour; scant 2 oz. shredded almonds.

Prepare the biscuit mixture as for pâte sucrée, working in the ground almonds with the flour, and chill for 1 hour.

Meanwhile prepare the topping. Sift the icing sugar into a small bowl, add the lightly beaten egg white, and work together to a thick spreading consistency. Stir in the shredded almonds.

Divide the biscuit mixture into pieces the size of a hen's egg and roll into balls on a floured board. Place on a buttered baking-tin and flatten well with the bottom of a tumbler. Cover each biscuit with a little of the topping and bake in a moderate oven (350° F. or Reg. 4) for about 10 minutes or until a pale golden brown.

Tuiles à l'Orange

2 egg whites; 4 oz. castor sugar; 2 oz. butter; 2 oz. flour; grated orange rind.

Whip the egg whites stiffly then add the sugar and beat thoroughly. Melt the butter and add to the mixture by degrees with the sifted flour. Add the flavouring. Spread out in teaspoonfuls on a well-greased baking-sheet, bake in a moderate oven (375° F. or Reg. 5) until golden brown (about 5 or 6 minutes). Take off at once and roll up or curl slightly on a rolling-pin. Put at once into an airtight tin if not using immediately.

Cigarettes Russes

2 egg whites; 4 oz. castor sugar; 2 oz. plain flour; 2 oz. butter;
2–3 drops vanilla essence.

Break the egg whites into a basin; add the sugar and beat until
smooth with a fork. Melt the butter and add with the sifted flour.
Flavour with a little vanilla. Spread in oblongs on a greased and
floured tin and bake in a moderately hot oven (375° F. or Reg. 5)
for 5 to 6 minutes.

Allow to stand for a second or two, then remove with a sharp
knife and place upside down on the table; wind tightly round a
wooden skewer or pencil, holding them firmly in the hand. Remove at once and cool quickly. Store in an airtight tin.

NOTE: Bake one first to test the mixture – if difficult to handle,
add a pinch of flour, or, if too firm and hard, add a teaspoon
of melted butter.

Orangines

2 oz. butter; 2 oz. blanched, chopped almonds; 2 oz. castor sugar;
1½ oz. flour; 2 oz. candied orange peel; 1 drop carmine; 1 tablespoon milk.

Chop the almonds and peel finely. Cream the butter, add the
sugar, and cream until white; add the peel and almonds, then the
flour, carmine, and milk. Butter the baking-sheets, put out
the mixture in half teaspoonfuls, and flatten out with a wet fork.
Bake in a moderate oven (375° F. or Reg. 5) until tinged with
brown (about 7 or 8 minutes), then leave for a few minutes before
taking off the tin.

Galettes Muscat

3½ oz. castor sugar; 3½ oz. ground almonds; 3 egg whites; a few
drops vanilla essence; 1 oz. plain chocolate.

Beat the whites to a light froth, add the sugar, cream well, then
beat in the almonds and vanilla essence.

Have ready some greased and floured baking-sheets. Spread
out the mixture through a metal or cardboard stencil in the shape
of an oak leaf. Bake in a moderate oven (370° F. or Reg. 4) for

7 to 10 minutes. Lift off, cool, and spread one side with melted chocolate. Mark with a knife, to represent the veins on the leaf, and leave until cold.

ICINGS AND FILLINGS

Butter Cream (1)

2 oz. sugar; scant ½ gill water; 2 egg yolks; 4 oz. unsalted butter.

Dissolve the sugar in the water, then boil till the syrup is sticky and will pull a thread between finger and thumb. Pour onto the egg yolks and whisk until thick. Cream the butter and beat in the egg mousse by degrees. Flavour as wanted.

Butter Cream (2)

¼ pint milk; 4 oz. castor sugar; 2 egg yolks; ½ lb. unsalted butter.

Put the milk and half the sugar in a saucepan and dissolve over gentle heat. Cream the egg yolks with the remaining sugar until light, then tip on the hot milk; return to the saucepan and stir until the custard coats the back of the spoon. Strain and allow to cool. Cream the butter until soft and add the custard by degrees, beating well between each addition. Flavour and use as required.

Butter Cream (3)

2 egg whites; 4 oz. sifted icing sugar; ½ lb. unsalted butter.

Place the egg whites and sugar in a pudding basin over a saucepan of steaming water and using a rotary beater whisk until the mixture is thick and firm. Cream the butter very well and add the cooked meringue mixture by degrees. Flavour and use as required.

Apricot Glaze

1 lb. smooth apricot jam; ½ gill cold water.

Place the jam and water in a saucepan over a low heat and stir until dissolved. Pass the jam through a wire strainer, then return it to the pan and bring to the boil. Boil gently until the glaze is quite clear and the desired consistency is obtained.

Stock Syrup

½ lb. granulated or loaf sugar; 16 oz. water.

Dissolve the sugar in the water over very gentle heat, then bring
to the boil and allow to boil steadily for 10 minutes or to 220° F.
on a sugar thermometer.

Glacé Icing

½–¾ lb. sifted icing sugar; 4–5 tablespoons stock syrup.

Put the sugar syrup in a saucepan and beat in the icing sugar
a spoonful at a time. Beat thoroughly with a wooden spatula.
The icing should look very glossy and be a little too thick to
pour easily. Place the saucepan over a very low heat and warm
carefully. The pan must not get hot; it is wise to test the bottom
frequently with the palm of the hand. Flavour the icing as
required.

Fondant Icing

1 lb. loaf sugar; ¼ pt. water; 1 teaspoon liquid glucose or a
good pinch of cream of tartar.

Place the sugar in a saucepan with the water over very gentle
heat and allow to dissolve; wash round the sides of the pan with
a clean pastry brush dipped in water to wash down any sugar
crystals not dissolved, then put the lid on the pan and bring to
the boil. Remove the lid, add the glucose or the cream of tartar
dissolved in a teaspoon of water, and boil steadily to the 'soft
ball' or 240° F. on a sugar thermometer. Remove the pan from
the heat, allow the bubbles to subside, and then pour the hot
syrup slowly onto a wet marble slab. Leave to cool for about 1
minute, then gather the syrup from the outside into the middle.
This will even the heat of the batch and the syrup is then ready
for working. Take a large wooden spatula and work through the
syrup with even strokes until it turns to fondant. Pick up the fondant a small piece at a time and knead until smooth. Pack into a
small basin and leave to mellow one hour before using. To store,
wrap the fondant in waxed paper and pack in an airtight tin or

jar. For use, warm gently with a little stock syrup to a smooth cream.

Royal Icing

1 lb. icing sugar; 2 egg whites; 1 teaspoon lemon juice or orange flower water.

Rub the icing sugar through a fine nylon sieve or strainer; whisk the egg whites to a froth and add the icing sugar a spoonful at a time, beating thoroughly between each addition of sugar. Stir in the flavouring and continue beating until the icing will stand in peaks. Cover the bowl with a damp cloth during use.

Almond Paste

1 lb. ground almonds; $\frac{1}{2}$ lb. castor sugar; $\frac{1}{2}$ lb. sifted icing sugar; 1 whole large egg or 2 whole small eggs; 1 egg yolk; juice of $\frac{1}{2}$ lemon; 1–2 tablespoons brandy or sherry; $\frac{1}{2}$ teaspoon vanilla essence; 2 drops almond essence; 2 teaspoons orange-flower water.

Place the almonds and sugars in a bowl and mix together; whisk the eggs with the lemon juice and all the flavourings and add all this to the mixture of almonds and sugar, pounding lightly to release a little of the almond oil. Knead with the hand until smooth.

Lemon Curd

$\frac{1}{2}$ lb. castor sugar; $\frac{1}{4}$ lb. unsalted butter; grated rind and juice of 2 large lemons; 3 eggs.

Place the sugar, butter, lemon rind, and the strained juice into a double saucepan and stir until the sugar and butter are melted. Add the strained beaten eggs and continue stirring until the mixture thickens. Take great care that the mixture does not boil or it will curdle. Pour into clean, dry pots.

Pastry Cream

1 whole egg; 1 egg yolk; 2 oz. castor sugar; $\frac{3}{4}$ oz. plain flour; $\frac{1}{2}$ oz. cornflour; $\frac{1}{2}$ pint milk; 1 vanilla pod or vanilla essence.

Cream the two egg yolks and sugar together until white; add
the flours and a little of the cold milk to make a smooth paste.
Scald the remaining milk with the vanilla pod, strain on to the
egg mixture, blend, and return to the pan. Stir over gentle heat
until the mixture boils. Whip the egg white until stiff, turn a
little of the boiling cream into a bowl, and fold in the white.
Return this to the pan and stir carefully for two or three minutes
over the heat to set the egg white.

Chapter 13

MENUS FOR ALL OCCASIONS

OVER the years the would-be cook-hostess has been showered with good advice such as not to exceed her capabilities or the facilities of the kitchen; have a cold first course and sweet; choose a main dish that will keep warm without spoiling, and one that needs no last-minute carving or finishing.

All excellent advice but negative and imposing a severe restriction on the menu. However there are many points that can help the busy housewife or the as yet inexperienced student to choose a meal with variety and interest.

SOUPS

There is no doubt that a home-made soup will be a winner every time, and the correct accompaniment so often omitted in restaurant service will lift it right out of the ordinary. Now many of the recipes for the fine cream soups call for an egg-yolk liaison, something that causes difficulty if the soup has to be kept hot for any length of time as the risk of curdling increases. Instead of the liaison have a generous amount of cream, say twice that called for in the recipe, and up to a quarter pint ready in the warm soup tureen; keep the soup over gentle heat and when the guests are seated pour the boiling soup on to the cream, whisking well.

FISH

The choice of recipe and the plan of work is most important. Fish is not good if over-cooked or if kept warm for a long period, and moreover the sauce will form a skin and look unattractive unless it has some sort of protective coating either in the form of cheese and crumbs or Hollandaise sauce. If a recipe with one of these toppings is chosen it is best to prepare and cook the fish early in the day and let it get quite cold. The timing to reheat will be quite easy and the dish will look good. If, on the other hand, the sauce has no protective finish it is best to spend time in the morning preparing a fish stock from the bones and trimmings of the fish and to complete the sauce. This should be turned into a double saucepan and be covered with a generously buttered paper; the paper must touch the surface of the sauce and in this way it prevents a skin forming. For this type of dish the fish should be placed ready for cooking and kept well covered in a cool place. Plan the cooking time carefully and as fish only needs a slow oven (325 to 350° F. or Reg. 3 to 4 – a temperature that would be 'safe' for most meat and poultry), it is a simple matter to have freshly cooked fish. The sauce will reheat perfectly in its pan with no attention and no danger of burning, and in this way the fish can be coated just before serving.

MEAT

For the inexperienced a casserole seems to be the obvious choice for a main course, but lean meat, particularly varieties that must be well cooked, are an excellent choice for roasting, pot-roasting, and sautés as they will keep warm without spoiling. Veal and pork fillets are particularly good-tempered in this way. Chicken, if French roasted or pot-roasted, will be succulent even if kept warm, but if it is in a good sauce then, like fish, it is better if allowed to cool completely and then reheated just before serving. Last-minute cooking such as pan-fried steaks, wiener schnitzel, or grilled chops can be coped with if the accompaniments are chosen carefully. A potato dish that is baked in the oven and will keep warm and a tossed salad that requires no cooking would be excellent if preceded by a soup and followed by a cold sweet.

A little thought with a programme on paper giving regular time-checks saves endless worry and heartache and is invaluable even to the most experienced cook, and it will help the inexperienced on the road from the 'red-cheeked, shiny-nosed cook with chaos in the sink' to the immaculate hostess serving exquisite food.

*

Recipes marked with a star may be prepared in advance or reheated.

Luncheon Parties

JANUARY
Prawn and Orange Cocktail
Sauté of Kidney Turbigo with Sautéd
   Artichokes
or
Roast Neck of Lamb with a casserole
   of Artichoke and Mushrooms
Potatoes Boulangère
Creamed Rice and Fresh Fruit Salad

FEBRUARY
Eggs Duxelles
Chicken Vichy with Potatoes Château
*Plum Suédoise and Cream

MARCH
Spaghetti Napolitana
Matelote Normande with Potatoes Maître
   d'Hôtel
Tartelettes aux Fruits

APRIL
*Cod's Roe Pâté
Sauté of Beef Chasseur with New Potatoes
   and Spinach
Scalloped Apples

MAY
*Cream of Spinach Soup
*Salmon Trout with Sauce Mayonnaise,
   New Potatoes, and Cucumber and Chive
   Salad
*Camembert Glacée

JUNE
Potted Shrimps
Escalopes of Veal à la Crème with Potatoes
   Fondant and Cucumber à la Crème
Danish Strawberry Cake

JULY
Tomato Salad
Chicken Sauté Parmesan with New Pota-
   toes and Petits Pois à la Française
*Griestorte with Raspberries

463

AUGUST
Eggs en Cocotte with Cream
*Galantine of Chicken Parisienne with Salad Niçoise
Sugared Fruit with Gâteau de Savoie

SEPTEMBER
Dressed Crab
Ragout of Veal Créole
Damson Cream Ice and Cigarettes Russes

OCTOBER
Melon
*Jugged Hare with Mousseline Potatoes and Braised Red Cabbage
*Crème Caramel

NOVEMBER
*Artichoke Soup
Braised Leg of Lamb with Pommes Savoyade and Céleri au Jus
*Tarte aux Pruneaux

DECEMBER
Eggs Aurore
Pheasant Flamande with Potatoes Mousseline
*Apples Bristol

Dinner Parties

JANUARY
Soup Madrilène
Poulet au Riz with French Beans
Angels on Horseback

FEBRUARY
Prawn or Lobster Bisque
Veal Forestière with Potato and Celeriac Purée
Fresh Fruit Salad

MARCH
Scallops Nature
Entrecôte of Beef Bordelaise with Roast Potatoes and Cauliflower
*Coffee Parfait

* A Prawn Bisque is made in the same way as a Lobster Bisque.

APRIL
*Walnut Soup
Loin of Lamb à la Doria* with Potatoes
Fondantes and Orange
Mint Sauce
*Lemon Soufflé

MAY
*Cream of Lettuce Soup
or
*Trout Vinaigrette
Devilled Grilled Poussins with Simla Rice
and Salad in season
Orange Compote and *Crème Brûlée

JUNE
Asparagus with Beurre Noisette
Lobster 'Cordon Bleu'
Vacherin Chantilly aux Fruits

JULY
Consommé en Gelée
Caneton aux Cerises and New Potatoes
Bombe Favorite

AUGUST
Brill Juliette
Beef Niçoise with Hot Anchovy Loaf and
French Beans, Tomato, and Cucumber.
Peaches with Sabayon†

SEPTEMBER
Sole Meunière
Chicken Paprika with Noodles and
Courgettes au Beurre
*Hazelnut Meringue Cake with Blackberries

OCTOBER
Cream of Barley Soup
*Partridge au Chou with Potatoes Mousseline
Apple Mousse Gatinaise

NOVEMBER
*Chestnut Soup
or
Scampi Provençale
*Braised Venison with Potato and Celery
Julienne
Pear Fresco

* Made as Cutlets of Lamb Doria.
† See recipe for Tangerine Sabayon.

DECEMBER	Sole Maintenon
	Coq au Vin
	Tangerine Mousse

CHRISTMAS BUFFET	Smoked Haddock Mousse
SUPPER PARTY	Prawn Bouchées
	Pheasant Turinois
	or
	Roast Stuffed Turkey en Gelée
	Apricot Moscovite

Christening Party

FAMILY LUNCH:	Tomato and Orange Juice Cocktail
SUMMER	French Roast Chicken, hot or cold, with New Potatoes and Salad in season
	Fruit Fool* and Biscuits

FAMILY LUNCH:	Tomato and Orange Soup
WINTER	Baked Cold Gammon with Potatoes in Jackets and Sour Cream and Cabbage Salad
	Fruit Fool and Biscuits

TEA	Cream Cheese and Chive Sandwiches
	Egg and Cress Rolls
	Honey and Date Bread and Butter
	'Christening Sponge'†
	Chocolate Cake
	Fruit and Cream – Strawberries or Raspberries or Fresh Fruit Salad

Children's Party

Buttered Egg Sandwiches	Individual Jellies and Ice Cream
Sausages on sticks or in Bridgerolls	Small Meringues and Fresh Fruit Salad
	Rich Fruit Cake (Cherry and Sultana)
Cucumber Sandwiches	Orange Cake Iced
Tomato Sandwiches	Chocolate Biscuits

* See the recipe for Gooseberry Fool.
† For example, a Gâteau au Citron.

Twenty-First Birthday Fork Buffet Supper

Egg and Prawn Mayonnaise
Salmon en Gelée with Sauce
  Mayonnaise
or
Chicken Bouchées (hot)
or
Chicken Bangkok

or
Chicken Pie Romaine
Chocolate and Orange Mousse
Pineapple Cake
Vacherin Chantilly aux Fruits
Soup – Spicy Tomato – to speed
    the parting guest.

Engagement Party Cocktail

Quiche (small)
Cheese Sablés
Smoked Salmon Rolls
Small Tongue Sandwiches

Hot Frankfurters and French
  Mustard
Anchovy Loaf
Egg and Prawn Croquettes*
Asparagus Rolls

And of course the usual nuts and olives and crisps.

Wedding Breakfast

FORMAL

Consommé
Sole en Évantail
Coq au Vin
Angel Cake with Strawberries

FORK LUNCH

Salmon 'én coquille'
Chicken Tourtière and Jellied Ham
    Bourguignonne
Salads
Sugared Fruit and Vacherin Chantilly
or
Crème Brulée
Cheese Sablés

Silver Wedding Dinner Party

Sole Joinville
Beef en Croûte with Madère Sauce and
    Potatoes Parisienne and Petits Pois
Pêches Carmen
or
Fraises Escoffier

* See Egg Croquettes, and add a few prawns.

Golden Wedding – Family Luncheon Party

Egg and Prawn Mayonnaise
Chicken Villeroy with Haricots Verts
Gâteau Mille Feuilles

Theatre Party

BEFORE

Hors d'œuvres en Coquilles*
Sauté of Veal Marengo with Potato
 Purée
Almond Fruit Flan

AFTER

Onion Soup
Cold Beefsteak and Pigeon Pie
Crème Margot

* See page 31

KITCHEN EQUIPMENT

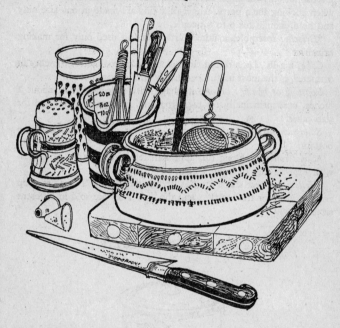

THE most important items have been given here. Those pieces marked * are not essential for a small kitchen but can be added later if and when desired.

BAKING-SHEETS

These should be thick and fit the oven. Two or three should be ample.

CAKE RACK, OR COOLING TRAY

A tray with a small mesh of fine wire. These are invaluable for cooling cakes, scones, etc., and are also useful when icing.

CAKE TINS

Angel: a tin which can be used either with or without the tube. Useful not only for angel cake but also for setting mousses or creams when cooking for a party. Angel-cake tins are made in one size only and hold enough for 6 to 8 people.

Brioche: resembles a fluted tartlet tin and used only for making brioches.

Cake: a 2-lb., i.e. a round tin measuring approximately 8 inches in diameter, is the most useful, preferably with a loose bottom.

Roasting or baking: oblong in shape with a deep edge of about 2 inches, used principally for meat roasting, but can also be used for slab cakes.

Sandwich: an 8-inch size for a family of four, with or without a loose bottom.

Swiss roll: an oblong tin, approximately 10 inches by 12 inches, with a raised edge of about 1 inch.

Tartlet: the best shape are the French tartlet tins. These are deep and are ideal for fruit tartlets and the like. They are sold in different sizes.

CASSEROLE OR COCOTTE

A heavy shallow pan with 2 side-handles and a lid. May be made of enamelled iron or steel; this sort is more useful than the earthenware kind as it can be used on a naked flame for browning. Made in different sizes.

CHOPPING BOARD

To last, this should be thick, heavy, and made of wood.

COLANDER

For straining vegetables, rice, etc. Made in enamel, polythene aluminium, or stainless steel. The two latter are the best.

*COPPER BOWL

For whisking egg whites, sponges, and meringues. See *Whisks, balloon.*

*DEEP-FAT BATH AND BASKET

These are sold complete.

DREDGERS

You need (a) one for sifting flour and pastry making, and (b) a finer one for castor or icing sugar.

FLAN RING

A 7-inch flan ring is a useful size. They are easier to use if bought as a plain ring to set on a baking-sheet rather than as a tin with a loose bottom.

*FORCING BAGS

1 large and 1 medium-sized bag made of nylon are enough for the average kitchen.

*FORCING PIPES

Two plain forcing pipes, 1 medium size and 1 smaller for éclairs. One 6- or 8-cut rose pipe for decoration.

GRATERS

The square type of stainless-steel grater is the best to buy, together with a Mouli cheese grater, which is an essential for grinding nuts and praline.

KNIVES

With the exception of a serrated-edged fruit knife, kitchen knives are best made of plain rather than stainless steel. As they are one of the most important tools in the kitchen they should be rubbed up after use and sharpened regularly on a steel or on carborundum. One knife of each of the following types should be ample for a household of four:

  Large chopping knife, for example, a Sabatier with a 7-inch blade.
  Medium chopping knife, say a Sabatier jeune with a 6-inch blade.
  A vegetable knife with a 3- to 4-inch blade.
  A palette knife with a 7-inch blade.
  A serrated-edged fruit knife with a 3- to 4-inch blade, of stainless steel.

*MARBLE SLAB

Primarily for making pastry, but useful for other things such as praline, fondant, and so on. Buy a piece from a stonemason; it will be better and cheaper. A useful size is 20 inches by 18 inches.

MEASURING JUG

A pint measure in aluminium or enamel.

*MEASURING SPOONS

A set of American measuring spoons is useful if American cookery books are being followed; so is an American measuring cup.

*MORTAR

Made of marble or composition. Choose a wooden pestle to go with it. It is less noisy than a composition one and just as efficient.

MOULDS

Charlotte: a plain round mould resembling a cake tin but smaller and with slightly sloping sides. Used not only for jellies and creams but a useful shape for hot steamed or baked puddings.

Dariole: small individual moulds, a Charlotte mould in miniature. Sometimes called a castle-pudding mould. Used for aspics and creams as well as for puddings (*babas*).

Moule à manqué: a mould common to the French cuisine and not easily obtainable here. The nearest equivalent is an American cake pan. Both resemble a deep sandwich tin with sloping sides. If a cake is to be iced it is inverted after baking so that the icing will run easily down the sides. This shape is also useful for setting a cream or bavaroise. Also obtainable in different sizes.

Savarin or Border: a plain ring mould used not only for savarins but for setting creams, both sweet and savoury.

PANS

Saucepan: a pan with a depth of 4 to 5 inches, depending on the pint-capacity. Saucepans are made of a variety of materials: aluminium, stainless steel, and enamelled iron are the most popular. Whatever the metal the pan should be thick and solid to conserve heat and avoid burning.

Sauté pan: like a frying-pan but at least 2 inches deep and with straight sides. The most easily obtainable are those of stainless steel, sold as frying-pans, with lids (which are an advantage).

Stew pan: a pan slightly shallower than a saucepan, with a depth of about 3 inches.

*PASTRY CUTTERS

Both plain and fluted for stamping-out pastry, scone dough, and bread for croûtes. These are sold in boxes of 6 to 8 different sizes, and though not all are essential for everyday use, they are a better buy when bought in this way.

PEELER

The Lancashire type, with a plastic or wooden handle, can be bought either for a right- or left-handed person. The metal is plated and so this type is generally used for paring the zest from lemons or oranges.

ROLLING-PIN

A good pin should be as heavy as possible. Avoid washing it too much and do not let it soak in water as this tends to warp it.

SCALES AND WEIGHTS

A set of ordinary household scales weighing up to 7 or 14 lb. is the best buy. With care and occasional adjusting they will last a lifetime.

SCISSORS

Ideally a kitchen should have 2 pairs, one for cutting paper, bacon rinds, and so on, and one pair of best quality with a serrated edge and a nick in the blade for cutting poultry and game, both raw and cooked. If kept for these jobs the scissors do not spoil.

SCRAPERS

Made in plastic or rubber. For scraping out bowls and so on the plastic ones are best; neither type should be put into any hot liquid.

SPATULAS

These are virtually wooden spoons but flat on both sides and are ideal for sauces, cake mixtures, and so on.

STRAINERS

Bowl: these are available in fine wire or nylon and in all sizes. The most useful is to have 1 medium-to-large wire one for straining small quantities of vegetables and sifting flour, and 1 medium-to-small nylon one for fruit juices, purées, etc.

Chinese or conical: a pointed strainer in aluminium or stainless steel. Intended for sauces or liquids. The shape of the strainer contains the sauce in a narrow stream so that it is easy to strain directly into a sauceboat or bowl.

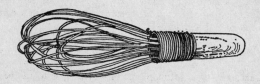

WHISKS

Balloon: used with a copper bowl. As the name implies, the wire is curved and fits the curve of the bowl. Balloon whisks have wooden handles and are made in 2 or 3 sizes to go with the size of the bowl.

Rotary or wheel: generally made the same size, but in different qualities and prices. It is wise to buy a good one as with care they have a long life.

Sauce: a small whisk made of plated or stainless-steel wire. These latter are the best though more expensive and are intended only for sauces and dressings.

Appendix B

COOKING TERMS EXPLAINED

TO BARD: To cover the breast of game or poultry for roasting with a slice of pork fat or specially prepared bacon fat known as larding bacon. This can be bought as 'spick' in some delicatessen shops. Barding gives additional fat and protects the meat which might otherwise become dry from the heat of the oven. The fat is taken off 6 to 7 minutes before the bird is dished to allow the breast to brown. See also *To Lard*.

TO BASTE: To spoon hot fat or liquid over food being roasted or poached in the oven. The object of basting is to keep the meat or other food (such as a whole fish) moist and juicy.

TO BAT: A term applied to flattening fillets of sole, lamb cutlets, and veal escalopes. A cutlet bat (see list of equipment) is the easiest tool to use. In default of this, the bottom of a heavy frying-pan or a flat-iron answers well. The object of batting is to give a wider surface for stuffing, in the case of fillets of sole, and better appearance, in the case of cutlets.

BEURRE MANIÉ (kneaded butter): One of the liaisons (see Chapter 10).

BEURRE NOIR, see under *Butter*.

TO BLANCH: Literally to whiten, but can also be applied to green vegetables. It is normally done to remove a strong taste. There are two forms of blanching: (a) in the case of onions, for example, put whatever is to be blanched into cold water, bring to the boil, and drain before further cooking. Certain meats are treated in the same way; (b) green vegetables, such as the cabbage tribe and peppers, should be put into boiling water and allowed to boil for $\frac{1}{2}$ to 1 minute before draining. They may be refreshed (*q.v.*) and further cooking carried out according to the recipe.

BOUQUET GARNI: In English 'a faggot of herbs'. A bouquet usually consists of a bayleaf, a sprig of thyme, and 3 or 4 parsley stalks. A spray of parsley may be used, but the stalks have more flavour and, moreover, do not disintegrate with long, slow cooking as the leaves are liable to do.

BRUNOISE: A garnish, as is Julienne, but the vegetables are cut into the smallest possible dice before being cooked.

BUTTER: (a) *Clarifying*: the object of clarifying is to take away the milk solids and salt in the butter, so giving a clear fat, free from all moisture. When heated it is not so inclined to burn as unclarified butter, and a greater temperature can be reached. It is used for frying sole, chicken, veal, etc., and gives a specially good golden colour.

To clarify, put ¼ lb. of butter into a pan and heat gently until a good foam comes to the top. Cook for another ½ minute, skim well, then pour off into a bowl. Do not allow the butter to brown. When cold, all sediment will have fallen to the bottom, which must be carefully scraped away from the cake of fat. This amount of butter will yield 2 to 3 oz. of clarified butter.

(b) *Noisette:* butter cooked to a light nut brown. When this stage is reached, a few drops of lemon juice are added and the butter poured at once over the dish for which intended, i.e. fish, meat, or vegetables.

(c) *Noir:* butter cooked to a dark nut-brown and sharpened by the addition of reduced vinegar. Used principally for fish and brains.

(d) *To pass through butter:* principally applied to such things that need very little cooking, e.g. tomatoes. Butter is melted in a frying-pan and the tomatoes are cooked in this for not more than 1 or 2 minutes so that they do not lose their shape.

CANAPÉ: A small round, 1 to 1½ inches in diameter, of fried bread, cheese, or short-crust pastry covered with a savoury mixture and served hot or cold.

TO CLARIFY BUTTER, see under *Butter*.

CONCASSER: To chop roughly. A term usually applied to tomatoes. Here the tomatoes are scalded and skinned, the seeds are taken out, and the flesh is sliced or chopped.

COURT BOUILLON: A quickly made vegetable stock, lightly acidulated. It is used for poaching all types of fish, and after the fish is cooked it may be turned into a sauce to accompany or strained off and kept for future use. (See page 123.)

CROÛTE: A round of crisply fried bread, fried in either oil, butter, or deep fat. Used as a raised base for savouries, tournedos, eggs, etc. The size varies according to what the croûte is intended for. If using shallow fat, care must be taken to see that the fat comes half-way up the sides of the croûte.

CROÛTON: Very small cubes of stale white bread fried in either shallow or deep fat until golden brown. When well drained they are lightly salted before being served with cream or purée soups.

CUISSON: Juices left in the pan or dish after meat, poultry, fish, and so on have been cooked.

DÉGORGER: This process is used to prepare aubergines, cucumber, etc. The vegetables are lightly salted after slicing, left for an hour or so, and then drained well. Further cooking or preparation can then be carried out. Like blanching (q.v.), this process removes any strong taste.

DÉPOUILLER: To skin or clarify. A term applied chiefly to brown sauces. See Chapter 10, on Sauces.

FLAMBER: To flame with brandy or fortified wine, e.g. sherry. This gives flavour to the meat or poultry, pancakes, etc., and at the same time gets rid of the alcohol. To flame, first heat the brandy to make the spirit more volatile and then set alight. Pour it at once, flaming, over the food. Red wine may be brought up to the boil and allowed to catch alight over a naked flame. Continue to boil hard until the flame has burnt out. If the wine does not catch light let it boil until reduced by about a quarter, then add to the sauce or dish. This process mellows the wine and reduces the alcohol content.

FLEURONS OR FEUILLETONS: Small crescent-shaped pieces of puff pastry used to garnish fish which is dished coated with a rich sauce. They are made by rolling out trimmings of puff pastry very thinly, brushing the surface with beaten egg and cutting crescents from this with a round fluted cutter $2\frac{1}{2}$ to 3 inches in diameter. Bake the fleurons in a hot oven for 7 to 10 minutes.

FUMET: A strong, well-reduced stock made from fish or game.

GLAZE: Reduced bone stock. Two to three pints of strong strained bone stock is needed to make approximately half a cupful of glaze. Boil the given quantity of stock until brown in colour and syrupy in texture. Pour off into a small jar and leave to set. A 'nut' of this added to gravies, soups, and some sauces gives flavour. Glaze is also used for brushing over cold tongue and galantine. Here a larger quantity is required and so a mock glaze can be made with well-reduced bone stock coloured with a drop or two of gravy browning with gelatine added to make it set.

JULIENNE: A term used to indicate the size and shape to which vegetables or other garnishes should be cut for certain dishes. A julienne strip is the length of a matchstick, about $1\frac{1}{2}$ inches long and about $\frac{1}{8}$ inch wide. A julienne garnish is generally composed of a mixture of root vegetables – carrot, celery, and leek, for example – and is cooked in a covered pan with a nut of butter only. It is then added to a soup or sauce.

JUS: Literally juice. In cooking it refers to that which runs from meat or game after cooking, found for example in the roasting-tin or griller pan.

TO LARD: Larding is done to give additional fat to cuts of meat that have little or none of their own, e.g. fillet of veal and fillet of beef. To lard, slice the larding bacon about ¼ inch thick and cut across into 'lardons'–match-like strips about 1½ inches long. These lardons are threaded into a larding needle and 'sewn' into the meat. At the end of cooking time the lardons should be nicely brown and crisp. (See also *To Bard*.)

MACÉDOINE: A term again to indicate a particular size and shape of cut-up vegetables or fruit. Here the pieces are large dice and are a mixture of vegetables such as carrots, turnips, or French beans, or of fruit such as peaches, pears, and pineapple.

MACÉRER: To soak. A term generally applied only to fruit soaked in liqueur or syrup.

MARINADE: To souse or soak. Applied to meat or game soaked in wine and oil with herbs and vegetables to flavour before cooking (see page 198). The object is to make the meat more tender, moist, and well-flavoured.

NOISETTE, see under *Butter*.

OLIVES: (a) *Green*. These are picked before they are ripe and preserved in brine. They are astringent in flavour and are eaten as an apéritif or as an addition to a sauce with rich meat such as duck. Green olives should be stoned before use; if they are to be shredded, cut small wedges or shreds from each olive with a small sharp knife starting from the outside down to the stone. To serve whole or to stuff with a savoury butter or a piece of pimento for an hors d'œuvre the olive must be 'turned' to take out the stone and yet retain the shape. To do this, choose a medium to large olive and, with a small sharp knife, make a small slanting cut across the top end. Still keeping the knife slantwise, continue to work round the stone in a spiral until the stalk end is reached. Then make a clean cut across and the stone will come away. Carefully reshape the olive.

(b) *Black*. Black olives are picked when ripe and, after a preliminary blanching in brine, preserved in oil. They are soft in contrast to the green, and slightly sweet. They are used principally in salads, e.g. Niçoise, and with certain veal and fish dishes. Black olives are stoned by slitting down the side and levering out the stone with the point of a small knife.

PANADA OR PANADE: A thick sauce which forms the base of most fish, meat, or vegetable creams. It may be made with a roux or like choux pastry, the latter where an especially thick one is required. A panade may also be of white crumb of bread, soaked in milk or water and beaten smooth before being used.

TO REFRESH: A term applied to a process which may follow blanching of vegetables and some meats. Once the food has been drained, a cupful or so of cold water is poured over. In the case of vegetables this 'sets' the colour. Where meat is concerned it helps to clean and wash away any scum, e.g. with brains, sweetbreads, etc.

RIBBON, BEAT TO THE: A term used when creaming egg yolks and castor sugar together for the base of a sponge cake or custard. A wooden spatula or spoon is used to work the yolks and sugar together until lemon-coloured and light in texture. This may take 3 to 4 minutes continuous stirring by hand or in a mixer. When the right stage has been reached the mixture should run from the spatula held above the basin in a broad ribbon.

RISSOLER: To brown slowly in fat.

ROUX: Forms the base of all flour sauces (see page 367 of Sauce chapter).

RUST: The underside of a bacon rasher or ham, opposite the rind. This is often hard or strong-flavoured and should be cut away.

SIPPETS: Small triangular pieces of dry toast served round a dish of minced meat or chicken.

TO SLAKE: In cooking a word usually applied to the mixing of arrow-root or cornflour with a small quantity of cold water before adding to a liquid for thickening. The proportions for mixing are one heaped teaspoonful of arrowroot, etc., to two tablespoons of cold water.

SOCLE: Only made for a *pièce montée*, i.e. a dish for a cold buffet. A socle is made from rice boiled to a pulp and, when cold and stiff, moulded to the shape required. It may then be covered with silver paper. The object is to raise the food off the surface of the dish and to give height. Lobster, cold stuffed chicken, galantine, etc., are served in this way. The socle is not eaten.

SUPRÊME: The wing and breast fillet removed in one piece from each side of a chicken carass.

TABASCO: A bottled sauce made of capsicums matured in sherry. It is very hot and spicy and so only a few drops are necessary to add to lobster dishes, prawn cocktails, and so on. Tabasco is also used to sprinkle over oysters.

Appendix C

EQUIVALENT MEASURES
ENGLISH AND AMERICAN

A STANDARD English measuring-cup holds 10 liquid ounces – that is,
½ pint (imperial measure), whereas an American measuring cup holds
8 liquid ounces, an American ½ pint. When dry ingredients are
measured in a cup their weight (avoirdupois) will obviously vary with
their density. A table showing some equivalent measures in American
cups is given below.

1 lb. flour (16 oz. avoirdupois)	= 4 cups sifted flour
½ lb. granulated and castor sugar	= 1 cup
½ lb. brown sugar	= 1¼ cups
½ lb. butter	= 1 cup

When spoon measurements are given, the spoons are rounded, that
is, they have as much above the bowl of the spoon as below.

METRIC

1 pint		= approx. ½ litre
1 ounce (oz.)		= approx. 28 grammes
1 pound (lb.)	= 16 oz.	= approx. 450 grammes

Appendix D

OVEN TEMPERATURES

	Degrees Fahrenheit	*Regulo (for gas cookers)*	*Degrees Centigrade*
Very slow	240–80	$\frac{1}{4}$–$\frac{1}{2}$	115–35
Slow	280–320	1	135–60
Warm	320–40	3	160–70
Moderate	340–70	4	170–85
Fairly hot	370–400	5–6	185–205
Hot	400–40	7	205–25
Very hot	440–80	8–9	225–50

INDEX

MORE ABOUT PENGUINS

Penguinews, which appears every month, contains details of all the new books issued by Penguins as they are published. From time to time it is supplemented by *Penguins in Print*, which is a complete list of all books published by Penguins which are in print. (There are over four thousand of these.)

A specimen copy of *Penguinews* will be sent to you free on request, and you can become a subscriber for the price of the postage – 30p for a year's issues (including the complete lists), if you live in the United Kingdom, or 60p if you live elsewhere. Just write to Dept EP, Penguin Books Ltd, Harmondsworth, Middlesex, enclosing a cheque or postal order, and your name will be added to the mailing list.

Another Penguin by the authors of this book is described overleaf.

Note: *Penguinews* and *Penguins in Print* are not available in the U.S.A. or Canada

THE PHILOSOPHER IN THE KITCHEN

JEAN–ANTHELME BRILLAT-SAVARIN

'Whoever says "truffles" utters a great word which arouses erotic and gastronomic memories among the skirted sex and memories gastronomic and erotic among the bearded sex.

'This dual distinction is due to the fact that the noble tuber is not only considered delicious to the taste, but is also believed to foster powers the exercise of which is extremely pleasurable.'

' "Rejoice, my dear," I said one day to Madame de V—; "a loom has just been shown to the Society for Encouragement on which it will be possible to manufacture superb lace for practically nothing."

' "Why," the lady replied, with an air of supreme indifference, "if lace were cheap, do you think anybody would want to wear such rubbish?" '

Jean-Anthelme Brillat-Savarin (1755-1826), Mayor of Belley, cousin of Madame Récamier, Chevalier de l'Empire, author of a history of duelling and of a number of racy stories (unfortunately lost), whose sister died in her hundredth year having just finished a good meal and shouting loudly for her dessert, is now best known for his *Physiologie du Goût*, here brilliantly translated as *The Philosopher in the Kitchen*, which was first published in December 1825. The work has a timeless appeal – being wise, witty and anecdotal, containing some of the best recipes for food and some of the most satisfactory observations on life.